The Conditions of Learning
and Theory of Instruction

FOURTH EDITION

The Conditions of Learning
and Theory of Instruction

Robert M. Gagné
Florida State University

Holt, Rinehart and Winston
Holt-Saunders Japan
New York   Chicago   San Francisco   Philadelphia
Montreal   Toronto   London   Sydney
Tokyo   Mexico City   Rio de Janeiro   Madrid

Publisher: Robert Woodbury
Acquisitions Editor: Earl McPeek
Project Editors: Herb Kirk and Biodun Iginla
Production Manager: Pat Sarcuni
Design Supervisor: Lou Scardino
Text Design: Caliber Design Planning, Inc.

Library of Congress Cataloging in Publication Data

Gagné, Robert Mills, 1916–
   The conditions of learning and theory of instruction.

   Rev. ed. of: The conditions of learning. 3rd ed. c1977.
   Includes index.
   1. Learning, Psychology of. 2. Learning. 3. Instructional systems. I. Gagné,
Robert Mills, 1916–   Conditions of learning. II. Title.
LB1051.G19   1984   370.15'23   84-22384

ISBN 0-03-063688-4 (US College Edition)
ISBN 4-8337-0228-2 (Holt-Saunders International Edition)

Printed in Japan, 1985

5 6 7 8 038 9 8 7 6 5 4 3 2 1
CBS COLLEGE PUBLISHING
Holt, Rinehart and Winston
The Dryden Press
Saunders College Publishing

Contents

Preface to
the Fourth Edition

The purposes and themes of this book, as set forth in the Preface to the Third Edition, have remained essentially unchanged. In revising, first priority has been given to bringing the contents up to date. The aim has been to reflect recent and current research on human learning, and the implications these advances in knowledge have for the formulation of what has come to be known as instructional theory.

Description of basic forms of learning, including classical and operant conditioning, has been moved to the first two chapters of the book. Next introduced are the two principal themes: varieties of learning outcomes and events of learning. These ideas are elaborated in subsequent chapters on intellectual skills, cognitive strategies, verbal information, problem solving, motor skills, and attitudes. A following chapter deals with these two dimensions of learning variables, drawing them together in an interrelated fashion as instructional theory.

Some implications of the theory of instruction, and of the learning principles related to it, are described in three subsequent chapters. These treat the topics of instructional design technology called task analysis, media selection, and instructional delivery.

It is my intention to give consideration to human learning as it occurs in a broad range of situations in which planned and intentional learning takes place. Sometimes, it seems best to illustrate the conditions of learning by examples from the schoolroom. On other occasions, examples come most aptly from situations of independent learning, or from instruction as it might occur in an industrial setting. To consider systematically the characteristics of learning in these different settings would require another volume. Rather than that, learning is represented here by a variety of tasks and situations that bring out features distinctive to each kind of outcome.

Tallahassee, Florida   **Robert M. Gagné**
January 1984

Preface to
the Third Edition

There have been many new research findings and theoretical developments since the publication of the second edition of this work. In addition, I have undertaken in the intervening years to examine what is known about learning conditions for five varieties of learning outcomes, some of which were only very briefly mentioned in previous editions. The emphasis in the present edition on interpretation of learning events in terms of the information-processing model will not come as a surprise to readers acquainted with my recent writings. I consider this form of learning theory to represent a major advance in the scientific study of human learning.

The considerable shift in orientation from its previous edition requires a very different organization for this one, and has occasioned its being largely rewritten to include much new material. This book, I feel, deserves a preface which is both frank and more than usually detailed.

In seeking to describe the conditions that affect human learning I have had in mind the question: What factors really can make a difference to instruction? The answer to this question is framed within two different themes that run throughout the book. The first of these themes is *varieties of learning outcomes.* A serious consideration of practical knowledge of learning, I believe, must go beyond the most general principles of the learning process, such as contiguity and reinforcement. One must recognize that learning results in retained dispositions which have different properties, different organizations, and which accordingly require that different conditions be established for their attainment. I call these learned dispositions by the general name of *capabilities.* Their five main varieties are called intellectual skills, cognitive strategies, verbal information, motor skills, and attitudes. Learning investigators and theorists often use these categories (not always by these names) in their accounts of learning—they are not entirely unfamiliar. Yet these same investigators often do not choose to make these distinctions explicit, as is done here. It should be noted that these five kinds of capabilities do not have simply ordered relationships with one another; and they are discussed in the order named mainly for convenience in presentation. As for how one kind of capability relates to another kind, that is a matter discussed within several chapters of the book.

The second main theme relating to the factors that make a difference to instruction may be identified as the *events of learning*. The description of these events begins with an account of the information-processing model of learning and memory, as posited by a number of contemporary investigators as a framework for learning research. This model, with its broad outlines of structures and processes, is shown to be both useful and illuminating as a basis for conceptualizing the conditions of learning. From the model, and from existing evidence regarding its functioning, one may form a description of conditions affecting the processes of learning and remembering. These conditions, some of which are internal to the learner and some external, make up the events of learning. Those events which are external, when deliberately planned and arranged, constitute *instruction*. Thus it is reasonable to define instruction as being made up of events external to the learner which are designed to promote learning.

The criterion of educational relevance for knowledge about learning results in a content which I recognize to be somewhat untraditional. Psychologists who study learning derive their problems for investigation from a variety of sources, not all of which relate to education. Sometimes, too, an original problem source which may have been educational in nature has over a period of years been virtually lost sight of, while the problem itself has become subtly altered in its definition. As a consequence, one cannot simply or automatically assume that names for topics in learning research (such as "verbal learning," "concept identification," "reasoning," and so on) are closely relevant to an understanding of planned instruction. By saying this, I do not mean to deprecate such research, which often has the most worthy purpose of finding explanations for general characteristics of the learning process. Selection of research findings for this book on the basis of their relation to instruction, however, is not the same as answering the question: What have investigators of learning been studying?

The book is addressed to a fairly broad audience and, it must be supposed, one which is heterogeneous in prior knowledge. I hope, first, that it will be used by those who are preparing for, or already pursuing, the teaching profession. Students in this category will need to acquire many new concepts and principles about learning and about their applications to education. This group of readers, I trust, will be rewarded by gaining a set of internalized models of human learning and instruction into which they will be able to incorporate the most important features of their varied experience with the practical affairs of teaching and learning.

A second group of students for whom the book is intended is of somewhat mixed composition, although possessing common goals. These are students of education who see their future careers as being concerned with educational management in its broadest sense. They may have teaching specialties in particular content areas, such as language, mathematics, science, or social studies. They may have chosen to orient their careers toward the establishment of educational quality in elementary, secondary, postsecondary, or adult education, or in vocational or industrial training. A knowledge of human learning is of value in all of these pursuits. Such knowledge is relevant to the practices of education that are known by such names as curriculum planning and development, instructional systems design, assessment of learning outcomes, and program evaluation. Educational leadership which includes a concern for the quality of instruction and the competence of student graduates must take into account the conditions of human learning and the means available for establishing them. Students of education in these varied fields will, I believe, profit from an understanding of learning conditions as described in this volume.

A substantial segment of the book's intended audience is expected to be composed of students of educational psychology at both undergraduate and graduate levels. For these students, a word of orientation perhaps needs to be said. The psychology of learning described in this book represents that body of theoretical and empirical knowledge about learning which, in my view, is most highly relevant to education. The selection of this knowledge has been made against the criterion of relevance to what I perceive to be taking place in classrooms or other places where deliberately planned instruction occurs. There is, in addition, some information which provides a historical-intellectual background, occurring chiefly in Chapters 1 and 4. This may be reviewed very briefly, or skipped, by students of educational psychology if it is already familiar to them. Otherwise, the contents of the book present an organization of knowledge about human learning that I consider worthy of appreciation by the student of educational psychology, and most promising as a basis for future research.

Naturally, it would please me as an author to learn, as this book is put to use, that students of a variety of backgrounds and interests in education have found it possible to acquire an organized schema of human learning as it occurs in situations of instruction. While I would expect each such student to contribute his or her own interpretations and amendments, I would nevertheless anticipate that such a schema will be valuable as a referential model against which the complex events of teaching and learning can be compared and evaluated.

Tallahassee, Florida
December 1976

Robert M. Gagné

The Conditions
of Learning
and Theory of Instruction

FOURTH EDITION

1

Introduction

The fellow human beings we know and associate with got the way they are largely because of learning. Their habits of living have been learned and can be changed by learning; so too can their stores of knowledge, their skills, and the human qualities that characterize them as individuals.

Adult human beings are marvelously adaptable, competently functioning persons. How they managed to progress from their beginnings as highly dependent and relatively incapable infants to such an advanced state is a question of great intellectual interest and importance. One part of the answer, to be sure, lies in human genetic makeup and in an understanding of the process of development through growth. The other part, relating to a different set of circumstances in the life of the individual, is learning. Human skills, appreciations, and reasonings in all their great variety, as well as human hopes, aspirations, attitudes, and values, are generally recognized to depend for their development largely on the events called learning.

One may, if one wishes, cease to wonder about learning at this point, having confirmed to one's own satisfaction that human development in all its manifestations must depend on the twin factors of growth and learning and their interactions with each other. One can say about a child, "He'll learn," just as one says, "She'll grow into it (or out of it)," and such statements are difficult to deny. But to consider learning and growth merely as natural events is to overlook the most important difference between them. The factors that influence growth are to a very large extent genetically determined, whereas the factors that influence learning are determined chiefly by environmental events. Once a person's genetic stock has been chosen at the moment of conception, growth cannot be altered very much, except by extreme measures. But members of human society, which itself is responsible for the care of a developing person, have a tremendous degree of control over events that affect learning. Experience, we are told, is the great teacher. This means that the events the developing person lives through—at home, in the geographical environment, in school, and in various other social environments—will determine what is learned and therefore to a large extent what kind of person he or she becomes.

This enormous dependence of learning on environmental circumstances implies a great responsibility for all members of human society. The situations in which developing children are placed, whether deliberately or otherwise, are going to have great effects on them. In fact, there is not a very clear understanding at present of what the limits of these effects may be. Are the situations in which the growing person is nowadays customarily placed the sort that will encourage the development of disciplined thinkers, of great artists and scientists? Or will they discourage such development and inhibit the full exploitation of human thought and intellect?

The realization that learning is largely dependent on events in the environment with which the individual interacts enables us to view learning as an occurrence that can be examined more closely and understood more profoundly. Learning is not simply an event that happens naturally; it is also an event that happens under certain observable conditions. Futhermore, these conditions can be altered and controlled, and this in turn leads to the possibility of examining the occurrence of learning by scientific methods. The conditions under which learning takes place can be observed and described in objective language. Relations can be detected between these conditions and the changes in human behavior that occur in learning. Thus we can make inferences about what has been learned. Also, scientific models and theories can be constructed to account for the changes observed, just as for other types of natural events.

Learning and Its Conditions

This book is about the *conditions of learning*. We shall consider the sets of circumstances that obtain when learning occurs, that is, when certain observable changes in human behavior take place that justify the inference of learning. A number of different kinds of changes brought about by learning will be described and related to the situations in which they occur. We shall not present a theory of learning but will draw some general concepts from various theories. Our major concern is to find a reasonable answer to the question, What is learning? This answer is to be phrased in terms of an objective description of the conditions under which learning takes place. These conditions will be identified, first of all, by reference to the situations of ordinary life, including those of the school, in which learning occurs. Their identification will also be aided in certain instances by reference to experimental studies of learning.

Learning is a change in human disposition or capability that persists over a period of time and is not simply ascribable to processes of growth. The kind of change called learning exhibits itself as a change in behavior, and the inference of learning is made by comparing what behavior was possible before the individual was placed in a *learning situation* and what behavior can be exhibited after such treatment. The change may be, and often is, an increased capability for some type of performance. It may also be an altered disposition of the sort called *attitude* or *interest* or *value*. The change must have more than momentary permanence; it must be capable of being retained over some period of time. Finally, it must be distinguishable from the kind of change that is attributable to growth, such as a change in height or the development of muscles through exercise.

The Elements of the Learning Event

Students in the sixth grade may learn to write sentences which use the participial form of verbs to modify the subjects of sentences, as in the example, "Seeing no obstacles, he went ahead with the plan." By such learning, they may acquire an alternate way of expressing thoughts which otherwise would require a separate clause, such as "Since he saw no obstacle, he went ahead with the plan." When they have learned to the extent that they can use this alternative, learners should have no difficulty in turning sentences with clauses into sentences which use participial phrases, and vice versa. In addition, they will readily be able to detect the incorrectness in a sentence such as "Trying to catch up, the tight skirt slowed Ruth's progress." In other words, learning has made it possible for students to use a new form of a sentence correctly, whatever its content may be.

How has this learning been brought about? What are the elements of the situation that can be abstracted as having to do with learning?

1. First there is a *learner*, who is a human being (it would be possible for the learner to be an animal, but that is another story, or more exactly, several others). Learners possess sense organs, through which they receive stimulation; brains, by means of which signals originating in the senses are transformed in a number of complex ways; and muscles, by means of which they demonstrate what they have learned. The stimulation that is constantly being received is organized into various patterns of neural activity, some of which are stored in the learner's memory in such a way that they can be recovered. Such memories may then be translated into action that may be observed as the movement of muscles in executing responses of various sorts.
2. The events that stimulate the learner's senses are spoken of collectively as the *stimulus situation*. When a single event is being distinguished, it is often called a *stimulus*.
3. Another important input to learning consists of content recovered from the learner's *memory*. Such content, of course, has an already organized form which has resulted from previous learning activities.
4. The action that results from these inputs and their subsequent transformations is called a *response*. Responses may be described more or less specifically. For example, one can speak of the movement of a particular muscle or of the action of the whole body in walking. For this reason and others, responses are often described in terms of their effects rather than in terms of their appearances. When so classified, they are called *performances*. For example, a response might be the movement of the finger

rhythmically over a small area of the scalp. But it may often be more useful to refer to the performance of scratching the head.

A learning occurrence, then, takes place when the *stimulus situation* together with the *contents of memory* affect the learner in such a way that his or her *performance* changes from a time *before* being in that situation to a time *after* being in it. The *change in performance* is what leads to the conclusion that learning has occurred.

At this general level of description, the student's learning to use a participial phrase correctly may be said to have come about in the following way. Before the learning, the students' performances in writing sentences showed no tendency to use participial phrases. Then a stimulus situation was introduced, which may have included a teacher who used verbal communications to get the students to attend to certain stimulus features of sentences and to make certain responses to them. A number of different sentences, some containing participles and some not, were also used as part of the stimulus situation. Students were required to recover certain concepts from memory, such as "subject," "modifier," "phrase," and "participle." A sequence of stimulus events was made to occur, at the end of which the students succeeded in using participial phrases and in distinguishing a sentence containing such a phrase from one using a clause. The teacher then verified that learning had taken place by asking the students to repeat their performances with some additional examples. The performance was again successful, and the inference was made that learning had taken place. What had been produced by this activity was a new *capability*, to be stored in the learner's memory.

This example is markedly oversimplified, of course. But the framework for the events of learning exhibits a constant set of elements. External to the learner is the stimulus situation, which may initiate and influence learning. Internally, the learning is affected by organized contents recovered from the learner's memory. Various transformations of these inputs result from internal processing and finally exhibit themselves in the learner's performance. As our discussion of the conditions of learning proceeds, many occasions will call for reference to these elements of the set of learning events.

This brief introduction to the events of learning shows that there are two main ideas that need to be understood. First is the question of *what is learned*. It is generally believed that the most elementary unit produced by learning is the *association*, which is established when two events (or ideas) occur together and become mentally linked. From such units, in a manner that is by no means clearly understood at present, are built up the new *capabilities* that make possible the great variety of human performances. For example, individuals learn capabilities that underlie the performance of reading, other capabilities for automobile driving, and so on. These learned capabilities possess different levels of complexity in their organization. If we are to make sense of them, we must have a way of distinguishing *general types* of capabilities having common characteristics rather than individual ones that make possible each performance. Chapter 3 will introduce these main types of learned capabilities. The second main idea pertains to the *processes* involved in learning, which are described initially in Chapter 4. As the previous example has indicated, a single instance of learning is made up of a number of events, some of which are internal to the learner, while others are external. Before dealing with these matters, however, it will be useful to review briefly some historically well-known phenomena that have influenced thought about the processes and outcomes of learning.

SOME PHENOMENA OF LEARNING

How people learn, and the conditions under which they learn, are questions that have been investigated by several generations of learning psychologists. Learning has been a favorite subject particularly for American writers and researchers, partly because of a philosophical tradition that places great emphasis on experience as a determinant of human knowledge. It is of some value, therefore, to describe the kinds of occurrences that are well known to investigators of learning, the phenomena that form the background of thought in the study of learning. These phenomena will point the way to influences that have shaped current learning theory, and to ideas that will undoubtedly affect future developments as well.

Research on learning has generated several typical models, or *prototypes*, which are frequently referred to by writers on the subject. Such prototypes include conditioning, trial-and-error learning, insight, and the "law of effect," among others. These commonly identified phenomena are often used to communicate basic similarities or contrasts among situations in which learning occurs. Knowledge of the prototypes of learning phenomena, and the situations in which they are typically observed, will aid in understanding the varieties of learned capabilities discussed in subsequent chapters.

Association

Perhaps one of the most durable ideas about learning is that it depends in a fundamental way upon *association* of mental events. Learning occurs when the coincidence of, say, the sound of a melody and its singer are associated in such a way that the melody continues to "remind" us of the singer. Learning occurs when, through deliberate pairing of events in instruction, we acquire an association between "week" and "seven days."

One of the oldest lines of thinking reflected in modern learning psychology derives from nineteenth-century British associationist psychologists, who formulated theories about how ideas are linked. These theorists were primarily concerned with how complex ideas, such as flower or number, are constructed in the human mind from elementary sense impressions in the first place. On this latter point, they were generally agreed that acquiring a new idea necessitated (1) *contiguity* of the sense impressions or simple ideas that were to be combined to form the new idea, and (2) *repetition* of these contiguous events. Some of these psychologists also discussed "mental concentration" (which is now usually called attention) as an important condition for learning new ideas by association (Mill, 1869).

American psychologists like William James and John Dewey added some distinctly new interpretations to the associationist tradition. The ideas of Darwin concerning the *functions* of living organisms in adaptation exerted a considerable influence on these American scholars. Accordingly, they sought to discover the functions of behavioral events like learning and thinking, rather than simply the composition of these events. A most important characteristic of learning was considered to be its function in the life of the organism. This view led them to place the *nervous system*, rather than "the mind," in a position of central importance in understanding how sense impressions are connected with behavior. And perhaps most significant, they assigned a critical role to *action* as a factor in learning. Action did not simply follow ideas, as British associationists had proposed, but became an essential feature of the process of behavioral organization called learning.

As the investigation of learning proceeded, association came to mean something other than relations among ideas. The strong tendency to avoid mentalistic conceptions of learning led to the formulation of "associations" as inferred links between the stimulus situation and the response (Robinson, 1932). They were also called, at one time or another, "connections" and "bonds." This conception of associations has persisted to the present day. The association is usually considered the simplest form of entity that is learned, under conditions of contiguity and repetition. As a fundamental building block, it enters into the learning of more complex types of learned capabilities such as human skills and knowledge. Most modern theories of learning simply assume the existence of associations rather than trying to explain them (J. R. Anderson and Bower, 1973; Hinton and Anderson, 1981).

Trial-and-Error Learning

A most important trend in the scientific study of learning was established in the use of animals for experiments on learning. Edward L. Thorndike (1898) was a pioneer in these efforts to understand the learning of animals by performing experiments rather than by collecting anecdotes about animal behavior. From his controlled observations of cats, dogs, and chickens escaping from problem boxes, he concluded that many previous accounts of animal thought were erroneous in that they attributed too much power to animal intelligence. His investigations suggested that all that was necessary to explain animal learning were specific bonds between "sense impressions" and "impulses to action." These associations he considered to be stamped in by the consequences resulting from the completed act (such as escape from the problem box). Thorndike believed that these associations also made up a large part, although not all, of what human beings learned and remembered.

A hungry animal, such as a cat, is placed in a box with slatted sides and a door that can be opened by pressing a wooden lever to release a latch, allowing the animal to reach food placed within its view outside the box. At first, the cat is observed to engage in a variety of acts, including scratching at the sides and door of the box. Sooner or later, these activities lead by chance to the depression of the latch that opens the door. The animal then immediately leaves the box and eats the food. When placed in the box again, the animal's behavior is obviously changed. It spends less time scratching at the sides of the box and more time making movements in the region of the latch. On this second trial, the animal takes much less time to release the latch and get to the food. Subsequent trials reduce the time still more, until the cat is releasing the latch only a few seconds after being placed in the box.

The view of learning represented by this prototype situation may be described briefly as follows. When confronted with a novel situation, the motivated animal engages in various tries to attain satisfaction. Sooner or later, largely by chance, it makes a set of responses that lead to motive satisfaction. The particular responses that are immediately followed by motive satisfaction (eating the food, in this case) become stronger in relation to others. Thus, when the animal is placed in the box a second time the latch-pressing responses occur sooner, whereas the other responses (such as scratching the floor of the box) tend to be shorter in duration or entirely absent. On subsequent trials in the box, these errors progressively weaken and disappear. The correct responses, in contrast, are progressively strengthened by being followed immediately by motive satisfaction. This generalization was called the *law of effect* by Thorndike. The learning situation does not differ in basic characteristics from that of the rat pressing a lever, employed later by Skinner (1938). *Reinforcement* is the term Skinner uses to identify the events that Thorndike called the law of effect.

Is the animal trial-and-error prototype representative of human learning? The answer is clearly no. It is, in fact, rather difficult to relate this prototype to learning that might occur in a human being. If human beings are put in a problem box, we know that they are likely to adopt a strategy of searching for a way out. They recognize latches, knobs, or other devices as having certain functions. They think out the consequences of their actions before they take them and choose the most likely alternative. Once they find their way out they are likely to remember the method immediately, and there will be no gradual error reduction on subsequent trials. How can such human behavior be in any sense comparable to trial and error? The strategies, the recalling, the recognizing, the thinking, the choosing, are all there in the person's behavior; they can readily be observed if the proper experimental conditions are provided.

Nevertheless, as we shall see in the next chapter, the law of effect—the principle of reinforcement—is a dependable and powerful generalization about human learning. Many kinds of behavior categories are learned without conscious attention on the part of the learner. If we observe closely, we can come to realize that quite a few of these behaviors are acquired because of the action of reinforcement, of which the learner may be completely unaware. At a dinner table, for example, how we seat ourselves, how we ask for the salt, how we fold our napkins at the close of the meal, all have almost surely been learned because of the action of the law of effect during a number of previous experiences.

Despite its origin in studies of animal learning, the partially accidental (trial-and-error) nature of learning is equally characteristic of much of the learning done by humans. So too is its quality of being affected by its consequences, which is the essential meaning of the law of effect. As we shall see later, complex patterns of behavior may be established, strengthened, or weakened and eliminated by alteration of their aftereffects, that is, by changing the conditions of reinforcement. Thus, the most important discovery of trial-and-error learning is now best described as reinforcement theory.

Reinforcement

The term *reinforcement*, which refers in general to the effects made upon learning by its consequences, continues to play a prominent role in the explanation of learning phenomena. In Thorndike's study of *trial and error*, learning was thought to be influenced positively when the animal attained through its activity a "satisfying state of affairs." However, reinforcement has more recently taken on several different meanings, and it is doubtful at the present time whether these can be conceived as entirely similar to each other.

One meaning of reinforcement is represented by the work of Hull (1943) and Spence (1956) and interpreted in the writings of N. E. Miller (1959). In this theory, reinforcement is typically considered to occur when a motive is directly satisfied—for example, when the fundamental drive of hunger undergoes a reduction in intensity. The effect of such reinforcement may be to strengthen a learned association or its recall or both. This general conception of motivation is often called *drive reduction theory*. Obviously, in the prototype learning situation to which it leads, the newly acquired response of the learner is followed as immediately as possible by the satisfaction of a drive. In the case of an animal, the intensity of the drive may be reduced by changing some internal state, for example reducing hunger with food. W. human beings, however, various other stimuli may acquire reinforcemei.. properties simply because they have been associated with drive reduction; these other stimuli become what are called *secondary reinforcers*.

Skinner's conception (1969) of reinforcement, which constitutes a central feature of his theoretical view of learning, does not necessarily depend on the notion of reward. To Skinner, reinforcement means a particular arrangement of stimulus and response conditions that bring about the learning of a new association. Specifically, a response that one wants the individual to learn must be made *contingent* on the occurrence of certain *stimulus conditions*, which in turn bring about another response. This theory may appropriately be called the *contingency of reinforcement* theory. Typically, in the learning situation the response desired from the individual is deliberately made to precede the occurrence of some other response which has a high probability of being made. Thus the cat's obtaining food (as in Thorndike's puzzle box) is made contingent upon its pressing the lever. The child's activity of coloring pictures is made contingent upon his or her reading the names of the colors printed within the picture outlines. Various arrangements of contingencies (some of which will be referred to later) are possible. They have the common characteristic that the activity to be learned must be followed by the occurrence of some chosen event. This event shortly comes to exert control over the activity, and one can then say that learning has occurred.

Conditioned Responses

I. P. Pavlov (1927) found that when a buzzer was sounded at the time food was shown to a hungry dog, and this set of events was repeated several times, the dog came to salivate at the sound of the buzzer alone. Whereas the salivation at the sight of food could be considered a natural (or unconditioned) response, salivation at the sound of a buzzer had to be acquired as a conditioned response. This learning occurred when the new signal (the buzzer) was presented together with the food in a number of trials.

John B. Watson (1919) championed the view of learning suggested by Pavlov's studies of conditioning in dogs. In Watson's writings, learning is viewed as a matter of establishing individual associations (conditioned responses) firmly based in the nervous system. More complex human acts are considered to be chains of conditioned responses.

Some investigators of Pavlovian conditioning believe it to be a special kind of learning, representative of the establishment of *involuntary* acts, including anticipatory responses such as the startled eye blinking that may follow a threatening gesture (Kimble, 1961). More generally, this kind of conditioning is thought to be particularly applicable to *emotional reactions* (Hill, 1981) such as worry or excitement. It is likely that human beings acquire many conditioned responses of this sort in the course of their lives. One may find oneself, for example, waking with a start at the slight click the alarm clock makes before it actually rings. Hearing an automobile horn from an unexpected direction may evoke a tensing of muscles in the hands on the wheel and in the foot on the brake. In the schoolroom, the teacher's pointing to an object to be described may become a conditioned signal for students to be alert for other stimuli from that direction. It is even possible that learned anticipatory responses may be largely what we mean when we speak of "paying attention" to something. Conditioned emotional reactions of an involuntary sort may be involved in reactions to snakes, spiders, or in other events accompanied by unexpected signals. Perhaps they also play a part in the determination of attitudes.

Despite the widespread occurrence of conditioned responses in our lives, the prototype remains unrepresentative of most learning situations. The learning of voluntary acts cannot adequately be represented by the pairing of conditioned and unconditioned stimuli. A child who wants to learn to ride a bicycle will get little help from some deliberate arrangement of conditions in accordance with the prototype of the conditioned response, because voluntary control of actions is not acquired in this way. The same is true, needless to say, for most other kinds of things a child must learn, beginning with reading, writing, and arithmetic. There can be little doubt that Watson's idea that most forms of human learning can be accounted for as chains of conditioned responses is incorrect, primarily because it is an overly simple conception of what is learned.

The Learning of Verbal Associates

Hermann Ebbinghaus (1913) carried out an ingenious set of experimental studies of learning and memorization. He used himself as an experimental subject, and series of nonsense syllables of the sort NOF-VIB-JEX, as materials. These constructed syllables were employed in the attempt to gain control over the unwanted variable of previous practice, since it was apparent to Ebbinghaus that an association like BOY-MAN was already more or less well learned. In committing to memory these series of nonsense syllables, he was able to study the effects of the variables of length of series, order of presentation, and many others. Later investigators saw in the nonsense syllable a versatile tool for the study of *verbal association.*

As research in this area continued, its focus shifted from serial lists of verbal units to sets of paired syllables or words, called *paired associates.* In sets composed of pairs like DAX-RYQ, or like KING-SAD, the first member was treated as the stimulus, the second as the response. Having been asked to learn, say, twelve of these pairs, the learner would be asked to respond by saying SAD when the first member of the pair, KING, was shown.

For some years, investigators of verbal associate learning apparently believed that their findings could account for the learning of *single* associations. But even Ebbinghaus's results showed that the commission of one syllable to memory was strongly influenced by the presence of other syllables. During the many years of research following Ebbinghaus, the factors that have been found to affect the learning of nonsense lists have constantly increased, and the difficulty of experimental control has similarly become greater. The learning of any single association in a sequence has been shown to be markedly affected by the *interference* of other associations both within the list and outside it. A great many characteristics previously thought to describe the learning of single associates are now attributed to the effects of interference.

The verbal associate prototype must also be considered to represent a very limited range of actual learning situations. The differences in learning and retaining logically connected prose and poetry, as opposed to nonsense lists, have been apparent for many years (see Ausubel, 1968; Estes, 1976); and it is doubtful whether the interference that occurs within these two types of material follows the same laws. There may be a limited number of instances in which human beings engage in the learning of material whose members are arbitrarily related, as in learning the alphabet, or π to ten places. But the vast majority of verbal learning that occurs must be affected strongly by its meaningfulness, as experiments on verbal associates have demonstrated.

Insight

Opposed to these associationist ideas of learning have been the writings and investigations of Gestalt psychologists. As conceived in their views, learning typically takes the form of an *insight*, which is a suddenly occurring reorganization of the field of experience, as when one "has a new idea" or "discovers a solution to a problem." Learning to solve mechanical puzzles like "rings and chains" frequently includes sudden flashes of insight leading to more rapid solution procedures.

Köhler used a variety of problem situations to study insightful learning in chimpanzees (1927). For example, a banana was suspended from the top of the animal's cage, out of reach. Several wooden boxes were available within the cage, but the animal could not reach the banana by standing on any one of them. A great variety of restlessness and trial and error was exhibited. On occasion, however, an animal was observed to act suddenly, as though it were carrying out a plan, by placing one box on top of another, then immediately climbing on this structure to reach the banana. As another example, one chimpanzee was observed, again after much trial and error, to put together two jointed sticks, which were then used as a single long stick to reach a banana placed outside the cage. Köhler called such learning *insight*, and emphasized its discontinuity with the previous trial-and-error behavior. The total successful act was put together and exhibited suddenly, without error, and as if by plan. Köhler's interpretation was that insight involved a "seeing" of relations, a putting together of events that were internally represented.

This form of learning in human beings has also been described by other Gestalt writers like Wertheimer (1959) and Katona (1940). For example, Wertheimer describes children's solutions, insightful and otherwise, to a geometric problem. Children who knew the formula for the area of a rectangle as $h \times b$ were asked to derive a means of finding the area of a parallelogram. Some proceeded in a rote fashion to multiply the length of the base times the length of the side, which, of course, is incorrect. Others were able to obtain the correct solution by cutting a right triangle from one side of the parallelogram, and attaching it to the other side, thus reconstructing a known figure, the rectangle. Still others were able to see the problem as one of dividing the entire parallelogram into little squares (a very sophisticated solution). Although a child may have tried several wrong approaches, a "good" solution was arrived at, according to Wertheimer, when the child could see the essential structure of the problem situation.

The most frequent criticism of the insight explanation of these learning events is, however, a very serious one. This is that animals and children solve these problems by *transfer from previous learning*. The chimpanzee is able to pile boxes one upon another because it has previously learned to do this, although not necessarily in the test situation. The child is able to identify the triangles as similar because he or she has previously done this with other right triangles. It cannot be said that such an explanation is not true, because in these Gestalt examples the factor of prior learning was not controlled. Despite the neatness of a theory that accounts for insight on the basis of the structure of the observed situation, the phenomena of insight in one instance after another have been shown to be affected by previous learning.

One of the most impressive modern evidences of the effects of prior learning on insightful behavior occurs in Harlow's studies (1949) of *learning set*. Harlow trained monkeys to solve problems in which the correct choice among three objects was the "odd" one, the object dissimilar to the others. By trial-and-error learning, in which they were consistently rewarded for doing so, monkeys learned to choose the odd one of three objects. In the next problem, three new objects were presented, including an odd one, and the monkeys again learned to choose the odd one, although somewhat faster this time. A third problem, again with a new set of objects, was solved faster than the second. After solving a few more of these oddity problems, the animal was able to solve oddity problems (involving objects it had not previously encountered) at once, without any hesitation. The animal had acquired, Harlow said, a learning set that enabled it to solve oddity problems correctly without trial and error.

This evidence implies that previous learning, acquired through a number of encounters with similar problems, can establish an internal capability that makes the animal quite different from naive monkeys of the same age and strain. It becomes an "oddity-problem solver" monkey, who displays insight when given an oddity problem to solve. Obviously, this capability for insight did not arise because of "structuring of the situation." Rather it came from accumulated experience based on many individual trials of previous learning.

What can be said about the representativeness of insight as a prototype of learning? On the one hand, it does appear to represent some common learning occurrences that are rather easy to identify. When children are led to "see" relations, such as those between addition and multiplication or between weight and the pull of gravity, they often display insight. On the other hand, it is difficult to find insight in the learning of a great variety of other things. Children cannot learn the names of plants or stars in an insightful manner. They cannot learn to read by insight, nor to speak a foreign language. Students of biology do not learn the structures and functions of animals by insight. In short, insight cannot be a prototype for a vast amount of learning that human beings ordinarily undertake. Perhaps it occurs when we learn by solving problems, but we also learn many, many things that are not problems. They may simply be facts or propositions or principles.

Information Processing

Contemporary theories of learning and memory reflect a distinct break with most of the views of learning so far discussed. The latter models largely reflect the idea that *associations* are formed and stored as a result of learning. Otherwise, they give only small emphasis to the *internal* processing supposed to occur when something is learned and retained. A marked contrast is shown in a number of newer cognitive theories, as described in such books as Tulving and Donaldson (1972), Estes (1978), and Anderson (1976). These theories propose an elaborate set of internal processes to account for the events of learning and remembering. The contrast between old and new conceptions is so great, particularly in terms of the number and variety of internal structures and processes proposed, that one pair of authors has described the recent theories as the "new mental forestry" (Greeno and Bjork, 1973).

Human learning and memory are currently interpreted in terms of *information processing*. These theories propose that the stimulation encountered by the learner is transformed, or *processed,* in a number of ways by internal structures during the period in which the changes identified as learning take place. The initial stimulation is transformed in the brain to a *registration* of the events seen, heard, or otherwise sensed. A second transformation takes place when this information is temporarily stored in the *short-term memory* (also called the *working memory*). Still another kind of processing occurs when the information is put into *long-term memory*. Again, a different transformation takes place when the information is *retrieved* from long-term memory, and when it generates the responses that lead to the observed performance of the learner. These theoretical notions will be described in greater detail in Chapter 4, where we shall consider their implications for identifying optimal learning conditions.

The conceptions of information-processing models of learning and memory derive from a number of sources. In part, they have arisen from the attempts of learning psychologists to formulate a mathematical learning theory, that is, to represent the variables of the learning process in mathematical equations. In large part they derive also from the formulations of computer science, particularly its attempt to explore the limits of intellectual processing possible to the computer. A third source of thought reflected in information-processing theories is that of linguistic science, which attempts to understand how human beings learn and use language. Modern theories of learning appear to have revived a concern with how ideas are learned and stored, as opposed to how stimuli are associated with responses. Initial stages of internal processing, for example, are often conceived as operating on *propositions*, in which form information is to be stored in memory.

The information-processing model of learning has important implications for an understanding of instruction. The stimulating conditions that are brought to bear on learners are not viewed simply as stimuli to which they react. Instead, these external stimuli may be conceived as initiating, maintaining, or otherwise *supporting* several different kinds of ongoing internal processes involved in learning, remembering, and performing. A second and related implication is the conception that several *phases of processing* occur during a single act of learning. The external stimulation involved in instruction may be designed to support a single phase of such processing or a combination of phases.

The Significance of Learning Prototypes

Throughout the course of scientific investigation of learning, there has been frequent recourse to certain typical experimental situations to serve as prototypes of learning. It is these prototypes which provide instances of the basic phenomena of learning, derived from trial-and-error learning, conditioned responses, verbal associates, and studies of insight. A distinct change in the nature of these prototypes has occurred with the emergence of the information-processing model, which derives in part from computer and linguistic sciences. The choice of prototype has had considerable influence on learning research. When contrasting predictions are made by learning theories, prototypes are often appealed to as concrete ways of settling the issues. And it is from these prototypes that experiments are designed to test theoretical predictions. In other words, these prototypes continue to be the models that investigators think about when they set out to study learning scientifically.

As examples, the prototypes themselves represent a variety of kinds of learning. It has not been possible to reduce one variety to another, although many attempts have been made. In addition, there are many instances of learning that these prototypes apparently do *not* represent. There seem, in fact, to be varieties of learning that are not considered by these standard examples; their representativeness of actual learning phenomena is not at all comprehensive.

These learning prototypes all have a similar history in this respect: each of them started out as a representative of a particular variety of learning situation. Thorndike wanted to study animal association. Pavlov was studying reflexes. Ebbinghaus studied the memorization of verbal lists. Köhler was studying the solving of problems by animals. By some peculiar semantic process, these examples became prototypes of learning, and thus were considered to represent the domain of learning as a whole, or at least in large part. Somehow, they came to be placed in opposition to each other: either all learning was insight or all learning was conditioned response. Such controversies have continued for years, and have been relatively unproductive in advancing our understanding of learning as an event.

THE VIEW OF LEARNING PRESENTED IN THIS BOOK

How can one determine what learning is? The plan followed in this volume is twofold. First of all, it is to identify the general *types of human capabilities* that are learned. These are the behavioral changes that a truly comprehensive learning theory must explain (and which no theory as yet does encompass). Once these varieties of learning outcome have been identified, an account can be given of the *conditions* that govern the occurrence of learning and remembering. This leads to a description of the factors that determine learning, derived insofar as possible from available evidence in controlled experimentation. By this means it is possible to differentiate the sets of conditions that support the learning of different human capabilities.

Types of Learned Capabilities

From a naturalistic viewpoint, we shall describe the major kinds of learning outcomes, that is, five types of human capabilities that are learned. The traditional prototypes described in the previous section are considered to represent only parts of the situations in which learning of these capabilities occurs and therefore to depict mainly the elemental forms of learning. The information-processing model has a great deal more flexibility, and apparently greater relevance, in accounting for the learning of major types of capabilities. The kinds of questions to be raised and answered by subsequent chapters are suggested by the following set:

1. How does an individual learn the skill of threading a needle, of parking an automobile?
2. What conditions are necessary for the student to learn to understand Newton's laws of motion?
3. How can one account for the learning of factual information, such as the events of history or descriptions of the natural world?
4. How does a learner acquire increased competence in finding new solutions to the many practical problems of life?
5. How can conditions be arranged to bring about the learning of positive social values such as honesty and respect for others' feelings?

All these human activities are learned. To suppose that one set of conditions governs their occurrence is to ignore the facts of common observation. A serious and comprehensive attempt to describe learning must take all these varieties into account. Naturally, it must make differentiations among them, and classifications of them, if these are possible. But to begin with the premise that "all learning is the same" would be quite unjustifiable.

The Conditions of Learning

The occurrence of learning is inferred from a difference in a human being's performance before and after being placed in a "learning situation." One may, for example, think of designing some conditions of learning to teach children how to form the plurals of nouns. The children could then be placed in the learning situation, and following this, their performance in making plural nouns could be observed. But it would be embarrassing to discover that their performance in making plurals was no better than that of children of equivalent age and ability who had *not* been placed in the same learning situation. The presence of the performance does not make it possible to conclude that learning has occurred. It is necessary to show that there has been a *change in performance*. The capability for exhibiting the performance *before* learning must be taken into account as well as the capability that exists after learning.

One set of factors contributing to learning is the capabilities that already exist in the individual before any particular new learning begins. The child who is learning to tie shoelaces does not begin this learning "from scratch" but already knows how to hold the laces, how to loop one over the other, how to tighten the loop, and so on. The theme is the same for other kinds of performances. The student who learns to multiply whole numbers has al-

ready acquired many capabilities, including adding and counting and recognizing numerals and writing them with a pencil. The student who is
learning how to write clear descriptive paragraphs already knows how to
write sentences and to choose words.

Previously learned capabilities make up the *internal conditions* necessary
for learning. These internal conditions are brought into play by a set of
transforming processes (as conceived by learning theory) which are to be
described in Chapter 4.

A second major category of learning conditions is *external* to the learner.
Let us suppose an individual possesses all the prerequisite capabilities
needed for learning the English equivalents of ten foreign words. Another
individual possesses all the prior capabilities for learning how to multiply
two negative numbers. There is no particular reason to suppose that the
external conditions needed for learning in one case are the same as the
external conditions needed for learning in the other. In the first case, common observation would lead us to expect that the pairs of words would
need to be repeated a number of times in order for learning to occur. But in
the second case it is not apparent that repetition would have a similar
effect. The differences between these two sets of external conditions, among
others, will be discussed more completely in the chapters to follow. At this
point, the important thing to note is that the conditions are not the same.
Two different *types of capabilities* are being learned. They require not only
different prior capabilities but also different external conditions for learning.

The point of view to be expanded on in this book is probably apparent
from previous paragraphs. Restated, it is this: There are several varieties of
performance types that imply different categories of learned capabilities.
These varieties of performance may also be differentiated in terms of the
conditions for their learning. In searching for and identifying these conditions, one must look, first, at the capabilities internal to the learner and,
second, at the stimulus situation outside the learner. The learning of each
type of new capability starts from a different point of prior learning and is
likely also to demand a different external situation. The useful prototypes of
learning are delineated by these descriptions of learning conditions.

ORGANIZATION OF THE BOOK

In Chapter 2 we provide an account of the conditions and characteristics of
learning as revealed by studies of *association*. We have pointed out in this
chapter the basic nature of associations as learned elements that are believed to link together all that is learned. We call these *basic forms* of learning. A great deal of research on learning has been devoted to investigating
the establishment of associations and chains of associations. These out-

comes of learning may best be considered, we believe, as *components* of learned human capabilities. In fact, they are usually treated as components in most contemporary learning theories. Much has been discovered about the characteristics of associations and chains of associations. Their properties are thought to be of fundamental importance to an understanding of the organized capabilities they compose. It will be desirable, therefore, to devote some attention to a description of the conditions of learning for these behavioral components and to some of their major properties.

A major theme of the book, introduced in Chapter 3, pertains to varieties of what is learned. Five categories of learning outcomes are defined and exemplified. These five classes form a descriptive basis for many of the later chapters. Next, in Chapter 4, there is a shift to a second theme, the events which take place during learning. These events, as related to the information-processing model of learning and memory, must be separately distinguished for *each* of the kinds of learned capabilities described in Chapter 3. By considering how these events relate to each kind of learning outcome, we describe in subsequent chapters the *conditions* for their learning.

The relationship of events of learning to varieties of learning outcomes and to learning conditions is shown schematically in Figure 1.1. Events of learning operate upon the learner in ways that constitute conditions of learning. When such conditions prevail, various learning outcomes in the form of human capabilities are the result. Thus the two themes, categories of learning outcomes (as initially described in Chapter 3) and the events of learning (Chapter 4) together provide a framework for our account of learning conditions. Both chapters 3 and 4 therefore lay foundations for material that is to follow by examining human learning from two different viewpoints.

Having set these foundations, we proceed to provide descriptions of the conditions of learning for each type of human capability. Chapters 5 and 6

Figure 1.1   The relations between events of learning, outcomes of learning, and conditions of learning, as these topics are to be treated in subsequent chapters.

consider these conditions as they apply to several subvarieties of *intellectual skills.* (This and other categories of capabilities are defined in Chapter 3.) Chapter 7 deals with *cognitive strategies* and their relation to the intellectual activities of learning, remembering, and thinking. Chapter 8 describes learning conditions for *verbal information.* The synthesis of capabilities involved in the human activity of *problem solving* are dealt with in Chapter 9. Proceeding with other learning outcomes, Chapter 10 describes learning conditions for *motor skills,* and Chapter 11 for *attitudes.*

Chapter 12 brings the implications of previous chapters together in a statement of *instructional theory.* Here the varieties of learning outcomes are separately related to the events of instruction, as originally outlined in Chapter 4. Systematic statements of theory describe the distinctive ways in which instructional events are designed for each variety of learned capability. Subsequent chapters explore the applications of theory. Chapter 13 gives an account of theory-based procedures for *analyzing requirements for learning.* A related topic, treated in Chapter 14, deals with a theory-derived model of decisions in *selecting media for instruction.* The final chapter, 15, relates the ideas of instructional theory to the *design of instruction.*

EDUCATIONAL IMPLICATIONS

The identification of varieties of learning in terms of the conditions that produce them obviously has some definite implications for education and educational practices. Some of these may be immediately evident as the reader becomes acquainted in subsequent chapters with the conditions of learning for each variety. Others, however, need to be separately specified, since they are so fundamentally related to educational procedures.

The discussion of educational problems in later chapters uses the fewest possible assumptions about the mechanics (or logistics) of education. None of these logistic elements is assumed as a given. Quite to the contrary, the point of view presented is that these features of the educational process should be determined by the requirement of getting students to learn efficiently. In discussing implications, therefore, it is assumed that neither a school building nor a set of books nor desks nor chalkboards nor even a teacher is necessarily needed. If these components of the educational system are shown to be necessary because of the requirements of learning, well and good. The only thing that must be assumed is the existence of a student who is capable of learning. This is the starting point.

How learning operates in everyday school situations is a most valuable kind of understanding. Such knowledge can make possible the successful accomplishment of activities of the following sorts:

1. *Planning for learning.* One important implication of the identification of learning conditions is that these conditions must be carefully planned

before the learning situation is entered into by the student. In particular, there needs to be planning in terms of the students' capabilities both before and after any learning enterprise. Where do students begin, and where are they going? What are the specific prerequisites for learning, and what will learners be able to learn next? The planning that precedes effective instructional design includes carefully specifying these prerequisites.

2. *Managing learning.* How can students be motivated to begin and to continue learning? How should the direction of interest and effort be guided? What can be done to assess the outcomes of learning? These questions pertain to the management of learning and the learning situation. They are general questions in the sense that their answers are not specifically dependent on the content to be learned or on the conditions of learning which prevail for that content. The management activities implied by these questions are necessary for any system whose purpose is to accomplish learning in an effective manner. Clearly, they are among the most important functions to be carried out by a teacher.

3. *Instructing.* The function of instructing derives in a specific sense from a description of the required conditions of learning. Instructing means arranging the conditions of learning that are external to the learner. These conditions need to be constructed in a stage-by-stage fashion, taking due account of each stage of previously acquired capabilities of the learner, the requirements for retention of these capabilities, and the specific stimulus situation needed for the next stage of learning.

In the most general sense, instruction is intended to promote learning. This means that the external situation needs to be arranged to activate, support, and maintain the internal processing that constitutes each learning event. At one point, instruction may support the process of attending, which is an early phase of learning. At another point, the external stimulation provided by instruction may activate an internal strategy for encoding a mass of facts. And at still another point, instruction may primarily function to provide cues that make a newly learned skill memorable or readily applicable to a novel problem encountered by the student. Whether instruction is given by a teacher, or is in some fashion provided by the student, it has several important functions in influencing the ongoing processes of learning.

GENERAL REFERENCES

Learning and Learning Theories

Bower, G. H., and Hilgard, E. R. *Theories of learning,* 5th ed. Englewood Cliffs, N.J.: Prentice-Hall, 1981.

Gagné, R. M. *Essentials of learning for instruction.* New York: Holt, Rinehart and Winston, 1974.

Hill, W. F. *Principles of learning: A handbook of applications.* Palo Alto, Calif.: Mayfield, 1981.

Hulse, S. H., Egeth, H., and Deese, J. *The psychology of learning,* 5th ed. New York: McGraw-Hill, 1980.

Kimble, G. A. *Foundations of conditioning and learning.* New York: Appleton, 1967.

Marx, M. H., and Bunch, M. E. *Fundamentals and applications of learning.* New York: Macmillan, 1977.

Melton, A. W. (Ed.), *Categories of human learning.* New York: Academic Press, 1964.

Travers, R. M. W. *Essentials of learning,* 5th ed. New York: Macmillan, 1982.

2

Association Learning

Over a period of many years investigators of human learning have struggled to devise learning tasks that would assure that the events to be observed were "pure learning" and not something else. The phenomena chosen for observation might not be learning; learners might be performing some acts reflexively, or they might simply be recalling something previously learned. Those who study the phenomena of learning have often tried to simplify the task to be learned to remove from it the possible contaminations of unwanted influences. As a result, what has often been studied is the smallest possible element involved in learning: the association. As we saw in the previous chapter, Thorndike conceived of trial-and-error learning as a matter of strengthening associations. The verbal units studied by Ebbinghaus and those who followed him were also looked upon as associations, as were the conditioned responses studied by Pavlov and the operant responses of Skinner.

We return to these basic prototypes of learning in this chapter in order to present a comprehensive picture of learning processes and the conditions that affect them. We want also to highlight the continuities that exist between these models of learning and those to be described in subsequent chapters.

THE STATUS OF BASIC LEARNING FORMS

Investigators of basic forms of learning have focused their studies on the *characteristics of learning by association*. Thus, the study of the conditioned response was undertaken to find and verify the conditions which governed the association of a new stimulus (such as the sound of a buzzer) with a response such as salivating. Those who studied animal trial-and-error learning were seeking to explore the conditions leading to an association between a stimulus situation (such as a maze or a problem box) and the animal's response of running or pushing. And those who investigated the learning of word pairs were seeking to describe the conditions of association of the first word as a stimulus with the learner's response of saying the second word.

Learning studies that employed these prototypes, whether conducted with animals or human beings, were dominated by the requirement of using learning situations in which an identifiable stimulus was in fact associated with a relatively invariant response. It was usually assumed, or sometimes deliberately postulated, that the learner was internally "associating," or "connecting," a stimulus (S) with a response (R). Thus the psychology of learning came to depend on what is called "S-R theory," in which interest centered upon accounting for the dash between the S and the R, a dash that, in fact, was the symbol of the learned association.

It is now generally recognized by those who conduct scientific investigations of learning that even the most deliberately simplified learning situation cannot be adequately accounted for merely as an association between an S and an R. Over a period of thirty years, for example, the brilliant theoretical account of paired-associate learning formulated by E. J. Gibson (1940) in S-R terms has given way to the recognition that such learning is an exceedingly complex act that requires the postulation of a number of different internal processes (Battig, 1968), each of which may be affected by a distinct set of external conditions (S. E. Newman, 1964; Saltz, 1963).

The Role of Association in Learning

It is virtually a certainty that more than association is involved in learning, even when learning is apparently of a very simple type. Nevertheless, the idea persists, with considerable justification, that association is *one* of the processes that occurs in learning. Furthermore, association seems to occur with such frequency that it deserves to be called a *basic* process.

The British associationist psychologists were impressed with the fact that when two "ideas" were commonly experienced together, the presentation of one tended to arouse the thought of the other. Thus, an individual seeing a picture of a dog is likely also to think of a cat, since the two are commonly experienced as household pets. People do possess these associations, which are to a considerable extent predictable on the basis of known common experiences (Deese, 1965).

Information-processing theories of learning and memory often begin with the assumption that what is learned (that is, what is "stored in long-term memory") are propositions. These are internal representations of sentences or sentence-like actions, each containing a subject and a predicate. "Mary gave John a book" is a simple example. When attempting to account for the storage of propositions and their retrieval, however, such theories find it necessary to assume that association is a basic process in learning. Propositions and their components may require the existence of networks of associations to account for the ways in which new items of information are learned and old ones recalled.

If association remains, even in modern theories, as a basic learning process, how shall its characteristics be studied? We have seen that various attempts to investigate association are now thought to be inadequate, because the simplified learning situations employed were not really simple. How to study a process like association is a puzzling problem to which no ready answer has yet been suggested. The study of basic forms of learning has provided a number of suggestions about how association "works," and what conditions govern the learning of associations. It is worthwhile to take some note of characteristics of association that have been revealed by these studies. At the same time, the reader must be aware of the possibility that what appear to be studies of "S-R learning" may turn out to have much more complex explanations than that implied by words such as *association* or *connection*.

Varieties of the Basic Forms of Learning

There are three prototypes of learning that have been examined with the intention of revealing the characteristics of "associative learning." First there is the conditioned response studied initially by Pavlov (1927) and many learning psychologists throughout the world. This type is called *classical conditioning* or *signal learning*, in which the learner associates an already available response with a new stimulus, or "signal." Second is the learning called *operant conditioning* by Skinner (1938), which is also frequently called *instrumental conditioning* (Kimble, 1961). This kind of learning is to be found in Thorndike's work (1898) with animals in problem boxes as well as in many other animal learning studies involving mazes, compartments, levers, and other devices in which a response of the learner is "instrumental" in leading to a subsequent reinforcing event.

A third way of studying associative learning has been with human beings learning to make verbal responses to stimuli that are words or pairs of words. Again, the intention has been to investigate the characteristics of association as a learned "connection" between one word and another, following the tradition of Ebbinghaus (1913). We call this *verbal association learning*.

To these three basic types of learning situations, we add another, which is closely related to the basic three. This is known as *chaining*, in which the individual associations are connected in sequence. Chains of associations are readily learned by animals, for example, as successive turns in a maze. In human beings, similar sequences may be learned as "mental mazes." Chaining is also exhibited in *verbal sequences*, such as lists of words, nonsense syllables, or the alphabet from A to Z.

CLASSICAL CONDITIONING

Most people are acquainted in one way or another with the classical (Pavlovian) type of conditioning, whether in common domestic animals or in other human beings. We have all observed one or more instances of such learning in household pets. For example, the cat or dog may run to the kitchen when it hears its food dish placed on the floor, or it may run from the driveway when a car approaches. George Bernard Shaw (1959) thought that these things were completely obvious and could not see why Pavlov had felt it necessary to "discover" them. Of course, in a real sense, Pavlov did not discover them; but, true scientist that he was, he attempted to measure them under carefully controlled conditions. In so doing, he gave us an account of the conditions and characteristics of conditioning that is as valuable today as it was in his time.

The Phenomenon of Classical Conditioning

Most educated adults know how Pavlov's dog learned to salivate in response to the sound of a buzzer. The type of conditioning situation seen here has also been extensively analyzed in human beings, namely, in studies of the blinking of the eye. There are many precise data on the learning of this association, and the results are particularly instructive concerning the question of what is learned.

When a small puff of air is delivered to the cornea of a person's eye, the eye blinks rapidly. This is the connection Pavlov called the *unconditioned reflex*, meaning that the action is there to begin with and is not conditional on any previous learning. But if a click is sounded about a half-second before the puff of air reaches the cornea, we have an important condition for the establishment of a learned association. The click (or any other "neutral" stimulus) is called the *conditioned stimulus* (the "signal"). When this sequence of events—click then puff of air—is repeated a few times, it is usually possible to demonstrate the existence of a newly learned connection, namely,

$$S_{click} \rightarrow R_{blink}$$

This is done by presenting the click by itself, without the puff of air, and noting that the blink response occurs.

Experimental studies have shown that the conditioned blink is not the same as the unconditioned blink (Kimble, 1961). The unconditioned blink is a more rapid response; it occurs in 0.05 to 0.10 second, whereas the signaled blink takes 0.25 to 0.50 second. With suitable methods of measurement, the two are clearly distinguishable as responses. Thus it appears that what is learned may be called an *anticipatory blink* to a signal. Such a blink does not avoid the puff of air; if it did, this would be an instance of operant learning, which we shall discuss next. But the learned blink anticipates the puff of air; it signals "puff of air to come."

How often does the pairing of signal and unconditioned stimulus have to be repeated in order for a conditioned response to be established? Although there is no single answer to this question, the evidence suggests that a number of repetitions must be used in order to establish a stable response, at least for the eye blink. Figure 2.1 shows the curves of learning obtained for three groups of subjects differing with respect to "ease of conditioning." These graphs show the frequency of occurrence of the learned response following various numbers of trials in which stimuli were paired. As can be seen, people who were fast at conditioning attained a 60% rate of conditioned responding in 20 trials, whereas people who were only intermediate in speed of conditioning required about 58 trials, and those who were slow seemed bound to take many more than 100 trials. Other instances have been reported, however, of signal learning taking place much more rapidly than this, depending particularly on the strength of the unconditioned stimulus. Signal-response associations have been shown to occur in a very few trials when the signal accompanies a stimulus arousing a strong emotion. This was the case, for example, when the child Albert was observed to acquire a conditioned fear of a white rat when a sudden loud sound (produced by a striking metal bar) was made behind his head at the time he was reaching toward the animal (Watson and Rayner, 1920). Following this conditioning, the child showed fear whenever the white rat was brought near him. In animals such as dogs, conditioned fears have readily been established in very few trials.

Conditions of Learning

With the help of these examples, it should not be difficult to state the conditions necessary for classical conditioning. Evidently, one must deal with

Figure 2.1 Learning curves showing the increase in frequency of conditioned eyeblinks in successive blocks of trials, for groups of learners whose rate of conditioning was found to be slow, intermediate, and fast. (Data of K. W. Spence, *Behavior theory and conditioning*. New Haven: Yale University Press, 1956.)

conditions that need to be present *within the learner* as well as with conditions that can be manipulated *in the learning situation*.

Conditions within the learner. In order for classical conditioning to occur, there must be a natural reflex—typically a reflexive emotional response (startle, fear, anger, pleasure)—on the part of the learner. It must be clear that an *unconditioned stimulus* can evoke such an *unconditioned response*. Further, there is much evidence of marked individual differences in the rapidity with which people acquire signal-response connections. Such differences are not markedly related to intelligence. But they *are* significantly related to the level of *anxiety* with which the individual typically faces life's problems and decisions. Many studies have shown that people who tend to be anxious acquire conditioned responses more rapidly than do less anxious people (Taylor, 1951).

Conditions in the learning situation. The conditions for signal learning that can be externally controlled are *contiguity* and *repetition*.

1. The conditioned stimulus and the unconditioned stimulus must be presented in close proximity to each other in the order named. These necessary time relationships have been tested in situations involving many kinds of signals and responses. Variations have been found to be very small, so that it is reasonable to think that they reflect some stable characteristics of the functioning of the nervous system. Learning occurs dependably when the conditioned stimulus precedes the unconditioned by an interval between 0 and 1.50 seconds and most readily when the interval is about 0.50 second.
2. As Figure 2.1 shows, repetition of the paired stimuli is also necessary. The amount required, however, may vary considerably depending on the response involved and on the intensity of the unconditioned stimulus. The connection appears to increase in strength (or dependability of occurrence) as the repetitions of paired stimuli increase in number.

Thus the conditions of classical conditioning are relatively simple to describe and easy to control. Besides the eye blink used in our example, conditioned responses have been established for many behaviors in the human being, including salivation, changes in electrical resistance of the skin, respiration changes, nausea, and hand withdrawal to an electric shock. Early investigators attempted to establish signal learning with the use of certain simple reflexes like the knee jerk and the pupillary reflex, but these have generally been found to be extremely difficult to condition. Diffuse emotional responses or their components are, in contrast, easy to condition. One response falling in this category, for example, is the galvanic skin reflex, which has been used frequently in the study of signal learning. When an electric shock is applied, say, to the individual's hand, physiological processes are set in motion that alter the resistance of the skin to the passage of a weak electric current. This change in resistance can be easily and precisely measured by means of simple electrodes attached to the skin and connected with a circuit including a galvanometer. Thus a means is provided for measuring the acquisition of a conditioned association. In practice, the subject is seated in a chair and electrodes are attached. Then the skin resistance (galvanic skin reflex, or GSR) is noted on the galvanometer until a fairly steady base reading is obtained. Conditioning then begins by the presentation of, say, a tone signal followed about half a second later by the shock, evoking the change in skin resistance. These events are repeated at suitable intervals, and the presence of the newly acquired signal connection is detected by a trail in which the signal tone is not paired with the shock. The conditioned response can usually be established in such circumstances after only a few repetitions.

Some Other Phenomena of Classical Conditioning

Some other events that occur in classical conditioning situations have great importance for an understanding of this form of behavior modification, as well as of other more complex forms dependent upon it. For one thing, there is the phenomenon of *extinction*, a kind of unlearning that results in the disappearance of the previously learned association. There is also *stimulus generalization*, the occurrence of responses to stimuli similar but not identical to the signal used to bring about learning.

Extinction.   Suppose that a conditioned response of blinking the eye to the sound of a bell has been reliably established. How may it be eliminated? The most dependable way to bring this about is by repeated presentation at suitable intervals of the signal (the bell) *without* the unconditioned stimulus (the puff of air). When these conditions are put into effect, the conditioned association undergoes a progressive weakening; in other words, it appears less and less dependably, until it fails to occur. The rate at which extinction occurs is illustrated in Figure 2.2. After an initial period of extinction, upon presentation of the signal, the conditioned response may appear again. Pavlov called this *spontaneous recovery*. However, the connection is obviously weaker and may be reextinguished in a few trials in which the signal is presented alone. Ultimately, under the extinction procedure, the newly learned connection does disappear completely.

Stimulus generalization.   The conditioned response, once established, may be elicited by signals other than the one used to establish it. The closer the physical resemblance between these other signals and the original one, the stronger the response obtained. Suppose that a galvanic skin response has been conditioned to a tone signal of 1000 cycles per second. It may then

Figure 2.2 A typical curve of extinction for the conditioned galvanic skin response (GSR), showing the decrease in percent of response in five extinction trials that followed immediately after the signal learning. (Data of C. I. Hovland, "Inhibition of reinforcement" and phenomena of extinction. *Proceedings of the National Academy of Sciences*, 1936, 22, 430–433.)

also be shown to occur, in somewhat reduced strength, to a tone of 1025 cycles or 975 cycles. The conditioned association, in other words, is not a highly precise one. *Generalization* may be shown to other stimuli that resemble the original stimulus as measured along some physical dimension. Hovland (1937) obtained the results shown in Figure 2.3 when he measured the strength of the GSR to stimulus tones differing from the original signal by increasing amounts of "just noticeable difference" (JND). Evidently, the *gradient of generalization*, as such curves are called, drops off sharply at first and then more gradually as the resemblance between the original stimulus and the test stimulus lessens.

OPERANT (INSTRUMENTAL) LEARNING

Another fundamental kind of learning, simple to observe and widespread in its occurrence, is called *operant learning* (Skinner, 1938). Thorndike called it *trial-and-error learning*, but this is probably not a good descriptive name. It is also called *instrumental learning* (Kimble, 1961), and this name makes two points: (1) it emphasizes the precise skilled nature of the responses involved, as in "using instruments"; and (2) it implies that the learned connection is instrumental in satisfying some motive. Such learning concerns a *single* connection between a stimulus and a response, not multiple or chained associations, which will be dealt with later. The stimulus and the response appear to become integrally bound together in such learning in a

Figure 2.3 The stimulus generalization gradient obtained for a conditioned GSR to a tone of 1000 cycles. Decreasing amplitude of response was found as the stimulus tones used to "test" the responses were made decreasingly similar to the original tone. (Data of C. I. Hovland, The generalization of conditioned responses with varying frequencies of tone. *Journal of General Psychology*, 1937, *17*, 125–148).

way that does not happen with classical conditioning. A bell really has nothing to do with the blinking of the eyes, except as a signal for it. But because of the occurrence of operant learning, a colored block may become for a child a thing to be picked up.

It is difficult indeed to find an example of human learning that might represent operant learning in the relatively pure form of a single learned association. Many instances that seem at first glance to be suitable examples turn out on closer inspection to represent the somewhat more complex forms of chaining or verbal association. Human beings rapidly acquire a background of prerequisite learning that enters into the subsequent acquisition of these more complex varieties.

This difficulty makes it necessary to turn for an example to the behavior of the very young human infant. Although the amount of systematic experimental evidence is very limited for infant learning, it can be assumed with some safety that not much previous learning has occurred. Accordingly, the example to be considered here is the infant's learned response of holding the nursing bottle in the proper position for feeding. Under what conditions does a child learn to perform this act?

At first, of course, there is the stage at which this behavior has not been learned. The parent must hold the bottle tilted at the proper angle in order for feeding to be possible. During the course of feeding, however, the infant will often grasp the bottle, somewhat unsystematically to be sure. Now suppose the parent begins to release the bottle so that greater pressure is exerted against the child's own hands. So long as the child's hands exert a sufficiently firm grasp in a sufficiently raised position, the feeding continues. Should this muscular tension be relaxed, a point will be reached in the tilt angle of the bottle where no formula reaches the mouth. Then perhaps the parent will push the bottle upward into position again, and feeding is restored. By gradually helping the child hold the bottle properly, and gradually removing the help so that the child's own responses are appropriate, the stimulus-response association becomes established. Eventually the child, once given the bottle, can reinstate the necessary response and has then "learned to hold the bottle."

This learning event appears to be not so much trial and error as a "successive approximation" procedure. The learning that occurs here, as Skinner says, is a matter of *shaping*. A set of stimuli, including the sight and feel of the bottle as well as the proprioceptive stimuli from the child's arm and hand muscles, becomes connected with a correct response of holding the bottle in a position from which the formula can be sucked into the mouth. At the same time, a slightly different set of stimuli, involving a slightly different feel (when the bottle is lower), results in no food in the mouth.

Conditions of Operant Learning

We consider here the nature of conditions necessary for operant learning (abbreviated as S → R learning). Learning conditions within the learner are distinguished from those outside the learner (in the learning situation).

Conditions within the learner. First of all, it is evident that there must be a terminating act that provides *reinforcement*. In the example given here, it is necessary for the infant to suck on the nipple and thereby obtain a mouthful of food. This produces what Thorndike called a "satisfying state of affairs." In modern usage, taking of food by sucking is the *reinforcer* that is made contingent upon the performance of holding the bottle.

A single S → R may be established when the terminal reinforcing act does not immediately follow the response, as in the sucking example, but is more remote. This is the more usual case when one is dealing with human behavior. For example, a correctly performed association may be followed by a word of praise ("Good!"), which in turn is connected with a response that ultimately provides the reinforcement. Thus, meeting this condition does not require that the terminating act be an innate one, such as the ingestion of food. For learning to occur, one needs only to insure that there is such a response, terminating in reinforcement, which can be performed by the learner.

Conditions of the learning situation. Turning to the conditions external to the learner, we see that the critical set of events is the occurrence of a *reinforcement contingency.* Reinforcement must take place when the act to be learned occurs and only when it (rather than some other action) occurs. As for the reinforcement, some theorists hold that this must be something that the learner already does vigorously, whereas others maintain that the act must lead to an external reward, such as food, praise, or relief of pain. It is not possible here to consider the essential nature of reinforcement, as discussed, for example, by Kimble (1961) and by Bower and Hilgard (1981). But the fact of reinforcement, which makes the learning of any new S → R association dependent upon the directly following consequences, is widely accepted. In the example of the infant and the bottle, the operant learning will not occur if the bottle is empty, and the sucking and swallowing of liquid does not occur (unless, of course, some other reinforcer is provided). Modern learning theorists call this condition the *empirical law of effect.*

Contiguity has an important part to play in the establishment of an S → R association. The shorter the time elapsing between the occurrence of the learned response and the occurrence of reinforcement, the more rapidly learning will take place. If the infant had to wait, say, five seconds between the time the bottle was tilted correctly and the time food arrived, it would be more difficult to learn than if this interval were only a second. This relationship between *ease of learning* and *delay of reinforcement* has been well established in laboratory studies of operant learning (Kimble, 1961, pp. 140–156).

Repetition of the stimulus situation is also a necessary condition for the occurrence of operant learning. As Thorndike's findings (1898) demonstrate, the amount of repetition needed may vary from a single trial to many, depending on the degree to which they conform with responding that is either innately determined or previously learned.

Other Phenomena of Operant Learning

Extinction. Just as there is a phenomenon of "unlearning" for classical conditioning, there is a comparable event in operant learning, also called *extinction.* In both cases, these events result in the disappearance of a previously learned association, and it is understandable on these grounds that the two forms of unlearning should be given the same name. But the conditions under which they occur are *not* the same.

Extinction of a learned operant occurs when the reinforcement that follows the learned response is omitted. Under these circumstances, the association gradually decreases its likelihood of occurrence when the stimulus situation is presented, until it dies away. It may be noted that extinction is not a matter of omitting an unconditioned stimulus (like a puff of air to the cornea, in signal learning) but of removing the reinforcing state of affairs. The latter can be done in various ways. For example, extinction of the infant's S → R association of holding the bottle may be brought about, as has been said, by omitting the milk. It may also be accomplished by making sure that the infant is not hungry when presented with the bottle (this might happen if the child were fed by the parent before being allowed to hold the bottle). Under such circumstances, little or no reinforcement would follow the learned response of bottle holding, and it would undergo extinction.

Generalization. The generalization of the learned connection to stimuli that resemble the set used in learning is another characteristic shared by operant learning and classical conditioning. Guttman and Kalish (1956) established learning in which pigeons pecked at a transparent plate that transmitted light of a given color. Then the birds were tested with this color and a range of other colors with wavelengths differing from the original color. As expected, the frequency with which pecking occurred to a color decreased regularly as the physical resemblance between it and the original hue was lessened.

The Basic Forms of Learning in Everyday Life

Responding to signals and executing simple motor responses are no more than a small portion of the capabilities that human beings can and do learn. Perhaps the phenomena they exhibit and the conditions of their learning can help us understand *associative learning* as a basic process. However, to complete our account, we shall describe a few examples of these forms of learning as they occur in everyday life and in the school.

Some examples of classical conditioning. Signal learning occurs in the lives of all of us. Sometimes it happens because of environmental accidents rather than as a result of planning by parents or teachers. We learn to respond to many kinds of signals, such as automobile horns, alarm clocks, and certain kinds of verbal outbursts of other people. Generally speaking, we acquire an association exhibiting a diffuse, imprecise, "emotional" response to such signals, because they are repeated together with other (unconditioned) stimuli that generate these responses initially and innately.

A number of children's fears are doubtless acquired by means of classical conditioning. Children may avoid certain locations, animals, or even people because there has been a pairing (whether adventitious or otherwise) of the stimuli they present with some unconditioned stimulus such as a frightening noise. It seems likely that pleasant emotions can also be aroused in essentially the same way through previous pairings with particular persons or situations. Possibly the young child's favorite teddy bear or blanket may become a signal for pleasant feelings, just as may particular scenes or melodies at a later stage of development.

Some examples of operant learning.   Operant learning has considerable usefulness. For children, it is a kind of learning that includes such things as reaching and grasping for toys or other objects, smiling at the proper people, positioning the body and limbs, and vocalizing utterances. As the child acquires a larger and larger repertory of these somewhat isolated associations, they begin to form into longer chains, and it becomes increasingly difficult to isolate "pure" examples of this kind of learning.

Operant learning is undoubtedly the main variety involved in the initial learning of words by children. An initial utterance like "nha-nha," overheard by a parent, may be *shaped* into a connection that yields the response "ma-ma" by suitable use of the procedure of differential reinforcement. A part of this procedure involves getting the child to respond to the proper external stimulus, which may be "ma-ma" spoken by the parent.

Reinforcement and the Learning of Receptive Behaviors

Since much school learning requires verbal communication directed toward the learner, one of the important events in instruction is the adoption by the learner of what may be called a *receptive set* toward such communications. While adult learners normally adopt a set for receptivity as a matter of course, the same cannot be said of many children. Accordingly, a good deal of the efforts of a kindergarten or prekindergarten teacher may well be devoted to guiding the learning of receptive behaviors in children. The child must learn to attend to verbal requests, to follow verbal directions. These are examples of what may be called *receptive sets.* Even though the effects of its learning are quite general, and bring about behavior that precedes the learning of many other things, a receptive set is learned under the same conditions as other more specific acts.

These conditions that pertain to the learning of receptive behaviors are those of operant learning. In particular, a proper selection of the conditions of reinforcement is involved; the *contingencies of reinforcement* must be suitably arranged so that the reinforcement is made *contingent upon* the occurrence of the behavior to be learned. In simple terms, this means that learning conditions must be arranged so that some reinforcing activity follows closely the occurrence of the desired receptive behavior. Some examples of the application of the reinforcement principle to the learning of receptive behaviors follow.

Increasing the "span of attention."   The young child may be highly inattentive and may follow the verbal directions of the teacher for only a few minutes at a time. The suggested conditions for learning are to follow each period of attention by reinforcement (perhaps initially a tangible reward), making sure that such reinforcement is given only for instances of attention which gradually become longer and is withheld when the span lapses to shorter intervals.

Involvement in learning tasks. Children are sometimes unwilling to become involved in learning tasks; that is, they are unreceptive to the verbal communications that are an essential part of the learning situation. Receptive behavior may be established, according to reinforcement principles, by first choosing a task the child likes to do and insuring that appropriate verbal directions precede it. As the application of reinforcement is continued, the teacher may then expand the preferred activity to include another that is not originally one that the child likes to do. For example, if the child likes to paste circles on construction paper, this activity may be preceded by a suitable communication and expanded to include the task of identifying particular sizes or colors before pasting.

Following directions. The preschool or kindergarten child may not follow directions well or consistently. Again, the idea of reinforcement can provide an important clue for the arrangement of learning conditions. One must begin with a task that is short and requires brief directions. Preferably, such a task has a specific starting and ending point. An example might be, "Pick up your pencil and place an X in each of the circles on this page. When you have marked an X in all of the circles, lay your pencil down." It is a task, in other words, for which the child *can* successfully follow directions. Working from this base, the teacher gradually expands the length of the task and the variety of directions required, making sure that there are definite checkpoints at each step along the way, and that the terminal part of the task is such that the child experiences both success and satisfaction in its completion.

These few examples show that working with reinforcement contingencies to establish receptive behaviors is something that requires a great deal of patience. But even more important is careful attention to the *sequence* of events that reflects the correct contingencies. The reinforcing state of affairs must *follow* the to-be-learned behavior, not precede it. The reinforcement must also have a great deal of *consistency*; that is, it must occur when the desired behavior appears and be omitted when the desired behavior does not appear.

The principle of reinforcement contingency is a powerful tool for the management of learning. Of course, its applicability is not confined to young children. Liking to read good books, being receptive to music and art, acquiring effective study habits, all may pose problems for students of any age and represent behavior modifications potentially attainable by proper application of reinforcement techniques (Skinner, 1968, pp. 145–168). Such techniques have also been of particular help in changing the behavior of "emotionally disturbed" children in classrooms in which routines of reinforcement were carefully planned and executed (Hewett, 1968). Still another important field of application is in the training of mentally retarded children (Orlando and Bijou, 1960).

CHAINING

Chaining is the connection of a set of individual associations (S → Rs) in sequence. Some sequences, such as turning on a television set or a washing machine, are made up of motor responses. Other sequences are entirely verbal, for example, the greeting "How have you been?" or the pledge of allegiance to the flag. For the acquisition of sequences that are nonverbal, the term *chaining* will be used. The subvariety involving verbal behavior deserves a separate description as *verbal association* or *verbal sequence learning*.

E. R. Guthrie (1935) tells the story of a girl who had acquired the habit of dropping her coat on the floor when she entered the house. Her annoyed mother had often scolded her and required her to go back and pick up the coat. But her chastisement was quite ineffective in overcoming the unwanted behavior. The mother, however, discovered an effective procedure. She made the girl go out of the house with her coat on, then come in, and hang it up properly. This illustration shows the importance of correct sequencing of events in a chain. The original chain troubling the mother had the following sequence: enter house → drop coat → see mother → mother says → "Pick up coat" → pick up coat → hang up coat. What had to be established was a shorter chain with quite a different sequence: enter house → keep coat on → approach closet → hang up coat. The mother displayed some useful wisdom when she realized the second chain could not be learned by simply adding links to the first one. What was necessary was the institution of the desired chain with correct links from start to finish.

The Conditions for Chaining

The conditions necessary to bring about chaining can now be described. There are, as usual, some conditions that exist within the learner and others that are external.

Conditions within the learner. Of utmost importance to the acquiring of chains is the requirement that each individual stimulus-response association be *previously learned*. One cannot expect a chain such as opening a door with a key to be learned in an optimal way unless the learner is already able to carry out the S → Rs that constitute the links. The learner must be able to (1) identify the key's upright position, (2) insert it into the lock fully, (3) turn it clockwise fully, and (4) push the door open. If a novice (a child, perhaps) complains that he or she cannot unlock the door after being shown how, one immediately suspects that the child has not fully mastered one of these links. Similarly, the chain learned in starting the motor of a car requires the previous learning of the individual links. Failure to learn on a single occasion usually indicates that one or more links have not been previously learned (pressing the accelerator as soon as the motor "takes hold" is an example).

Conditions in the situation. Several conditions in the situation are important to chain learning. Assuming that the links are known, the first condition for the establishment of a chain is getting the learner to *reinstate them* one after the other *in the proper order.* Two different approaches to this sequencing are possible:

1. One can begin with the terminal act and work backward, as Gilbert (1962) suggests. This insures that the link one is trying to connect at any given point in the chain will always be introduced in the correct order. To connect link 4 with link 3, one waits for the occurrence of link 3 and then immediately follows it with link 4 (the act leading to reinforcement); then one observes the occurrence of link 2, and follows it with links 3 and 4, and so on. This *progressive part* method, it may be noted, follows the procedure of operant learning *for each successive link.*
2. A *prompting* method may be used, in which additional external cues are employed to insure the reinstatement of the links in the proper order beginning from the start of the chain.

Both these methods work. Whether one is more effective than the other, in some or all circumstances, is a question awaiting further evidence.

A second condition is the familiar one of *contiguity.* The individual links in the chain must be executed in close succession if the chain is to be established. The smoothly executed chain pertaining to unlocking a door, for example, requires that the insertion of the key be followed by turning it to the right. Some of the stimuli for the second of these links arise out of the responses made in the first. Should there be a delay between the two links, the stimuli for the second connection will not be like those of the performance aimed for, and the chain may be learned with difficulty. This does not mean, of course, that it is not possible to learn chains that have delays deliberately built into them. Such instances may certainly be acquired; for example, one learns to await a dial tone after the coin has dropped fully into a public telephone.

A third condition relates to the *repetition* variable. Presumably, if all other conditions were fully met, repetition would be unnecessary. The chain would tend to form on the first occasion. Practically speaking, however, it is difficult to insure that all the conditions have been fully met. The individual links may be only partially learned, the prompting may be not fully effective, or some delays may creep into the execution of the chain. Given these practical circumstances, repetition of the sequence has the function of smoothing out the rough spots, and some practice is almost always desirable for this reason.

The fourth, and final, condition of *reinforcement* is present in the learning of chains. The terminal link must provide reinforcement—the food pellet is obtained, the engine is started, the door is opened. Should the final link cease to be a reinforcer, extinction will occur, and the chain as a whole will then disappear. It has been found that the reinforcement needs to be immediate in order for chain learning to occur most readily. The introduction of a delay in reinforcement markedly increases the difficulty of learning.

Chains and Procedures

Although chains are widespread throughout human experience, they are essentially humble in nature. In the early grades of school, a number of important chainlike skills must be learned. Buttoning, fastening, tying, using a pencil, erasing, and using scissors are chain activities. At a slightly more complex level are the chains involved in printing and writing, which are of considerable importance as components of more elaborate activities to be acquired in school. Throwing, catching, and kicking balls, and many other fundamental athletic skills are also acquired as chains in the early years of the individual's life. Even the earliest encounters with computers require the learning of chains.

In the later years of school, varieties of additional chains must be learned. Sometimes these take the form of *procedures*, complex and lengthy chains that often incorporate simpler chains as components. Students may learn in science courses to carry out many measurement procedures, such as weighing and the pouring of liquids. Later still they may learn to adjust and use a variety of scientific instruments, including microscopes, voltmeters, centrifuges—each of them requiring the learning of procedural chains. Vocational students are likely to have to learn a large number of procedures as basic tasks of the occupation they plan to enter. Students of art may learn procedures such as brush techniques, students of music the complex procedures of playing an instrument.

The individual motor chains that are learned, many early in life, contribute to the more complex, purposeful activities called *motor skills*, which are the subject of Chapter 10. Chains of motor responses become the components of motor skills, often as "part-skills." The latter are combined into organized motor performances which continued practice invests with smoothness and precise timing.

VERBAL ASSOCIATION

If it is true that people are capable of a tremendous variety of performances with the use of their legs, arms, and hands, it is also even more strikingly true that their verbalizations show enormous versatility. Although the individual sounds human beings can make are limited in number, the patterns that can be constructed from these sounds are virtually limitless. Such patterns, at least the simplest ones, are learned as chains. But the tremendous variety of these chains as well as the subtlety of resemblances and differences among them make verbal behavior a subject of special interest from a learning standpoint. Here we shall deal with only the most elementary kind of verbal behavior, the learning of verbal associations and verbal sequences. Chapter 8 will describe the learning of the more highly meaningful forms of verbal learning as *verbal information learning*.

Probably the simplest verbal chains are illustrated in the activity of *naming*. A youngster is told while being shown a three-dimensional object, "This shape is called a tetrahedron." If conditions are otherwise right, the next time this particular object is seen, the child will be able to say that it is a tetrahedron. But other conditions are important. It is fairly easy to identify some that would insure that the learner would *not* be able to say "tetrahedron." To mention two of the most obvious: (1) the child may not have distinguished the object as a stimulus and (2) may not have learned to say its name.

The act of naming a specific object like a tetrahedron seems likely to be a chain of at least two links. The first of these links is an observing response, an association that connects the appearance of the object with some responses involved in observing the triangular character of its sides and that at the same time serves to distinguish it from other three-dimensional objects of roughly the same size and color. The second link is the association that enables the individual to say "tetrahedron" (that is, to say it is a voluntary response, in the manner of stimulus-response learning). As a diagram, a simple act of naming is represented by this kind of chain:

$$S_{object} \rightarrow R_{observing} \sim s_{tetrahedron} \rightarrow R_{\text{"tetrahedron"}}$$

The small *s* stands for the internal representation of the object resulting from its observation. Internally generated stimuli of this sort are called *mediators*.

Verbal Sequences

Chains of verbal associates may be longer than two links. Relatively brief verbal sequences of words can readily be learned as chains in a single presentation.

Verbal chains may be very long indeed, if we think of the memorization of digits twenty-eight places beyond the decimal point, or, for that matter, of the verbatim learning of verses of poetry or books of the Bible. If presented with an entire verse of poetry, the learner may break it up and put the pieces together in various ways. On the whole, the evidence suggests that under many circumstances the most efficient procedure is what is called the *progressive part* method, in which the learner adds a new part (like a line of the poem) while continuing to rehearse the older parts (McGeoch and Irion, 1952). On the first try, the learner may attempt to say line 1; on the next, lines 1 and 2; on the next, lines 1, 2, and 3; and so on. Such a procedure not only insures that parts are chosen that are within the span of immediate memory but also allows for the continued practice of earlier learned parts that may be forgotten because of interference.

In the case of lengthy verbal chains, some aspects of the sequence may have been previously learned, as well as the individual links. The English language displays some remarkably predictable sequences, as is illustrated by the completion of such phrases as "Boy meets _____," and "Now is the _____." The predictability of such sequences means that the ordering of English words has in many cases been learned previously (G. A. Miller, 1951). Longer chains may be taken in as a "chunk" under such circumstances. Another implication is that the learning of many prose sequences has already been partially accomplished.

Conditions of Learning Verbal Sequences

It should now be possible to state in more formal terms the important conditions for the establishment of the capability of reinstating verbal associates and verbal chains.

Conditions within the learner.   The previous discussion leads to the following summary of the conditions for optimal learning.

1. Each link of the chain to be acquired must have been previously learned as an S → R association. This means, of course, that the verbal unit must have been discriminated as a stimulus from other units resembling it in a physical sense. Also implied is that this unit should be discriminated as the response portion of the association; in other words, it should be a highly familiar response (Underwood and Schulz, 1960).
2. Mediating connections between each verbal unit and the next must have been previously learned. The greater the learner's available supply of these *coding* connections, the more rapidly will learning take place. Evidence clearly shows (Noble, 1963) that verbal associates are learned more rapidly, the greater the number of verbal "free associates" there are to the syllables or words being chained. But verbal codes are not the only mediators usually available. Visual images or auditory images (as in rhymes) may also serve this function extremely well.

Conditions of the learning situation.   When conditions within the learner are satisfied, the learning of a verbal chain is a fairly simple matter.

1. The verbal units must be presented in the proper sequence. Various methods may be employed, the two most common being presenting the entire chain to be read from left to right or presenting the units in the chain one after another. This latter method has been extensively used in laboratory studies of verbal sequence learning.

2. As is true for nonverbal chains, learning is aided by the use of external stimuli that furnish cues for order. Such an extra cue is provided, for example, by mnemonic devices that may have been previously learned. Students of neuroanatomy sometimes learn the names of the cranial nerves in order by learning the rhyme "On old Olympus' towering top. . . ," the first letters of which cue the order of the nerves: olfactory, optic, oculomotor, and so on. Pronounced poetic meter serves such a function for chains of medium length, as in "The cur'few tolls' the knell' of par'ting day'." Other kinds of prompting stimuli may also be used.

3. For words that have not previously been learned in a sequence, the limit of verbal chain length that can be apprehended as a single event (for previously unchained material) appears to be seven plus or minus two. In other words, the individual's span of immediate memory determines the length of a chain that can be learned all at once. There is no limit, apparently, to the length of a verbal chain that can be learned part by part, for people have memorized entire books verbatim. For long chains, the progressive-part method has usually been shown to be the most efficient one.

4. Confirmation of correct responses must be provided for in the learning situation. This is often done by showing the learners a printed form of the entire verbal chain immediately after they have tried to reproduce it or each link of the chain following each response.

The Effects of Interference

One of the most important phenomena that occurs in the learning of verbal associates and sequences is *interference*. Many experimental studies of such learning have shown that the linking of one verbal unit with another (1) tends to reduce the retention of another such linking that has *preceded* it in time and (2) reduces the probability that a *subsequent* linking will be retained (Hill, 1981; Underwood, 1964). In the first case, the interference works backward on something previously learned and so is called *retroactive*; in the second, the interference works forward on something yet to be learned, and is termed *proactive*.

Suppose that one is to learn a verbal chain of twelve links, beginning CAT RED SIT LAM TIN ROW, and that each one of these links has been well learned as an individual word. If one were to require the learning of chains involving two words at a time, such as CAT-RED, or RED-SIT, it is obvious that each chain could be learned immediately on a single occasion. Yet when the twelve words are put together as a chain, and exposed one after another, they probably cannot be learned with perfect accuracy on a single occasion. Why is this so? The most probable explanation is that in the process of connecting a particular link, other links (both previous and subsequent ones) become *harder to remember* because of interference.

If one has learned CAT RED SIT in the chain of twelve links used in our illustration these links will be available in memory when one is trying to recall TIN (as a later part of the chain), and the recall of TIN will to some extent be made less likely. Similarly, once TIN has been learned, it will be available in memory when CAT, RED, or SIT are being recalled; and this in turn will reduce the likelihood of recall of each of those words in the chain. The longer the verbal chain, the greater will be the effects of interference on any link.

Another condition of importance to the establishment of verbal sequences is one which overcomes interference by making the items highly *distinctive*. For example, it is known that a highly unusual word occurring, say, in the fourth position of a ten-item sequence will be recalled in this position better than most other items in the sequence. An example of an unusual unit in a five-unit sequence is as follows: PAL BOY CAT 8 SIR. This factor of distinctiveness may also partially account for the better retention of items at the beginning and at the end of a sequence.

Meaningful Verbal Learning

While the learning of verbal sequences, including those containing meaningful words, may be usefully conceived as a process of "chaining," it appears doubtful that this conception is capable of encompassing the whole of what is meant by verbal learning. When students "learn" a chapter in their history text, for example, one does not expect them to demonstrate this learning by a verbatim oral reproduction of the text. Instead, one may expect them to be able to reproduce in the proper order the "ideas" that are contained in the text. Is such a performance achieved solely by the processes of association and chaining, or are some other processes at work? There are several reasons for believing that the learning of meaningful propositions (or *verbal information*, as we call it in Chapter 8) requires internal processing that is different from, and may be more complex than, verbal chaining. Some of the major reasons follow.

1. Learning the substance (that is, the ideas) of meaningful verbal material is accomplished more rapidly than learning the same material as verbal chains to be reproduced verbatim (Briggs and Reed, 1943; Jones and English, 1926).
2. The retention of ideas, as contrasted with the verbatim reproduction of meaningful passages of prose, shows considerable superiority in recall (English, Welborn, and Killian, 1934).

3. The effects of interference, which are prominently involved in the retention of nonmeaningful material, have in a number of studies failed to appear as influences on the retention of meaningful passages (Ausubel and Blake, 1958; Hall, 1955; Newman, 1939).

4. The system of memory for meaningful material permits the retrieval of information that was not directly stored in it rather than being confined to what was specifically presented (Bartlett, 1932; Tulving, 1972).

Such evidence has led a number of learning theorists to hold that verbal chaining is entirely inadequate to account for the learning of meaningful material. Chapter 8 is devoted to a description of conditions affecting meaningful verbal learning, which we call *verbal information learning*.

Some Educational Implications

Human performances that involve the use of learned verbal chains can be found in everyday life both in and out of school. Children *do* sometimes learn the sequence of letters in the alphabet, whether or not this is considered good pedagogical practice. Students memorize formulas, or key numbers like the square roots of 2 and 3, and occasionally much longer numbers. Children are often expected to learn the Lord's Prayer, the first verse of "The Star-spangled Banner," the Pledge of Allegiance, and a number of other verses, sayings, or quotations. Students often have to memorize the school cheer and may, of course, learn many lines as amateur actors. But all these tasks seem to lack an essential purpose, urgency, when considered in terms of the larger goals of education. The sequence of the alphabet, after all, is not involved in learning to read. Formulas can easily be looked up. And although "The Star-spangled Banner" may be of some use in social gatherings, its words can gradually "sink in" after being heard many times. Although few educators today would be inclined to say memorization is bad, it is generally thought to be unimportant. Perhaps it is a matter of priority. Students must acquire knowledge and the ability to think, and these goals are heavily emphasized in today's curricula.

Priorities, however, have changed in American schools. Seventy-odd years ago there was much verbal memorization: the alphabet, the multiplication table, numerical quantities and formulas, poetry, prose writings like the Gettysburg Address, the Preamble to the Constitution, and so on. Students practiced reciting the verbal passages they had learned, and declamation contests rewarded oratorical skill. Verbal memorization is still emphasized today, we are told, in schools in many parts of the world, particularly in Asia and to some extent in Europe.

Is there an educational value to the memorization of verbal sequences? What considerations should enter into a determination of priority for instruction of this sort? The answer to these questions lies in a recognition of the most important uses of recalled verbal phrases, sentences, or passages.

The time saved by recalling a formula rather than looking it up is not that important. The major use of recalled verbal sequences is in the area of language itself, specifically in the construction of verbal utterances that communicate ideas. The question is, What degree of skill is it important for students to have to express their ideas in oral form, whether in simple conversation, in informal conference, or in lectures and speeches? To what extent are we interested in providing students with skills of communication and persuasion?

It is no accident that some of the most renowned American orators of previous generations knew such literature as the Bible and the writings of Shakespeare to the extent that they could repeat whole passages verbatim. These and other literary sources are fundamental to our language. People who are skilled in oral communication are able to recall words, phrases, or entire passages of flowing English and to weave them into their own vocal utterances in highly effective ways. They are able to do this not simply because they have *read* these classics of English literature, but because they have *memorized* them. In the terms used in this chapter, they have learned many varieties of verbal sequences and can recall them readily. They are able to utilize at will such historic phrases as "dedicated to the proposition that all men are created equal" or "a tide in the affairs of men" or "with what measure ye mete, it shall be measured unto you."

Naturally, such memorized verbal sequences may also become a source of clichés in both writing and speaking. Phrases such as "stark naked," "utterly exhausted," "starry-eyed wonder," "justifiable wrath," and "global diplomacy," since they have been encountered so frequently in reading material and in everyday speech, become memorized portions of the individual's language repertoire. An orator may sometimes deliberately exploit the appeal such clichés have for an audience. But a skillful speaker is one who has also learned to "play the changes" on such familiar materials so that the overly familiar is avoided. And it is even more important for the writer to avoid excessive use of such phrases, even though they form an important part of his or her background.

In sum, then, the most direct and obvious employment for memorized verbal sequences is in the construction of created language, particularly in oral speech. The construction of effective original speech does not depend simply on an understanding of rules for grammatical expression. It requires the ready recall of a large fund of verbal sequences that can be woven into novel passages of spoken English in a countless variety of patterns.

GENERAL REFERENCES

Classical Conditioning

Bower, G. H., and Hilgard, E. R. *Theories of learning*, 5th ed. Englewood Cliffs, N.J.: Prentice-Hall, 1981. Chapter 3.

Kimble, G. A. *Hilgard and Marquis' "Conditioning and learning."* New York: Appleton, 1961.
Pavlov, I. P. *Conditioned reflexes.* Transl. by G. V. Anrep. London: Oxford University Press, 1927. (Also in paperback, New York: Dover, 1960.)

Operant Learning

Bower, G. H., and Hilgard, E. R. *Theories of learning,* 5th ed. Englewood Cliffs, N.J.: Prentice-Hall, 1981. Chapter 7.
Kimble, G. A. *Hilgard and Marquis' "Conditioning and learning."* New York: Appleton, 1961.
Skinner, B. F. *Contingencies of reinforcement: A theoretical analysis.* New York: Appleton, 1969.
Mayer, G. R. *Applying behavior-analysis procedures with children and youth.* New York: Holt, Rinehart and Winston, 1977.

Chaining

Gilbert, T. F. Mathetics: The technology of education. *Journal of Mathetics,* 1962, *1,* 7–73.
Keller, F. S., and Schoenfeld, W. N. *Principles of psychology.* New York: Appleton, 1950. Chapter 7.

Chaining Verbal Associates

Cofer, C. N. (Ed.). *Verbal learning and verbal behavior.* New York: McGraw-Hill, 1961.
Cofer, C. N., and Musgrave, B. S. (Eds.). *Verbal behavior and learning: Problems and processes.* New York: McGraw-Hill, 1963.
Dixon, T. R., and Horton, D. L. (Eds.). *Verbal behavior and general behavior theory.* Englewood Cliffs, N.J.: Prentice-Hall, 1968.
Hulse, S. H., Egeth, H., and Deese, J. *The psychology of learning,* 5th ed. New York: McGraw-Hill, 1980.
McGeoch, J. A., and Irion, A. L. *The psychology of human learning,* 2nd ed. New York: McKay, 1952.
Underwood, B. J., and Schulz, R. W. *Meaningfulness and verbal learning.* Philadelphia: Lippincott, 1960.

3

What Is Learned—Varieties

Now that we have seen what the basic prototypes of learning can accomplish in terms of associations and chains, we need to examine some more complex forms of human performance. We shall look at some major categories of learned human capabilities as they occur in everyday life and in educational settings. In addressing the question of how such complex forms of behavior are learned, we shall return in Chapter 4 to the ideas of *information processing* as a model for learning. As an essential piece of background knowledge, however, we must begin in this chapter with the question "What kinds of things do people learn?"

During their lifetimes, people learn many things. In early childhood they learn to interact with their environment in basic patterns of sensorimotor coordination: to move their bodies and limbs, to manipulate objects, and to respond appropriately to their protectors. Quite early, children learn to speak and to use language, an enormously powerful set of skills that will have the most profound effect on all their subsequent learning and that will set them apart from all other animals for the remainder of life.

As beginning schoolchildren people face two major learning tasks. One is to continue their socialization by learning to interact with other children and adults in ways that will achieve moment-to-moment goals without conflict and that will support the needs of others with kindness and consideration. A second task is to learn to respond appropriately to symbols that represent the environment in miniaturized fashion: pictures, diagrams, printed words, and numerals. This last is the intellectual task of reading, writing, and manipulating numbers. While children continue to elaborate and supplement what they have learned of oral language, this distinctly new form of symbol use adds another dimension to their capabilities as human beings.

Once these basic language and symbol-using skills are acquired, schoolchildren are capable of learning many things. They learn about the earth, its peoples, and its geographic and physical properties. They learn about human society and its institutions. They learn how to deal with the environment not only by direct interaction with things and people but by solving problems constructed in imagination. As they continue to acquire competence in symbol-using activities, children learn skills which prepare them for adult life: comprehending passages of printed language, composing communications in both oral and written form, solving practical quantitative problems with numbers.

As education continues, individuals learn more and more specialized knowledge and more highly complex skills. They may learn things that will be useful in pursuing an occupation, such as typing or drawing or the procedures of real-estate transfer. They may learn knowledge and skills that pertain to the role of a citizen, such as the structure of local government, the rules of jury trial, and the laws of voter registration. And the chances are that they will learn things that give them pleasure, such as listening to music, reading fiction, and participating in sports.

FIVE VARIETIES OF CAPABILITIES

How is it possible to think about learning in all the varieties in which it occurs during the lifetime of the individual? How can we find common ground among the many instances of learning, considering the vast array of differences that are so apparent in what is learned?

As a first step, we must focus on *what is learned*, rather than upon the conditions that exist when learning occurs. Learning conditions are not the same for different varieties of what is learned. Therefore, it is first necessary to distinguish as clearly as possible the *types* of outcomes that learning has—the *varieties of learned capabilities*. These capabilities, as we have seen in Chapter 1, must be observed as human performances. What must be looked for, then, are types of human performances that have common characteristics, even though their specific details vary. From these performances inferences can be made about the learned capabilities that make them possible.

Consider, then, what major categories of human performance may be established by learning. The following list will be expanded upon in the remainder of this chapter.

1. **Intellectual skills.** An individual may learn to interact with the environment by *using symbols*. The child uses oral language to deal with the environment symbolically, for example when saying "Open!" as a request to a parent to open a door or as a response to such a parental request. Reading and writing and using numbers are basic kinds of symbol use learned in early grades. As school learning continues, symbols are used in more complex ways: for distinguishing, combining, tabulating, classifying, analyzing, and quantifying objects, events, and even other symbols. Mentally converting 24 ounces into pounds is a simple example; making a singular verb agree with a singular subject in a written sentence is

another. This kind of learned capability is given the name *intellectual skill*. It is "knowing how," or *procedural knowledge*.

2. **Verbal information.** A person may learn to *state* or *tell* a fact or set of events by using oral speech or by using writing, typewriting, or even drawing a picture. Obviously, a person must *have* some intellectual skills in order to posit statements. In other words, the person must know how to construct at least a simple sentence. But the purpose of the learner's act is to *tell information*, not merely to display the intellectual skill of sentence construction. A simple statement may vary in its skill from one person to another, yet the information (the ideas) conveyed may be indistinguishable. What is stated may be a single idea or a set of ideas that are ordered in some way (as in recounting a set of events). Being able to *state* ideas is a learned capability called *verbal information* ("knowing that," or *declarative knowledge*).

3. **Cognitive strategies.** The individual (in this case, a young woman) has learned *skills that manage her own learning, remembering, and thinking*. She has learned certain ways of reading different parts of a text, for example. When asked to learn a set of apparently unrelated object names, she approaches the task by searching for relationships among the names, or relationships with other more familiar names. Perhaps the learner has acquired a particular skill that enables her to recapture the details of a scene she has witnessed, or to remember the main points of a lecture she has heard. She has also learned certain techniques of thinking, ways of analyzing problems, and approaches to the solving of problems. These skills, which control the learner's own internal processes, are given the general name of *cognitive strategies*.

4. **Motor skills.** The learner has learned to *execute movements* in a number of organized motor acts, for example in threading a needle or throwing a ball. Often these individually coherent acts form a part of more comprehensive activities such as playing tennis or driving an automobile. The unitary acts are referred to as *motor skills*.

5. **Attitudes.** A learner acquires mental states that *influence the choices of personal actions*. One person may tend to choose actions that increase the likelihood of selecting golf, for example, as a preferred recreation. Another may choose to study physics rather than English literature during the time available for study. Such "tendencies," which are seen as *choices* to the learner rather than as specific performances, are called *attitudes*.

Here, then, are the five main categories of capabilities that human beings learn. These categories are comprehensive. Any learned capability, regardless of how it is otherwise described (whether mathematics, history, economics, or whatever), has the characteristics of one or another of these varieties.

How are these organized outcomes of learning related to the learned associations discussed in Chapter 2? The answer is that they are more complex units which, according to theory, are held together by learned associations. As we saw in the previous chapter, isolating a single association for study is very difficult, if not impossible. What gets learned and stored in memory are these complexes called *capabilities*. We shall see in later chapters what conditions support the learning of each of these capabilities. First, though, we shall give some additional examples of each type.

INTELLECTUAL SKILLS

A person who takes a saw and cuts a piece from the end of a board is, of course, interacting with the environment in a *direct* manner. This action, however, may have been preceded by other actions, for example planning that involved measuring a length like $22\frac{3}{16}$ inches, finding the difference between that distance and $24\frac{1}{8}$ inches, and perhaps using a tool with a straight edge to draw a line at a right angle to the board's edge. Many of the activities involved in this type of planning require the individual to interact with the environment *indirectly* through the use of symbols. The learner represents linear measurements by the symbols "$22\frac{3}{16}$" and "$24\frac{1}{8}$" and proceeds to operate on these symbols rather than directly on the lumber itself. Some symbolic operations are done "in the learner's head"; others may need to be worked out on a small writing surface. But these operations are very different from the actions that would need to be done directly to the wood, were such symbolic activity not possible. The capabilities that make symbol use possible are what we mean by *intellectual skills*.

An individual learns many simple and complex intellectual skills. The content of school mathematics, for example, is virtually all intellectual skills. However, intellectual skills pertain also to symbols other than numerals and number operations. In a larger sense, the symbols used to represent the environment to the learner constitute *language*. A relatively simple intellectual skill in the use of language symbols is the grammatical rule of the objective form of a pronoun following a preposition ("from her"). A more complex skill is involved in using a metaphor ("seeking the bubble reputation"). Since language is used to record and communicate the relationships (concepts, rules) that exist in any subject, the learning of such relationships can be expected to involve the learning of intellectual skills. It may be seen, therefore, that such skills are in many ways the most important types of capability learned by human beings and the essence of what is meant by "being educated."

Conditions of Learning

How do individuals learn to use symbols in an intellectual skill? It is apparent that some conditions for this learning must exist within the learners (*internal* conditions), while others are *external* to the learners and may be arranged for in instruction. These conditions will be described in subsequent chapters. Here, we shall give a few examples to illustrate what is meant by the conditions of learning.

Suppose that some youngsters are expected to learn how to find the difference between a linear extent measured as $22\frac{3}{16}$ and another measured at $24\frac{1}{8}$, and assume that they don't already know how to compute this. They can learn this particular skill (applicable to all mixed numbers containing eighths and sixteenths) quite readily, provided certain internal conditions are present. Particularly significant among these conditions is the availability of certain *component* or *subordinate skills*, which may be identified as "forming equivalent fractions by multiplying numerator and denominator by the same (small) number" ($1/8 \times 2 = 2/16$), "forming equivalent fractions by dividing numerator and denominator by the same (small) number" ($6/16 \div 2 = 3/8$), and "finding a difference by subtracting fractions having common denominators" ($4/8 - 1/8 = 3/8$). Of course, if these subordinate intellectual skills have not been previously learned and stored in memory, they will not be available to the learners and must therefore be learned. But if they are present as internal conditions, learning of the new skill can proceed with little difficulty or delay.

The external conditions for acquiring the new skill may begin with a reminder that the subordinate skills will need to be recalled. Often this is done by means of verbal communications, such as "Remember how to subtract fractions like $\frac{3}{16}$ from $\frac{4}{16}$." A second kind of verbal communication may be used to inform the learners of the learning objective, that is, of what the specific purpose of the performance will be after it has been learned. This may be represented by some such statement as "The distances $22\frac{3}{16}$ and $24\frac{1}{8}$ are different; what you want to do is to find the amount of this difference." A picture and an example might also be used to convey this objective.

The next event that makes up the external conditions of learning for this skill is a communication that suggests "putting things together," that is, combining subordinate skills to make the new one. Actually, the learners may already see how to do this or may be able to "discover" it themselves, in which cases no additional stimulation is needed. Often, though, some statement or hint may be valuable, such as "If you change $\frac{1}{8}$ to $\frac{2}{16}$, can you then find the difference?" Then, if the learners state the difference they seek as "$\frac{1}{16}$," only one more step is needed. This is the provision of a new example (such as the distances $1\frac{7}{8}$ and $1\frac{1}{4}$) on which the learners can demonstrate the application of their newly learned skill.

Thus, the *internal conditions* for learning an intellectual skill consist of (1) the previously learned skills that are components of the new skill and (2) the processes that will be used to recall them and put them together in a new form. Several distinct events make up the *external conditions*, and some of the most important have been mentioned in the example described. Notice that these external events have the purposes of (1) stimulating recall of the subordinate skills; (2) informing the learner of the performance objective; (3) "guiding" the new learning by a statement, question, or hint; and (4) providing an occasion for the performance of the just-learned skill in connection with a new example. These events are perhaps the most obvious features of the external conditions of learning; they serve to illustrate a set that will be described more fully in later chapters.

The Nature of Intellectual Skill

The most typical form of an intellectual skill, exemplified by the instance just described, is called a *rule*. When learners have acquired a rule, they are able to exhibit behavior that is *rule-governed*. Such behavior does not mean that the learners are able to formulate or state the rule. Quite the contrary is often the case; young children evidence rule-governed behavior in their use of oral language and in many other ways. The external observer of behavior (the learning investigator, for example) is able to draw the conclusion that a rule has been learned.

Performance is rule-governed when its regularity can be described only by a rule statement rather than by the relation of a particular stimulus to a particular response. A rule statement relates *classes* of stimuli to *classes* of responses. In the fraction example mentioned previously, the learners acquired a capability which does not relate to the *particular* stimulus situation ($22\frac{3}{16}$, $24\frac{1}{8}$), but to a *class* of situations having certain characteristics (mixed numbers including eighths and sixteenths). Accordingly, the performance of which the learners become capable does not consist of a *particular* response ($\frac{1}{16}$), but of an entire class of responses (any differences of the mixed numbers presented, expressed as eighths or sixteenths). Thus the performance made possible by learning is perfectly regular, and it can be described by a rule statement ("finding the differences in mixed numbers containing eighths and sixteenths as fractional parts"), which relates an entire class of stimuli (any mixed number of the sort described) to a class of

Applying a rule: A performance involving an *intellectual skill.*

performances (any difference obtained). This is what is meant by rule-governed behavior. The individuals, then, can be said to have *learned a rule.*

It should be emphasized that when learners have acquired a rule (as shown by its use), they may be quite incapable of describing what has been learned, in other words, of *stating* the rule. In fact, learners are likely to think that stating the rule is a rather silly thing to do. It may also be a very difficult thing to do, because rule statements can quickly become enormously complicated in a linguistic sense. The most straightforward way of determining whether learners have learned a rule is to simply ask them to perform on an instance of the rule not previously encountered during learning. If the rule is one of finding differences in mixed numbers of the sort described, then a new instance such as $3\frac{1}{16}$ and $3\frac{5}{8}$ may be given. If the rule is one of using pronouns in the objective case following prepositions, an example might be "The captain was silent, and I waited to receive a signal from _____."

Subcategories of Intellectual Skills

We have seen that when component skills are already available in the learner's memory, rule learning is typically a matter of *combining* simpler component skills into a new pattern. Are these component skills also rules that are analyzable into even simpler skills? In general, the answer to this question is yes. A complex rule may usually be shown to be composed of simpler rules, each of which in turn may be further analyzed into previously learned components. However, as this process continues, the nature of the components changes somewhat, and they need therefore to be separately identified and described.

Concepts.   A fairly simple rule is represented by the statement "A gallon of liquid consists of four quarts." It can be seen that a rule is a *relation* between two or more *things.* In this case, there are three *thing-concepts:* gallon, liquid, and quart. The primary *relational concept* is the verb "consists of," with a secondary relation represented by the quantity "four." Thus, an initial step in the further analysis of a *rule* produces the new category of intellectual skill called a *concept.* The concept is a component of a rule and is thus subordinate to it. Learning the simplest rule is a matter of combining some previously learned concepts in a particular way. If the learner has previously learned the concepts *gallon, liquid, quart, four,* and *consists of,* learning the new rule "A gallon consists of four quarts" may be readily accomplished. (Note particularly, however, that learning the new rule does not mean learning to state the rule, which is not the same capability. Rather than stating it, the learner who has acquired this rule will be able to show that four quarts of liquid make up a gallon.)

Discriminations.   Intellectual skills can be analyzed still further. Concepts can be seen to require even simpler skills called *discriminations.* The things concepts represent have characteristics that may be described (in the ultimate sense) in physical terms. For example, a dime possesses certain object properties: it is round, of a certain thickness and diameter, a particular weight, silver in color, and metallic in its "feel." (As we shall see in a later chapter, these object properties are themselves concepts of a basic sort called *concrete concepts.*) In order to learn to identify a dime, that is, to learn "dime" as a concept, these object properties must be distinguished from each other and from those of other objects. The learner must be able to *tell the difference* between objects varying in these particular qualities: between a color that is silver and one that is not silver, between a shape that is small and round and one that is not, and so on. Telling the difference between variations in some particular object-property is called a *discrimination.*

Obviously, colors, shapes, sizes, texture, and most other discriminations important for further learning are learned very early in our lives. Kindergarten children are likely to have learned to tell the difference between the color red and some other color, as shown by an exercise in which they match the reds in an array of various colors with a red sample. But not all the necessary discriminations have been learned; the children may need to learn to tell the difference between tones of nearby pitch or letter-sounds that are similar (such as the short vowels "e" and "i"). Quite a few children must learn discriminations of printed letter patterns (for example, L and J) as prerequisite capabilities for learning the letter concepts *d* and *b.* The necessity for learning additional discriminations sometimes becomes apparent in later school grades and in adult learning. For example, the pronunciation of certain sounds in a foreign language may need to be preceded by discrimination learning so that the students first learn to hear the differences between the new sounds and sounds more familiar to their native languages. Consider also how many fine discriminations must be learned by a tea taster or a wine taster!

Higher-order rules.   Just as rules may be analyzed to reveal the necessity for simpler skills (concepts, discriminations), the reverse process also occurs. Rules may be combined by learning into more complex rules, which may be called *higher-order* rules. Such rules have greater generality, that is, they apply to a greater variety of situations than do any of the component rules of which they are composed. Higher-order rules may be learned under conditions similar to those for other rules. It is often true, however, that higher-order rules result from the learner's *thinking* in a *problem-solving* situation. In attempting to solve a particular problem, the learner may put together two or more rules from very different content domains in order to form a higher-order rule that solves the problem.

Procedures.   Another way that rules get more complex is simply by becoming longer. The rule for long division, for example, is relatively lengthy and deserves to be called a *procedural rule* or simply a *procedure.* Just as is the case with other rules, the long division procedure may be analyzed into simpler subordinate rules, including those of multiplying whole numbers, estimating a quotient, subtracting whole numbers, and others. Additionally, though, the procedure is a chain of simpler rules that must be applied in a particular sequence in order for division to be done correctly. This means that in addition to knowing each of the simpler rules (and the concepts of which they in turn are composed) the learner must be able to reinstate a *sequence of action steps.* Often, as in the case of long division, remembering the sequence is not too difficult following practice because the steps repeat themselves as the performance proceeds. When procedures become very long and nonrepetitive, they usually require an external checklist, or something similar, as an external aid to remembering the sequence of steps.

Prerequisites in the Learning of Intellectual Skills

The very important learned capability called *intellectual skill* has a number of forms, some simple and some more complex. Distinguishing these forms of intellectual skill is important for two reasons. First, a significant characteristic of intellectual skills is that the learning of any one skill depends upon the prior learning of one or more simpler skills. Second, as we shall see in later chapters, certain notable differences exist in the conditions of learning required for each type of intellectual skill.

A summary of the interdependence of intellectual skills, and their dependence upon basic forms of learning, may be given as follows:

Higher-order Rules
require as prerequisites

Rules
that require as prerequisites

Concepts
that require as prerequisites

Discriminations
that require as prerequisites

Basic forms of learning:
Associations and Chains

Subsequent chapters will devote attention to conditions for learning the following forms of intellectual skill: discriminations, concepts, rules, and higher-order rules. The significance of the internal conditions brought about by prior learning of prerequisite skills will again be emphasized in these descriptions.

COGNITIVE STRATEGIES

A second and most important kind of capability learned by human beings is called a *cognitive strategy*. These are the skills by means of which learners regulate their own internal processes of attending, learning, remembering, and thinking. These internally organized skills have been given different names by various authors. Bruner (1971) refers to them as "cognitive strategies," which he relates primarily to processes used in finding and solving novel problems. These strategies appear to be related to the "mathemagenic activities" described by Rothkopf (1971) and to the "self-management behaviors" referred to by Skinner (1968). They are called "executive control processes" by a number of learning theorists who favor information-processing conceptions (Greeno and Bjork, 1973).

Besides the increasing repertoire of competencies for dealing with their environment (intellectual skills), learners acquire increasingly skillful strategies that they use to activate and regulate the learning, retention, and use of their own skills. Rather than being oriented to specific kinds of external content, such as language or numbers, cognitive strategies are largely independent of content and generally apply to all kinds. If learners have improved their strategies of attending (one kind of cognitive strategy), this strategy will apply to the learning of any subject, regardless of content. Similar generality of application would be true of strategies of encoding, strategies of memory search, strategies of retrieval, and strategies of thinking.

A "mnemonic system" for remembering the sequence of ideas in a speech is an example of a cognitive strategy for retrieval. Such a system is of limited usefulness and is not advocated here as something to be learned. Nevertheless, mnemonic systems of this sort have been used by prominent orators for a great many years. One strategy is to create an imaginary position for each point to be made somewhere in a highly familiar room. For example, the speaker might begin with the high cost of oil, imagining that this idea is located at the left of the doorway to the room. Then, proceeding clockwise, the speaker might locate the next point (say, the scarcity of food supplies) as the closet door along the lefthand wall. If the next item is about the incidence of starvation, this might be located in the left corner of the room. Thus, the speaker would continue this process until all the main points have been located in the room. The imagined locations become cues for the retrieval of the main points of the speech in the proper order. In using this method of cueing to remember a speech, the speaker has deliberately chosen a cognitive strategy, in this case a strategy for retrieval.

This particular cognitive strategy for remembering a sequence of ideas appears to have limited usefulness. The cognitive strategies that apply to

Originating an interpretation of unfamiliar data: a performance using a *cognitive strategy.*

remembering in a more general sense are undoubtedly more complex and subtle in their operation. It is likely, though, that everyone has learned *some* strategies for remembering, as well as some for attending, learning, and thinking. The strategies that some people possess appear to be better than those of others, because the *quality* of their learning and thinking is better or faster or more profound. How to bring about improvement in cognitive strategies, so that every learner is "working up to potential" is one of the challenging problems of education.

Cognitive strategies may be fairly simple and easy to understand. For example, children who are given the task of learning a set of objects shown in pictures may be told to commit them to memory in terms of categories. Likewise, children who are learning pairs of words (BOY-COW) may be told to think of a sentence connecting the words ("The BOY rode the COW"). Strategies of this sort can readily be acquired and used so as to improve the performance of remembering (Brown, 1978; Rohwer, 1975). There are also cognitive strategies that are more abstractly described, such as those applicable to the solution of mathematical puzzles, which are obviously more difficult to acquire and use (see Wickelgren, 1974). It seems probable that many of a learner's cognitive strategies improve in increments over long periods of time, rather than being totally learned in a few days, weeks, or months.

Internal conditions. Since cognitive strategies are internally organized skills, they must have something internal to work on. Thus, it is reasonable to suppose that if an encoding strategy for the learning of facts is being learned, and if the strategy involves putting the facts in familiar categories, the learner must have a repertoire of convenient categories, previously learned and recallable for use. Similarly, if what is being learned is a strategy of thinking that can be used to solve problems of light refraction, the learner needs to have available some previously learned rules relevant to light refraction. Thus, although cognitive strategies are themselves free of specific content they cannot be learned or applied without some specific content. These mental operations, in other words, must have something to work on—they cannot be exercised in a vacuum.

The capabilities that need to be recalled from previous learning in support of the learning and refinement of cognitive strategies are usually intellectual skills. This necessity is illustrated in the previous examples: in one instance concepts (such as categories) must be recalled by the learner, in the other rules of light refraction. In addition, information is sometimes the kind of capability that must be recalled. For example, the exercise of cognitive strategies in composing an original essay on the distribution of electric power obviously requires the recall of a great deal of information about the subject. The effectiveness of the learner's cognitive strategies may be indicated by the originality of the essay, but the facts must be available in any case.

External conditions.   The identification of specific external conditions affecting the learning of cognitive strategies is perhaps least well known. In view of the absence of exact knowledge of what these strategies are and how they operate internally it is perhaps not too surprising that our knowledge of these external factors is limited. Arranging external conditions to establish and improve cognitive strategies is, after all, an attempt to exercise external control in an indirect fashion over the learning of capabilities that are internally managed.

Practical means of arranging optimal external events for learning cognitive strategies usually come down to encouraging the learners to practice the use of cognitive strategies in a variety of novel situations. For example, various kinds of learning materials may be presented, so that the learners are faced with decisions about strategies for attending, strategies for encoding, or strategies for retrieving. A succession of extremely varied, novel problem-solving situations may confront the learners, requiring them to select and use different strategies in solution. The educational implications of these approaches call for the inclusion in courses of instruction of frequent occasions on which the students are challenged to discover new ways of managing their own learning and thinking (see Bruner, 1961, 1971).

VERBAL INFORMATION

A third major category of learned capability is verbal information. We expect individuals to learn verbal information during the course of their lives and to retain a great deal of such information so that it is immediately accessible.

We know that individuals have learned some verbal information when they are able to "tell about it" or state it. What they state, of course, is basically in the form of one or more sentences (or propositions) having a subject and a predicate. Information is thought of as verbal, or more precisely, capable of being verbalized, because we know it in sentence form. Learners' statements often have the purpose of "telling" some other person or persons. However, learners often may be "telling" themselves.

Information is an important capability for a number of reasons (see Gagné and Briggs, 1979, pp. 78–84). First, the individual may need to know certain facts, such as the days of the week, months of the year, names and locations of cities, states, and countries, simply because they are "common knowledge" that every adult is expected to have. Second, verbal information functions as an aid and accompaniment to learning. The study of the principles of economics, for example, requires that the learner make use of a broad base of organized information about production, markets, banking, and so forth. And third, information is important as specialized knowledge, which must be possessed by experts in any field. A trained chemist, in addition to knowing how to use the rules of chemistry, also knows a great deal of information about the subject.

Conditions of Learning: Verbal Information

The learning of verbal information requires its own set of internal and external conditions. Consider the following passage as containing information to be learned:

> The action of a volcano consists of the expulsion of heated materials to the surface of the earth from the interior. A volcano is a conical hill composed mainly of materials which have been thrown up from underground, and have built up around a central vent of eruption. The volcano has a truncated summit, and a cup-shaped cavity called a crater. In large volcanoes, rents appear on the sides of the cone, from which steam, hot vapors, and streams of molten lava are poured out.

This passage may be perceived as being composed of several propositions, which may be listed as follows:

Proposition 1:   Function of volcanic action (expulsion of heated materials, etc.)
Proposition 2:   Characteristics of a volcano (conical hill)
Proposition 3:   Function of volcanic hill materials (thrown up from underground, etc.)
Proposition 4:   Characteristics of conical hill (truncated summit, cup-shaped crater)
Proposition 5:   Relation of cone to rents (rents form on sides of cone)
Proposition 6:   Function of rents (hot vapors and lava pour out from them)

Let us assume that we are not immediately concerned with how the previous passage is presented—whether in print or by some auditory source. How are these propositions learned? What conditions must be present in order for the learner to "tell" someone what the passage contains?

Internal conditions.   Certain internal conditions for learning this material are immediately apparent. The learner must have available, from previous learning, linguistic rules (intellectual skills) that make possible the comprehension of a sentence as a structure composed of agent, action, location, object, and so on. If the passage itself has a complex syntactic structure, the learner must be able to interpret it as a proposition with conjunctions, dependent clauses, modifiers, and other elements. Apparently, the learner must also "know the meaning" of at least some of the words, although the

". . .Now we are engaged in a great civil war, testing

Testing what?

Stating *verbal information.*

extent of this requirement cannot be clearly specified. For example, the sentence "Tilgem reduces gorbil" is readily learnable as information even though the thing-concepts "tilgem" and "gorbil" are not known from previous learning.

Still another internal condition influencing the learning of information has been emphasized by a number of learning theorists (Ausubel, Novak, and Hanesian, 1978). This is the availability to the learner of cognitive structures of meaningfully organized information. Such structures of organized knowledge are considered to have been previously learned. They are related in some meaningful sense to the new information to be learned. For example, the passage about volcanoes would, according to Ausubel (1978), be related to a more inclusive cognitive structure, previously learned, probably pertaining to hills, mountains, and other geographical features of the earth, including those having the name "volcano." The new information is conceived as being acquired when it is subsumed in this larger meaningful structure.

External conditions.   Two sets of conditions are of particular importance to the learning of information. The first is stimulation that makes a cognitive structure readily accessible to the learner—that reminds one of the larger meaningful context into which the new information will fit. Studies by Ausubel and his associates (Ausubel, 1960; Ausubel and Fitzgerald, 1962) and more recently by Mayer (1976, 1978) have shown the effectiveness of what is called an *advance organizer* in accomplishing this purpose and thus improving learning and retention of information. The advance organizer is a communication given to the learner prior to the encounter with the set of information to be learned. Its purpose is to remind the learner of the meaningful context already available in memory and relevant to the new learning.

A second condition which may be externally arranged is that of *informing the learner of the objective* of the learning. In any passage of meaningful propositions, certain features of the information may represent the desired goal of learning while others may be incidental. For instance the objective may be to learn definitions of new technical terms, to learn the dates of the events described, or to learn new names for familiar things. The particular objective chosen, of course, will be reflected in the test given to assess the learning of the information. Informing the learner of the objective may be done in a number of ways, including a directly informing statement. A way that has been much investigated is to include within a passage of text the type of questions the learner will be expected to answer once the learning is completed (Frase, 1970; Rothkopf, 1970, 1971).

What about repetition as an external condition? Will not the information be better learned and retained if it is gone over several times? Practically speaking, repeated hearing or reading of an informational passage does improve its learning. The weight of evidence, however, attributes this result to variations in the internal processing of the information from one occasion to another. Certain facts within a total paragraph may be processed when it is read the first time, certain others when it is read a second time, and so on. But the reading of the *same* fact more than once does not make it "stronger" in memory. Thus if a learner is asked to learn ten disconnected facts, repetition of the list increases the number of facts learned. It does so, according to most modern theories, because additional facts are taken in with additional repetitions.

Varieties of Information Learning

Just as intellectual skills come in varieties that are more or less complex, one might expect similar degrees of complexity among sets of information. It is true that certain distinctions can be made along this dimension of information, although the categories are primarily for convenience of description.

The simplest kind of information is a *label* or *name*. This elemental form of information probably should be conceived as a *verbal chain* in which an instance of the object is associated with its name. The verbal response itself may be of any variety. It is important to note that learning the *name* of an object is not the same as learning the *concept* that the object represents.

The most typical form of unitary information is the *fact*, which is expressed as a simple proposition such as "Jet engines generate noise," or "The boy captured the model airplane." Single facts appear to depend for their learning on the internal presence of the "larger meaningful structure." Their learning may also be strongly influenced by the simultaneous presentation of other related facts. Information may also be learned sets of interrelated facts, or *bodies of knowledge*. The organization of these sets of facts, the ways in which the individual components are related to each other, may have a considerable effect on learning and retention. Organized knowledge often takes the form of a *schema*, having interesting properties to be described later.

MOTOR SKILLS

We turn now to a different and familiar kind of capability usually easy to distinguish in human performance: a motor skill. (Note that there is no particular reason for considering this type of learning outcome, or any other type, in a particular order; each type is different.) Many examples of motor skills come to mind. In the young child, there are motor skills involved in such activities as dressing and eating. At the start of school, if not before, the child learns to make particular kinds of designs, including letters, with pencil and paper. Throughout the years of school, the individual learns the various motor skills involved in games and sports: throwing a ball, hitting a ball, jumping over hurdles, climbing. In many different kinds of courses, the student is likely to learn a number of tool-manipulation procedures that include motor skills. While not often given a central place in the curriculum, a variety of motor skills are involved in school learning.

We say that individuals have acquired motor skills not simply when they can perform certain prescribed movements but when these movements are organized to constitute a total action that is smooth, regular, and precisely timed. The smoothness and timing of performances reflecting motor skills indicates that these performances have a high degree of internal organization. As a consequence, it is typical for a motor skill to improve in precision and smoothness with continued practice over long periods of time (Fitts and Posner, 1967).

Internal conditions.   Motor skills are usually composed of a sequence of movements. Thus, the action of driving a golf ball consists of the sequence of (1) positioning the body and the club, (2) raising the club over the shoulder, (3) aiming the club at the ball, and (4) making a full swing with involvement of arms and body. Printing the letter E requires a sequence of movements in which each of the four lines composing a letter is first (a) positioned and then (b) drawn to a particular length. The *procedural sequence* of a motor skill must be learned. Often, it is learned along with the motor skill itself. This procedure, which has been called the "executive subroutine" (Fitts and Posner, 1967), has the character of a rule by which the learner knows "what comes after what." A procedural rule of this sort must be available to the learner as improvement in motor performance with practice continues.

The separate parts of a motor act can often be learned and practiced separately as *part-skills*. These too may be prerequisites established by previous learning. Swimmers, for example, sometimes practice separately the

Planing the edge of a board:
a *motor skill.*

part-skills involving leg movements and those involving arms and head. A child who is learning to draw a square may "put together" the previously learned part-skills of line drawing and corner drawing.

External conditions.   The most important set of external conditions for motor skill learning is provided by periods of practice. The sequence of motor acts gets repeated again and again in a situation that provides *feedback,* or *knowledge of results.* Sometimes, the feedback is an inherent part of the act being performed, as is the case when a musical instrument is being played. In other instances, additional feedback may be provided by a coach or instructor. In any case, an important part of the stimulus situation for motor skill learning is provided by internal feedback from the muscles. Apparently, it is this system of kinesthetic sensing over successive periods of practice that brings about the gradual improvement in smoothness and timing of motor skills.

ATTITUDES

The final kind of learned capability to be introduced in this chapter is attitude. We define attitude as an internal state that influences (moderates) the choices of personal action made by the individual. Attitudes are generally considered to have affective (emotional) components, cognitive aspects, and behavioral consequences (Triandis, 1971). Some investigators consider attitudes to have their origin in discrepancies of beliefs and ideas; others presume that attitudes arise from emotional states. Here, we emphasize the effects of attitudes upon behavior, that is, upon the choices of action made by the individual. The internal states that influence these actions may well possess both intellectual and emotional aspects. However, it is their outcomes in human performance that provide the point of reference for our description of attitudes as learned dispositions.

The kinds of actions taken by human beings are obviously influenced greatly by attitudes. Whether one listens to classical music or rock, whether one obeys the posted speed limit while driving, whether one encourages one's spouse to express independent ideas, whether one votes for candidates who demonstrate concern for the public good—all are influenced by attitudes. These internal moderating states are acquired throughout life from situations encountered in the home, in the streets, in the church, and in the school.

Of course, the course of action chosen by an individual in any particular situation will be largely determined by the specifics of that situation. An individual who has a strong attitude of obedience to laws may nevertheless exceed the highway speed limit when in a hurry and no patrol cars are in sight. A child who has a strong attitude of honesty may steal a penny when no one is paying attention (Hartshorne and May, 1928). But the moderating tendency that persists over a period of time and that tends to make the individual's behavior consistent in a variety of specific situations is what is meant by an attitude. Obviously, observing and measuring the strengths of such tendencies is not an easy matter, since the effects of specific situational variables must be ruled out.

Attitudes are learned in a variety of ways. They can result from single incidents, as when an attitude toward snakes is acquired because of an instance of fright experienced in childhood. They can result from the indi-

Making a choice of personal action: the influence of an *attitude*.

vidual's experiences of success and pleasure, as when children acquire strong positive attitudes toward video games by experiencing increasing success at them. And frequently, they are learned by imitation of other people's behavior, as when a child learns how to behave toward strangers by observing the actions of a parent. Regardless of these variations, there are some common factors in the learning and modification of attitudes.

Internal conditions. Attitudes must have some behavioral means of expression; this implies that certain capabilities appropriate to that behavior must be available to the learner. If the personal action to be influenced involves intellectual skills, these skills obviously must have previously been learned. For example, if an attitude of liking to solve mathematical puzzles is to be acquired, the learner must have some previously learned skills of numerical computation. If someone is to develop a strong attitude toward avoiding harmful drugs, some information about the drugs (such as their appearance and names) is a prerequisite. The learner who is to learn to like playing the piano must already have the motor skills to make such a choice of action possible.

When attitudes are acquired by imitation (or human modeling) it is necessary that the learner have respect or admiration for the person whose behavior is being imitated. This condition often exists between child and parent or between child and teacher. As is well known, the imitation of peers is likely to replace the imitation of parents during the preadolescent and adolescent periods, when the earlier unquestioning admiration for parents is replaced by a kind of rejection. In adults, attitudes are often established by modeling of people who are respected or admired for various qualities: physical attractiveness, virtuosity in sports, moral probity. But admiration for the model must exist, if the attitude exhibited in his or her behavior is to be acquired by the learner.

External conditions. Since a variety of situations may lead to the modification of attitudes, their common features are not easy to identify. Apparently, there must either be (1) an emotionally toned experience on the part of the learner in following a course of action or (2) the observation of a "good" or "bad" effect of the behavior of a human model. The latter condition leads to the presumption that the success (or, alternatively, the failure) of the model is vicariously experienced, that is, the learner is vicariously reinforced (Bandura, 1971).

A word should be said here about the inadequacy of certain external conditions in bringing about changes in attitudes. It has frequently been found that verbal statements intended to persuade are quite ineffective in changing listeners' attitudes (Hovland, Lumsdaine, and Sheffield, 1949). Whether based upon appeals to moral principles, to emotional states, or to rational arguments, these statements appear to be equally ineffective. Thus, it seems that a frequently important condition for attitude change is the presence of a human being who can serve as a model, whether in actuality or in the learner's imagination. When the persuasion is attempted by a respected model, a change in the learner's attitude is likely; persuasive statements without such a model are notoriously ineffective.

As is true for other learned states, the feedback of accomplishment, reward, or success is also an important condition for the learning of attitudes. The learner who succeeds at ice skating will very likely acquire a positive attitude toward that activity. The learner who has modeled an attitude of kindness toward animals will be more likely to maintain this attitude if his own acts of kindness to animals are rewarded in some fashion.

A SUMMARY OF TYPES OF LEARNING OUTCOMES

The five major categories of learning outcomes have now been described and exemplified. As a summary, we include Table 3.1, which lists these learned capabilities and gives a single example of each. The first category, intellectual skill, contains a number of subordinate categories, listed in order of their increasing complexity. The five major categories, however, are arbitrarily ordered in the table. They are simply different capabilities (Gagné, 1984).

Subsequent chapters of this book describe conditions of learning for the categories of human capabilities shown in Table 3.1. Chapters 5 and 6 are devoted to *intellectual skills*, from discriminations to rules. Chapter 7 considers the higher-order rules involved in human problem solving and goes on to discuss the category of *cognitive strategies* as it applies to the control of various learning processes. The learning of *verbal information*—the stating or "telling" of names, facts, and ideas—is taken up in Chapter 8 and followed in Chapter 9 by an account of the capabilities involved in *problem solving*. Next we consider the learning of the class of capabilities called *motor skills*, in Chapter 10. The category of *attitudes*, in Chapter 11, completes the roster of major classes of learning outcomes.

EDUCATIONAL IMPLICATIONS

Human beings learn many different things during their lifetimes. One way to make sense of the enormous variety of outcomes learning produces is to consider them as *performance categories*. Although these categories cut across the subject matter (content) of what is learned, they possess certain distinguishing features. Each category implies that a different kind of capability has been learned.

When viewed in this manner, there are five major categories of learned

TABLE 3.1   Five Major Categories of Learned Capabilities, Including Subordinate Types, and Examples of Each

Capability (Learning Outcome)	Examples of Performance Made Possible
Intellectual Skill	Demonstrating symbol use, as in the following:
Discrimination	Distinguishing printed *m*'s and *n*'s
Concrete Concept	Identifying the spatial relation "underneath"; identifying a "side" of an object
Defined Concept	Classifying a "family," using a definition
Rule	Demonstrating the agreement in number of subject and verb in sentences
Higher-order Rule	Generating a rule for predicting the size of an image, given the distance of a light source and the curvature of a lens
Cognitive Strategy	Using an efficient method for recalling names; originating a solution for the problem of conserving gasoline
Verbal Information	Stating the provisions of the First Amendment to the U.S. Constitution
Motor Skill	Printing the letter *R*; skating a figure eight
Attitude	Choosing to listen to classical music

capabilities: intellectual skills, verbal information, cognitive strategies, motor skills, and attitudes. Not only do these differ in the performances they make possible; they also differ in the conditions most favorable for their learning. These learning conditions are partly *internal,* arising from the memory of the learner as a consequence of previous learning. In addition, some learning conditions are *external* to the learner and may be deliberately arranged as aspects of *instruction.* In the following paragraphs we summarize some of the main points made in this chapter that apply to the planning of instruction.

For the learning of *intellectual skills* (procedural knowledge) the most important internal condition is the recall of prerequisite skills that are components of the new skill to be learned. External conditions, often in the form of verbal directions, guide the combining of these simpler skills. Intellectual skills have several varieties, increasing in complexity from *discriminations* to *concepts, rules,* and *higher-order rules.* Rules with many steps are called *procedures.*

The learning of *verbal information* (declarative knowledge) depends upon the recall of internally stored complexes of ideas that constitute "meaningfully organized" structures. In addition, certain basic linguistic skills must be present so that information can be stored in propositional form. Externally, the conditions of learning operate to relate the information to be learned to these previously learned structures, which serve as cues for retrieval and as organizing schemas.

Cognitive strategies are internally organized skills that learners use to manage their own processes of attending, learning, remembering, and thinking. They require as internal conditions the recall of intellectual skills and information relevant to the specific learning tasks being undertaken. Externally, what is apparently required is frequent opportunity to practice these strategies; over the course of practice, their use is refined and improved.

The learning of *motor skills* is attended by the recall (or prior learning) of an executive subroutine that provides the sequence and pattern for the performance and often by the recall of part-skills that are combined into the total motor act. External conditions are mainly provided by repetition of the performance, that is, by practice

Attitudes are internal states that modify choices of personal action toward objects, persons, or events. They are learned in a variety of ways. One of the most dependable is by modeling, which requires a preexisting or previously learned respect for a real or imagined person. When this method of attitude change is employed, the external conditions consist of display of the desired behavior by the model and the observation of a successful outcome (or reward). The experience of success following a behavior choice usually has a direct positive effect upon the learner's attitude.

GENERAL REFERENCES

Varieties of Learned Capabilities

Gagné, R. M. Learning outcomes and their effects. *American Psychologist*, 1984, 39, 377–385.

Gagné, R. M. The learning basis of teaching methods. In N. L. Gage (Ed.), *The psychology of teaching methods*. 75th Yearbook, National Society for the Study of Education. Chicago: University of Chicago Press, 1976.

Gagné, R. M., and Briggs, L. J. *Principles of instructional design*, 2nd ed. New York: Holt, Rinehart and Winston, 1979.

Intellectual Skills

Klausmeier, H. J., Ghatala, E. S., and Frayer, D. A. *Conceptual learning and development: A cognitive view*. New York: Academic Press, 1974.

Resnick, L. B., and Ford, W. W. *The psychology of mathematics for instruction*. Hillsdale, N.J.: Erlbaum, 1981.

Verbal Information

Anderson, J. R., and Bower, G. H. Recognition and retrieval processes in free recall. *Psychological Review*, 1972, 79, 97–123.

Ausubel, D. P., Novak, J. D., and Hanesian, H. *Educational psychology: A cognitive view*, 2nd ed. New York: Holt, Rinehart and Winston, 1978.

Cognitive Strategies

Bruner, J. S. The act of discovery. *Harvard Educational Review*, 1961, *31*, 21–32.

Bruner, J. S., Goodnow, J. J., and Austin, G. A. *A study of thinking.* New York: Wiley, 1956.

Brown, A. L. Knowing when, where, and how to remember: A problem of metacognition. In R. Glaser (Ed.), *Advances in instructional psychology*, Vol. 1. Hillsdale, N.J.: Erlbaum, 1978.

O'Neil, H. F., Jr. *Learning strategies.* New York: Academic Press, 1978.

Motor Skills

Fitts, P. M., and Posner, M. I. *Human performance.* Monterey, Calif.: Brooks/Cole, 1967.

Singer, R. N. *Motor learning and human performance*, 3rd ed. New York: Macmillan, 1980.

Attitudes

Bandura, A. *Principles of behavior modification.* New York: Holt, Rinehart and Winston, 1969.

Ringness, T. A. *The affective domain in education.* Boston: Little, Brown, 1975.

Triandis, H. C. *Attitude and attitude change.* New York: Wiley, 1971.

4

The Processes of Learning

In the previous chapter, we described the five major kinds of *outcomes* learning can have. In this chapter we take a different view of learning, this time as a *process*, or more precisely a *set of processes*. A single act of learning has (at least for purposes of analysis) a beginning and an end. Each instance of learning takes a certain time, even if only a few seconds. During the course of an act of learning, a number of different processes are at work. One can analyze these processes into phases, each of which performs a different kind of processing. The processes may occur in sequence, but it is also possible for two or more to take place simultaneously, or "in parallel."

The processes of learning form the basic structure of information-processing theories of learning. These theories have adopted a model that posits internal *structures* of the human learner and the kinds of *processing* accomplished by each of these structures. The processes and structures described by learning theories are inferred from empirical studies of learning. Presumably, these processes and structures reflect the action of the human central nervous system and are compatible with what is known about the neurophysiology of the nervous system. The structures and their activities remain as postulated entities, however, since they have not yet been related to particular locations or operations of the brain.

From the model of learning and memory employed in modern theories, one can identify the phases of processing that take place from the beginning to the termination of an act of learning. These events of learning provide us with valuable indicators of what conditions of learning are needed for the completion of each phase. The purpose of this chapter is to describe the events of learning postulated by the information-processing model and the conception they provide of human learning and memory.

THE INFORMATION-PROCESSING MODEL

The model of learning and memory that forms a basis of information-processing theories (for example, J. R. Anderson and Bower, 1973; Atkinson and

Shiffrin, 1968; Rumelhart, Lindsay, and Norman, 1972) postulates a number of internal structures in the human brain and some corresponding processes that they carry out (Greeno and Bjork, 1973). A version of this model is shown in Figure 4.1.

The Flow of Information

From the environment, the learner receives stimulation that activates receptors and is transformed to neural information. Initially, this information enters a structure (or structures) called the *sensory register*, where it persists for a very brief interval. The investigations of Sperling (1960) and Crowder and Morton (1969) have shown that information from the various senses is "registered" in more or less complete form for a few hundredths of a second. The components of this sensory representation that persist for a longer period must be the object of the process of *attention*. The remaining components simply die away and no longer affect the nervous system.

From sensory register to short-term memory. The entire "picture" recorded in the sensory register does not persist. Instead, the information is transformed into patterns of stimulation, a process called *selective perception*. Instead of random stimuli, such invariances as edges, textures, slants, and three-dimensional objects are synthesized (J. J. Gibson, 1950). Selective

Figure 4.1 Model employed by information-processing theories of learning and memory. (From R. M. Gagné, *Essentials of learning for instruction.* Copyright 1974 by the Dryden Press, a division of Holt, Rinehart and Winston. Reproduced by permission of Holt, Rinehart and Winston.)

perception depends upon the learner's ability to attend to certain features of the contents of the sensory register while ignoring others (Palmer, 1975). The perception of features forms a new kind of input to the short-term memory.

Short-term memory storage.   The transformed information next enters the short-term memory, where it can persist for a limited period, generally thought to be up to twenty seconds. Some evidence exists for two forms of storage in the short-term memory: (1) an acoustic form, in which the information is internally heard by the learners, and (2) an articulatory form, in which the learners "hear themselves saying" the information. In retrieving a telephone number for the time needed to dial it, for example, one has the impression of hearing oneself repeat the number (Lindsay and Norman, 1977, pp. 256–299). It is also quite possible, however, that the learner uses other kinds of storage, such as visual imagery, in remembering pictures of scenes he has witnessed (Paivio, 1971).

The capacity of the short-term memory is limited. A number of studies have suggested its capacity may be similar to that of the "immediate memory span," that is, to a number of individual items equal to seven plus or minus two (G. A. Miller, 1956). The items themselves may be letters, numbers, or single-syllable words. Once this capacity has been exceeded, old items must be "pushed out" as new items are added to the store. However, an interesting additional property of the short-term memory is its ability to carry out silent, mental repetition of the information, a process called *rehearsal*. Obviously, rehearsal extends the capacity of the short-term memory to store items for longer time intervals. The rehearsal process may also aid the encoding of information as input to the next structure, the long-term memory. But the *number* of items stored in the short-term memory is not increased by rehearsal.

From short-term to long-term memory.   From the standpoint of learning, the most critical transformation of information occurs when it leaves the short-term memory and enters the long-term memory. This process is called *encoding* (see Melton and Martin, 1972). The information available as certain perceptual features in short-term memory is now transformed into a *conceptual*, or meaningful, mode. Apparently it is stored not as sounds or shapes but as concepts whose meaning is known and can be correctly referenced in the learner's environment. The information that is stored is *organized* in various ways rather than being merely collected. A number of modern theories, for example, postulate that one basic form in which learned material is encoded is as meaningful *propositions* (J. R. Anderson and Bower, 1973; Kintsch, 1972; Rumelhart, Lindsay, and Norman, 1972). Some propose even more complex forms of encoding involving hierarchical relations of concepts (Quillian, 1968) or topical organization of the sort occurring in paragraphs (Crothers, 1972). At the same time, it is generally recognized that visual and other kinds of imagery may form a basis for the encoding that characterizes the input to long-term memory (Bower, 1969; Paivio, 1971).

Apparently, then, the process of encoding takes many forms. What is learned may be encoded in meaningful verbal units like sentences or perhaps even more comprehensive units. Encoding processes may take the form of tables, spatially arranged matrices, diagrams, or detailed images, or "pictures," of the information being learned. The main characteristic of encoded material (for entry into long-term memory) is that it is *semantic*, or meaningfully organized.

Storage in long-term memory. Information in encoded form is stored in long-term memory. Some evidence suggests that storage is permanent and does not suffer loss through time (see Adams, 1967). However, it is evident that what is stored may become inaccessible for a number of reasons. *Interference* between newer and older memories may block the accessibility of stored information. Mainly, though, the phenomenon of forgetting may result from the ineffectiveness of search and retrieval processes. Other than these few points, little is known about what specifically happens to learned material during the time it is stored in long-term memory.

Retrieval. In order to be verified as learned, entities must be retrieved from long-term memory. It is generally supposed that the process called retrieval requires that certain *cues* be provided, either by the external situation or by the learner (from other memory sources). The cues are employed to match or "link" what is learned, in a *search* process. The entities so located are considered to be "recognized," and may then be retrieved.

Often, what is retrieved is returned to the short-term memory, which has the character of a "working memory," or perhaps a "conscious memory" (Atkinson and Shiffrin, 1968). Here the learned material becomes readily *accessible* to the learner, so that it may be combined with other inputs to form new entities (that is, new encodings). Or it may be transformed to activate the response generator, which provides an organization for various human performances. Sometimes, as in the case of automatized skills, learned entities are directly transformed as inputs to the response generator.

Recall of what has been learned may be exhibited within a short time after the internal events of learning have taken place. Within limits, such remembering is spoken of as being "immediate." Many times, however, the performance is not called for until a future time—hours, days, or weeks later. In such circumstances, the internal processing that occurs may be somewhat different. Presumably, search and retrieval processes of the long-term memory are involved in both cases, but additional kinds of processing may be necessary in delayed recall.

The processes of recall apparently sometimes require a *reconstruction* of the events remembered, rather than simply a reinstatement of them. For example, people can usually answer correctly a question about the number of windows in the house or apartment in which they live. How do they do this? Apparently, they first retrieve a visual image of each room, and then, while holding it in mind, count the windows. When asked to recount a set of events observed months ago or a story read in the distant past, the learner may fill in the gaps by a *construction* that seems to makes sense, and at the same time be quite convinced that the remembering is accurate (see Bartlett, 1932).

When the recall of what has been learned involves application to a new situation or to a novel problem, *transfer of learning* occurs. Although this phenomenon has not been extensively studied as an information-processing problem, it appears that special processes or particular combinations of processes must be involved. An individual who is required to bring knowledge or skill to a novel problem must often conduct a *search* process that is more complex and extensive than that used for familiar situations. It is likely also that the *cues* which are employed to retrieve what is learned (and to be "transferred") are of a different sort than those used for immediate or even delayed recall. Novel problem situations requiring transfer of learning may involve internal processing of the sort called *generalizing* as well as that of active *construction* (see Lindsay and Norman, 1977, pp. 400–406).

The working memory.   In addition to its function as a temporary store for incoming information, an important characteristic of the short-term memory is its role as an *active* or *working memory* (Shiffrin, 1976). Search processes may be initiated in the working memory to retrieve material stored in long-term memory. As a result, material may be returned to working memory in a form that matches the coded nature of newly received inputs. In this way the working memory makes possible the combining of material to be learned with the contents of memory established by previous learning. As a simple example, in learning the new intellectual skill of finding the length of the hypotenuse of a right triangle, the working memory retrieves and combines the subordinate skills of identifying sides, adding squares, and taking square roots.

Response generation.   The next transformation along the route of information flow is accomplished by the *response generator*. This structure determines, first, the basic form of human responding, that is, whether the performance will involve speech, the large muscles of the trunk, the small muscles of the hand, or whatever. Second, it determines the pattern of the performance, the sequence and timing of the movement involved in the action to be accomplished. In general, the processes associated with the response generator insure that an organized performance will occur.

Performance. The penultimate stage of information processing consists in the activation of the effectors; this results in patterns of activity that can be externally observed. If what has been learned is a capability of stating the sense of a set of propositions, then "telling" is the performance that shows learning has occurred. If a motor skill such as writing with a pen has been acquired, then this performance may be exhibited, and its occurrence verifies (to an external observer) that the capability has been learned.

Feedback. Learning is a process that appears to require the closing of a loop that begins with stimulation from the external environment. The final link of this loop is an event that also has its origin outside the learner, in the environment. *Feedback* is provided by observation of the effects of the learner's own performance. This is the event that provides the learner with the confirmation (or verification) that learning has accomplished its purpose. If someone has set out to learn to ride a bicycle, feedback is provided when the person actually rides the bicycle. If the purpose of learning has been to acquire the intellectual skill of finding the area of triangles, feedback is provided by the successful computation of the area of one or more triangles. Although feedback usually requires an external check, its major effects are obviously internal ones that serve to fix the learning, to make it permanently available. This is the phenomenon called *reinforcement*, about which we shall have more to say later.

A summary of information-processing flow. Our account of the internal processing that constitutes the events called learning and memory is not complete, and some very important processes have yet to be described. Nevertheless, it appears desirable to review the main features of the flow of information from the external environment through the learner's nervous system, out to the environment, with another link to internal processes through feedback. Figure 4.2 displays the structures of the information-processing model (Figure 4.1) in a vertical linear fashion. Its right-hand column indicates the processing associated with each structure.

Stimulation from the learner's environment activates receptors to produce patterns of neural impulses. These patterns persist in the sensory register for a brief interval (some hundredths of a second), from which they may be processed by selective perception into perceived objects and object-qualities, or features. This "information" may then be stored in short-term memory as auditory, articulatory, or visual images, which are subject to rehearsal. As input to the long-term memory, the formation is semantically (or meaningfully) encoded, and then stored in this form. Processes of search may be instituted, followed by the process of retrieval. At this point, the

STRUCTURE

PROCESS

Receptors

(input)

(output)

Sensory register

RECEPTION OF
PATTERNS OF NEURAL IMPULSES

SELECTIVE PERCEPTION
OF FEATURES

Short-term memory

SHORT-TERM STORAGE
REHEARSAL

SEMANTIC ENCODING

Long-term memory

LONG-TERM STORAGE

SEARCH

(Short-term) working memory

RETRIEVAL

Response generator

RESPONSE ORGANIZATION

PERFORMANCE

Effectors

FEEDBACK ➔ REINFORCEMENT

Figure 4.2 Processes of learning and memory as inputs to and outputs from postulated structures of the information-processing model.

information may be returned to the short-term memory, which is conceived as a "working" or "conscious" memory. From this structure, or directly from long-term memory, the response generator is brought into play to generate a suitable response organization. The signal flow from this structure activates effectors which exhibit the human performance. Feedback is provided via the learner's observations of this performance, and the phenomenon of reinforcement establishes the learned entities as capabilities available for future recall, exercise, and use. Since these events are displayed linearly in the figure, the feedback loop is not indicated as part of the diagram, but must be imagined by the reader.

Control Processes

Our description of information flow and the processes involved in it provides a conception of the internal events of learning. In computer language, these processes might be called *routines*. Obviously, though, as these processes occur in human learning, they have a richness and complexity that goes beyond their basic functioning. The ways in which an individual learner may approach, engage in, and execute an act of learning all display the characteristics of variability, flexibility, and ingenuity. How are these qualities of learning, remembering, and generalizing to be conceived and brought into the total picture?

The answer lies in the processes listed at the top of Figure 4.1, *executive control processes* and *expectancies*. Both these processes have been largely acquired by the individual in previous learning. For that reason, they constitute another separate portion of long-term memory. Their function is to determine (or choose) the particular kinds of information processing in which the learner engages to accomplish particular kinds of learning tasks. In other words, they determine the learner's approach to one or more ways of processing information—how a person goes about attending and storing and encoding and retrieving information.

It may be noted that the arrows leading from the boxes labeled *executive control processes* and *expectancies* are not connected with other structures in the model. Actually, this incompleteness is intended to illustrate, on the one hand, that these control processes are capable of affecting any and all of the phases of information flow, and on the other, that their interconnections have not yet been fully worked out.

Executive control processes. The *cognitive strategies* described in the previous chapter are executive control processes. They are called by various names by different writers. For example, they appear to be equivalent to the *mathemagenic activities* described by Rothkopf (1970) and the *self-management behaviors* referred to by Skinner (1968). Bruner (1971) makes frequent reference to cognitive strategies and considers their learning a most important educational goal. As control processes, they occur prominently as part of the model of information-processing theories of learning and memory (Atkinson and Shiffrin, 1968; Greeno and Bjork, 1973).

Control processes influence attention and selective perception by determining what features of the contents of the sensory register will be entered into the short-term memory. They may determine what is rehearsed in short-term memory and thus what is retained for longer storage. They may influence the choice of an encoding scheme—whether the learner finds meaning in small chunks or large—and thus determine how the information is stored in long-term memory. They may affect the learner's scheme of search and retrieval and thus determine how much or how well one remembers. Probably also, they have an effect on the choice of a format for responding and so influence the kind of response organization chosen for the learner's performance. And by no means of least importance, they determine the learner's strategies for generalizing and problem solving and so influence the quality of the individual's thought.

A simple example from the psychological laboratory may illustrate the essential nature of an executive control process and its functioning in learning. Rohwer and Lynch (1966) gave children the task of learning twenty pairs of words such as LION-HORSE, STICK-COW. The subjects studied the total list and later were asked to respond with the second word when given the first. The encoding strategy deliberately employed with half the children was to use the words in a sentence such as "The STICK hurts the COW." For the other half of the children, randomly chosen, a different encoding strategy was used; the words were presented in a phrase such as "the STICK and the COW." A considerably greater number of words were remembered after two review trials by the group using the first strategy than by the group using the second. Of course, these children did not choose the strategies in this instance. But these approaches are examples of strategies that can be readily learned and employed as executive control processes for this particular kind of learning task.

Expectancies.   Expectancies are another subclass of executive control processes. They represent the *specific* motivation of learners to reach the goal of learning that has been set for them or that they have set for themselves. What learners intend to accomplish can influence what they attend to, how they encode the learned information, and how they organize their responses. An expectancy is a continuing set, oriented toward the goal accomplishment, which enables learners to select the outputs of each processing stage. Thus, if learners have the expectancy of learning how to find resistances of electric circuits, they may selectively reject the perception of the shape of the resistors or the location of the circuit in a piece of equipment. They will encode certain characteristics of the circuit relevant to its resistance and ignore others. They will choose a response organization that reports or identifies a numerical value of ohms and not some other physical property. In other words, all of their internal processes will be responsive to the goal that these learners "have in mind," which is an expectancy.

Although the concept of expectancy is not commonly included as an integral part of information-processing theories of learning, it has figured prominently in the work of one modern theorist, namely Estes (1972). His proposal has been adopted for the account given here. Estes considers that the feedback effects of reinforcement influence learning and memory not because they are "rewarding," but because they convey information to the learner. Information that informs the learner that the goal has been reached or is relatively close has a reinforcing effect. In other words, feedback is useful because it *confirms the learner's expectancy*, and this is what is meant by the term *reinforcement*. While this view of reinforcement denies none of the empirical facts about reinforcement (see Skinner, 1969), it provides a novel interpretation of this important concept.

The role of executive control.   The two interrelated sets of processes called *executive control* and *expectancy* play crucial roles in any information-processing account of human learning and memory. It is apparent to the theorists who use the model shown in Figure 4.1 (or a similar one) that learning and remembering cannot be fully accounted for in terms of a simple diagram of information flow. There must also be processes by which the learner *selects* the nature of processing at each of the stages shown. How the attention of the learner is directed, how the information is encoded, how it is retrieved, and how it is expressed in organized responses are all matters that require a choice of strategies. This choice is the function of the executive control processes, including expectancies established before learning is undertaken. These processes have the effect of making the learner a truly intelligent being—one who can "learn to learn," and therefore one who can engage in a large measure of self-instruction.

It is of interest to note that control processes must themselves be learned, as we indicated in the last chapter when cognitive strategies were being described as one type of learning outcome. Of course, some very elemental control processes are probably determined largely by innate genetic factors (for example, the organization of visual perception or the basic structure of language). Nevertheless, learning most probably plays a major part in the formation of useful strategies of learning, remembering, and thinking, particularly as they apply to the subjects acquired in school. As for expectancies, these too are influenced by learning in the sense that they must be related to various persisting motives possessed by the learner. In addition, though, expectancies are capable of being changed in their specific content in the manner of a set (or "mental set") Thus, an expectancy to "find the multiplication product of two-place numbers" on one occasion may give way to an expectancy to "convert decimals into fractions" on another occasion. The two expectancies do not conflict with each other, since they are temporary. Both may be equally effective in selecting specific processes to serve the learning goals they represent.

EFFECTS OF EXTERNAL EVENTS ON LEARNING PROCESSES

Up to this point, our account of the events of learning has been concerned almost entirely with the *internal* structures of learning and memory and with the processes they mediate. To be sure, we have assumed that some external stimulation is present to begin the information flow, and that feedback from the external environment reinforces the learning. But our account of learning events is still incomplete; while these internal processes are occurring other things can happen *externally*, and these have only been hinted at. Of utmost importance is the fact that these additional external events can have substantial effects on learning—on how it takes place and on how effectively it accomplishes its purpose.

External events that transpire, or are made to transpire, during the course of a single act of learning can have the effect of *promoting* learning and memory. Alternatively, of course, external events may do the opposite; they may hinder learning. But we are mainly concerned here with the positive aspects of these events, with the effects that lead to the furtherance of learning and remembering.

Early Phases of Learning

In the very brief period before something is stored (and therefore "learned"), the learner's processes are concerned with "taking in," or *apprehending*, the stimuli relevant to learning. These preparatory phases consist, first, of an alertness to stimuli that goes under the general name of *attention*. Second, there is the very important screening and organizing of the raw stimulation, or what we have described as *selective perception;* this leads to a storage of relevant stimulus features in the short-term memory. From this point, the transformed information is ready to be again transformed (encoded) to enter the long-term memory.

External events in alertness.   It is easy to grasp the idea that learners who must respond to some stimulation in order to learn must first *receive* this stimulation. This means that their senses must be oriented toward the source of the stimulation, and that they must be ready to take it in. Attending may be thought of as the initial event of learning, made possible by an internal state that can often be detected by observing what learners are looking at or listening to. This internal state is believed to be in part a function of a central neural system called the *reticular activating system* (Lindsley, 1958), and the state itself is one of "arousal" or "alertness."

The kinds of external stimulation that produce alertness are fairly well known. Increases in the intensity of stimulation, such as those made by bright lights or loud sounds are usually dependable stimuli for the command of attention. More generally, any sudden change in stimulation, up or down, is likely to constitute an effective stimulus to alert the learner. The sudden dimming of lights in a theater alerts the audience; a sudden turning off of the sound of a radio similarly commands the attention of a listener.

External events in selective perception.   The processing of information that has been registered in the *sensory register* proceeds with *perception*, which is selective in its operation. One who is looking at another person may selectively perceive that individual's face or hands or clothing, or, under other circumstances, his or her totality as a person. Similarly, one may perceive a window as a part of a wall or, alternatively, as twelve individual panes of glass. Selective perception is guided by a control process that includes a temporary (mental) *set* (see Hebb, 1966, pp. 82–101), which may be activated by verbal instructions or other forms of stimulation. Thus, a common external event affecting perception is the verbal communication that activates such a mental set.

Other kinds of stimuli are frequently used to influence selective perception. For example, the learner who is reading a text may encounter pictures that illustrate key concepts, and italic type or underlining that indicate important terms. If pictorial material is being presented, diagrams may emphasize important features. Or arrows and heavy outlining may be employed to differentiate the features to be learned. In general, the purpose of these additional stimuli is to facilitate selective perception by increasing the differences between relevant and irrelevant features of the objects or events being observed.

The process of perceiving implies that the individual is differentiating the stimulus from other stimuli or parts of the stimulus from other parts. The limits to what someone is able to do in this respect depends largely on previous learning of stimulus discriminations. This prior learning, determining the limits of what can be perceived, is often called *perceptual learning* (E. J. Gibson, 1969). Selective perception appears also to be influenced by the context within which an object or event is viewed. For example, Wheeler (1970) found that brief presentations of the single letters of words like READ resulted in 10 percent better identification when the letters were contained in the word than when the letters were exposed by themselves. Features of an object that are chosen to be perceived by the learner thus depend upon the object plus the context in which it occurs (see Anderson, 1980, pp. 43–52).

Encoding

In order to enter and be stored in the long-term memory, the material of learning must be *encoded*. That is, it has to be transformed into a form that is *semantic,* or *meaningful.* The directional meaning of *starboard,* containing no inherent clues to the landlubber, may be encoded as "The *star boarder* is always *right.*" A long sequence of numbers such as 1 4 9 1 6 2 5 3 6 4 9 6 4 8 1 may be encoded as "squares of successive whole numbers."

The process of encoding, and the subsequent entry of the encoded information into long-term memory, may be considered the central and critical event in an act of learning. The phases of processing that precede this one are preparatory; the phases that follow it are confirmatory in the sense that they "prove" that learning has occurred. Encoding, however, is the critical process by which incoming information is transformed into learned and memorable capabilities.

This pivotal process of encoding may obviously be affected by events in the learner's environment or events planned as a part of instruction. A particular scheme for encoding may be directly communicated to the learner. For example, a teacher may organize a set of facts about the farm products of the various states in a table that divides the states into regions and the products into several convenient categories. The table then becomes an encoding scheme, and quite an effective one. As a second possibility, learners may be encouraged to provide their own individual encoding schemes. Some may use visual images, others rhymes, others a network of superordinate concepts. In this case, the external stimulus is functioning to activate a learner's mental *set,* which thereafter brings to bear one of the learner's cognitive strategies for encoding.

Memory Processes

Storage.   Having been acquired, the new capability must be *stored* in order to qualify as something that has truly been learned. The change that has been brought about by the process of encoding now is retained over a period that might be a few minutes or a lifetime.

One intriguing possibility, supported by some clinical evidence, is that retention in long-term memory persists for a lifetime, and in this sense is permanent. Penfield (1951) has reported instances in which patients whose brains are electrically stimulated under medical treatment have reproduced in startling detail childhood memories—episodes involving recall of situations, sounds, conversations, and other aspects of past events. Such events have been forgotten in a practical sense, but traces of them may persist in the brain. If memory traces are in some sense permanent, the reasons for forgetting must be sought in other events such as interference from other stored memories or obstacles to retrieval. The idea that storage in long-term memory is permanent, however, is by no means well proven, for it is entirely possible that reported memories for long-past events may be substitutions rather than the actual events (Loftus and Loftus, 1980). A conservative view of the matter is simply that some memories last a long time (see Neisser, 1982).

The storage of learned items in long-term memory can presumably be influenced by external events, particularly by the learning of other items. Research has been conducted on the retention of verbal information (of the sort which forms meaningful propositions), to determine whether *interference* (Postman, 1961; Underwood, 1964a) occurs, and whether it follows the same course as it does with unconnected words or word-pairs. Previously learned propositions might conceivably influence the storage of propositions to be newly learned (*proactive interference*); or the learning of new propositions might interfere with the storage of some that are already learned (*retroactive interference*). Evidence for interference of both types has been obtained with meaningful information (Crouse, 1971; Slamecka, 1959, 1960). However, it appears that such interference occurs when the specific propositions learned directly negate each other (R. C. Anderson and Myrow, 1971). Under conditions in which entire passages of text contain different, or conflicting, information, evidence of interference is not found. For example, Ausubel, Robbins, and Blake (1957) found that the retention of ideas learned from a passage on Buddhism was not diminished, but slightly enhanced, when followed by the reading of a passage on Christianity.

Search and Retrieval.   The processes of *search* and *retrieval* seem to be definitely subject to the influence of events external to the learner. Having learned a set of verbal items (in this case, unconnected words) the learner's retrieval of these items is markedly improved when *cues* in the form of categories are provided (Tulving and Pearlstone, 1966). For example, the recall of words in the category "vegetable" may be cued by that category name. Cues of this general sort may even be provided by the learner when such a strategy is suggested (Dong and Kintsch, 1968).

The provision of cues to search and retrieval is obviously an external event of great importance to remembering. Such cues can be incorporated into the situation designed for initial learning and encoding (Thomson and Tulving, 1970). Presumably, they can also be effective at the time of recall if they are able to suggest to the learner a search strategy that is relevant to the encoding already accomplished. Cues for retrieval can take a variety of forms. In addition to the "categorization" function already referred to, cueing can be accomplished by matrix or tabular organizations or by pictures (see Paivio, 1971).

Performance and Its Organization

The transformation brought about by the structure called the response organizer (Figure 4.1) are surely affected by events external to the learner. Somehow, these external events must indicate to the learner the general form of this performance; this is usually given in the initial learning situation and is typically a verbal communication. (Of course, in the case of young children, other means may be used.) The kinds of performances indicated to the learner are those described in the previous chapter. That is, the external communication establishes a set for the learner (1) to *tell* something, (2) to *demonstrate* how to do something, (3) to *execute* a skilled movement sequence, (4) to *choose* a course of personal action, or (5) to *originate* a solution to a novel problem.

Establishing the correct set for the learner's performance is normally done in instruction by "informing the learner of the objective" of the learning. It is easy to understand that gross errors of performance are avoided by the learner who possesses a correct impression of the performance aimed for. If the student has learned about Ohm's law, telling about it is one kind of performance; demonstrating its application to an electric circuit with particular values of voltage and resistance is quite a different kind of performance. Originating a way of teaching Ohm's law understandably to sixth-graders would be still another kind of performance.

Processes of Executive Control

We have now considered the ways in which external events may influence the flow of information in the model of Figure 4.2. What about the executive control processes of this model? Can they also be influenced by external events? What can be done outside the learner to affect the operation of these control processes (which we equate to the *cognitive strategies* of Chapter 3)?

Executive control operations can be selected and activated by external events. One example of such effects is to be seen in the activation and selection of particular kinds of *attentional sets* by instructions or by questions (Frase, 1970; Rothkopf, 1970). When questions interspersed in textual passages refer to particular categories of content (such as technical terms or dates), these categories are selectively perceived by the learner. Apparently as a consequence of these external events, classes of content involved in the interspersed questions are learned and remembered to a greater extent than other kinds of content. Thus, particular strategies for selective perception are activated and selected as a result of these events.

Activation and selection of a similar sort may be seen in the effects of instructions or hints on encoding strategies. When learners are encouraged to encode items to be learned in terms of vivid imagery, learning and retention are improved over items learned without such instructions (Bower, 1970; Rohwer, 1975; Wittrock, 1974). Again, the activation of particular types of sets for retrieval of information, such as the use of concrete or "picturable" cues, sets into motion strategies of retrieval that are superior to other strategies in their effects on recall (Paivio, 1971). Over periods of practice in problem solving, instructions to children demonstrating the use of such strategies as "waiting until all the evidence is in" and "systematically reviewing the facts" have been shown to activate strategies leading to improved solving of "detective story" problems in fifth-grade children (Olton and Crutchfield, 1969). Thus, external instructions, suggestions, and other similar events appear unmistakably to affect the selection and use of various control processes and to exert influence on many different internal learning processes.

Expectancies, too, are often influenced by external events such as verbal instructions. Typically, verbal communications that "inform the learner of the objective" of learning establish specific expectancies. This sort of communication, externally delivered, may influence any or all of the internal processes of learning by enabling the learner to "keep on the track" and to avoid gross errors. A specific expectancy established in this manner enables the learner to know when learning is complete—the learner is able to perform in the desired manner and to receive reinforcement thereby

A SUMMARY OF EXTERNAL EVENTS THAT INFLUENCE INTERNAL PROCESSES

Table 4.1 summarizes the relationships described in the previous section, indicating the kinds of external events that can affect ongoing internal processes.

TABLE 4.1   Internal Processes of Learning and the Effects That Can Be Exerted upon Them by External Events

Internal Process	External Events and Their Effects
Attention (Reception)	Stimulus change produces arousal (attention)
Selective perception	Enhancement and differentiation of object features facilitates selective perception
Semantic encoding	Verbal instructions, pictures, diagrams, suggest encoding schemes
Retrieval	Suggestion or display of cues such as diagrams, tabular arrays, rhymes, aids retrieval
Response organization	Verbal instructions about the objective of learning inform the learner about the class of performance expected
Control processes	Instructions establish sets that activate and select appropriate strategies
Expectancies	Informing the learner of the objective establishes a specific expectancy for performance

In early stages of the learning act, abrupt stimulus changes can arouse the learner's attention. Once the information is received in the sensory register, emphasis on features of objects (by underlining, colored printing, or other forms of enhancement) contributes to the process of selective perception. Beginning with the process of semantic encoding (for entry into long-term memory), a variety of forms of "learning guidance" may be employed. Often, instructions are delivered orally or by printed text. Pictures, diagrams, tables, lists, or combinations of these vehicles may be employed as external stimuli. Their purpose is to provide, or to suggest, schemes for encoding and cues for search and retrieval. Verbal instructions are also frequently used to define for the learner the pattern of responding, that is, the type of performance expected (in particular, one of the five kinds of learning outcomes described in the previous chapter).

Executive control processes, including expectancies, are also influenced by external events. Verbal instructions establish (mental) sets that put in operation various cognitive strategies available to the learner. These strategies (or control processes) may in turn influence any and all phases of information processing involved in an act of learning. Expectancies are also established, typically, by verbal communications that tell the learner what the objectives of learning are.

EDUCATIONAL IMPLICATIONS

The information-processing model of learning and memory is of great significance for the planning and design of instruction in educational programs. The model tells us that an act of learning, however brief or extended, is composed of several phases. Learning begins with the intake of stimulation from the receptors and ends with the feedback that follows the learner's performance. Between these events are several stages of internal *processing*. Instruction, then, is not simply a matter of presenting an initial stimulus—instead, it is composed of several different kinds of external stimulation that influence several different processes of learning.

As a whole, the stimulation provided to the learner during the instruction has the function of *supporting* the various kinds of internal processing taking place in the learner. The external events called instruction may support internal processes by *activating* a mental set that affects attention and selective perception. Or an external event may *enhance* the internal process of encoding, by providing an organization that is adopted by the learner. Another possibility for instruction is to *maintain* the operation of an executive control process, such as an expectancy of performance outcome, so that internal processing preserves a particular direction. As the learning act is completed, the external event called *feedback* is a particularly important function of instruction. Taken together, these various external events make up what is called *instruction*. In appropriate ways, they support the operation of internal learning processes.

Assuming that some motivation exists, the internal processing that constitutes learning is ongoing. When the outcomes of learning are deliberately planned, the events of instruction can likewise be planned to achieve these outcomes. Naturally, learners can influence the internal processes by means of their own executive control processes (cognitive strategies). In fact, as experience is gained, learners can be expected to gain an increasing degree of control over their own processes, and this control will probably become more and more effective. Thus, learners become capable of engaging in self-instruction to an increasing extent as learning continues. The kinds and amount of support required in externally provided instruction may be expected to vary with each learner's own sophistication in self-instruction.

The five varieties of learning outcome described in the previous chapter are supported by some instructional events that affect their learning in the same ways, and by some events that affect them differently, depending on what is being learned. An example of the former sort is feedback, which is an essential condition for all learning. An example of the latter sort is instruction that supports encoding, the nature of which differs for each kind of learning outcome. The conditions of learning to be described in subsequent chapters are concerned with the external events that support the different types of learned capabilities, as well as with the internal events (processes) these external events influence. These conditions provide a basis for the design of effective instruction.

A NOTE ABOUT CHAPTERS TO COME

Chapter 5 begins an account of the conditions of learning for intellectual skills, and the following chapters continue the story for other types of learned capabilities. In each chapter, a description is given of the *internal* and *external* conditions of learning. In a primary sense, internal conditions partake of the capabilities that have been learned previously and stored in the learner's long-term memory. To be useful for new learning, they must be retrieved to working memory for further processing.

External conditions are those events in the learner's environment which can influence internal learning processes, in the various ways suggested by Table 4.1. To provide the best support for internal learning processes, these external events need to be differentially designed for each of the five learning outcomes. These external events that support learning processes are also described in the individual chapters to follow.

The ideas about internal and external events for each variety of learning outcome are brought together as a *theory of instruction* in Chapter 12. This chapter summarizes and integrates the discussions of previous chapters pertaining to conditions that contribute to the effectiveness of learning. A systematic account is given of the external events that collectively are called *instruction* and of the ways in which these events influence the *internal processes of learning.*

GENERAL REFERENCES

The Information-Processing Model of Learning and Memory

Atkinson, R. C., and Shiffrin, R. M. Human memory: A proposed system and its control processes. In K. W. Spence and J. T. Spence (Eds.), *The psychology of learning and motivation*, Vol. 2. New York: Academic Press, 1968.

Gagné, R. M. *Essentials of learning for instruction.* New York: Holt, Rinehart and Winston, 1974.

Klatzky, R. L. *Human memory: Structures and processes*, 2nd ed. San Francisco: Freeman, 1980.

Lachman, R., Lachman, J. L., and Butterfield, E. C. *Cognitive psychology and information processing: An introduction.* Hillsdale, N.J.: Erlbaum, 1979.

Lindsay, P. H., and Norman, D. A. *Human information processing: An introduction to psychology*, 2nd ed. New York: Academic Press, 1977.

Processes of Learning

Anderson, J. R. *Cognitive psychology and its implications.* San Francisco: Freeman, 1980.

Gibson, E. J. *Principles of perceptual learning and development.* New York: Appleton, 1969.

Norman, D. A., and Rumelhart, D. E. (Eds.), *Explorations in cognition.* San Francisco: Freeman, 1975.

Paivio, A. *Imagery and verbal processes.* New York: Holt, Rinehart and Winston, 1971.

Wessels, M. G. *Cognitive psychology.* New York: Harper & Row, 1982.

External Events and Their Effects on Learning

Gagné, R. M., and Briggs, L. J. *Principles of instructional design*, 2nd ed. New York: Holt, Rinehart and Winston, 1979

5

Intellectual Skills: Discriminations; Concrete Concepts

The learned associations described in Chapter 2 may be put together in a sequential fashion to generate chains and verbal sequences. These associations and the chains constructed from them may also be the objects of further learning, as we shall see in this chapter. First, we should point out that *sets* of associations (or sets of chains) may become increasingly differentiated in the sense that the individual members become more readily distinguishable from one another. Through learning, an initially undifferentiated stimulus object may eventually be responded to in ways that distinguish its parts, dimensions, or characteristics. Second, once these fundamental distinctions have been made, another learning possibility becomes available to the learner: the capability of responding to stimulus objects as members of a common class or category.

Suppose an individual has learned a simple S → R association to the stimulus provided by a door key. We have already seen that this link may be combined with others to form a chain, such as using the key to open a door. But there are other ways of responding to a key and to collections of keys. Here we will consider the learning of capabilities that may be briefly described as follows:

1. The individual is given a set of three keys, one for each door in an office. Initially the keys all look and feel alike. Soon, though, the individual can tell them apart by the number of notches and the depth of the first notch.
2. The individual responds to a specific collection of keys as door keys and to another collection as padlock keys and is able to identify an entirely new key as belonging to one of these categories.

Both of these occurrences begin with stimulation provided by collections of stimulus objects or events. However, these are two rather different kinds of capabilities, the first being somewhat simpler than the second. In the first kind of performance, the individual becomes capable of distinguishing one key from another, or from several others, and makes different responses to the different members of a particular collection. This is called *discrimination*, or when several distinctions are involved (as in the example given), *multiple discrimination*. In the second type, the learner is able to respond in a single way to a collection of objects as a class; this class extends beyond the members that were originally present. This second kind of learning is called *concept learning*. Notice that in the second example, the learner is able to distinguish keys also but now is distinguishing *classes* of keys (and has learned two different concepts) rather than merely distinguishing a specific key from others (discrimination). Both these forms of learning are of considerable importance in a practical sense. As will be seen, the second kind is really dependent on the prior learning of the first, and there is a marked contrast in the versatility of behavior produced by learning of the second kind as opposed to the first.

This chapter, then, deals with two different kinds of learning that may occur when an individual is confronted with a set of stimulus objects. In some circumstances of discrimination learning, the learner may have to acquire a response that differentiates (by name or otherwise) the stimulus features of a single member of a set from those of other members. Or the learner may distinguish several different members of a set, making a different response to each. Having previously learned to make these distinctions, the learner may be required to acquire the capability of responding to the set of stimuli as a class and distinguishing members of the class from non-members; this is what is meant by "learning a concept." Of course, the learner may be required to respond to a stimulus set in *both* these ways on different occasions, and such a response is perfectly possible.

LEARNING DISCRIMINATIONS

Acquiring discriminations is obviously an undertaking of great importance in everyday life and in school learning. Young children must learn at a very early age to distinguish among the parts of their environment: colors, brightnesses, shapes, sizes, textures, distances, loudnesses, and pitches. Adults, too, are constantly called upon to acquire new discriminations of stimulus objects, such as the locations of doors or streets, the distinctions among newly encountered faces, the taste of wines. As for learning in the school, the student is confronted early with the necessity of learning discriminations among printed colors, shapes, letters, numerals, and among the sounds of speech. Considerably later on, students learn distinctions, perhaps, among the microfeatures of body tissue, or among the apparent brightnesses and sizes of stars. E. J. Gibson (1969) describes the relevance of *perceptual learning*, conceived as a matter of increasing differentiation of parts of the environment, for the early years of the child's learning. Discrimination learning leads to perceptual differentiation, she points out, within five media: objects, space, events, representations, and symbols. The child's earliest learned perceptions pertain to objects and space, while discrimination learning of events comes a bit later, as the child becomes able to manipulate objects and to move about. Still later, and much emphasized in early school grades, is the learning of discriminations of representations (pictures) and symbols. Thus, it is important to realize that many discriminations of a basic sort have already been acquired when the child first goes to school.

Discrimination learning is often concerned with the *distinctive features* of stimulus objects. Thus the child learns to respond differentially to the characteristics that serve to distinguish objects from one another: shapes, sizes, colors, textures, and so on. Similarly, the child learns to distinguish phonemes, the smallest units of speech, by means of such distinctive features (here, technically named) as grave-acute, lax-diffuse, vocalic-nonvocalic. The young schoolchild learns to discriminate the distinctive features that will be needed to distinguish pictured or drawn representations and also letters.

The discrimination learning engaged in by children when learning to differentiate printed letters provides an instructive example of the process. Suppose the children first learn to make the response "gee" to the printed letter g. In its simplest form, this may be S → R learning of the following sort:

$$S \longrightarrow R$$
$$\text{printed } g \qquad\qquad \text{oral "gee"}$$

The response connection thus learned is of no particular significance for the learning of the discrimination—it is simply a response different from others that the children might make. The critical learning is that of using this response for g, and *not* for a or p or q. Thus, the learning has to involve reinforcement when the response "gee" is made to the letter g and an absence of reinforcement when this response is made to other letters. The children must learn to indicate by their response that they can distinguish the critical features of g (a loop above the line, a tail on the right that extends below the line and curves inwards) from the features that are "not g."

Consider another example—the discrimination of a circle and an ellipse—which young children may be asked to learn (without their names). Initially, two figures may be presented on a set of cards, some containing two circles, others two ellipses, and still others a circle and an ellipse. In the procedure of learning, the children are asked to say whether the two figures are "the same" or "different"; or they may be asked to say "Yes" or "No" to whether the figures are alike. As a response is made to each card, the children are told whether it is correct or incorrect (by a nod of the head, the statement "Right," or some other signal). As the trials proceed, the learners obviously increase their probability of being "right" and their confidence in their answers. They have acquired the discrimination when it becomes evident that they "see" the difference in the figures without appreciable error. This performance may then be checked with a *matching* task in which the children select one of the figures from a set containing both circles and ellipses by matching it with whichever shape has been designated in the directions.

Discrimination learning of this sort commonly takes the form of presenting a single letter (such as *g*) along with other letters, one at a time, in mixed order. The learner is asked to respond to the *g's* by saying "gee" and to make no response to the other letters. Alternatively, pairs of letters may be presented, one a *g* and the other a different letter, and the child asked to point to the *g*. The child who has learned to say the names of several letters may be asked to name each of them when they are presented successively in a mixed order. At this stage, of course, the child may be learning *multiple discriminations*, or several discriminations at once. All of these methods of presentation are examples of *contrast practice*. The learner is given an indication of being "right" when an appropriate response to a letter is made, and "wrong" when an incorrect response occurs. By means of such differential reinforcement, the learner comes to respond correctly to the differential features of the letters.

Pupils are asked to learn different names for printed letters so that they can make consistent distinctive response to these letters on a page. In some forms of early instruction, children are asked to learn the sounds of letters as responses (g as "guh") rather than their names, since these sounds will later be involved in oral reading. There may be some advantage for later learning in acquiring responses that "sound" letters rather than "name" them. The important thing to be noted, however, is that what is being learned at this stage is *not* the names of the letters (which the child may well have learned previously as oral responses), but the *discriminations* among their physical appearances.

Interference in Discrimination Learning

When multiple discriminations are learned, it is apparent that the task of discriminating the stimuli one from the other increases in difficulty as more stimuli become involved. When *g* is presented alone, the discrimination task is not very demanding, but when *g* is presented along with *y*, the chances of confusion are increased. This trend continues when the letter *p*, which is even more similar to *g* than is *y*, is added. The possibilities of confusion in the appearance of *p* and *g*, *d* and *b*, and *m* and *n* are well known to teachers of young children. As a set of stimuli, all of these letters must be distinguished from each other by multiple discrimination. A learning technique is sometimes used to magnify the differences among the letters when they are initially being learned, for example, by emphasizing the left and right positions of the "tail" on the letters *d* and *b*. Another technique, again designed to make stimulus differences more prominent, is to have children feel cut-out letters; this provides additional tactual and kinesthetic cues to their differences.

A major change in the multiple-discrimination as opposed to the single-discrimination situation is that great potential for *interference* exists in the former. That is to say, the similarities between stimuli tend to favor the occurrence of *confusion errors*, increasing the difficulty of learning. Once the discrimination that permits different responses to be made to *p* and *b* has been acquired, a distinction must be learned between *d* and *g*. The occurrence of interference shows up when the learner attempts to recall any of these.

Learning is thus made more difficult when a multiple set of discriminations is being learned. One solution (a practical one, which may or may not be the best) is to proceed to learn the single discriminations one by one and then to provide additional practice one by one, using a mixed-up order of presentation. The question of how many single discriminations to learn before undertaking recall and repetition is one that has not received a clear answer from laboratory experimentation. Likely to work well for this purpose is "progressive part" learning, in which new discriminations are introduced while old ones are reviewed (see McGeoch and Irion, 1952). Another approach is to initially exaggerate the differences among the stimuli and in successive practice trials to gradually reduce these differences to those that are normal. The most efficient technique for multiple discrimination of stimuli such as the set of letters may turn out to be one that incorporates both these approaches.

CONDITIONS OF LEARNING DISCRIMINATIONS

The various examples described should make possible a formulation of some propositions regarding the conditions necessary for learning discriminations.

Conditions within the Learner

One condition that must exist within the learner is the ability to recall and reinstate the different response chains necessary to exhibit the discrimination. If this is a matter of "knowing the name" of an object or object-quality, this requirement appears not to be an overly demanding one. The S → R or response chain is learned in the manner described in the previous chapter as a verbal label or as some other kind of response. When discriminations are learned to multiple stimuli, of course, the learner must be able to exhibit as many different responses as there are differences in stimuli.

Conditions in the Learning Situation

A discrimination is usually established by the selective reinforcement of correct versus incorrect responses to the stimulus (an object or object-quality). For example, if young children are learning to distinguish *closed* and *open* plane figures (curves), positive reinforcement is provided when they are shown sets of figures both closed and open and distinguish them correctly. This may be done in various ways: (1) The children may be asked to identify closed figures and then be shown pairs (closed and open) in which they point to the correct one; (2) a large set of figures, closed and open, may be shown in which the children must point to either the closed or open ones; or (3) closed and open figures may be shown one by one and the children asked to say "closed" or "open." In any of these situations, it is understood that differential reinforcement will be employed, that is, some indication will be given that correct and incorrect responses have been made in each trial.

Procedures such as these have the purpose of permitting a *selection* of the correct stimulus features to be made. Initially, the learner may respond to some stimulus features that are correct and to others that are incorrect. The child, for example, may be responding at first to large versus small gaps in the figure rather than to continuity versus discontinuity of the curve. As additional trials are given, the responses to incorrect aspects of the stimulus are progressively subject to *extinction*, and the correct discrimination becomes established. When correct responses are made by the child, their correctness is confirmed by a teacher; when the responses are incorrect, such confirmation is omitted.

When multiple discriminations are learned, the learning task becomes more difficult because of confusions among the stimuli to be discriminated. In other words, there tends to be *interference*. Consequently, a greater amount of contrast practice is required so that the responses to "incorrect" stimulus features will be suitably extinguished. Although the different responses learned in multiple discriminations are commonly *names* for the objects differentiated, they need not be. The sender of Morse code learns a set of key-tapping patterns to differentiate the individual letters of the message to be transmitted. The student of the clarinet learns to distinguish a set of printed notes by means of a set of fingering responses, each of which bears a specific relationship to a particular note. The operator of a panel controlling industrial or other machinery may have to have a number of different key-pressing responses to distinguish the various signals received. In all these instances there are strong tendencies to interference among the individual response chains; this interference is overcome by the use of contrast practice.

Educational Implications of Discrimination Learning

Discrimination learning is deceptively simple, and the need for it may be overlooked. The discriminations most of us are able to exhibit have been acquired early in life and without deliberate intent. We tend to think that everyone is able to "see" (that is, discriminate) the difference between green and yellow, red and pink, pointed and curved, rough and smooth. It is common, therefore, to assume that the discriminations needed for further learning are already available to the learner. But the need for discrimination learning is often made apparent when we encounter new kinds of stimuli to be incorporated in learning—stimuli that are not common in the sense of having been previously encountered. Thus, learners who tackle a foreign language may be confronted with sounds they have not heard before—the umlauted "u" in German, or the uvular "r" in French. The student who looks through a microscope for the first time may similarly encounter a new field of view, containing many features to be discriminated. The student of music may face the task of discriminating tonal differences not previously attended to.

Multiple discriminations are frequently required in the learning that takes place in schools. Young children must learn distinguishing features for a great variety of things and events in their environment: rocks, birds, stars, flowers, and coins are a few examples. Children must learn to make different responses to many kinds of printed symbols, including letters, numerals, words, and other signs. Students acquire a multitude of discriminations of the stimulus features involved in the objects encountered during education—in gases, liquids, solids, parts of the earth and universe, animals, plants, music, works of art. All their lives, people must learn new discriminations of novel objects, symbols, faces. In addition to being a widespread type of learning outcome, discrimination also plays an important role in other more complex learning activities yet to be described.

LEARNING CONCRETE CONCEPTS

One way the individual can learn to respond to collections of things is by distinguishing among them. Another way, even more important as a human capability, is by putting things into a class and responding to any instance of the class as a member of that class. In a sense this latter learning seems just the opposite of the first kind. But it is more than that, because it incorporates the first kind as one of its preconditions. This latter learning, which makes it possible for the individual to respond to things or events as a class, results in the kind of learning outcome called a *concept*.

At this point, it is important to note that the term *concept* has several meanings. Obviously, it will not be possible to deal with them all at the same time, and it would doubtless be a mistake to try to do so. First, we should consider the most fundamental meaning, which is exhibited in individual behavior by responding to object-qualities such as those implied by the names *red*, *double*, *circular*, and *smooth* or by common objects such as *cat*, *chair*, *tree*, and *house*. It is customary to refer to these as *concrete* concepts, since they can be denoted by being pointed out; in other words, they are *concepts by observation*. Later on, it will be possible to describe *concepts by definition*; these are abstract in the sense that they involve relations. Some examples are physical concepts of mass and temperature, language concepts of subject and object, mathematical concepts of square root and prime number. Further descriptions of defined concepts will be undertaken in the next chapter.

An Example of a Concrete Concept

Suppose one were to show a seven-year-old child a set of three hollow blocks on a tabletop. Two of these blocks are identical for practical purposes, but the other is different. The child is told that a small piece of candy is under one of the blocks but not under the others. The point is to try to "guess" where the candy is, and lift one or more blocks to get it. (We may call the blocks A, A, and B.) Unknown to the child, the experimenter follows the rule of always placing the candy under the *odd* block, the one that is unlike the other two. Initially, of course, the child really does guess, and the association $S_B \rightarrow R_{lift}$ is reinforced. Now the experimenter places a new set of hollow blocks, of different appearance, C, C, and D, on the table, with the candy under D. (Of course, the spatial placement of the blocks is unsystematic in all cases.) Now the child, after one or more errors, chooses block D, and the association is reinforced. Other combinations may be tried, such as BBA, DDC, BBC, EEF. Eventually, the child *chooses the odd one*. Once this happens, the child is able to perform the task without error for *any* set of blocks. It may then be said that the child is *using a concept* or behaving conceptually.

In order for such a statement about the child's behavior to be valid, certain things must be true. First, it must be known that the behavior could not have been learned as a simple $S \rightarrow R$ connection or as a chain of such connections. If one used only a single set of blocks, like AAB, the child could learn to choose the odd one (B) on the basis of its appearance alone, as an $S \rightarrow R$ association. Similarly, if one placed the blocks in the same spatial order so that the odd one was always on the extreme right the child could learn a simple stimulus-response association to a particular location as the stimulus. In order to state that the child is using a concept, one must demonstrate that the performance is impossible on the basis of simpler forms of learning. This can be done, as in the example given, by presenting the child with novel stimulus objects in novel positions. If the response is correct, it may be justifiably said that the child "knows what the *odd* one is" or knows the concept *odd.*

The example illustrates a way that individuals have of responding to collections of things, which is different from multiple discrimination. In this case the collections of objects may vary widely in appearance. Individuals naturally must distinguish among them. But what is important is that people respond to them in terms of some *common abstract property*. In a real sense, people *classify* them.

What a young girl does in this situation with the blocks may be inferred to be something like the following. She may initially think, "Oh, it's B." Having found that this doesn't work when CC and D are presented, she may say to herself, "It's the one on the right" or "It's the blue one." But none of these responses is successful; they are unreinforced and become extinguished. Eventually, she says to herself, "It's the odd one," and this works every time. Does she *actually* think these things? It is difficult to obtain evidence as proof. But so far as the ultimately correct performance is concerned, the child behaves *as if* she says to herself, "It's the odd one." To be able to state that the child uses a concept, one has only to demonstrate that such an "as if" clause is true.

From Discrimination Learning to Concept Learning

It has often been shown that discriminations are prerequisite to the learning of concepts. The nature of concept learning and its relation to the discrimination learning that precedes it is suggested by the stages depicted in Figure 5.1.

Assume that learning begins with the discrimination of a straight line, to be distinguished from (curved) lines that are not straight. Learners first master the discrimination shown as stage 1, so that they respond positively to the straight line and negatively (or in some different fashion) to the curved line. Stage 2 then introduces the same straight line, paired with various curved lines; none of these are straight, but they differ in a number of ways. Another way to say this is that the curved lines vary in their irrelevant dimensions (such as amount of curvature and orientation). Contrast practice is continued under these conditions until learners show convincingly that they discriminate "straight" from "not straight." Thus there is *generalization* of the original discrimination learning.

Prototype or clear case.   There are differences of opinion based on research evidence as to how a new concept is first represented in memory. In

STAGE 1: DISCRIMINATION

Straight   Curved

STAGE 2: GENERALIZATION

STAGE 3: VARIATION IN IRRELEVANT DIMENSIONS

Figure 5.1 Stages of learning beginning with a discrimination and leading to the learning of a concept.

terms of Figure 5.1, this is the question of what is first stored in memory at stage 2, so that "straight line" can be generalized to lines that differ in length, thickness, orientation, or other irrelevant attributes while retaining the "straight" quality. Rosch (1978) presents evidence indicating that the representation of a concrete concept is one that is typical, that is, a *prototype* that reflects the best instances of the category. Brooks (1978) argues that the learner is likely initially to acquire a concept representation based upon a particular instance. This may be the first instance encountered by the learner, and thus it may not necessarily be a "best" instance. Subsequent encounters with other instances bring about changes that may alter the stored representation of the concept toward the direction of typicality. However, such changes, according to Brooks, will continue to depend upon the particular instances and situations encountered by the learner.

Although the nature of the initial mental processing of a concrete concept is still under investigation, there is general agreement that the process of generalization, indicated as stage 2 in Figure 5.1, is an essential aspect of concept learning (Markle and Tiemann, 1969; Tennyson, Woolley, and Merrill, 1972).

Varied contrast practice is again continued in stage 3 (Tennyson and Park, 1980). In this stage, there is variation in the irrelevant dimensions of the nonstraight lines and also in the irrelevant dimensions (orientation, thickness, etc.) of the straight lines. Once the learning of this stage has been mastered, there is convincing proof that the learner has "abstracted" the relevant object-quality and acquired the *concept* of line straightness. To make a final check on the learning of the concept, it is customary to choose a brand-new example not used during learning. A new straight line may be drawn, with a different nonstraight line. We say that the concept has been acquired when the learner can identify such a *novel instance*. Note that what the learner is doing is placing this new instance into the category "straight," in other words classifying it.

The three stages illustrated in Figure 5.1 are somewhat comparable to those described by Klausmeier, Ghatala, and Frayer (1974). These investigators have described four levels of concept attainment, each requiring a different kind of intellectual processing. The first level is *concrete*, in which the learner discriminates the object from other objects. Second is the *identity* level, which involves recognizing the object in a different situation or from a different perspective. The third level (comparable to stage 3 of Figure 5.1) is the *classificatory* level, which may be inferred from learners' behavior when they are able to identify newly encountered examples. As for the fourth level, it is called the *formal* level and is attained when learners can define the class of objects in terms of its attributes. This level is equivalent to the *defined concept*, to be described in the following chapter. Of course, it should be understood that every concrete concept, although it may initially be learned by observation, can also be learned by definition. Concrete concepts that are learned by young children are often given fuller meaning and greater precision when they are later brought to the formal level (as *defined concepts*) by learning in school.

Verbal Instructions in Concept Learning

The meaning of concrete concept is illustrated by the examples we have given. But the description of concept learning is not yet complete. A concept may be acquired by means of the contrast practice procedure, employing a succession of instances varying in their irrelevant dimensions. But this procedure is not necessarily typical when the learner can be guided by language.

Suppose that a child capable of using language does not know the concept *edge*. Assume it is desirable for the child to exhibit the capability of identifying an edge by name, and more importantly, of identifying any one of a class of things called edges in novel situations. How can such learning come about?

The first step might be for the child to acquire the word as a self-generated $S \rightarrow R$ connection, so that when the instructor says "edge" and then asks that the word be repeated, the pupil says "edge." Next the pupil will learn to say the word "edge" to that part of an object, and to refrain from saying "edge" to other parts that are not edges, such as a *side*, a *top*, or a *corner*. This is the generalization stage, previously described. The important event in each case is a firm and precise attainment of *edge* discriminations, even when other dimensions of the object are varied. Now greater variety is introduced into the situation. Edge is learned as a feature of a flat-surfaced object such as a piece of paper, involving distinctions between *edge* and *surface* and *corner*. It is learned again with reference to a drawn two-dimensional figure, which may show *shading* as well as clear edges.

How many situations need to be used to assure a sufficient number of variations in which edge is distinguished from features that are "not edge"? There appears to be no known answer to this question. But it is important to conduct the learning within stimulus situations that *represent the actual range of the concept being learned*; otherwise the concept that emerges will be incomplete in some sense. Concepts that are *inadequate in range* are frequently learned by all of us, owing to the peculiarities of the situations we have encountered. For example, a young child who has seen only one or two bears may have an inadequate concept of this class of animals. An inadequate concept, in this sense, however, is *not incorrect* and may in fact be useful for many purposes. Extension of the range of a concept can readily be brought about by additional learning occasions.

When the learner is able to say "edge" to several different specific stimulus situations, it is reasonable to suppose that the concept has been learned. The instructor might confirm the learning by using a verbal communication presenting three of the stimuli at once (the three-dimensional object, the paper, the drawing). The teacher might say, "each of these has an edge. What is this? (An edge.) And what is this? (An edge.) And what is this? (An edge.)" Finally, one more step is taken and the pupil is shown a new object or drawing with which the word "edge" has not previously been associated. The instructor then says, "Where is the edge?" The pupil points to it. A concept has been acquired!

It is not entirely clear whether the use of the final new example is necessary for the learning, or whether it is merely a test of what has already been learned. Quite probably, the former is the case. At any rate, the instructor will probably wish to make a more reliable determination that concept learning has really happened by asking the student to respond to one or two additional examples, each a novel one

What is the role of the verbal label, the word "edge," in this set of events? Obviously, it provides an important shortcut to the learning of a concept. Without it, one would have to conduct a greater number of trial-and-error situations in order to insure that the responses to the concept of "edges" and "nonedges" were correct. When the word is known, however, it can be used to *cue* the correct responses to stimulus to recall, which makes it relatively easy to structure the situation required for learning.

Thus it may be seen that the learning of a concept is not *necessarily* a verbal matter, since concepts can be learned in other ways by animals as well as by human beings. But using verbal cues makes concept learning a relatively easy task for human beings who have already mastered the prerequisites. In the design of instruction for the learning of a concrete concept, the defining attributes of the concept are first identified. These attributes are then used to devise systematic variations in the instances of the object presented to the learner (Gagné, Wager, and Rojas, 1981). An example of this technique is illustrated in Figure 5.2.

The verbal directions and cues of Figure 5.2, however, need to be carefully distinguished from the verbalizing that presents a definition. As an example of the latter, an edge might be defined as "a region of abrupt change in intensity of the pattern of light waves reflected to the eye from a surface." In the case of a triangle, a definition might be "a simple closed plane figure having three line segments as sides." It should not be supposed that verbal definitions of this sort would be very effective in bringing about the learning of a concept. (Learning of concepts does sometimes occur this way in highly sophisticated adults, but that is another story.) The learner must instead begin with concrete situations, to which common verbal associates may be brought. When this condition obtains, using words like those in parentheses in the figure as "instruction" is a convenient way of generating the proper conditions for concept learning.

Adults learn new concepts in much the same way. Suppose, for example, an adult who is studying physiology must learn the concept of *striated muscle*. In such a case one assumes that the basic learning of the words has already been accomplished. But the verbal chains that connect several instances of observed tissue samples (actual or pictured) to the response "striated muscle" must be established. Furthermore, a number of multiple discriminations must probably also be acquired; the individual must learn to distinguish muscle tissue from other forms and to distinguish striated from smooth and heart muscle. Once these differences have been mastered, the basic instructional conditions for concept learning can be carried out. That is, various instances of striated muscle can be shown at one time (or in quick succession) and identified by the student, who should then be ready to classify a new example of striated muscle as a member of the concept class.

Is this all the adult must learn about a concept in order to be said to "know" it? The answer is yes, so long as the word "know" means nothing more than to use the new entity as a concept. Of course, an adult will probably go on to learn more about striated muscle in the form of rules (to be discussed in the next chapter). How striated muscles work, where they occur in the body, their embryological development, and many other things may also be learned. But these additional learnings will be useless except as sheer verbalizations, unless the learner first knows the concept by reference

THESE ARE TRIANGLES:

THIS IS A TRIANGLE:

THIS IS NOT:

(THREE SIDES)

THIS IS A TRIANGLE:

(STRAIGHT SIDES)

THIS IS NOT:

THIS IS A TRIANGLE:

(CLOSED FIGURE)

THIS IS NOT:

THIS IS A TRIANGLE:

(SIMPLE FIGURE)

THIS IS NOT:

Figure 5.2   Example of instruction in the concrete concept "triangle," using a few verbal directions. The varied attributes shown in parentheses may be used as part of the instruction with learners who recognize their referents.

to a *class of concrete situations.* It may be noted that this observation about concepts has profound implications for educational practice. For example, the fundamental reason for laboratory work in science instruction is to give such concrete examples. Concepts may be aroused by verbal means, as we have seen. In human beings, their learning is almost always verbally mediated. But to be accurate tools for thinking about and dealing with the real world, concepts must be referable to actual stimulus situations. These provide concepts with an "operational" meaning that can come in no other way.

Concepts in Intellectual Development

Seven-year-old children show marked differences from four-year-olds in acquiring concepts, presumably because the younger ones have not yet acquired the words that make concept learning an easy matter (Kendler and Kendler, 1961). This has been shown by giving children of two age groups a task like that illustrated in Figure 5.3. In the first task, the children were asked to choose between two exposed squares, one large and one small. Although the relative position of the squares was varied, the "large" one was always correct, and the child received a marble for choosing it. Once this task had been learned, each child was given a second task in which the "small" square was now correct. (Another group of children first responded to "black" as correct, and then were shifted to "white.") The seven-year-olds took an average of eight trials to make this shift, whereas the four-year-olds required twenty-three. It seems probable that the older children in this study were able to use the concept of *opposite* quite readily, whereas the younger children had difficulty with it and tended to continue responding to the situation by learning anew a reverse discrimination. The pre-availability of language has been shown in other studies to make considerable difference in children's acquiring of concepts.

Klausmeier and his associates (Klausmeier, 1976; Klausmeier and Allen, 1978) tested the attainment of several different concepts in students in grades kindergarten and 3, 6, and 9. The concrete concept *cutting tool* was

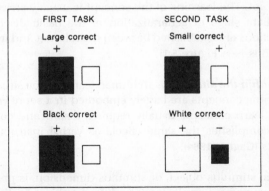

Figure 5.3 Two examples of discrimination reversal problems learned by children of two different age groups (four and seven). After learning the first task, the children were shifted to the second (reversed) task. (Kendler, H. H., and Kendler, T. S., Effect of verbalization on reversal shifts in children. *Science*, 1961, *141*, 1619–1620.)

attained (at the classificatory level) by 76% of the kindergarteners, by 83% of the third-graders, and 100% of the ninth-grade students. In the case of the concept *equilateral triangle*, the comparable percents for children in kindergarten were 42%, for sixth-graders 80%, and for ninth-graders 100%. Quite probably, the striking difference in achievement of these two concepts at the kindergarten level is a direct result of a difference in the frequency with which they are encountered. Even before attending school, children are likely to have had some experience with saws and knives and other cutting tools, but they are not so likely to have encountered equilateral triangles. By the time they are in grade 3, however, children have probably had a number of instructional experiences with equilateral triangles.

The results obtained by Klausmeier and associates also confirm the learning difficulty of a concept like *noun*, which is an example of a defined concept (see next chapter) requiring verbal statements to represent it. The concept *noun* could not be identified (at the classificatory level) by kindergarten children, although it could be by 70% of the sixth graders and by 82% of the ninth graders.

The Conditions of Concept Learning

It is now possible to summarize in a more formal way the conditions for the learning of concrete concepts.

Conditions within the learner.   Prerequisites to the learning of concepts are capabilities that have previously been established as discriminations. These must be recalled by learners at the time they undertake concept learning. When verbal instructions are employed, verbal labels must have previously been learned as associates to the stimulus features that represent the concept. The learning of the concept is usually arrived at through the intermediate stage of generalization of the basic discrimination, in which distinctions are established between the relevant and irrelevant stimulus dimensions (see Figure 5.1).

Conditions within the situation.   In human learners, the situational conditions for learning concepts are largely embodied in a set of *verbal cues*. To have animals learn concepts usually requires a slow and complex procedure that accomplishes the same effects as verbal instructions do with human beings (Gagné, 1964).

1. The specific stimulus object, or stimulus dimension, is presented as an instance along with a noninstance (a different object or dimension). The learner identifies the dimension by name. In terms of the example used here, the instructor asks "What is this?" or "Show me the edge." The learner's response confirms the presence of the discrimination.

2. In the generalization stage, the instructor introduces the instance along with various noninstances. Again, the identification of the discriminated feature (such as the edge) is asked for and obtained in each case.
3. Now the stimulus feature that is to become the concept is itself varied and presented along with various noninstances. The new capability may be verified by asking for the identification of several additional instances of the class, agai   using stimulus objects not previously employed in learning. If these are successfully identified, one may conclude that a new concept has been learned.
4. The condition of *reinforcement* is present in the concept-learning situation. The learner's correct responses to "edge" and "nonedge" must be confirmed if the concept is to be learned. *Contiguity* also appears important to concept learning, as illustrated by the contiguous presentation of several instances involving the same discrimination. The absence of contiguity may well be the factor mainly responsible for the slowness of concept learning done in a trial-and-error fashion. When all the specific instances on which the concept depends are "lively" in memory at the same time, concept acquisition is rapid. As for *repetition*, it does not appear to be necessary when other conditions are optimal. The provision of one or more new examples may merely serve the purpose of "testing" the presence of the concept. There is no available evidence whether these additional instances aid in concept retention, although this may be true.

Generalizing with Concepts

The possession of the capability generated in the learner when a concept is acquired is distinguished from all other forms of learning so far described by the characteristic of *generalizability*. Having acquired the concept of *edge*, learners should be able to generalize this concept to different stimulus situations that have not played a part in the learning. They can immediately and unhesitatingly identify an edge on a roof, a cliff, an automobile fender, a lampshade, or any of a great variety of stimulus situations. (Of course, this assumes that the initial situations used to exhibit the concept were sufficiently representative of the total class covered by the concept.) If they have learned the concept *raise*, they will be able to recognize this class of event in such diverse circumstances as the raising of an arm, a flag, or a window. *The effect of concept learning is to free the individual from control by specific stimuli.* This kind of learning, then, is obviously of tremendous importance for most kinds of intellectual activity engaged in by human beings. We read in terms of concepts, we communicate with concepts, we think with concepts.

It is not surprising, then, that the "test" for the presence of concepts is a matter of demonstrating that generalizing can occur. Regardless of what stimuli have been used for learning, the acquisition of the concept of *odd* or *edge* or *raise* is tested by presenting a stimulus situation that was not involved in the learning. There must be a demonstration that the learner can generalize the concept to a variety of specific instances of the class that have not been used in learning. Otherwise, the learning may not be a concept but merely a collection of specific chains.

The generalizing capability provided by concept learning goes far beyond the *stimulus generalization* that is a fundamental property of S → R learning. Of course, this latter property is still present in the connections used to establish or to arouse the concept. But it is limited by the physical resemblances of objects or events. Generalizing by means of concepts, in contrast, is not limited by physical resemblances. When using a concept, the individual experiences no difficulty in identifying the edge in a large round swimming pool or in a tiny letter on a printed page. The property held in common by such widely different stimulus situations cannot be described in terms of the resemblances of physical stimulation. An edge, in other words, is an abstraction from all the specific situations in which it occurs. This is apparently what some writers mean when they refer to concepts as "relationships of stimuli."

The world experienced by human beings is largely organized by means of concepts. We think of our environment, as well as ourselves, primarily in terms of concepts of objects, places, and events. We communicate with other people, and they communicate with us, to an overwhelming degree by means of concepts. There are concepts of things and places, like *chairs, tables, trees, lawns, houses, automobiles, top, bottom, side, corner*. Things in conceptual form are the nouns of sentences. Then there are concepts of relations, which generally are represented by verbs, such as *go, stay, take, put, raise, lower, sit, accept, deliver, reject*. Because of the accidental character of their experiences with them, children sometimes acquire these words as concepts in a trial-and-error fashion. But a new concept such as that represented by a technical term may readily be taught in the more systematic manner just described.

An Example—Letter and Phoneme Identification

An example of concept learning of considerable educational importance, and illustrative of many of the characteristics previously discussed, is learning to identify printed letters and syllables as parts of words.

As pointed out in the early portion of this chapter, one prerequisite learning is that of acquiring discriminations such as d = "duh," b = "buh," k = "kuh." Once such discriminations have been learned, a firm foundation has been laid for the acquiring of letter-sound concepts. The distinction is that letters must now be identified as corresponding to an entire *class* of acoustic stimuli, depending upon their context within a syllable or word. In terms of actual response characteristics, the flat "a" is pronounced with considerable difference in the words "frantic" and "stagger"; yet as a concept to be acquired for the purpose of reading or listening, it is still a member of the class of letter a. In the word "dumb," the "d" has a good deal of force behind it, with the tongue far back; in "dirt," however, the "d" is much closer to a "t" in sound. But both sounds are members of the class d. For each printed letter there is a class of *phonemes*.

Following the learning of basic discriminations, the child who is learning to read must learn to identify phonemes by recognizing a single printed letter for each letter-sound contained in the class. Thus, phonemes constitute an educationally important concept. The acquisition of these concepts takes place under learning conditions comparable to those for other concepts. The different instances of the class must be presented and each identified (recognized) as belonging to a single class of printed letters. For example, the sound of "d" in "dirt" must lead to recognition of "d," and the sound of "d" in "dumb" must lead to the same recognition; the sound of "b" in "book" must be identified as b, and also as the sound of "b" in "table." The conditions for learning, then, may be described as consisting of the presentation of a sufficient variety of positive and negative instances of the phoneme class accompanied by suitable provisions for reinforcement.

It seems that difficulties in learning the pronunciation of printed words may sometimes result from an unsystematic sequence of learning events. The systematic sequence is (1) learn to identify the letters, as d—"duh," and so on; (2) learn to put letters together in longer chains, sometimes called "blending," as in "buh"–"a"–"tuh" for "bat"; (3) learn to pronounce the entire printed word as "bat." At this third stage, however, the concepts called phonemes are of particular importance. The children must recognize the printed t, for example, as a member of the phoneme class "t" that has a particular sound in this context. By so doing, they learn to match the letter combination at to a familiar sound in their oral repertoire. Similarly, having also recognized the phoneme b, they learn to match the entire printed word to the word "bat" in their oral vocabulary.

Some Educational Implications

It would be difficult to overemphasize the importance of concept learning for formal education. The acquisition of concepts is what makes instruction possible. One cannot take the time to present even a small fraction of all the specific situations in which students may encounter an edge or an odd one or a cell or a striated muscle. But if the use of a few examples can help learners to acquire these concepts, one may expect that generalizing will occur to the whole of the learners' experience. Students are freed from the control of specific stimuli in their environment and can thereafter learn by means of *verbal instruction*, presented orally or in printed form. They can also communicate their intentions, actions, and thoughts to other people—again because the specific words employed arouse concepts in their hearers that function just as their own do.

Young children arrive in kindergarten with many concepts learned and many not yet learned. They probably have already acquired concepts for a number of common objects in the environment, such as chairs, floors, ceilings, streets, flowers, animals, and trees. Most probably, they know such place concepts as *above, below, on top of, underneath, next to, middle*. Similarly, the youngsters will doubtless respond conceptually to words like *start* and *stop, go* and *come, sit* and *stand*. But children still need to learn many other concepts that will form the basis of much of their later learning. They may not yet know what *the one before* means, or *the next one* or *double* or *like* and *unlike*. Kindergarten children probably have not yet learned to conceptualize word sounds as printed letter combinations as a basis for reading and writing. They may not be able to use number names for quantities (whether or not they can recite a verbal chain such as "one, two, three") but will need to learn these foundations of arithmetic. In fact, it would be valuable to know with some confidence which concepts the typical kindergarten child does not yet have or which ones will have to be learned first. The problem is clearly an important one.

As students progress in school, they continue to acquire concepts. Once the fundamental skill of reading has been acquired, concepts can often be introduced by means of instruction with accompanying pictures or diagrams. In mathematics this is fairly easy because the stimulus situations that must be responded to with concepts are usually marks on a printed page; adding can be represented by + and subtracting by −. Languages can also be represented in print, so that the concepts pertaining to language structure (subject, verb, and so on) are learned in response to printed sentences such as "John's hat is on the table." But in other subjects, there may be greater difficulty in presenting the fundamental situations to be conceptualized, and pictures and diagrams are often employed. Thus, at some stage of science learning, the concept *fulcrum* may be introduced with the presentation of several diagrams depicting levers; or the concept *cell* may be presented by means of an idealized diagram. Most difficult of all are likely to be abstract concepts like *family* and *legislature*, of the types that make up the social science disciplines.

The great value of concepts as means for thinking and communicating is that they have *concrete references*. The importance of this characteristic cannot be overemphasized. But since concepts are learned by the human being via language, there is often a danger of losing sight of this concreteness. Learning can become oververbalized, which means that the concepts learned are highly inadequate in their references to actual situations. The learner "does not really know the meaning of the word," even though it can be used correctly in a sentence. For example, the verbal information obtained by reading that striated muscles are made up of bundles of long narrow cells is unlikely to provide a student of physiology or anatomy an adequate concept of striated muscles. The danger of verbal superficiality, and the necessity for avoiding it, has been recognized in several educational doctrines. "Learning by doing" is one of these. Another recognizes the importance of the laboratory and the demonstration in science teaching. The concepts of science deal with the real world and therefore must be based on "operations" that are equally concrete.

In addition to having concrete references, concepts possess the additional property of freeing thought and expression from the domination of the physical environment. As will be seen in the next chapter, concepts in their generalized form may be linked together in various ways to form principles. "Water boils" is a simple sentence recalling two different concepts to the individual who has already acquired them. But the linking of these concepts results in the conveying of information, that is, *knowledge* in propositional form. The tremendous variety of knowledge imparted by means of verbal communication is, of course, a fundamental fact of education. Once concepts have been mastered, the individual is ready to learn an amount of knowledge that is virtually without limit.

GENERAL REFERENCES

Discrimination Learning

Estes, W. K. *Handbook of learning and cognitive processes*, Vol. 1. Hillsdale, N.J.: Erlbaum, 1975. Chapters 5 and 6.

Gibson, E. J. *Principles of perceptual learning and development.* New York: Appleton, 1969.

Riley, D. A. Discrimination learning. In M. H. Marx and M. E. Bunch (Eds.), *Fundamentals and applications of learning.* New York: Macmillan, 1977.

Concept Learning

Bourne, L. E., Jr. *Human conceptual behavior.* Boston: Allyn and Bacon, 1966.

Harlow, H. F., and Harlow, M. K. Learning to think. *Scientific American*, 1949, *181*, 36-39.

Rosch, E., and Lloyd, B. B. (Eds.), *Cognition and categorization.* Hillsdale, N.J.: Erlbaum, 1978.

Trabasso, T., and Bower, G. H. *Attention in learning.* New York: Wiley, 1968.

Children's Concepts

Flavell, J. H. *The developmental psychology of Jean Piaget*. New York: Van Nostrand, 1963.

Klausmeier, H. J. *Learning and teaching concepts*. New York: Academic Press, 1980.

Levin, J. R., and Allen, V. L. (Eds.), *Cognitive learning in children: Theories and strategies*. New York: Academic Press, 1976.

Sigel, I. E., and Hooper, F. H. *Logical thinking in children*. New York: Holt, Rinehart and Winston, 1968.

6

Intellectual Skills: Defined Concepts and Rules

Some concepts can be learned by direct interaction with the learner's environment, while others must be learned by the use of language. The latter kind of concepts are really rules for classifying objects and events.

This chapter deals with the learning of concepts and rules, varieties of intellectual skills highly representative of human intellectual capabilities. To some readers it may seem, at last, that the types of behavior being described are those with which formal instruction most typically concerns itself, and this is probably the case. It should be emphasized, however, that these forms of learning build upon learnings that have preceded them. Although the learning of defined concepts and rules may well represent some frequent goals of a formal schooling process, it would be a mistake to believe that these goals can be reached by simply ignoring all other forms of learning or by pushing the latter into a trash can of unimportant events. The varieties of learning described here are possible only because they have been preceded by the acquisition of a set of simpler prerequisite capabilities.

Many concepts cannot be learned in the manner described in the previous chapter, that is, as concrete concepts. Instead, they must be learned by *definition* and, accordingly, may be called *defined concepts*. Sometimes they are called abstract, in order to distinguish them from the concrete variety. For example, the concept *diagonal* is a defined concept, not a concrete concept. The statement "A diagonal is a line connecting opposite corners of a quadrilateral" represents a relation ("connect") between the two concepts "line" and "opposite corners of a quadrilateral." Another example is the concept *pivot*, which may be defined as the relation, "pointed end of a shaft on which an object turns." In this instance, it may be seen that the defined concept is composed of other concrete concepts, including "pointed end," "shaft," and "turns." This is not always the case, of course; a defined concept may be composed of one or more concepts that are themselves defined rather than concrete.

Rules and Their Names

The inclusive subject of this chapter is the *learning of rules*. The defined concept is, in a formal sense, one type of rule. The relation expressed by a defined concept may be used, as its name implies, to enable the learner to identify the relation and distinguish it from others: The concept of *uncle* is distinguished from *aunt* or the concept of *mass* from *weight*. Rules are also used for other purposes. They operate to guide the individual's behavior in meeting a host of particular problems. The rule that is symbolized in mathematics as $a + b = b + a$ guides the individual's behavior in selecting a combination of seven objects and two objects as being equivalent to a combination of two objects and seven objects; or four objects and five objects as equivalent to five and four. It is not necessary to learn each individual combination of numbers in a rote fashion as verbal chains. Instead, the rule is applied to whatever combination of numbers is being dealt with at the moment. Students learn to *apply a rule*, and their behavior may be said to be *rule-governed*.

The ability of human beings to respond to an enormous variety of situations and to operate effectively—despite almost infinite variety in the stimulation they receive—makes it at once apparent that rules are probably the major organizing factor, and quite possibly the primary one, in intellectual functioning. The $S \rightarrow R$ connection, once proposed as the unit of mental organization, has now virtually been replaced by the rule in the theoretical formulations of many psychologists. Even those who still favor the connection as a fundamental entity of neural functioning are forced to concede that the preponderance of observed human behavior occurring in natural situations is rule-governed. When a young child constructs the imperfect sentence "Daddy, in" to express the desire that the father enter the house, the child is applying a rule—perhaps an inadequate one by adult standards, but a rule nonetheless. One knows this not from observing the single instance of the child calling the father but from additional observations that indicate the child can construct the same kind of sentences for the mother, a dog, or other people. The stimuli in these other situations are all different and may actually not have occurred previously in the child's life. Yet sentence-constructing behavior can be seen to be *regular*, or rule-governed.

Rules have found a solid place for themselves in modern accounts of cognitive psychology and information processing. The *production system* (the name is borrowed from computer science) forms a basic idea in Newell and Simon's (1972) account of problem solving. A production system is typically exemplified in the following way:

IF the subject of the sentence is plural and
  a verb is to represent the subject's action
THEN use the plural form of the verb

The production system idea includes an emphasis on the "action" quality of a rule. That is to say, the production system is the learner's representation of knowing how to *do* something.

More generally, rules may collectively be given the name of *procedural knowledge*. An if–then relation obviously has the characteristic of a procedure, since it involves at least two steps. This phase is used to provide a contrast with *declarative knowledge*, here called verbal information (Chapter 8). More than this, though, is implied by the phrase procedural knowledge. There is a recognition that some rules involve a lengthy set of steps (for example, pencil-and-paper long division). As we shall see later, *procedures* (or *procedural rules*) have some characteristics that make it convenient for them to be separately considered as a subcategory. Their principal qualities, however, are those of the rule.

DEFINED CONCEPTS

A defined concept is a rule that classifies objects or events. Examples: The set of *prime numbers* is classified by the definition of any number divisible only by the number one and by a number with the same value as itself. A *circle* is a closed plane curve on which every point is equidistant from a fixed point. A *jungle* is an area of land overgrown with masses of vegetation. A *cousin* is the son or daughter of an aunt or uncle. These concepts require verbal definitions if they are to be learned in an adequate form.

Some of these examples, like *circle*, may have been learned previously as concrete concepts. This is not an unusual occurrence. However, the concrete form of a concept such as circle has some inadequacies when compared with its defined form. For instance, the child who has attained the concrete concept of circle might identify as circles plane figures that are not quite circles, for example, figures in which the points on their curve might not all be equidistant from a fixed point. Of course, the concrete concept of circle may be perfectly useful in many situations over a period of years. Yet the defined concept is more precise and consequently applicable to an even greater variety of situations.

Some concepts can only be learned in a defined form. *Cousin* is an example. One cannot identify instances of the class *cousins* on the basis of their appearance, by picking them out or pointing to them. It is necessary to apply a definition to show that one knows what a cousin is. Exact words do not have to be employed, of course, but the relation between son or daughter and aunt and uncle must be shown in a way that follows the definition. (It is interesting to note that in doing this, aunt and uncle have to be defined first.) As one might expect, abstract concepts like *family*, *city*, *transportation*, and *justice* also have to be learned as defined concepts. They have no concrete counterparts that can be identified by their appearance. These abstractions must be understood and communicated by means of the statement of a *classifying rule*, which is also called a *definition*.

Definition

Definitions are statements that express rules for classifying. An individual who has acquired a defined concept has learned this kind of a rule and is able to apply it to any instance of the class. Notice that it is not essential for the individual to learn the rule *statement* itself (that is, the definition) in order to show us that the concept has been learned. The definition merely represents the classifying rule that has been learned.

In the simplest case, a definition represents one or more objects (which may be called *thing-concepts*) and a relation (or *relational concept*). Consider the definition of *saucer*: a dish (thing-concept) for holding (relational concept) a cup (thing-concept). While this is the basic form, most definitions are more complex. They are modified primarily by additional descriptions of the features of the thing concepts they contain. The definition of *bottle*, for example, might begin with a container (thing-concept) for holding (relational concept) liquid (thing-concept). For increased adequacy, the definition must contain additional modifiers so that it becomes "a rigid container with a round narrow neck and no handle, made to hold liquid."

This analysis shows us that when *objects* are defined, their definitions have four essential parts:

1. A thing-concept that is the superordinate class (as "dish" is superordinate to "saucer," "container" to "bottle")
2. A set of characteristics or features of this superordinate concept ("rigid," "narrow-necked,"and so on)
3. A relational concept that tells what the object does or is used for ("holding")
4. Another thing-concept that is the object of this verb ("cup," "liquid")

In some accounts of concepts, all of these parts are considered "relevant features" (for example, Klausmeier, 1971). There seems to be some usefulness, however, in the distinction between "features" (1 and 2) and "function" (3 and 4).

Definitions of concepts that are themselves *relations* have somewhat different components. Such definitions appear to require the use of a near-synonym, usually a simpler and more familiar relational concept, such as that expressed by a verb. Defining the relation *homogenize*, for example, begins with the familiar verb "break up." A liquid (such as milk) is homogenized by "breaking up" its particles into uniform size. The relational concept *swaddle* appears to require "wrap" in its definition, followed by the modifiers "completely or almost completely." Thus, the typical components of a definition for a relational concept are these:

1. A relational concept that is familiar to the learner, and a near-synonym ("break up," "wrap")
2. A thing-concept that is the object of this relational term ("liquid," or a concept as general as "thing")
3. Modifier words, such as adverbs or prepositional phrases, that function as the characteristic of the relation (and are thus comparable to the adjectives that represent the characteristics of thing-concepts). Examples are "into uniform size," and "completely or almost completely."

Defined concepts, whether they are things or relations, must apparently be represented by definitions composed of other concepts. These latter components are already familiar to the learner, that is, they have been previously learned. Unless the definitions are to be completely circular, this means that some concepts must originally be learned *without* definitions. As we have seen, *concrete concepts* are learned on the basis of encounters with class instances that can be directly sensed by the learner. If the concept of a *pentagon* must be learned from a definition containing the concepts "straight" and "side," the latter are likely to have been learned as concrete concepts at some earlier time. Or if *tabulate* is to be learned as a concept by definition, the familiar relational concept "list" presumably has been acquired previously, and quite possibly as a concrete concept.

Concepts as Classifying Rules

Defined concepts are rules for classifying. When learners have acquired such a concept, they are able to follow the definition in actually classifying some object or some relation. (Remember that this does not necessarily mean that they can state the definition.) If learners have acquired the concept *hackney*, one expects that they will be able to follow the definition in showing that this means a trotting horse used chiefly for driving. In an ideal sense, learners will be able to identify instances of horses (perhaps in pictures) that are trotting and used for driving as opposed to other animals that are not trotting and not used for driving. Of course, when the assumption can reasonably be made that they know the meaning of component concepts, learners may satisfactorily use words to identify the concepts *horse*, *trotting*, and *used for driving*. It is important to note, however, that acceptance of these verbal statements as evidence that learners have acquired a defined concept *does* involve an assumption. In essence, the evidence that the concept has been learned derives from a *demonstration* that the definition can be used to classify instances.

Consider another example. Suppose that learners must acquire the concept *courtesy*, represented by the definition "well-mannered behavior indicating respect for others." One way to determine whether such a concept has been acquired would be to present learners with instances of behavior (either shown in pictures or described). Some of these behaviors would be well-mannered, some not; some would indicate respect for others, while others would not. The conclusion that learners could *classify* these instances in accordance with the definition would be shown by their identifying instances that are "well-mannered" and that "show respect for others" and their rejection of instances could not be so classified. Again, it would be possible to ask learners to use verbal responses by asking them to "tell why" they had classified each instance. This would be a convenient method, but it obviously requires the assumption that learners know the meaning of the words they use. One might be more inclined to accept this assumption, and therefore the evidence that the concept has been learned, in a twelve-year-old student than in a six-year-old.

LEARNING DEFINED CONCEPTS

Defined concepts are usually learned by means of their definitions. In contrast to concrete concepts, defined concepts cannot be readily acquired simply by the presentation of a variety of instances and noninstances whose characteristics can be directly perceived by the learner. Instead, the component concepts of the definition are typically communicated to the learner Thus, the verbal statement that represents the defined concept (that is, the definition) may be communicated. This means that the learner is reminded of the *thing-concepts* and the *relational concepts* that comprise the new concept to be learned and is able immediately to "grasp" the meaning of the new concept.

By this means, it is fairly easy for a suitably prepared learner to acquire a new concept. Suppose one communicated the concept *caliche* (a concept unknown to many Americans and used in a speech by President Lyndon Johnson) by means of the statement "a crust of calcium carbonate which forms on the top of soil in arid regions." Obviously, this verbal communication is an adequate means by which an adult learner can acquire this new concept. The statement of the definition provides memory cues for previously learned concepts such as *crust, calcium carbonate*, and *forms.*

At the same time, it is apparent that the learner *cannot* acquire the concept by means of these verbal cues if the referential meaning of the component concepts is unknown. If the concept *calcium carbonate*, is not known, the *caliche* concept will not be learned in adequate form. If the learner does not know the concept *arid*, the new concept cannot be adequately formed. And, of course, if the relational concepts *form* and *on top of* are not known, the newly defined concept will not be learned.

Definitions and Examples

When college students were asked to recognize previously unfamiliar concepts (such as *atavistic* and *excoriate*) after being shown their definitions, they correctly selected over 90 percent of them in most cases (Anderson and

Kulhavy, 1972). However, the definitions of defined concepts are not always simple. On the contrary, they often are lengthy and complicated rule statements.

Markle and Tiemann (1974) investigated the learning of *morpheme*, a linguistic concept unfamiliar to the college students who participated in their study. Their definition, designed to include three critical attributes, was "a linguistic unit which carries a stable meaning from one construction to another, contributes that meaning to the construction in which it appears, and cannot be further subdivided into units having meanings related to that construction." *Webster's Third New International Dictionary* contributes the examples of a free form (pin, load), a bound form (the "s" of pins, the "hood" of childhood). Markle and Tiemann tested the acquisition of the *morpheme* concept by means of fifty test items of examples and nonexamples. The provision of examples in addition to a definition was found to be a condition that improved the generalization of the concept to new examples.

A number of studies (reviewed by Tennyson and Park, 1980) have verified the importance of including examples in the teaching of defined concepts. Thus, although it is significant that a verbal definition can teach a great deal, the use of carefully chosen examples and nonexamples appears to be a requirement for what may be called "full understanding" of a defined concept. To be most effective, such examples should cover as full as possible a range of essential and nonessential (or "variable") attributes.

External and Internal Conditions for Defined Concept Learning

The typical conditions for learning a defined concept can be seen as comprising both internal and external events.

Conditions within the learner.   Learners must have access in their working memory to the component concepts represented in the definition of the concept to be learned. These are (1) the thing-concepts (nouns), which are the subject and object of the verb, and (2) the relational concept, which is represented by the verb. As noted previously, the latter relation may either "have the characteristics of" or "function to" or both. These component concepts are simply the basic requirements. Of course, as definitional concepts become more complex, the meaning of modifier words such as adjectives and adverbs must also be known.

One other internal condition needs to be noted and is often assumed. Learners who are to respond adequately to a verbal statement must have previously acquired the intellectual skill (rule) of representing the *syntax* of such a statement to themselves. That is to say, they must be able to distinguish the subject (the "actor") from the verb (the "relation") and both from the object. This very fundamental language skill is usually learned during the early years.

Conditions in the learning situation.   Externally, the conditions for learning a defined concept usually consist in the presentation of the definition in oral or printed form. The learner is confronted with a statement such as "A roof is the outside cover of a building." Such a proposition calls upon the learner's syntax skills of language understanding to maintain the proper order of the component concepts. The words themselves are *cues* to make these component concepts reaccessible in one's working memory. Thus one is able to acquire a concept that has previously not been learned. We know the concept has been acquired when the learner can demonstrate what a roof is, perhaps by drawing a building and indicating the part called "roof." Alternatively, the learner may be presented with a number of different examples of roof to identify. Preferably, these should extend over the entire range of variation in instances of the concept.

Additionally, the external conditions for learning defined concepts should include both instances and noninstances. According to the evidence from quite a number of studies (see Tennyson and Park, 1980), it appears that most effective learning results are obtained when the examples extend broadly over the range of positive instances included in the concept, and when the nonexamples represent closely similar instances that exhibit critical differences. In the case of a concept like *morpheme*, the range of positive examples would include *drop* and *manor* and *gangster*, whereas a nonexample might be as closely similar as *pumpkin* (a stable meaning, but not one that is contributed to the word in which it appears). Examples and nonexamples contribute some important elements to the learning conditions, because they enable the learner to recognize the distinguishing features of concept instances to be encountered in the future.

RULES

A defined concept is a particular kind of rule, a rule that classifies. Thus a rule must be an internal state that governs one's behavior and enables one to demonstrate a relationship. A rule must be more than the verbal statement by which it is represented, for instance, the proposition, "the perimeter of a square is four times the length of one side." It must be something that accounts for regularity of behavior in the face of virtually infinite variations in specific stimulation: all sizes of squares in whatever setting they may occur. *A rule, then, is an inferred capability that enables the individual to respond to any instance of a class of stimulus situations with an appropriate instance of a class of performances.* The latter performances are predictably related to the stimuli by a specific class of relations.

An illustration follows: An individual responds to a class of stimulus situations (2 + 3, 3 + 4, 7 + 5) with a class of performances (adding 3 + 2, 4 + 3,

5 + 7) that are predictably related to the stimuli by a relation that may be expressed as "independence of order."

The rule that governs this behavior may be represented by the statement "Adding the class of numbers *a* to the class of numbers *b* is independent of the order in which *a* and *b* are combined." We as external observers may *represent* the rule by this verbal statement. In fact, we *must* represent it in some way if we are going to talk about it. However, we do not know how the individual being observed would represent the rule, and at this point we are not concerned with that question. We can observe that a rule is being *applied* when the individual responds regularly to a large class of specific situations.

Consider another illustration: pronouncing English words with long "a" or short "a." Children learn to pronounce printed words like "mate," "dame," "sane," with a long "a" and words like "mat," "ram," and "fan" with a short "a." If their behavior is rule-governed, this may be demonstrated by asking them to pronounce a word new to them, such as "concentrate" or even a novel pseudoword such as "jate" or "raf." When the children respond to these situations correctly, one may say that they are exhibiting a class of performances (pronouncing the medial letter *a*) to a class of stimuli (various *a* and *ae* combinations of printed letters) that are related to each other by a class of relations (long when *e* follows, short when *e* does not follow the intervening consonant).

Typically, a rule is composed of several concepts. In the example just given, there is the concept "long 'a,'" the concept "*e* at end of syllable," and the relational concept "follows." An individual who possesses the rule as a capability can be observed to identify these component concepts and also to demonstrate that they relate to one another in the particular manner of the rule. In accordance with the theoretical position taken here, the individual must have learned these component concepts as prerequisites to learning the rule. Assuming that these concepts have been acquired, learning a rule becomes a matter of learning their correct *sequence*—it is the *e* that follows the *a*, not the other way around.

Rules are obviously of many types insofar as their content is concerned. They may be defined concepts, serving the purpose of distinguishing among different ideas; and they may be capabilities that enable the individual to respond to specific situations by applying classes of relations. In language learning, the individual acquires rules for pronouncing, for spelling, for punctuating, for constructing ordered sentences. In mathematics, all number operations require the learning of rules. In science, the individual learns many rules in the form of defined concepts, such as those for force, mass, density, and energy, and many others that relate these concepts, such as $F = ma$. Evidently, rules may vary in such properties as abstractness and complexity, although the dimensions of these characteristics have not been specified.

Rules and Verbalizations

One of the essential distinctions that must be made is between a rule as *an inferred capability* and the representation of a rule as *a verbal statement* (or a *verbal proposition*). The process of communicating rules, or describing them as learned capabilities, requires that one use words and other symbols to represent the rules. But the term "rule" should not mean the same thing as its representation as a verbal proposition.

When a student is able to state the proposition that represents the rule, one does not usually assume that the rule has, in fact, been learned. For example, a student may be able to state the verbal proposition "A millimeter is four hundredths of an inch," but the statement of this rule is unlikely to be taken as convincing evidence that the student "knows the rule." To determine whether the rule, rather than merely its verbal statement, has been learned, one must find out whether the student can (1) identify the component concepts, namely, *inch* and *four hundredths*, and (2) show the relation between these concepts that constitutes a millimeter. There are various ways of doing this, but all of them appear to reduce to the act of *demonstrating* what a millimeter is. The student might be shown a scale of inches divided into hundredths and asked, "If each of these major divisions is an inch, show me how to determine how many millimeters an inch contains." The expected performance would be for the student to identify the "four hundredths," and by counting, obtain the number twenty-five.

While "knowing the verbal statement" does not necessarily mean "understanding the rule," it is important to recognize that verbal statements usually are crucial in the process of *learning* a new rule. Once a child has learned to use language, the process of learning is vastly facilitated by the use of verbal statements as *cues* to the learning of new defined concepts and rules. Adult learning, in many spheres, is largely carried on by the use of verbal statements read in textbooks or other written materials. A student reading for the first time that "a gene is an element of the germ plasm that transmits hereditary characteristics" is able to learn a great deal from this verbal statement, particularly if its component concepts (*germ plasm, transmits,* and so on) have been previously learned. Thus, the communicative function of such verbal statements and their role in learning need to be affirmed without question, even though the student's recall of them as verbalizations is inadequate evidence that the rule has been learned.

Some learning theorists have suggested that rules are initially learned as verbal information ("declarative knowledge") (see, for example, Neves and Anderson, 1981). If one thinks of the learning of rules of grammar in a foreign language by high school students, or the learning of rules in algebra and geometry, such a view does not seem unreasonable. A student of French may learn the verbal statement, "a masculine noun takes the article 'le'", or some paraphrased equivalent. The student may then use this verbal statement as a guide to generating a correct phrase such as "le chapeau." However, it is important to note that rules are often learned *without* a verbal phase. For example, children learn the rules of their native language (such as agreement of nouns and verbs, formation of plurals, and so on) and use them with evident skill without ever being able to state these rules as propositions. Some children are able to solve arithmetic word problems before being able to state them as arithmetic expressions (Riley, Greeno, and Heller, 1983). In older children and adults, rules of musical performance on an instrument are often acquired and used without being possessed as verbal statements.

Procedures

Rules are sometimes called *procedures,* or as part of the set of human capabilities we have named intellectual skills, *procedural knowledge.* This name is mainly intended to distinguish "knowing how" (procedural knowledge, or intellectual skill) from "knowing that" (verbal information). Some rules are very simple, in the sense that they require only a few procedural steps. For instance, a mathematical rule of addition contains the following steps:

(1) $a = b$ (a subordinate rule, given)
(2) $c = d$ (a subordinate rule, given)
(3) $a + c = b + d$ (the addition rule)

Step 1 requires the learner to keep in mind a simple rule that is given (an "if" rule); step 2 requires the same for a second simple rule. The third step is the "then" part of the rule, concerning the addition of the other two subordinate rules. The whole rule, then, consists of three steps. While such a rule is a procedure, it is short in length.

Other rules involve lengthy procedures, sometimes with conditional steps. Even the procedure of multiplying with numerals on paper requires the following steps, as in the example "multiply 253 by 27":

Step 1:   Write down multiplicand and multiplier
          in vertically aligned columns: 253
                                            27

Step 2:   Multiply the number in the ones place of the multiplicand by the number in the ones place of the multiplier (7 times 3).

Step 3:   If a single-place result, record below the right-hand column; if a two-digit result, record the ones portion in the right-hand column, "carry" the value of the tens place (1, carry 2).

Step 4:   Multiply the number in the tens place of the multiplicand by the number in the ones place of the multiplier, and add the carried value from step 3 (35, plus 2).

Step 5:　If a single-place result, record below the tens column; if a two-digit result, record the tens portion in the tens column, carry the value of the hundreds place (7, carry 3).

Step 6:　Multiply the number in the hundreds place of the multiplicand by the number in the ones place of the multiplier, and add the carried value from step 5 (14, plus 3).

Step 7:　Record the result in the appropriate column or columns.

$$
\begin{array}{r}
253 \\
27 \\
\hline
1771
\end{array}
$$

Step 8:　Multiply the number in the ones place of the multiplicand by the number in the tens place of the multiplier.

And so on.

Using a hand calculator to perform multiplication of this sort reduces the number of steps in the procedure from twenty steps to eight. Even eight steps, however, does not turn out to be the shortest of procedures. It is not at all inappropriate, therefore, to conceive of intellectual skills as making up a collection of *procedural knowledge*. Such knowledge is composed of rules, and many of these rules are procedures involving few or many steps.

Work procedures.　Real-world jobs are often largely composed of procedures. Office procedures, for example, may consist of lengthy sequences of checking, verifying, recording, compiling, filing, and other operations on printed paper forms. Airplane and helicopter pilots are accustomed to carrying out fairly lengthy procedures prior to and during flight. Relatively short procedures for troubleshooting household appliances are usually included in the packages for the use of those who purchase them. These may be contrasted with procedures of great length described in user's manuals for industrial and military equipment. It is not surprising that the job descriptions of people who are responsible for maintaining and repairing complex equipment are full of procedures.

In their fundamental nature, procedures are rules. They are composed of steps that *relate concepts to other concepts* in a number of different ways. (In how many ways can one thing be related to another?) The steps typically involve (1) identifying the concepts; and (2) carrying out, or showing, the relations among them. The steps of procedures may be few, in which case they can readily be retrieved and kept in mind (maintained in working memory). When procedures contain many steps, cues to their sequence may need to be stored as a verbal chain in long-term memory; alternatively, an external memory aid such as a checklist may be used. Neither the remembered nor the external verbal statement, of course, is the procedure itself (the rule stored as an intellectual skill capability of the learner).

RULE LEARNING

It will be most useful to begin our description of rule learning with examples of some very simple rules that might be learned by a child, and later show how such rules can grow in complexity.

Examples of Rule Learning

A young child may be told "Round things roll." Such a statement represents two different concepts: (1) *round things* and (2) *roll*. Under what circumstances might it be expected that learning has occurred from such a statement? What are the conditions under which one can be reasonably certain that the child has learned the rule that round things roll?

It seems fairly evident that if learning the rule is expected, the child must already know the concepts *round things* and *roll*. If the concept *round* has not already been acquired, the child may end up learning a more restricted rule, such as *Balls roll*, and therefore be unable to show that a half-dollar or a saucer will roll. Accordingly, if the rule is to be acquired in its fullest sense, the learner must know the concept *round* in its full sense, as it applies to a variety of objects, including discs and cylinders a well as spheres such as balls.

Similarly, the concept of the event *roll* should have been previously acquired. Naturally, rolling must be distinguished from such events as *sliding* and *tumbling*. The concept of *rolling* may be considerably more difficult to learn than *round*, since the stimulus events of rotating about an axis may not be easy to discriminate from other events involving the motion of bodies. But again, the child must have acquired the concept *roll* to adequately face the task of learning the full rule and not just a partial one.

With these prerequisites, the remainder of the learning situation is provided by a representative set of stimulus objects and by a set of verbal instructions to which the learner responds. The stimulus objects might include an inclined plane and a set of unfamiliar blocks, some of which are round and some not. The instructions might go like this: "I want you to answer the question, What kinds of things roll? . . . You remember what 'roll' means (*demonstrate with one round object*). . . . Some of these objects are round. Can you point them out? . . . (*Learner responds*). . . . Do all *round* things roll? (*Learner answers 'Yes'*). . . . Show me. . . . (*Learner responds by rolling two or three round objects*). . . . Good! . . . What kinds of things roll? (*Learner responds, 'Round things roll'*). . . . Right!" With the completion of this exercise, it is reasonable to conclude that the rule has been learned. However, to test this, a new and different set of blocks may be presented to the student, who is asked to answer the question, Which of these will roll?

To many adults, this instruction may seem elaborate and detailed, but it surely will not have this appearance to a kindergarten teacher. Why does one not simply say to the children, "Rounds things roll; remember that"? There are two major reasons. First, the children may not recall the concepts *round* and *roll* at the time they are presented in the sentence. Special pains must be taken to be sure that these concepts are highly accessible at the moment the rule is stated. The second reason is to insure that the children do not simply learn the words "Round things roll" as a verbal chain. This, of course, is very easy for them to do, since the statement is a short chain and they already know the links. But the purpose of the instruction in this case is not the learning of a verbal sequence; rather, it is the learning of a *rule*. Consequently, the children must be asked to exhibit terminal responses possible only if they can, in fact, put together the concepts *round* and *roll*. Knowing the rule means being able to demonstrate that round things roll, not simply to say the words.

Adults often have to learn principles that are structurally more complex than this. A student of biology, for example, may encounter the rule (which might be equally well termed a defined concept) "Metamorphosis occurs when the larva of an insect turns into a pupa." It seems quite evident that in this case, too, in order to learn the principle, the adult must not only have learned the relatively well-known concepts *insect* and *turn into* but also the less familiar concepts *larva* and *pupa*. One may suppose that the adult who has the intention to do so can learn the new rule entirely from the verbal statement. To do this properly, the learner might think of an actual example or two of insect larvae turning into pupae, that is, exhibiting metamorphosis. It may be noted, though, that this new rule is more likely to be learned adequately if the adult has seen metamorphosis in the laboratory or museum, on a field trip, or in a picture. For one cannot be sure that an adult who is confronted with the verbal proposition, "Metamorphosis occurs when the larva of an insect turns into a pupa" will, in fact, learn it as a rule, although this may be the assignment. Just as the child can learn this statement as a verbal proposition, so too can the adult.

For adults, then, the external conditions of learning rules are often reduced to verbal statements in textbooks or lectures. Provided that the component concepts have been previously learned, verbal instruction *can* be sufficient, although it may not be. The test, of course, is to provide an instance that requires students to *demonstrate*. The test must probe for the rule, not simply for the sequence. A test that says "Metamorphosis occurs when the _____ of an insect turns into a _____" (or something equivalent) is commonly employed. Notice, though, that such a test makes the assumption that learners are able to identify the concepts involved. In contrast, a test that presents pictures of an insect in various stages of development, including the larva and pupa, and requires students to "show what is meant by metamorphosis" (or something equivalent) will be able to determine whether the rule has been learned.

As these examples indicate, rules having the simplest formal structure are composed of two concepts. Often these can be thought of as having the form, "If A, then B" (Gagné, 1964). Although the two-concept rule may be simplest, it is probably not as typical or frequent as the three-concept rule, which is the form of many defined concepts as well. An example is the rule, "A pint doubled is a quart." This statement verbally represents the three concepts *pint, quart,* and *doubled.* It is interesting to note another typical characteristic, namely, that two of these are thing-concepts while one is a relational concept.

Rules can become much longer than those illustrated so far. The simple rule "birds fly" can be expanded to "birds fly south in the winter," which contains four concepts rather than two. Classifying rules (defined concepts) can sometimes become quite lengthy, as in the following examples: (1) "Forgetting is a decrease in performance from the level exhibited immediately following the learning which has produced that performance, occurring after a time interval during which no practice has occurred." (2) "Mass is that property of an object which determines how much acceleration will be imparted to the object by the action of a given force." Usually such rules are stated verbally at the end of a sequence of instruction rather than at the beginning. To learn them typically requires breaking them up into simpler parts, which are finally put together as a total rule.

Conditions of Rule Learning

The conditions of rule learning that derive from these examples may now be drawn together.

Conditions within the learner.   The prerequisite for acquiring the chains of concepts that constitute rules is knowledge of the concepts. *A pint doubled is a quart* is easily learned as a rule when the learner has already learned *all three* concepts involved. There is, of course, a "partial" learning of a rule that may result when the individual knows only some of the component concepts. Should a learner know all the concepts except *doubled,* some kind of rule could still be learned, but it would be an inadequate one.

As previously emphasized, knowledge of the concepts means being able to identify any members of the class. It is only when such prerequisite concepts have been mastered that a rule can be learned with full adequacy. Otherwise, there is the danger that the conceptual chain or some of its parts will be learned merely as items of verbal information, without the full meaning that inheres in a well-established rule. Unfortunately, inadequate rules *can* be learned. It is a challenge for instruction to avoid these, and it is a challenge for measurement techniques to distinguish them from adequate ones.

Conditions in the learning situation. The major external conditions of rule learning are embodied in *verbal instructions.* The sample instructions used with "Round things roll" will be useful to recall here.

1. The conditions of rule learning often begin with a statement of the general nature of the *performance expected when learning is complete.* In the example, the instructor says, "I want you to answer the question, What kinds of things roll?" Why was this said? Was the instructor simply stating the rule, giving it away, so to speak? The main reason for making such a statement, which learners "hold in mind" during learning, appears to be this: it provides learners with a means for obtaining immediate reinforcement when they have reached the end of learning. Having this statement for a model, they will be able to know when they have *finished learning* and, in many cases, when they have acquired the correct rule. Since rules may be long chains, learners may need a conveniently retained reference to tell when the end is reached. The instructor, though, cannot be said to be "telling the rule." The teacher is not stating the rule itself, but only the kind of performance that will demonstrate the attainment of the rule.

2. Verbal instructions continue by *invoking recall of the component concepts.* The instructor says, "You remember what 'roll' means. . . . You remember what 'round' means." In many cases, the recall of these concepts is stimulated entirely by verbal means. In others (as in the example previously given), the class of stimuli that represent the concept may also be shown; students may be asked to recall the *roll* event by identifying one and the *round* thing by picking out one. Pictures, of course, may be used for this purpose as well.

3. Verbal cues are next given for the rule as a whole. In our simple example, the verbal statement "Round things roll" accomplishes this purpose. However, it should be noted that these verbal cues to the rule need not be an exact statement of the entire rule; they are so in this example only because the rule is such a short one. If the rule were from elementary geometry, for example, "An angle is formed by the intersection of two rays," the verbal cues might be contained in such statements as "Here are two rays. They intersect. We have an angle." Such statements do not correspond exactly to an acceptable verbal definition. Yet they function as well or better in providing verbal cues to stimulate the learning of the rule.

4. Finally, a verbal question asks the students to demonstrate the rule. The instructor says, "Show me." The exact form is not of great importance as long as it truly requires the students to demonstrate the rule in its full sense. Students may also be required to state the rule verbally, as when the instructor asks, "What kinds of things roll?" But such a verbal statement is not essential to the learning of the rule, nor does it prove the

students have learned the rule. Then why is it done? Probably for a very practical reason: the instructor wants the students to be able to talk about the rule later on, and so they are taught the right words to say. This ability is undoubtedly useful, but it is important to note that this kind of information learning is not an essential part of rule learning.

5. The presence of some familiar learning conditions may be recognized in rule learning. *Reinforcement* is provided when the rule is demonstrated in its complete form. The instructor may say "Right!" Even prior to this, the students may receive reinforcement by noting the match between their terminal act and what they have been told is their learning objective. If it means the repeated application of the rule to examples immediately following learning, *repetition* has not been shown to be an important condition for this kind of learning (Gagné and Bassler, 1963). However, when repetition takes the form of *spaced review* (Reynolds and Glaser, 1964), it is likely to have a marked effect in enhancing retention.

Events of instruction. The conditions for learning rules that are in the situation, then, are incorporated into a sequence of instructional events. Perhaps it will be worthwhile here to recapitulate that sequence, since it may be considered to represent the steps for instruction of rules, whether practiced by a teacher, a film, or textbook:

Step 1: Inform the learner about the form of the performance to be expected when learning is completed.

Step 2: Question the learner in a way that requires the reinstatement (recall) of the previously learned concepts that make up the rule.

Step 3: Use verbal statements as cues that will lead the learner to put the (new) rule together with its concepts in their proper order.

Step 4: By means of a question, ask the learner to demonstrate one or more concrete instances of the rule, and provide feedback as to correctness in each case.

Step 5: (Optional, but useful for later instruction.) By a suitable question, require the learner to make a verbal statement of the rule.

Step 6: Provide for "spaced review" a day or more following learning to aid retention of the newly learned rule. Present new instances for recall and demonstration of the rule.

LEARNING HIERARCHIES

Although it is useful to discuss the learning of a single rule, most rules are not learned in isolation, except perhaps by the young child. Instead, the school student or the adult typically learns related sets of rules pertaining to a larger topic. What is learned is an *organized set of intellectual skills*. The individual rules that compose such a set may have demonstrable relations to each other in a logical sense. They are also related to each other in the *psychological* sense that the learning of some are prerequisite to the learning of others, just as concepts are prerequisite to the learning of rules. Here our interest centers on the psychological organization of intellectual skills and not on the logical organization of verbal information that may be involved in their learning.

The psychological organization of intellectual skills may be represented as a *learning hierarchy*, often composed largely of rules. As previously shown, two or more concepts may be prerequisite to (and in this sense subordinate to) the learning of a single rule. Similarly, two or more rules may be prerequisite to the learning of a superordinate rule. Once the latter is learned, it may combine with another rule, and so on. The entire set of rules, organized in this way, forms a learning hierarchy that describes an *on-the-average* efficient route to the attainment of an organized set of intellectual skills that represents "understanding" of a topic.

An Example of a Learning Hierarchy

Many subjects taught in schools have an organization that can readily be expressed as a learning hierarchy. The rule, or set of rules, that is the learning objective may be shown to be composed of *prerequisite* rules and concepts. The learning of the intellectual skills that are the "target" of instruction is a matter of *combining* these prerequisite skills, which have been previously learned. (They may have been *just previously* learned or recalled from learning that took place a while ago.)

An example of such a learning hierarchy, applicable to a topic in physics, is shown in Figure 6.1 The intellectual skill of demonstrating the calculation of horizontal and vertical components of forces using vector diagrams, is seen to depend on the prerequisite learning of several subordinate rules. In order to acquire the target skill the student must previously have learned to (1) use rules to verify the conditions for equilibrium, (2) represent the magnitude and directions of forces as parts of triangles, and (3) employ trigonometric rules to represent the relationships in a right triangle (sine, cosine, tangent, and so on). If these three sets of subordinate rules have been learned and can be made accessible in the learner's working memory, the learning of the target skill (shown at the top of the hierarchy) can proceed without a hitch. If these subordinate rules are not known, however, the learning of the target skill is not possible. Of course, this "strong" statement is not intended to exclude the possibility that the three subordinate rules and the target skill may be learned "all at once" or on a single occasion by the learner. The important point is that the component skills (rules) are indeed prerequisites, and must be available to the learner when the target skill is "put together."

VECTOR RESOLUTION OF FORCES

Figure 6.1 A learning hierarchy showing the analysis of a rule to be learned (top box) into prerequisite components, which are subordinate rules and concepts.

Each of the subordinate rules may be analyzed to reveal other subordinate rules or concepts that are prerequisites to its learning. For example, as Figure 6.1 shows, the skill of representing magnitudes and directions of forces as parts of triangles requires that the learner know the prerequisite concepts that identify the parts (angles, sides) of triangles, and that the learner also know how to identify the magnitudes and directions of forces (as these may be represented verbally or pictorially). Still other "lower-order" skills, such as the identification of right triangles and the distinguishing of vertical and horizontal directions, are not shown in Figure 6.1, but could surely be identified as underlying those that are illustrated.

Many other topics learned in school have the character of organized sets of intellectual skills and may be represented as learning hierarchies. The rules of syntax and punctuation in English obviously can be depicted in learning hierarchy form. All sciences, as well as mathematics, are composed of sets of rules that build upon each other. In the social sciences, the total structure is often a looser one, but individual topics—classifying family relationships, comparing and contrasting systems of government, formulating predictions of social trends—can be viewed as examples of intellectual skills having a hierarchical character. A variety of learning hierarchies can be used to represent the learning of a foreign language, beginning with the elementary concepts of word-sounds and proceeding through the complex rules governing the generation of communicative speech. Some additional examples of learning hierarchies are given by Gagné and Briggs (1979), and their uses in instruction have been previously discussed in Chapter 3.

Cumulative Learning

Since learning hierarchies indicate some requirements for *prior learning*, when any new intellectual skill is to be learned, they imply certain conclusions about *readiness* for learning. Developmental readiness for learning any new intellectual skill is conceived as the presence of certain relevant subordinate intellectual skills. The individual who is to engage in problem solving to acquire a new higher-order rule must have first acquired some other simpler rules. These in turn depend for their acquisition on the recall of other learned entities, rules, or perhaps concepts. As we have seen in previous chapters, concepts in their turn depend for their learning on the recall of other prerequisites, the discriminations that are specifically related to them. The learning history of the individual is *cumulative* in character. The discriminations that are learned form a basis on which concepts are built. Concepts contribute positive transfer to the learning of rules, and the latter support the learning of more complex rules and the capabilities of problem solving.

Learning has the specific effect of establishing the capabilities necessary for the performance of any intellectual task. It also has cumulative effects. When a particular rule is learned, for example, the individual establishes a capability that can transfer to the learning not only of a single more complex rule but also to several others. As a specific instance, learning rules regarding the factoring of numbers up to one hundred may be shown to contribute to the learning of the higher-order rules involved in adding fractions. The factoring rules are also prerequisite to other mathematical tasks, such as completing ratios and simplifying equations. When learning of the latter tasks is undertaken, these subordinate rules of number factors do not have to be learned all over again. They are already available in the learner's memory. Learning is cumulative, then, because particular intellectual skills are transferable to a number of higher-order skills and to a variety of problems to be solved. As individuals develop, they continually increase their store of intellectual skills. This means that the possibilities of transfer to the learning of higher-order capabilities multiply as each new intellectual skill is learned. These cumulative effects of learning are the basis for observed increases of intellectual "power" in developing human beings.

An Example of Cumulative Learning

The effects of cumulative learning may be illustrated in a task of liquid conservation, similar to that used by Piaget (Piaget and Inhelder, 1964) and by other investigators interested in studying aspects of his theory. The task to be performed is illustrated in Figure 6.2. When the liquid in a container shaped like A is poured into a container B (top row), many children below age seven are inclined to say that the taller container has more liquid. In another variant of the task, children at this age level tend to say that the volume in the shallower container (second row), exhibiting a larger surface area, is "more." Thus a few children at age seven are "conservers" in this task, while most are "nonconservers." To Piaget, these differences in performance reflect a critical point in intellectual development, marking the difference between a "preoperational" phase of thought and a "concrete operational" phase. The logical operation particularly relevant to such a task is considered to be the *multiplying of relations* (recognizing that an increase in height may be compensated by a decrease in width). Such operations are dependent on others that appear at an earlier stage of development, particularly reversibility (carrying out an inverse operation).

From the standpoint of a cumulative learning theory, performance of this conservation task may be accomplished when the individual has acquired the specific intellectual skills that are relevant to it. The set of intellectual skills required may be derived in the manner described in the previous section to yield a learning hierarchy shown in Figure 6.3.

It may be noted, first of all, that this particular hierarchy has been derived under the assumption that the children to be tested are uninstructed in

Figure 6.2 Two tasks of "conservation of liquid" in rectangular containers. (From R. M. Gagné, Contributions of learning to human development. *Psychological Review*, 1968, 75, Figure 2, p. 183. Copyright 1968 by the American Psychological Association and reproduced by permission.)

Figure 6.3   A learning hierarchy which shows the cumulative learning of intellectual skills leading to the task of judging equalities and inequalities of liquid volume in rectangular containers. (From R. M. Gagné, Contributions of learning to human development. *Psychological Review*, 1968, *75*, Figure 3, p. 184. Copyright 1968 by the American Psychological Association and reproduced by permission.)

mathematical concepts of volume, specifically in the relation volume equals height times width times length. Obviously, one *could* construct a learning hierarchy that proposed that children learn this exact mathematical relation in order to perform the final task. This possibility was not followed in the present instance in order that fewer assumptions about prior learning could be made.

According to Figure 6.3, reading from the top down, the child needs to have learned the rule that volume of liquid in rectangular containers is determined by length, width, and height. Volume will be changed if any of these is altered. Proceeding one step further in the analysis, we find three rules about compensatory changes in two dimensions when the third dimension remains constant. (The fact that Piaget considers compensatory multiplying of relations essential to this task is noteworthy.) If the width of a liquid remains the same in two different containers, the two can have the same volume if a change in height in one is compensated by a change in length in the other.

Figure 6.3 illustrates that a child must have learned three other rules relating to change in only one dimension at a time in order to learn these complex rules. For example, if height is increased while width and length remain constant, volume will increase. The learning of these rules is in turn supported by the prior learning of other rules. One is that volume of a container is produced by accumulating "slices" of the same shape and area. A second is that volume can be projected from area in any direction, up or down, to the front or back, to the right or left. Following these rules, one can identify considerably simpler rules, such as those comparing areas of rectangles by compensatory action of length and width and the idea that length and width determine area. One who chooses to trace the hierarchy still further downward encounters the concepts of rectangle, length, width, and an even simpler one, the concept of length of a line.

In its right-hand branch, the hierarchy describes the intellectual skills dealing with liquids in containers. Included here are rules having to do with changes in shape of liquid in containers and liquid volume as cumulative slices of area. This branch is necessary because at the level of higher-order rules, the child must distinguish the volume of the liquid from that of the container. It is notable that this branch also includes the concept of liquid "identity"—that is, matching a liquid poured from one container to another as "the same liquid." This concept of identity is generally considered to be arrived at very early in the intellectual development of the child.

The cumulative learning theory proposes a conception of "what is learned" (or "what develops") that differs from Piaget's theory. The latter states that performing conservation tasks depends on the development of logical processes such as "reversibility," "seriation," and "compensation." The proposal of the cumulative learning theory, in contrast, is that development results from the learning of relatively specific intellectual skills having to do with liquids, containers, volumes, areas, lengths, and heights. Specifically, it is supposed that the child does not acquire a general ability of "compensatory multiplying of relations" all at once at some particular stage of development. Instead, the specific intellectual skill of "identifying equal volumes given compensatory changes in length and width, height remaining constant," is acquired through learning. In addition, and at approximately the same time, the child may acquire a number of other intellectual skills such as those shown in Figure 6.3. If necessary specific capabilities are learned, perhaps by being taught in some systematic fashion, the child will be able to perform the conservation task.

Do the intellectual capabilities of the child remain this specific? Of course not. That well-known property of learning, *transfer of learning*, occurs. Suppose that a child has learned to judge equalities of liquids in rectangular containers. Suppose, further, that one then undertook to have the child learn to judge volumes of liquids in cylindrical containers. Presumably, such learning could be based upon another learning hierarchy, which would have certain skills in common with that of Figure 6.3, but would also have some new ones dealing with areas of circles and volumes of cylinders. Having learned to judge volumes in *both* kinds of containers, a learner would then have some intellectual skills of great value for *generalizing* to still other problems. One might, for example, have the child try the entirely new problem of judging volumes of liquids in irregularly shaped containers. Since the learner would already know how to equate volumes in rectangular and in cylindrical containers, we would expect that these skills would transfer to the new problem, dealing with shapes that were partly and roughly rectangular and partly and roughly cylindrical. Transfer of previously learned skills to the entirely new problem seems highly predictable.

Once learners have acquired a repertoire of learned specific skills, their performance of conservation-type problems is likely to become progressively easier, because an increasing number of these subordinate skills will exhibit transfer of learning to any new conservation task devised. Thus the specific intellectual skills learners acquire provide the basis for the formation of skills of increasing generalizability, of the sort described in the next chapter as *cognitive strategies*. At some stage in their development, one might then choose to speak of children as "conservers," or to say that they possess the learned capabilities that make possible the solution of novel conservation problems regardless of their specific composition.

The conception of cumulative learning, then, is that any type of intellectual skill, although learned as a relatively specific entity, will generalize through the mechanism of learning transfer to the learning of many other skills and to the solving of many previously unencountered problems. Readiness for new learning is thus a stage of development, to be sure. But the readiness stage of development for any learner depends first upon what relevant prerequisite skills have already been learned, and, second, upon what capabilities have yet to be acquired in order to meet the learner's particular objective. Stated simply, the stage of developmental readiness of any learner is determined by what is already known and by how much is yet to be learned in order to achieve some particular learning goal.

SOME EDUCATIONAL IMPLICATIONS

The learning of *rules* is obviously of vast educational importance, if only because of the fact that rules make up the bulk of what is learned in school. An important component of rules is the kind of learned entities typically referred to as *defined concepts*. While the distinction between rules and defined concepts needs to be maintained, we emphasize that these two entities, considered as human capabilities, are formally alike. In the case of the defined concept, the individual is using a rule in order to *identify* something that embodies a relation; in the case of another kind of rule, the individual may be concerned with demonstrating the relation itself. But in both cases one is dealing with a sequence of subordinate entities that in the simplest instance contain the components concrete concept → relation- → concrete concept. An example is *A latch* (concrete concept) *closes* (relational concept) *a window* (concrete concept). The entire range of the category *rule*, then, includes defined concepts, rules that pertain to language (such as pronouncing *ie* as "ee"), rules that have the character of scientific principles (such as $F = ma$), and even very complex rules (such as those for the division of fractions). As will be seen in the next chapter, the category also encompasses a very important variety of rule applicable to the learner's own behavior, called a *cognitive strategy*.

The performance learners are capable of when they learn a rule is called *rule-governed behavior*. Unlike simpler categories of performance, rule-governed behavior exhibits the learners' capability of responding to entire *classes* of stimuli with *classes* of responses. For example, drivers are able to respond to *any* red signal light by bringing to a stop by *any* means *any* vehicle they are driving. It would be an entirely inadequate description of such behavior to say that these individuals had learned the S → R connection $S_{red} \rightarrow R_{stop}$. They may, of course, also have learned this connection, but their behavior goes far beyond what such a capability would make possible. Their behavior in making classes of response to classes of stimuli is regular and, therefore, is called rule-governed.

Another distinction of great relevance to education, emphasized in this chapter, is that between the *rule* (the inferred capability that makes possible the regular performance) and the *verbal representation* of the rule (often called a *proposition*). The individual may learn a rule without learning the proposition, although the human adult often learns both, because the proposition may be used as a cue to the learning of the rule. The learner may also be able to demonstrate the rule without being able to verbalize the proposition or to recall it as a verbal statement. Many examples of this latter state of affairs may be given. The individual who correctly doubles the consonants in words ending in *ing* probably cannot recall the verbal statement of the rule, although the person may originally have learned it as a verbal proposition. The rule continues to be present as a capability, but the verbal statement is gone from memory.

However, the important role of verbal statements in the learning of new rules must be recognized. Much adult learning is accomplished by reading printed verbal statements in textbooks and other materials. Such verbal statements communicate the rule to be learned and often constitute the first step in its learning, particularly when the component concepts have previously been learned. Reading that "hydrogen is a univalent element" may make possible little learning (except that of a verbal chain) if the student has not previously learned the component concepts *univalent* and *element*. If these have been learned, however, such a statement becomes an effective communication for learning a new rule. When followed by an action that demonstrates the learner's application of the rule to one or more specific situations, the learning of a new rule can be inferred to have taken place.

Much school learning is a matter of learning rules, including rules that define. Typically, the learning of a topic or part of a course of study can be viewed as a *hierarchy* in which the most complex rules (representing "target" objectives) require the learning of simpler rules as prerequisites to efficient attainment. These simpler rules in turn imply the learning of still simpler ones, including defined concepts, which in their turn may rest upon previously learned concrete concepts. While such an analysis can theoretically be carried to the point of revealing underlying discriminations, chains, and even simpler associations, it is not often useful to do so, since students usually are assumed to have already acquired such intellectual skills, perhaps in the earliest grades. Accordingly, learning hierarchies most often represent an ordered set of rules and concepts that the student needs to learn in order to achieve an understanding of the topic to be acquired.

Learning hierarchies imply that learning has a *cumulative* character, in which the acquisition of specific rules establishes the possibility of transfer of learning to a number of more complex, "higher-order" rules. Because of this property of transfer, each newly learned intellectual skill increases the intellectual power of the individual in a manifold sense. The specific rules that are learned make possible the learning of other more complex rules that are increasingly general in their applicability. Human intellectual development may be conceived as resulting from the learning of many specific intellectual skills that enter into the learning of other more complex and more general intellectual skills. Cumulative learning ultimately results in the establishment of capabilities that make it possible for the individual to solve a great variety of novel problems.

GENERAL REFERENCES

Learning Defined Concepts

Johnson, D. M. *A systematic introduction to the psychology of thinking.* New York: Harper & Row, 1972. Chapters 2 and 3.

Klausmeier, J. H. *Learning and teaching concepts.* New York: Academic Press, 1980.

Klausmeier, J. H., Ghatala, E. S., and Frayer, D. A. *Conceptual learning and development: A cognitive view.* New York: Academic Press, 1974.

Tiemann, P. W., and Markle, S. M. *Analyzing instructional content: A guide to instruction and evaluation.* Champaign, Ill.: Stipes, 1978.

Rule Learning

Anderson, J. R. *Cognitive psychology and its implications.* San Francisco: Freeman, 1980.

Bruner, J. S., Goodnow, J. J., and Austin, G. A. *A study of thinking.* New York: Wiley, 1956.

Gagné, R. M., and Briggs, L. J. *Principles of instructional design,* 2nd ed. New York: Holt, Rinehart and Winston, 1979.

Johnson, D. M. *A systematic introduction to the psychology of thinking.* New York: Harper & Row, 1972. Chapters 4 and 7.

Tighe, T. J., and Shepp, B. E. (Eds.), *Perception, cognition and development.* Hillsdale, N.J.: Erlbaum, 1983.

7
Cognitive Strategies

This chapter deals with the kind of cognitive capability that is more general and also more generalizable than intellectual skills. Cognitive strategies are internally organized skills whose function is to regulate and monitor the utilization of concepts and rules.

The varieties of intellectual skills we have described in Chapters 5 and 6 constitute some of the most valuable capabilities that individuals learn. They provide the basic structures for the learning that takes place in school. They are brought to bear on the solving of problems, as we have seen. Yet as learners proceed to learn and store intellectual skills and other capabilities, they are also developing ways to improve their self-regulation of the internal processes associated with learning. In other words, they are learning *how* to learn, *how* to remember, and *how* to carry out the reflective and analytic thought that leads to more learning. It is apparent as individuals continue to learn that they become increasingly capable of *self-instruction* or even of what may be called *independent learning*. This is because learners acquire increasingly effective strategies to regulate their own internal processes. This new function of control over internal cognitive processes is what distinguishes the capabilities to be discussed in this chapter from the intellectual skills described in the last two chapters.

SOME VARIETIES OF COGNITIVE STRATEGIES

As our description of the information-processing view of learning has indicated (Chapter 4), the processes of learning are modified and regulated by some internal processes of *executive control*. These internally directed processes are called *cognitive strategies*. By acquiring and using them, learners are able to regulate such internal processes as (1) attending and selective perceiving; (2) encoding incoming material for long-term storage; (3) retrieval; and (4) problem solving.

Cognitive strategies are often assigned a high priority as learning outcomes by writers on educational topics. For example, Bruner (1971) acknowledges the basic importance of intellectual skills in school learning but distinguishes these skills in solving problems from *problem finding*, which requires the location of "incompleteness, anomaly, trouble, inequity, and contradiction" (p. 111). Presumably, both the identification of novel problems and the translation of known rules into a form that can readily be put to use in solving such problems represent the kinds of human capability that deserve to be classified as cognitive strategies. They are ways that individuals use to focus their knowledge and skills on problem situations that may not previously have been encountered. Cognitive strategies are ways of "using one's head."

Cognitive Strategies in Attending

The use of executive control skills in attending to and selectively perceiving particular parts of printed texts has been explored in experimental studies by Rothkopf (1970), Frase (1970), and others.

The general procedure used in these studies is illustrated by one carried out by Rothkopf and Bisbicos (1967). High school students read a passage from a book by Rachel Carson, *The Sea Around Us*, consisting of thirty-six pages. After each three pages, two questions were interspersed with the text. One group of students saw questions that required a numerical quantity or a proper name as an answer. Another group saw questions inquiring about either a common English word or a technical term. After completion of the passage, the retention of information was tested in each of these categories for all students. Retention of numerical quantities and proper names was enhanced in the students who had answered questions during their reading on numerical quantities and proper names (different questions, of course, but in the same categories). Similar results were obtained for the students who had answered questions on English words or technical terms.

This series of experiments suggests that interspersed questions had the effect of *activating a strategy of attending* to facts of a particular category. These investigations appear to demonstrate that learners are able to exercise control over their own attention in learning from a text by utilizing a cognitive strategy that is available to them and that may previously have been learned. Thus learners are employing an executive control process to direct their own attention and to selectively perceive portions of what they read.

Cognitive Strategies in Encoding

In the learning of word-pairs (COW-BALL, ROCK-BOTTLE) many studies have demonstrated improved learning when the learners are given "elaboration" instructions (for a comprehensive review, see Rohwer, 1975). Often, the elaboration takes the form of sentences the learner is encouraged to construct without any assistance. Examples might be "The COW chases the bouncing BALL," or "The ROCK breaks the BOTTLE." Substantially improved learning has been shown to result in children and in adults from the use of these "explicit prompts," when the amount of learning is compared with that obtained under simple "memorization" instructions.

Another explicit prompt may be employed when learners are instructed to imagine a mental picture formed by the word-pairs or to use a visual image (Bower and Winzenz, 1970; Paivio and Yuille, 1969). In this case, too, studies have revealed enhanced learning in children of various ages and in adults (see Rohwer, 1975). In a number of instances, the prompts that learners devise and use themselves have been shown to be more effective than those deliberately given to them as learning and memory aids. Thus these tasks of word association appear to be readily learned when the learners are encouraged to use particular cognitive strategies, such as sentence-forming strategies or image-forming strategies. Of course, a learner who has practiced using such strategies may be able to easily excel over a naive learner who has not used them and who may not even be aware of them.

Presumably, such cognitive strategies represent *ways of encoding* word-pairs to be learned. Encoding strategies employed in the learning of concrete concepts have also been studied in the laboratory (Bruner, Goodnow, and Austin, 1956). In this group of studies, learners were asked to identify a classifying concept in sets of cards, each containing drawn figures that could be categorized in various ways: on the basis of shape of figure, color of figure, number of figures, and number of borders. The concept sought, for example, might be the class of cards containing *two yellow rectangles*. Learners were required to arrive at the correct concept by viewing the cards one by one and stating (initially guessing) whether each did or did not represent the concept. After each identification, the learners were told whether their guess was "right" or "wrong."

Two main strategies were employed by the learners in acquiring the correct concept. In one, the entire set of features on the card first identified as a positive instance was used as the basis for a hypothesis. For example, if the first "correct" card showed three yellow rectangles, this would be the learners' hypothesis. They would then compare subsequent cards with their memory of this initial one, looking for features in common with it and ignoring others. This strategy was called "focusing." Other learners adopted a strategy called "scanning." Using this method, they would choose one feature of a card (such as color) as belonging to the concept being sought. They would then have to change their hypotheses to select a different feature whenever they encountered a negative instance. At the same time, they would have to remember other features of cards that had been called positive instances in order to form a new hypothesis. This study found that when learners were put under time pressure, the focusing strategy was more frequently successful than the scanning strategy.

Other kinds of strategies were also adopted by a certain number of learners in this investigation. Some of these strategies were "conservative" in the sense that a wrong choice did not require starting all over again with a new hypothesis. Others were "risky" in the sense that they jumped to a hypothesis before the evidence was complete. The study confirms the idea that various strategies are used in discovering concepts and that particular kinds of strategies tend to be favored by particular people. It also makes clear that concept learning under these conditions may be undertaken with more than one kind of cognitive strategy.

Strategies of Retrieval

Strategies that enable people to retrieve names, dates, and unconnected events from their memories have been known for a long time (Yates, 1966) and are often called *mnemonic systems*. Mental images of "places," such as the parts of a familiar room, have been used by orators as cues to the successive points of their speeches. This practice is described by Cicero. Other "systems" require the association of names or events with certain previously learned coding systems, such as the letters of the alphabet, numerals, or the signs of the Zodiac. Rhyming words and novel images are often prominent features providing cues for the retrieval of masses of information (see Paivio, 1971).

Cognitive strategies of this sort appear to be useful for the memorizing and retrieval of special kinds of information, particularly information that is not otherwise related by its meaning or by the meanings it shares with other knowledge. Of course, these strategies make possible the demonstration of amazing feats of memory by professional mnemonists. The average person has little need to remember such disconnected information under most circumstances, unless simply to impress friends. What remains of "mnemonic systems" as techniques of perhaps broader usefulness for retrieval are *visual images* and *rhyming sounds* (which may possibly by viewed as auditory images).

Cognitive strategies of retrieval have been compared in children and young adults by Salatas and Flavell (1976). The learners were required to learn a list containing words belonging to certain categories (for example, toys, clothes, and tools). Upon learning the total list, each learner was asked under three different conditions to recall the words contained in it. In one condition, recall was asked for without mention of the category names (spontaneous use). In another, learners were explicitly asked to use the categories (explicit instructions). And in a third condition, they were asked to recall a word from one category, then a word from another, and so on (flexible use). Young children did not use the categories as retrieval cues spontaneously, although a substantial proportion did use them when asked to do so. Many college students did not use the categories spontaneously, but all did so when explicit instructions were given. Flexible control of the strategies was evident for half the kindergarten children, most third-graders, and all of the college students who participated in the study. The strategy of categorizing thus seems to be available to many learners for retrieval of word lists, and perhaps might be learned as a strategy even by very young children.

It is of some importance to discover what cognitive strategies are available to young children and how these strategies develop with increasing age (presumably by means of learning). Several retrieval strategies have been studied in elementary school children, including rehearsal (Belmont and Butterfield, 1971) and deliberate restudy of missed items (Masur, McIntyre, and Flavell, 1973).

One more example of remembering strategies in children will be briefly described. A memory task requiring a delayed response to objects (toys) placed under inverted cups was employed to study such strategies in three-year-old children (Wellman, Ritter, and Flavell, 1975). Each child was told a story involving one of the toys, which was then placed under one of four cups arranged in a semicircle on a table. Some children were told to "remember" where the toy was, some simply to "wait." After a delay of forty seconds each child was asked to locate the toy in question. Most children were able to do so with little hesitation. Interest in the study centered on the question of what kinds of strategies the children used for deliberate remembering during the delay period. These were inferred from the children's behavior in deliberately looking at and deliberately touching the "correct" cup. Children who were told to "remember" engaged in these activities more often and for longer durations than did children told to "wait." Evidently many of these young children possess the strategies of visual rehearsal and of tagging (by touching) the cup to be remembered. When faced with the task of remembering, they are capable of using the retrieval strategies available to them. The various ways that have been investigated for bringing about improvements in remembering have been given the name of *metamemory*, as a subcategory of the more general concept *metacognition* (Flavell, 1976). The latter term refers to learners' knowledge concerning their own cognitive processes and products. Metacognitive processes include cognitive strategies that monitor and regulate the various processes involved in learning, remembering, and thinking. Confining attention for the moment to metamemory, this is said by Brown (1978) to include strategies that (1) predict the memory system's capacity limitations; (2) make use of various routines for remembering; (3) identify and characterize the particular memory task at hand; (4) monitor the effectiveness of the routines employed; and (5) evaluate the success of memory routines so that they can be appropriately terminated. It would appear, then, that the set of cognitive strategies that make up metamemory are neither few nor simple. Yet specific strategies that aid remembering can be learned by children and adults.

Cognitive Strategies in Problem Solving

When students practice solving novel problems, they presumably learn not only rules applicable to those problems but also general ways of accomplishing problem solving. That is to say, they learn ways of exercising control over their own thought processes: how to seek relevant features of the problem, how to keep in mind what has been tried previously, how to weigh the probabilities of their hypotheses, and so on. These capabilities of self-control are the cognitive strategies of thinking.

Research investigators who study the learning of cognitive strategies applicable to human problem solving are faced with two major difficulties. The first is identifying exactly what these strategies are. Although it is easy enough to understand what they do in exerting control over internal thought processes, it is not at all clear at the present time that these strategies can be named appropriately or that the investigator can control the problem situation sufficiently to know which strategies are being engaged by the learner. Are there a great many cognitive strategies of problem solving or only a few? What specific processes of thought do these strategies control or influence? The problem of identifying cognitive strategies differs markedly from that of identifying the intellectual skills described in previous chapters; the concepts and rules applicable to solving problems in specific areas like language and mathematics are quite definite and readily identifiable.

The second difficulty experienced in the investigation of cognitive strategies is demonstrating their generalizability or transfer. If a cognitive strategy has been learned in the course of problem solving (rather than only a higher-order rule), one must expect transfer of learning to a variety of other problem-solving situations to be exhibited. It is not sufficient to demonstrate that learning has brought about improvement in solving problems of the same type. For example, if students have learned and practiced a cognitive strategy tentatively identified as "holding several hypotheses in mind at once" in problems dealing with geometric proofs, it is not sufficient to show that the learners can use this strategy with some new geometric proofs. If a cognitive strategy has been learned or improved by practice, it must then be shown to be capable of transfer to an entirely different domain of problems, such as solving anagrams or finding the roots of simultaneous equations. It is often not an easy matter to arrange conditions so that this transfer can be demonstrated.

Problem solving in plane geometry.   In a study of problem solving in plane geometry, Greeno (1978b) identified a set of cognitive strategies that could be installed in a computer program called Perdix and that were also used by students from a geometry course. As is typical of problems in this area, the task was one of constructing a proof of the size of an angle contained in a geometric diagram. One of the problems used by Greeno is shown in Figure 7.1. In this figure, angle p is known to be 40 degrees. The problem set for the students was: What is the angular value of angle q?

In attempting to solve this problem, the students had at their command certain geometrical axioms (rules). Examples are (1) the rule that vertical angles are equal and (2) the rule that an angle supplementary to a given angle forms a straight angle (180 degrees). The students needed to make use of these rules in gaining confirming evidence that various angles in the figure were congruent, and therefore equal, while others were supplementary. But when and in what order do these rules need to be applied, in order to arrive at a value for angle q? The selection and ordering of these rules requires the use of *cognitive strategies*.

The strategies employed in Greeno's computer program, and whose use was also verified by observing students' performances, are shown in Table 7.1, reprinted from Greeno's article. Strategy 1, while obviously useful, fails here because no quantitative relation between angles p and q can be directly inferred. Next, a problem solver might try to employ strategy 2. This, too, is found to be inadequate; although geometric relations among angles are found, they do not "reach" as far as angle q. Strategy 3, by analyzing the features of angles, makes use of rules about vertical and supplementary angles, but does not manage to find a relation between angles p and q. By using strategy 4, which seeks a relation between angle p and some angle spatially between it and angle q, and forming a chain of quantitative relations, the logical link between angles p and q is established and the problem solved.

Given a ∥ b, and m ∥ n,
measure of < p = 40°.
Find the measure of < q.

Figure 7.1 A problem used in Greeno's study of problem solving in geometry. (From Greeno, J. G., A study of problem solving. In R. Glaser (Ed.), *Advances in instructional psychology*, Vol. 1. Hillsdale, N.J.: Erlbaum, 1978. Copyright 1978 by Lawrence Erlbaum Associates. Reproduced by permission of the publisher and author.)

**TABLE 7.1   Cognitive Strategies Which May Be Employed in Greeno's
Geometry Problem**

1. If the current goal is to find the measure of an angle, this can be achieved if you know the measure of another angle that is related to the unknown angle by some quantitative relation. If that is not true, set the goal of inferring a quantitative relation between the unknown angle and some angle whose measure is known.
2. If the current goal is to infer a quantitative relation between two angles, this is possible if a geometric relation is known between the two angles, or if the two angles are both related to a third angle by quantitative relations. If that is not true, set the goal of inferring a geometric relation between the angles.
3. If the current goal is to infer a geometric relation between two angles, set the goal of analyzing the features of the angles, using the procedure for pattern recognition.
4. If the current goal is to infer a quantitative relation between two angles, and it has already been determined that there is no geometric relation between the unknown angle and any angle with known measure, then set the goal of finding an angle that is spatially between the two angles and that is congruent to one of the angles. When that is accomplished, try to relate that angle to the other angle in the original goal, forming a chain of quantitative relations.

Source: From Greeno, J. G. A study of problem solving. In R. Glaser (Ed.), *Advances in instructional psychology,* Vol. 1. Hillsdale, N.J.: Erlbaum, 1978. Copyright 1978 by Lawrence Erlbaum Associates. Reproduced by permission of the publisher and author.

Three points derived from the study of strategies in this problem in plane geometry are worth mentioning:

1. In addition to the axiomatic rules brought to bear on the problem, not one but several different strategies were employed.
2. The cognitive strategies that could readily be identified were relatively specific rather than general. They dealt with lines and angles; accordingly, they deserve to be called *task strategies*.
3. Successful solutions were attained by students who were able to select and use these task strategies in an appropriate order just when each was most needed. Does this imply that a kind of *executive strategy* was also employed?

Some general strategies.   In a review of research on the involvement of cognitive strategies in problem solving, White and Wittrock (1982) found evidence of the presence of several kinds of strategies that are general in nature and presumably applicable to many kinds of problems. First and most important, they say, is the strategy of *searching for deep meaning*. In a variety of problem situations, the superficial meaning of the problem tends to be misleading or at least unproductive in leading to a successful solution. Learners who use principles to solve problems are better off than those who deal only with facts. A second general strategy that shows itself in problem-solving studies is *tolerance for part-goals*. Rather than attempting to take a single large step, the successful problem solver uses a step-by-step, "hill-climbing" approach (Wickelgren, 1974), chaining together sub-goals of the problem.

Flexibility of approach appears to be another valuable strategy in problem solving. Successful problem solvers refrain from getting "stuck" in one mode of thought. For example, problem solvers in mathematics may switch the problem statement from words to diagrams or to an analogy. The fourth strategy to be identified is a strategy of *synthesis of parts*. The problem solver must be able to "put things together."

Differences in Experts and Novices

A number of recent studies of problem solving have sought to identify the possible differences in cognitive strategies employed by "experts" in contrast with those of "novices," or "nonexperts." Physics problems have been used in several investigations. Selecting kinematics problems from a textbook employing algebra but no calculus, Simon and Simon (1978) looked for differences in two students, one expert at these problems, the other new to the subject but having fair skill in algebra. The problems dealt with motion in a straight line, such as:

A bullet leaves the muzzle of a gun at a speed of 400 meters per second. The length of the gun barrel is half a meter. Assuming that the bullet is uniformly accelerated, what is its average speed within the barrel?

What differences could be observed in these two students who differed so markedly in experience? The investigators asked the students to "think aloud" and recorded what they said as steps in their thinking.

When these records were examined, several things could be noted about the problem solving engaged in by the two students. First, the "expert" needed only fourteen "steps" to arrive at a solution of the problem, whereas the nonexpert took twenty-nine steps to arrive at an incorrect answer, deciding that "something was wrong" with the problem. Despite this most striking difference, there were many similarities in the recorded comments of the students: observing that a mistake had been made, pausing to confirm the current state, stating plans, questioning moves, and the like. Such strategies as these were apparently held in common by the expert and the novice.

Another strategy, however, was suggested by the differences in performance of the two students. It appeared that the more experienced student moved from the problem statement to a representation (such as a drawing or image) of the physical situation and from that representation to a set of mathematical equations. In contrast, the inexperienced student tended to move directly from the problem statement to the equations. In doing so, she tended to take a longer time and to have greater difficulty in choosing the correct equations. In this evidence, then, is the suggestion that an expert may be using a strategy that the nonexpert has not acquired. Studies of other tasks of problem solving (Larkin, et al., 1980) provide confirming evidence that the strategy of representing the physical and spatial features of a problem is a commonly employed technique used by experts. Progress can then be made with confidence to a step (mathematical, in the case of physics problems) that can lead to solution by using familiar rules.

Cognitive Strategies of Thinking

Suggestions concerning the identity and nature of cognitive strategies of thinking have come from a variety of sources. They occur in studies designed specifically to study the process of thinking, such as those by Bruner, Goodnow, and Austin (1956); in theories of problem solving like those of Newell and Simon (1972) and Wickelgren (1974); in the theory of cognitive development of Piaget (Piaget and Inhelder, 1964); in the studies of human abilities previously mentioned (Guilford, 1967; C. W. Taylor, 1958); and in many other writings that attempt to analyze human thinking.

The development of thinking skills and cognitive strategies has been studied by Crutchfield, Covington, and their associates with the use of a systematic instructional program called *The Productive Thinking Program* (Covington, Crutchfield, Davies, and Olton, 1973; Olton and Crutchfield, 1969; Olton, Wardrop, Covington, Goodwin, Crutchfield, Klausmeier, and Ronda, 1967). This program consists of sixteen cartoon booklets containing lessons centered on "mystery" problems, presented in story form, that students attempt to solve. As students work individually on a lesson, each is called upon to generate ideas, to look for and evaluate the meaning of discrepancies, to ask questions, and to practice other strategies of thought. The strategies identified and practiced in these series include the following: (1) generating new and unusual ideas (divergent thinking), (2) avoiding premature judgments, (3) breaking mental sets to look at a problem differently, (4) clarifying the essentials of a problem, and (5) attending to relevant facts and conditions of the problem. In addition, these investigators consider that evidence obtained in the use of this program implies the existence of a "master thinking skill" that governs the management of other skills and strategies. Such a "master" strategy, for example, would be used by the learner to determine, at a particular point in problem solving, whether the best course would be to develop new hypotheses or, in contrast, to examine critically those already developed.

In connection with his analysis of a variety of verbal, mathematical, and other problems, Wickelgren's theory (1974) of problem solving includes procedures that fall into the category of general strategies of problem solving. This sophisticated analysis emphasizes first the strategy of drawing inferences, by which is meant making transformations of the goal of the problem or of the "givens." Additional strategies are (1) classifying action sequences as opposed to randomly choosing them; (2) defining an "evaluation function" over all states involved in problem solution and choosing actions at any given state with an evaluation closer to the goal (called "hill climbing"); (3) breaking up a problem into parts, thus making it possible to solve a set of simpler problems; (4) identifying contradictions that prove that the goal cannot be obtained from the given; and (5) working backward from the goals to new statements that imply the goal statement. The applicability of these strategies to chess problems, to algebraic and geometric problems, and to such "brain twisters" as Nim and the Tower of Hanoi are explicated in detail by Wickelgren. It is evident that the learning of such strategies and their practice in connection with such problems (often characterized as "puzzles") would provide the learner with powerful tools for their successful solutions. Presumably, these strategies would also have more general applicability to the solution of problems occurring in everyday life, even though the latter usually have structures that are formally simpler.

Transferring Cognitive Strategies

Perhaps the most important question about cognitive strategies is not whether they can be learned as specific ways of approaching problems, but whether as human capabilities they can be shown to generalize to new problem-solving situations. Can the learner, by practice in solving problems or in particular strategies of thinking, become a better problem solver? Can the efficiency and quality of the learner's thought be improved by instruction systematically designed to bring about such a goal? Can strategies be learned that will make someone a better thinker about every kind of problem—personal problems, social problems, environmental problems, political problems, as well as mathematical and logic-verbal problems?

No one disagrees with the educational goal of making people better thinkers. If there is disagreement, it concerns the feasibility of this goal. At one end of this spectrum are those who tend to believe that basic capacities for original thinking are inborn, although they must be influenced by environmental events that provide the motivation and the occasion for productive thought. At the other extreme are those who think that it should be easy to teach students how to think and, over a period of time, to turn them into excellent problem solvers. Those who hold the latter view tend to look at school learning as being simply perverse. Why is education not *concentrated* on teaching students to think as a matter of highest priority? Such a view can be simplistic, however. Students must have a firmament of basic skills and of knowledge that makes up the content of their thinking: one cannot think in a vacuum. Once this premise is admitted, it becomes apparent that much time and effort of school instruction must be expended in giving students the foundations on which their thinking can be based. Thus the time spent on teaching knowledge and intellectual skills does not necessarily imply that problem-solving strategies are being neglected.

Children's learning and transfer.   An experimental study by Wittrock (1967) exemplifies the conditions necessary to demonstrate that learned cognitive strategies are *generalizable*, that is, capable of transfer to new and unfamiliar tasks. Second-grade children were individually set the task of matching pictures shown in slides on the basis of common concepts. Matching was sometimes to be based upon color concepts (blue, green, yellow, and red); sometimes on shape concepts (cat, circle, diamond, and house); sometimes on size (large or small); and in other instances on number (one, two, three, or four). The children learned to match cards containing these concepts with those shown in slides by hanging the cards on four hooks in front of them. Two different strategies were taught to two groups of children. In the "nonreplacement strategy," the children removed cards that were incorrect matches from the hooks and turned them face down (this effectively eliminated them as incorrect matches on subsequent trials). In the "replacement strategy," children were not instructed to turn the incorrect cards face down, and many used these cards again for matching.

The results of this study showed clearly that the nonreplacement strategy led to superior performance not only on the concepts used in learning but also on the matching of entirely new concepts. These latter tasks of new learning were presented to the same children without any "strategy" instructions. Thus evidence was clearly obtained that strategies of concept learning acquired in one situation could be transferred and used to advantage in another situation involving entirely new concept learning.

Another example of the transfer of cognitive strategies is provided by *The Productive Thinking Program* discussed earlier in this chapter. The learning of various strategies and their transfer to successively presented new mystery problems was shown by tests of performance that included (1) number of ideas, (2) quality of ideas, (3) number of puzzling facts noted, (4) number of inventions suggested, and (5) number of available elements used in solution. Performance scores indicated significant gains in these aspects of productive thinking, and these gains transferred from one problem situation to another.

ACQUIRING COGNITIVE STRATEGIES

The skills of executive control called cognitive strategies are often readily acquired, and their use by learners typically becomes more dependable with increased practice. Effective strategies, when employed to select, initiate, and modulate processes of learning and thinking, can bring about striking changes in human intellectual performances. In considering the learning of cognitive strategies, we must attend not only to their initial acquisition, but also to questions of their persistence and transfer.

Learning Conditions for Cognitive Strategies

The many examples we have mentioned provide a basis for the identification of conditions applicable to the learning of cognitive strategies. Bear in mind as we proceed to describe learning conditions that cognitive strategies are routines that may influence any of the phases of learning, remembering, and thinking.

Conditions within the learner.   It is not difficult to perceive that a single set of conditions within the learner may affect the learning of cognitive strategies. Such strategies may, after all, be extremely simple, as is true of the strategy for remembering "say it over to yourself several times." For strategies of that degree of simplicity, all that appears to be required as internal conditions is understanding of such concepts as "say it to yourself" and "several times" and the capability of responding appropriately to verbal directions of this sort. Many strategies of attending, encoding, and retrieval appear to have the character of simplicity as well as internal requirements that are not highly demanding.

Other cognitive strategies are quite complex. The task strategies described by Greeno (1978b), for example, and given in Table 7.1, identify relatively complex procedures. In such cases, the internal conditions include the presence of certain task-relevant concepts such as the "measure of an angle," "quantitative relation," "geometric relation," and the like. While the instructive sentences could use different and simpler language, the relevant concepts must be present, in any case.

Even when highly general cognitive strategies are to be learned, the internal requirements still appear quite simple. For example, "begin at the end and work backward," "split the problem up into parts," "be prepared to switch your approach," and similar strategies seem quite easy to understand and describe. It would appear, therefore, that the internal requirements for acquiring cognitive strategies are limited to the concepts that make up simple rules and to the ability to comprehend the verbal statements of these rules.

Conditions in the learning situation.   It may be supposed that many cognitive strategies of the task-oriented variety are discovered by learners. Students may discover how to "say things over to themselves" (as in *rehearsal*) without being told to do so. Other strategies of remembering (such as clustering items belonging to a larger class or using visual images) may in many instances be discovered by learners. Likewise, strategies of encoding (such as embedding words in sentences) may be tried and used by learners without specific instruction. And discovery may be responsible, in some instances, for the acquisition of various strategies of problem solving by learners. "Breaking the problem into parts" is surely not a remote idea to a learner who is struggling to solve a problem. If the strategy leads to successful solution, its further use in other problem situations is made more probable.

Most cognitive strategies can readily be established or activated by verbal instructions. Again we emphasize that such strategies usually take the form of simple rules, like "attend to each topic sentence," or "group the ideas into categories," or "break the problem into its natural parts." Of course, such instructions do not in themselves ensure that any particular learner will use the strategy described. Assuming, though, that learners have the desire to attend, to learn, to remember, or to solve a problem, communicating a strategy by verbal means appears to be an appropriate procedure.

SOME EDUCATIONAL IMPLICATIONS

Cognitive strategies are a kind of human capability that affect many internal processes of critical importance to the learner. The question of *how* intellectual skills, verbal information, and other learned capabilities are attended to, encoded, remembered, and used in productive thinking is a question of which cognitive strategies can be brought to bear upon these processes.

There is increasing evidence that the kinds of cognitive strategies applicable to thinking and problem solving can be learned, and that when learned they exhibit transfer to new problem situations of the same general sort (Greeno, 1978; Hayes, 1976).

Studies of cognitive strategies to date have not demonstrated that these capabilities establish the basis for thinking or for the large generalizing effects they are expected to exhibit. While it is easy to demonstrate that some people employ better strategies in solving problems than do others, it has not been easy to show that deliberate attempts to teach cognitive strategies result in consistent and substantial learning and transfer of learning. Regardless of the nearly universal agreement on the educational goal of "teaching students to think," the evidence that this goal can be successfully accomplished by deliberate teaching of cognitive strategies is quite meager.

We have seen that there are many hypotheses concerning what useful strategies of thinking may be, and that these hypotheses come from different lines of investigation—from studies of intellectual development, individual differences, productive thinking, and problem solving. Surely the firmest evidence tends to show the relevance of relatively specific *task strat-*

egies. Perhaps the most useful course of action would be to try the deliberate teaching of these strategies, one by one, in order to find each strategy that can be learned and that shows evidences of transfer of learning—which would be a convincing test of the acquisition of the strategy as a learned internal state.

In contrast with task strategies, effective cognitive strategies that are truly general may take a long time to learn. The kind of puzzle-solving techniques described by Wickelgren (1974), for example, appear to be learnable in a relatively short time, but they also seem to be specific to particular puzzle forms. In the initial study of productive thinking by Crutchfield and Covington (1965), children seemed to acquire new strategies after only a small amount of instruction. Yet the fifth-graders in Wisconsin learned the same or similar strategies only gradually and incompletely during sixteen hours of instruction. Many adults have been convinced by their own experiences that strategies of thinking are seldom acquired quickly, but may require years of practice to reach the stage of refinement at which they are transferable to novel problem-solving situations. The question of how rapidly cognitive strategies can be learned, and how much generalizing experience is needed to make them broadly transferable, obviously relates to the matter of direct instruction. If such strategies can be directly taught in a short time, that would be a highly important fact to be taken into account in the design of school curricula. If, in contrast, learning of strategies takes years (because of the variety of learner experiences required), the implications for curriculum design would be quite different. In the latter case, the curriculum must provide for the learning of many other kinds of capabilities during the time that cognitive strategies are gradually being developed and refined.

GENERAL REFERENCES

Cognitive Strategies

Brown, A. L. Knowing when, where, and how to remember: A problem of metacognition. In R. Glaser (Ed.), *Advances in instructional psychology.* Vol. 1. Hillsdale, N. J.: Erlbaum, 1978.

Bruner, J. S., Goodnow, J. J., and Austin, G. A. *A study of thinking.* New York: Wiley, 1956.

Inhelder, B., and Piaget, J. *The growth of logical thinking from childhood to adolescence.* New York: Basic Books, 1958.

O'Neil, H. F. (Ed.), *Learning strategies.* New York: Academic Press, 1978.

Thinking Strategies

Klahr, D. (Ed.), *Cognition and instruction.* Hillsdale, N. J.: Erlbaum, 1976.

Siegler, R. S. (Ed.), *Children's thinking: What develops?* Hillsdale, N. J.: Erlbaum, 1978.

Tuma, D. T., and Reif, F. (Eds.), *Problem solving and education: Issues in teaching and research*. Hillsdale, N. J.: Erlbaum, 1980.
Wertheimer, J. *Productive thinking*. New York: Harper & Row, 1959.
Whimbey, A., and Lochhead, J. *Problem solving and comprehension: A short course in analytical reasoning*. 2nd ed. Philadelphia: Franklin Institute Press, 1980.
Wickelgren, W. A. *How to solve problems*. San Francisco: Freeman, 1974.

8

Verbal Information Learning

One of the most familiar categories of learned capabilities is verbal information, sometimes called declarative knowledge. From early childhood on we learn a large mass of information—*names* and *facts* and a great many collections of *organized ideas*. Some is stored in our memories for a relatively short time, apparently, before it is forgotten. Other items and sets of verbal information are retained for a very long time, sometimes over the entire span of our lives. Some verbal information seems isolated and unconnected with any other items, for example, the name of a person we once met years ago on a trip to a foreign land. Most individual items, however, appear to have many connections to a variety of other information, so that recalling a single fact leads readily to the recall of others associated with it in some way.

Verbal information in the sense used here refers to information that is *verbalizable*. As a human performance, the capability is one of being able to *tell* or *state* a fact or idea in the form of a proposition. We know that learners have acquired and stored an item of verbal information when they can tell us what it is; that is, when they can communicate it in a form that has a subject and a predicate. Thus, verbal information is not learned when learners can simply repeat words; this may be simply an indication that they have learned a verbal chain. Acquiring verbal information means being able to reinstate *propositions*. These may be as complex as the first sentence of the Declaration of Independence, "When in the course of human events . . . ," or as simple as naming an object a "table" in the understood sentence, "[That is a] table."

Although knowing verbal information means being able to state propositions, it is not always the case that information is stored as propositions. As we shall see, various kinds of systems are proposed in contemporary theories for the storage of verbal information. After all, the main requirement for a system of storage is that the learner be readily able to gain access to the information so that it can be stated in a form that communicates, as propositions do. The storage itself must represent the words and their relationships, and this function can be performed by an image as well as by other kinds of cognitive structures.

Another essential characteristic of verbal information is that some of the words of which it is composed have *meaning.* In a fundamental sense, this means that certain words of the proposition must be known as *concepts* in the sense that they are described in Chapters 5 and 6. We have already seen that a set of words, such as *mountain typewriter baseball,* is not information because the words, while meaningful, do not form a proposition. Consider next the set of pronounceable "words," *senjux glemrik femtol.* These also are not information for the additional reason that the words themselves convey no meaning; they have not been learned as concepts. An interesting change occurs, however, when a new "word," seeming to have the function of a verb, is substituted, as in the sequence: *senjux glings femtol.* Reading this sequence, we have the impression that it would be meaningful if only we knew what *glings* meant. Now if we make the substitution of an actual and familiar verb, we have: *senjux breaks femtol.* In this form, it seems reasonable to classify the sequence as a genuine example of verbal information—minimal verbal information, perhaps, and surely not highly useful to the learner. It is, however, in propositional form, and contains at least one word (the verb) with a known meaning. Thus it shares a basic characteristic with a set of words forming a true sentence, such as *boys break windows.*

VARIETIES OF VERBAL INFORMATION

Meaningful information that is learned occurs in varying degrees of complexity, depending upon its propositional structure. It seems useful for purposes of exposition to distinguish information in the form of (1) *names* or *labels,* (2) single propositions or *facts,* and (3) collections of propositions that are *meaningfully organized.* This last set of information is often presented as *connected discourse* and is received by the learner either visually or auditorially. Generally, such organized sets of propositions are often referred to as *declarative knowledge* or as *bodies of knowledge.* We shall discuss what is known about the nature of the organization of such knowledge later in this chapter.

Many experimental studies have been performed to investigate the learning of single words or word pairs as labels; consequently, many of the conditions affecting the learning of such labels can be identified and exemplified. Considerably fewer studies have been done on the learning and retention of single facts or of longer passages making up connected discourse. However, new studies of this latter sort are appearing every day, and by this time some of the major influencing factors can be identified.

Learning Labels

Labels that are the names for objects or classes of objects are often learned as single events when concept learning occurs. Thus young children may learn the label "dish" at the same time they acquire the concept *dish*. As we have seen, knowing *dish* as a concept means being able to identify instances of the class. Although such performance is not dependent upon knowing the word "dish," this label is usually employed (by the parent or other teacher) as the way of assessing the children's learning of the concept. Thus, in the natural situation, the learning of new labels does not seem a very difficult learning task. The word "dish" is used by the parent on many different and widely spaced occasions when an actual dish is visible; the children soon begin to say "dish" on similar occasions, and the word as a verbal response is reinforced.

Many studies of label learning have required learners to acquire several labels at once rather than one at a time. Such a learning situation bears some resemblance to the task faced by the individual at a party of strangers who wishes to acquire the names of twenty new acquaintances at once. Obviously, this is a much more difficult task; and the difficulty increases with the number of new labels to be learned (see the discussion of verbal associates in Chapter 2).

In many instances of everyday life, and also in the school, people learn one or perhaps two labels at a time. Kindergarten children, for example, may learn the label "elephant" from seeing the animal in a zoo or in a picture. But rarely are children expected to learn the names of all the animals they see at the same time. Thus a *contextual distinctiveness* usually prevails when we learn a single label for a newly seen object. However, sometimes children or adults *are* expected to learn ten or twelve labels all together. An example might be the learning of names of different leaves ("oak," "maple," "birch," and so forth) in a science lesson for elementary pupils. When a number of labels have to be learned all at once, such learning is likely to be more difficult (or take more time) than would be expected by adding up the difficulties (or times taken to learn) of single labels.

Paired-associate learning.   When one learns to read a foreign language, it is not uncommon to acquire a large number of "translation responses," such as *donner*-"give" or *acheter*-"buy." The traditional prototype for such learning is the *paired associate*, sometimes used in nonsense form such as RIV-GEX. The exposure to the learner of the paired words (or syllables) over a number of practice trials results in acquisition of the performance of stating (or writing) the second member of the pair when only the first is shown. A great deal is known about paired-associate learning, and a great deal more remains to be studied (see Hall, 1971; Murdock, 1974). In terms of conditions for acquiring verbal associates, these appear to be the most important findings:

1. Nonsense syllables do not perform the function that Ebbinghaus intended for them, that is, of being equivalently meaningless and unfamil-

iar. The learning of an association between two verbal elements, whether syllables or words, is markedly affected by previous discrimination learning of both the first member and the second (Goss, 1963).

2. Most investigators agree that the efficient learning of a two-element verbal association requires the use of an *intervening link* having the function of *mediation* or coding. The increased ease of learning resulting from the deliberate use of well-chosen mediation links is striking (Jenkins, 1963). Such links are usually implicit ones; that is, they occur inside the learner and do not appear as overt behavior. In the case of the association "give"-*donner*, an effective coding might be "give" → "donate," → *donner*. Many other mediating links are possible.

3. It is difficult to separate the phenomena of learning *single* associates from those of *multiple* associates. The typical paired-associate learning study, after all, uses ten or twelve pairs like RIV-GEX, not just one. Increasing the number of pairs makes each disproportionately harder to learn.

The reason usually given for this heightened difficulty of learning with increasing number of items is *interference*. The learning of label a for object A, b for object B, c for object C, and so on becomes difficult because the associations of labels with objects tend to be confused with each other or to cancel each other out. Having learned A-a, the individual next attempts to learn B-b; but since B is not completely unlike A, one may tend to learn B-a or fail to recall A-a once the new label B-b is learned. When A-a interferes with the learning of B-b, it is called *proactive interference;* the opposite, when learning B-b interferes with the recall of A-a, is called *retroactive interference.* Both of these phenomena take place in the learning of sets of labels of any considerable number. Both have been studied extensively in the psychological laboratory with the use of paired-associate syllables or words (Keppel, 1968; Kausler, 1974).

An example of a study showing the effects of interference in the learning of names is one by E. J. Gibson (1941). Two different sets of drawn figures were constructed, each containing thirteen figures. In one set the figures were similar to each other, while in the other they were highly dissimilar. Six of the figures used in each set are illustrated in Figure 8.1. In both cases these stimuli were first presented to learners one by one, together with their labels (syllables). On subsequent trials, the stimulus was first presented, and after a brief delay during which the learner attempted to supply its "name," the combination of figure and label was again exposed. The labels for highly similar figures required an average of 19.8 repetitions, whereas the set with dissimilar forms was learned with only 8.9 repetitions.

Storing of labels in memory.   The occurrence of interference among labels learned close together in time is a factor that works against rapid learning—

Figure 8.1 Examples of figures used in a study of learning verbal (nonsense) names for sets of figures which were highly similar (Task 1) and highly dissimilar (Task 2). (Based on E. J. Gibson, Retroactive inhibition as a function of degree of generalization between tasks. *Journal of Experimental Psychology*, 1941, 28, 93–115.

a factor to be overcome. What can be said, in contrast, about factors that aid the learning of information in the form of labels or names? The answer to this question makes us recall the information-processing model of learning processes described in Chapter 4. In terms of this model, the learning of a label is a matter of transforming the memory of the word as it may exist in short-term memory, possibly as a word-sound, to the form it takes in long-term memory. This transformation process involves changing its coded form, most likely by *semantic encoding*. The temporary form the label has assumed in short-term memory is encoded for long-term storage into another form, presumably one that will make the label most readily accessible when the learner wants to recall it.

How does a label get encoded when learned for storage in long-term memory? There are various theories of the organization of such memories. Basically, a label is conceived as being stored as a word having certain distinctive stimulus features. More importantly, though, encoding a label means establishing many associations with other words that are related to it (Bower, 1975). These related associations may be of several types, including superordinate (dog-animal) and subordinate classes (dog-spaniel). Labels are also considered to be stored in relation with the concepts they represent, that is, to their *referents*, the intellectual skills that involve identifying or otherwise using concepts. And not to be overlooked is the possibility that a label may be encoded as an *image* (Paivio, 1971). All of these ways of encoding may be involved in storing the "meaning" of a label. Of course, as a single word, a label may enter into other more complex forms of organizations such as sentences. This will be discussed later.

The coding of names or labels often involves the use of an intervening word association, or *mediating link* (Jenkins, 1963). Thus when newly learned labels have mediating links already in the learner's memory, the process of coding may be both rapid and effective. For example, if the French name is being learned for the English word "give," the word "donate" may serve as a mediating link. As we have noted earlier, the coding would be "give" → "donate" → *donner*.

Other examples of coding links for certain French words are shown in Figure 8.2. Verbal links may be formed by choosing English words already well known to the learner that bear some similarity to the French word and that have some previously learned association with the English associate. Often, a pictorial link of the sort indicated in the second column of Figure 8.2 works better for most people (see Paivio, 1971). Another method for learning at least equally effective is to require the learners to generate their own coding link—a word, an image, or anything they think of that will link the stimulus object with its label.

After reviewing studies of the "keyword method" of learning foreign language vocabulary, Pressley, Levin, and Delaney (1982) summarize the steps in an optimal method as follows: First, the learner must acquire a stable association between the new foreign word and a familiar English word that sounds like the foreign word or a prominent part of it. (Example: *moon* for the Spanish word *mundo*.) The English word is the keyword. Next, the learner relates the meaning of the foreign word to the keyword (*moon* calls up the meaning "earth" for *mundo*). The evidence gives some suggestion that older children and adults may prefer to think of their own keywords and the visual images to accompany them. The advantage of this particular technique over that of receiving preselected keywords and images, however, has not been clearly shown.

Another kind of coding of single words (labels) that has been extensively studied is called *clustering*. When asked to learn lists containing as many as sixty nouns, learners tend to recall them in "clusters" of common categories (Bousfield, 1953). The nouns in one list represented the categories of animals, names, professions, and vegetables. Although presented in random order, the items tended to cluster into these categories when recalled by the learner. Other studies (for example, Watts and Anderson, 1969) have shown that nouns presented in organized categories are learned and stored much more rapidly than lists composed of equally familiar nouns not organized

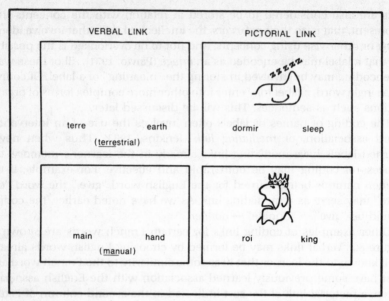

Figure 8.2 Some examples of verbal and pictorial links that can mediate English names for French words.

into categories. The process of coding, so far as single names are concerned, can be aided by clustering, or the placing of names into previously learned categories. Obviously, this kind of coding is definitely meaningful, or *semantic*.

Still another kind of meaningful coding of names and labels has been investigated with both children and adults. This coding is called *elaboration* and is exemplified by placing the word to be remembered in a phrase or a sentence. Rohwer (1966) investigated the learning of word-pairs like COW-BALL, in which the word BALL is to be given as an associate ("label") when the word COW is exposed to the learner. Rohwer compared the following ways of presenting the key words:

No elaboration:	COW	BALL
Conjunction:	The running COW and the bouncing BALL	
Preposition:	The running COW behind the bouncing BALL	
Verb:	The running COW chases the bouncing BALL	

In recall, the word COW was presented and the learner asked to state the associated word BALL. When a phrase using a conjunction was employed, the amount of recall was not increased over the no-elaboration condition. Increased recall was found, however, when a preposition was used; and recall was greatest when a true sentence including a verb was presented.

This initial study has been followed by a series that have repeatedly confirmed the substantial advantage for retention of the use of elaborations that include verbs to form whole sentences (see Rohwer, 1975).

From these studies of word coding, we can see that several fairly definite things are known about the learning of labels. First, learning a single name for an object on a single occasion is quite an easy task, one that is natural for the human memory. Thus, a person who encounters a new object for the first time and is told its name not only begins the process of acquiring the concrete concept of which the object is an instance but also readily learns to associate the object with its name. When several names must be learned for several different objects all at once, the task becomes more difficult. Presumably, this is because confusions attributable to the process of *interference* tend to occur. A number of ways of overcoming these interference effects may either be suggested to the learner or adopted as self-initiated strategies. Generally, these include ways of making each label increasingly *distinctive* and *meaningful* by associating it with other components of memory and thus coding it so that it becomes more readily retrievable. Labels may be encoded by being associated with other words that are themselves meaningful so that they form "mediating links." Coding may also take the form of imagery; the objects themselves, if they are highly distinctive, may aid this process. Labels may also be encoded in other meaningful ways, for example, by clustering into previously acquired categories or by being deliberately formed into sentences.

Learning Facts

A common form of verbal information that is acquired and stored by a human learner is a *fact*. We readily learn a variety of facts: a week contains seven days, chlorine is a poisonous gas, Calvin Coolidge declined to run for another term as President, Caesar described Gaul as having three parts. There are, of course, many kinds of facts. Some are quite specific and concrete, as when we know that "the Statue of Liberty holds a torch in her hand." Others are abstract, as in the saying "Necessity is the mother of invention."

Obviously, facts are composed of words. They may not always be stored in memory as words, or at least this may not be the entire form they take in memory. Presumably, one can store many of the facts shown in a picture as visual images. Yet somehow the words must also be stored, because the means we have of knowing whether a fact has been acquired is for the person to *state* the fact, and this statement requires words. It is reasonable to suppose that memory of facts requires the storage of words in some linguistic form. Information-processing theories of memory commonly make this assumption (Tulving and Donaldson, 1972).

However, a fact is more than a string of words. Sequences of words that form sentences are learned more rapidly and recalled with much greater facility than are word lists of the same size that are meaningfully unconnected (Briggs and Reed, 1943; English, Welborn, and Killian, 1934). For example, one does not expect a student who is learning facts from a history text to demonstrate this learning by making a verbatim reproduction of parts of the text. Instead, one might expect the learner to be able to reproduce in some ordered fashion the "ideas" contained in the text. The individual words may themselves be associated by means of the various linkings that apply to labels. But beyond this, there is reason to believe that factual information is learned and stored as *meaningful propositions.*

One prominent theory of the learning and retention of meaningful facts is that of Ausubel (1968; Ausubel, Novak, and Hanesian, 1978). He proposes that meaningful new ideas are learned by being *subsumed* in an already existing *cognitive structure* (an interconnected network of knowledge), which in turn has been established by prior learning. For example, if the learner is to acquire a new set of ideas about the principles of Buddhism, these newly incorporated ideas become organized into an already existing structure. An example of such a structure might be the principles of Christianity or something even more general such as the principles of comparative religion. In the latter case, one would speak of *derivative subsumption* (Buddhism being a specific example of a more general concept); in the former case, of *correlative subsumption* (Buddhism being in this case an extension or modification of previously learned propositions about Christianity).

The preexisting cognitive structure in the learner's memory may be actuated, according to Ausubel, by first presenting to the learner an *advance organizer.* The content of an advance organizer, relative to that which is to be learned, is at a higher level of abstraction, generality, and inclusiveness; it is intended to provide an ideational framework for the material presented for learning (Ausubel, 1960, 1978). When suitably designed, an advance organizer may aid in the retention of verbal information in the form of facts. The technique has also been found to help retention and transfer of learning of intellectual skills (Mayer, 1979).

Storing propositions in memory.   Learning theories of the information-processing variety conceive of facts being stored as propositions, usually within a network linking one proposition with another through concepts held in common. Each proposition has a definite syntactic structure, at least a *subject* and a *predicate.* Most theories that deal with learning and storage of facts propose additional features of syntax, such as *agent, object, location,* and *time* (Anderson and Bower, 1973). A scheme that depicts the representation of a fact in terms of the relations among verbs is illustrated in Figure 8.3. The most notable aspects of theories about the storage of facts would appear to be these: (1) facts are stored as propositions having inher-

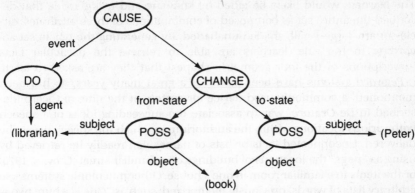

Figure 8.3 A representation of the factual sentence "The librarian gave the book to Peter." (Figure 8.15 from D. A. Norman and D. E. Rumelhart, *Explorations in cognition*. San Francisco: Freeman, 1975. By permission of the copyright owner, W. H. Freeman and Co.).

ent syntactic structures; (2) facts are not stored as either disconnected words or disconnected concepts; and (3) stored facts are linked with other facts through the concepts they hold in common.

This conception leads to the theoretical idea that the representation of facts in memory includes *paths* that connect one fact with others (Anderson, 1980). If the learner is asked to recognize a particular fact, the response is slower the more paths there are leading to other facts. In contrast, if the learner must recall facts, rather than simply recognize them, a greater number of paths to other facts appears to have the effect of enhancing retention (E. Gagné, 1978).

Organizational factors.   The learning and remembering of factual information is often aided by an organization that is different from the facts themselves. Three kinds of organization described by Bower (1972) are (1) *generative rules,* (2) *pegword systems,* and (3) *hierarchical retrieval plans.*

A *rule* may be used to generate access to facts. For example, the series of numbers 1 4 9 1 6 2 5 3 6 4 9 6 4 8 1 may readily be retrieved by recalling the simple rule that the numbers are the squares of successive whole numbers. Suppose students are asked to remember the following set of geometric figures:

The learners would likely be aided by knowing and using a rule that described the entire set as composed of combinations of three attributes: circle-square, large-small, shaded-unshaded. By generating the whole set according to the rule, learners are able to retrieve the particular facts (descriptions of the four geometric shapes) that they are asked to learn.

Pegword systems have been used for a great many years. As has been mentioned, a commonly used device for orators at the time of Cicero (described in *De Oratore*) was to associate the succeeding ideas of a speech with various locations within the auditorium in which the speech was to be delivered. Unconnected facts or lists of names can readily be retrieved by using as "pegs" the locations of buildings on a familiar street (Crovitz, 1970) or the items in a familiar room in one's house. Other mnemonic systems use arbitrary lists of words, previously memorized, such as "One is a bun, two is a shoe, three is a tree, four is a door." The words in such a list are meaningfully associated with the facts to be recalled. Sometimes images are formed that incorporate the concepts of the pegword and the fact to be remembered.

A *hierarchical scheme* for retrieval organizes facts to be learned and remembered in terms of categories of increasing specificity. It is one kind of "cognitive structure" that might be suggested by Ausubel's theory. One might remember the causes of fire in a garage, for example, by means of a hierarchical scheme such as that illustrated in Figure 8.4.

Organization provided by textual passages.   In addition to the organization that may originate within knowledge structures previously acquired by the learner, an organization for factual learning may come from the context in which individual facts are presented to the learner. New facts to be learned are usually presented in a text or oral discourse in a way that suggests organization. An example is the use of a topic sentence to organize a paragraph of text in which a number of different facts are presented.

Topic sentences, of course, are only one of many possible kinds of organization that may be employed in the presentation of facts and that may influence the learning of factual information. Facts may be organized in tabular form: the table exhibits a number of organizational factors. Its title is, in a sense, a topic sentence. The headings of its rows and columns provide clues for generative rules pertaining to the individual facts listed in them. In some instances, the table's format may provide a set of "pegs" based upon the spatial location of its contents. And the organization of a table is often a hierarchical one, exhibiting superordinate-subordinate relationships among its items. For all these reasons, the tabular presentation of factual information may be expected to provide organizing factors that aid the storage and retrieval of factual information.

Figure 8.4 A hierarchical arrangement of the possible causes of fire in a garage.
(Gagné, R. M., and Fleishman, E. A. *Psychology and human performance*. Copyright
1959 by Holt, Rinehart and Winston. Reproduced by permission of Holt, Rinehart
and Winston.)

Many of these characteristics may likewise be seen when a graph or diagram is used as an organizing device for presenting facts. Additionally, a
diagram may be recalled as a visual image and thus provide another advantage for retrieval. Figure 8.5 gives an example of a picture that provides
organization for a science principle.

Organization by inserted questions.   Still another way in which organization may be given to factual information is by inserting questions into passages of text. These effects have been studied extensively by Rothkopf (1970)
and by Frase (1970), among others. It was found that the performance of
students on items they had "practiced" in the inserted questions was sub-

Suppose you breathe onto a cold glass surface like a window or a drinking glass. Water droplets will form on the glass. The warm moist air of your breath cannot hold its moisture when cooled by the glass. As a result, moisture is given up in the form of water droplets.

Figure 8.5 A picture which helps to organize the description of a science principle.

stantially better than their performance on items that they had not previously encountered. Thus, the insertion of questions had a definite organizing influence on the facts learned and remembered.

Another and somewhat different effect of the inserted questions was also noted. When given items on which they had no specific practice, students remembered facts in the *categories* suggested by the inserted questions better than those in other categories. The group that had encountered questions on distances, dates, and proper names remembered facts in these categories better than other facts; and results were similar for the students who had seen questions on common words and technical terms. In other studies, this "general" effect of inserted questions has been found to occur when the questions are given *after* successively presented textual passages but not when they are inserted *before* the passages. There may thus be more than one way in which inserted questions exert their organizing effects on the learning of facts.

Learning Organized Verbal Knowledge

Students who are given a text to study, such as a chapter in a book on American history, are not usually expected to learn and remember only the specific facts contained in the chapter. One expects instead that they will learn and recall the *main themes* or *main ideas* and a sufficient number of facts to exemplify or elaborate these ideas. For example, a chapter dealing with the economic aspects of the Depression of 1929–1938 might describe the financial speculation in the stock market, business failures and their causes, bank failures, unemployment, and the government actions of the "New Deal." These and other main themes are what students may be expected to remember. The learners might also recall names of specific stocks or of banks or of governmental officials in order to demonstrate that they can provide instances of knowledge rather than "mere verbalizations." (It is not suggested here that such information learning is the major aim of instruction in American history, only an essential first step.)

Recall of the content of connected prose in a text may be influenced by conditions occurring at three different points in the course of learning and retention (E. Gagné, 1978). Factors having favorable effects on retention of organized knowledge may take place (1) before the reading of the text, (2) during the reading, or (3) during the interval between reading and recall.

Prior to the beginning of learning from a text, knowledge that has previously been learned and that is relevant to the new learning may be activated and made readily accessible. Brief passages of advance organizers may accomplish this end, as may also topic sentences or reminders of a more general category to which the new knowledge belongs. Other kinds of communications capable of having beneficial effects on retention include prequestions about the content to be learned and other ways of informing the learners about the objective of their learning.

Characteristics of the content to be learned from the reading of a text that have some effect on retention include the following: (1) the relative importance of the information in relation to the entire passage; (2) the extent to which the passage stimulates imagery in learners; (3) the presence of questions inserted within the passage (Rothkopf, 1976); and (4) the amount of repetition given to particular ideas. The factors that operate after the time of initial learning mainly have to do with review. Usually, questions are used to ask learners to state the meaning of main and subordinate ideas that have been read, in a nonverbatim fashion (in the learner's "own words"). There is an advantage in retention to reviews that are spaced rather than conducted in close succession.

Organization by Schema

How do passages of connected discourse become organized (encoded) in long-term memory? According to current theory, the strongest influence on understanding of verbal knowledge is exerted by previously acquired knowledge, already organized into what is called a *schema* (R. C. Anderson, 1977; Rumelhart and Ortony, 1977; Schank and Abelson, 1977). A schema is a collection of ideas and the relationships among them that form a category that the learner "understands." Understanding means that the learner is able to recognize specific examples of the schema. Thus, learners who have sufficient experience will possess schemata (plural of "schema") that pertain to "restaurant dining," to "baseball game," to "buying an automobile," and to many, many other human activities. Schemata represent the way people's knowledge is organized in long-term memory.

In general, schemata are the generic ideas underlying objects, events, and actions. They are the knowledge "structures" that the learner brings to a text or to an oral communication whose contents are to be learned. Schemata are abstract in the sense that they contain "slots" or "place holders" for each interrelated idea that they contain. When presented with new information in a particular text or message, the learner is able to fill these slots with the ideas conveyed.

An example of the effects exerted by a schema on the learning, comprehension, and retention of new verbal information is provided in a study of the "baseball schema" (Spilich, Vesonder, Chiesi, and Voss, 1979). Two groups of college students were selected, one high in baseball knowledge, the other low. Each group heard an audio tape describing a half inning of a fictitious baseball game and then were asked to recall as much of it as they could in a written account. The high-knowledge group recalled considerably more about the events of the game than did the low-knowledge group. Even more striking were differences in the quality of the recall as judged in terms of the "goal structure" of a baseball game. High-knowledge students remembered more information about actions that produced changes in significant aspects of the game: scoring, actions of batters and runners, number of outs, batting averages of players. Thus, while students in both groups recalled the main points of the half-inning's events (the score, who was winning, number of balls and strikes), there were striking differences in both the quality and quantity of remembered information. The differences was attributable to the *nature of the schema* each brought to the learning situation. High-knowledge students, we can suppose, have baseball schemata with many "place-holders," whereas low-knowledge students have schemata with many fewer "place-holders." What each learns and remembers is influenced accordingly. This example tells us that learning new verbal information is strongly influenced by the schemata into which our previously learned knowledge is organized.

Another striking example of how recall of a prose passage is influenced by the prior knowledge and interests of learners is provided in a study of Anderson and Pichert (1978). The material to be learned was a story about two boys who stayed away from school to play in one boy's house. Some of the information about the house was judged to be of interest to a prospective home buyer—new siding, a fireplace, a damp basement. Other information would more likely interest a burglar—the locations of bicycles, color television, and the fact that no one was home on Thursdays. Two groups of students read the passage, one group under instructions to take the perspective of a home buyer, the other under instructions to take the burglar perspective. As expected, recall of ideas that matched each of the perspectives was greater than for those ideas that did not match.

Following this first recall, half of the students were told of the alternate perspective, that is, the one different from that which they originally had. The other half of the students were not told of the alternative perspective. Then all were asked to make a second recall. The students given knowledge of the alternate perspective were able to recall information relevant to this new point of view. They recalled more information relevant to the new perspective than did students who were uninformed about it. The schemata activated by the two different perspective instructions thus had some notable effects on what was remembered, even after learning had initially taken place.

Schemata can take many forms. They can be *prototypes* of concepts, for example, of the human face or of an animal species. They can be schemata of action, illustrated by the difference in meaning between the sentences "the player kicked the ball," and "the addict kicked the habit." They can be *scripts*, reflecting a sequence of events such as that which occurs in restaurant dining (Schank and Abelson, 1977). As these authors also indicate, schemata can have the form of *plans* and *goals*. And of particular importance is the fact that schemata typically provide a basis for problem solving, as we shall see in Chapter 9. To solve a problem, a learner must first possess a schema that represents the problem in terms that make possible the application of the relevant rules that will lead to solution. In any of these forms a schema is one of the most significant ways in which verbal knowledge is organized in human long-term memory.

CONDITIONS OF LEARNING: VERBAL INFORMATION

Whether a student or not, a person obviously learns and remembers a great deal of verbal information. Somewhat arbitrarily perhaps, one can divide the learning of information into the categories of labels (or names), facts, and connected discourse, or organized knowledge. However, some general principles of learning appear to run through these categories, and these shared principles can be viewed as optimal conditions for learning. As is true for other categories of learning outcomes, learning conditions are conveniently seen as partly internal to the learner and partly external.

Internal Conditions

Which internal conditions of the learner favor learning and retention of verbal information? Which factors of internal disposition have been shown or suggested to support the coding, storage, and retrieval of information?

A preexisting set of organized knowledge. Some previously learned information, interconnected in some manner, needs to be present in the learner's memory. This preexisting knowledge is what Ausubel calls a "cognitive structure," into which newly learned information is subsumed. Among information-processing theories of memory, there are several concepts of this organized information as stored in the long-term memory. Computer simulation models initially attempted to account for the learning of paired associates and proposed a network of associations that formed a discrimination net (Simon and Feigenbaum, 1964). A memory model proposed by Quillian (1968) proposes that all factual information is stored as either a "unit" or as a "property"; the *unit* is the representation of an object or event, whereas the *property* represents a prediction (such as is implied by a verb or adjective).

Contemporary views of the nature of storage of verbal information usually begin with the assumption that *propositions*—including both the concepts they contain and the subject-predicate relation—are stored in long-term memory. This is the case with theories of memory proposed by investigators who favor computer-simulation models, such as Anderson and Bower (1973); Kintsch (1972); and Norman and Rumelhart (1975). The notion that a proposition is a "normal" unit of storage in long-term memory has the following implications for the learning and retention of individual names and specific facts: (1) new verbal information in the form of names and facts is learned by being incorporated into propositions that are parts of a larger network of propositions; (2) when information of this unitary sort is to be retrieved, the learner must gain access to propositions, not simply to isolated words.

Specific items of verbal information are stored within a network of propositions that are connected with each other through links with shared concepts. The greater the number of links with which a particular item is connected, the better will be its retention. Presumably, this is because a greater number of cues are available for retrieval of the item. Additional cues may also come from images of the items or events described in printed or orally delivered prose. As illustrated in Figure 8.2, mnemonic systems such as the *keyword method* take advantage of these characteristics of memory by suggesting the incorporation of single words into meaningful propositions (*arbre* sounds like *arbor* and means "tree"). An image of the keyword may add an extra link to this proposition and thus favor ready retrieval.

A principal mode of storage for organized bodies of verbal knowledge is the *schema*, a set of interrelated and interlinked concepts belonging to a superordinate category of objects, events, or actions. The schema has a particularly important function to play in preparing the learner for learning new knowledge. As a unit of organized knowledge, the schema represents the main features of what is most familiar and traditional to the learner. At the same time, the schema contains "place-holders" into which new specific knowledge may be fitted. For example, a restaurant-dining schema has place-holders such as "being shown to the table," "reading the menu," "ordering a meal," "eating food," and "paying the bill," among others. Having these characteristics, schemata enable the learner to anticipate the form of structure of whatever knowledge is to be newly learned and thus aid in encoding it for long-term storage.

Encoding Strategies.   If verbal information is stored in long-term memory in propositional form or in some other organized fashion, this must mean that it is encoded that way. Thus, the learner must have available some methods of information processing (encoding) that transform the perceived stimulation into the form of an "organized network." Generally, this means that the learner has available some *rules* for forming concepts and propositions. Additionally, the learner generates images as a way of storing concepts or relations (Collins and Quillian, 1972; Paivio, 1971). The process of encoding occurs on a number of levels, depending upon what intentions the learner has for later recall of the information (Craik and Lockhart, 1972).

However encoding is done, its most important function is to make the learned information memorable as well as transferable to situations the learner will later encounter. Effective encoding must therefore provide cues for later retrieval (Thomson and Tulving, 1970). In part, this means that the encoding structure (the image, the tabular format, or whatever) must provide *distinctive* cues. In part also, it means that there must be "deep processing" of the information in which a variety of relationships are established between the newly learned and the preexisting knowledge. The effects of such processing are to make greater ease of retrieval possible.

External Conditions

The external conditions for learning, as we have seen in Chapter 4, are the environmental events that lend support to the internal processes of learning. The critical events for verbal information learning, therefore, are evidently those that activate and maintain the processes of encoding, storage, and retrieval.

Providing a meaningful context.   The external situation for learning new verbal information needs to "make contact" with the organized knowledge that is already in the learner's memory. If names or labels are to be learned, associating them with others that are already learned is known to be effective. Or, the new labels may be "clustered" into more inclusive categories that have been previously acquired. Labels may also be more effectively learned and remembered if they are made a part of sentences and stored as propositions, as the work of Rohwer (1970) demonstrates. The sentences may be provided, or the suggestion made that the learner form some of his or her own. Another suggestion would be that the individual form images relating the new label with others that have already been learned.

Whatever method is used to activate internal processes, the function served by these external events is obviously to transform a nonmeaningful stimulus (a label to be learned) into one that is associated with meaningful information already available to the learner. Thus the new label is effectively encoded, stored in long-term memory, and can be more readily retrieved when needed.

Sometimes, to be sure, labels need to be memorized or learned verbatim, and no harm to the learner results from doing so. Usually, the names of the days of the week and the names of numerals and many other labels are learned this way, being simply "committed to memory." Useful jingles or rhymes, such as "Thirty days hath September . . . ," may also be acquired by children without elaborate attempts to provide related meanings. But these instances are the exceptions, not the rule. Most new learning of labels is greatly enhanced by provision of a large meaningful context.

Placing the newly learned *fact* within a context of meaning is likewise a condition for its optimal learning. A single fact about the atmosphere of Mars is more readily learned and retrieved if it is presented in a meaningful context with deals with other planets and other planetary characteristics (see Frase, 1969). Even the topic sentence of a paragraph, which suggests a larger context for the individual facts within it, may have this effect on learning. The method used by Ausubel (1968) to provide a context of meaning involved the use of an *advance organizer*. Before learning an organized set of new factual information, the learners are provided with a brief textual passage that orients them to the subject matter and relates the latter to the preexisting knowledge they already have.

As a practical method, questions or statements of objectives may be introduced before or after the presentation of facts. One effect these may have is to direct the learner's attention to the categories of information to be learned. An even more direct effect, however, is to influence the kind of encoding that the learner undertakes with the material and thus to enhance its retrieval (Frase, 1970; Rothkopf and Kaplan, 1972).

As for the learning of larger bodies of information, this too is presumably influenced by the degree of meaning the passages convey to the learner or by the amount of "deep processing" the learner does with them. Presumably, external conditions must accomplish the activation of internal processing strategies that favor the *constructive* aspects of memory described by Bartlett (1932). Stimuli must activate one or more schemata that provide a basic framework for the new information to be learned and that receive the new information into preexisting place-holders. By this means, memory is enhanced not only for the main themes of the new information, but for the details as well.

Increasing distinctiveness of cues.   While the retention of verbal information is sometimes enhanced by the subsequent learning of other, new information (as when new facts are added to an existing body of knowledge), it is also true that *interference* can occur. Thus, R. C. Anderson and Myrow (1971) demonstrated that high school students remembered fewer facts about a fictitious primitive tribe when they subsequently were asked to learn "similar but confusing" facts about another primitive tribe. External conditions or learning can be designed to reduce the probability of interference among potentially confusable information. The external cues for the recall of one set of facts can be made as distinctive as possible. In part, this may be done by tabular organization of facts to be learned or by the images suggested by location maps or diagrams. Also, physical cues of different colors, shapes, type styles, and so on may be used in the presentation of text. Still a different approach to increasing distinctiveness is by requiring learners to engage in "deep processing" of what they read by such activities as paraphrasing and drawing inferences (Glover, Plake, and Roberts, 1981).

The effects of repetition.   Sheer repetition of labels or facts, in a kind of "overt rehearsal," does not necessarily lead to better encoding or retention (Tulving, 1966; Meunier, Ritz, and Meunier, 1972). However, when *retrieval* is practiced, substantial improvement occurs in the later recall of learned information. An early study by Gates (1917) demonstrated that "recitation" was clearly more effective than "reading" for the memorization of passages of text. Similar findings have come from studies that dealt with the learning of the substance of factual passages (T. H. Gilbert, 1957; Ausubel and Youssef, 1965). The text-inserted questions used in the studies of Rothkopf (1970) and Frase (1970) may also be considered to have the effect of introducing practice of the items of information whose retention was later assessed.

The practice of verbal information items, when it involves retrieval on the part of the learners, constitutes a *review* of the information being learned and stored. Such review can provide the occasion for additional and more elaborate encoding. It can also increase the variety of retrieval cues learners have at their disposal. Thus, while repetition in the form of mere rehearsal does not appear to be an effective condition for the learning and retention of information, repetition which takes the form of review is highly effective.

EDUCATIONAL IMPLICATIONS

Students in schools learn a great deal of verbal information—names of objects; technical terms; facts of history, science, and social living; main themes of fiction and philosophical and political thought. In applying knowledge about learning to school instruction aimed at imparting verbal information, we need to consider two questions: (1) of what use to the individual is factual verbal knowledge; and (2) what conditions of learning, internal and external to the student, can be reflected in the design of instruction?

Usefulness of Verbal Information

It is not uncommon to hear disparaging statements about "facts" and "mere verbal knowledge" among teachers and other educators. The major reason for this point of view may be a desire to emphasize high-priority goals that are more difficult to attain, such as "teaching students to think creatively." Verbal information, after all, is learned quite readily, and much of it will be acquired incidentally in study that has other primary objectives. However, the priority assigned to information (knowledge) should be tempered by considerations of the positive usefulness of this type of human capability.

Verbal information of some kinds has a usefulness that extends throughout the individual's lifetime. We all need to know the names of common objects, the names of numerals, the days of the week, the months of the year, and many other facts simply essential for daily living and communication in society. Of course, many labels and facts of this sort are normally learned in the early grades of school. In later grades, depending upon the occupational specialty chosen by the individual, a great many additional items of information must be learned. A person who becomes a carpenter must learn many names and facts about lumber and the tools used for building; one who becomes a botanist must learn many names and much other information about plants.

Another use for verbal information is as a component in the learning of other kinds of capabilities. Such information forms the "content" of the specific instances to which intellectual skills (concepts, rules) are applied and in connection with which they are learned. The student who is learning a principle of government such as "the separation of church and state" must use many different items of verbal information about particular instances of the principle. Similarly, other kinds of capabilities, such as cognitive strategies and attitudes, require specific informational content in order to be exhibited by the learner. In general, except at the most elementary level, learning takes place against a background and within a context of verbal information. It is true, of course, that the necessary information can always be looked up; but a complete dependence on this method would be very inefficient. Much information, carried "in the head," is prerequisite to other learning.

A third and very important use for verbal information is as a vehicle for thought. One should not lose sight of the fact that the great thinkers we admire are likely to be men and women who have vast stores of knowledge. How is deliberative and reflective thought carried out? In part, no doubt, by means of images. But the relational, connective, functions of thought seem to require the propositional form presumably taken by information in the organized mode it assumes in human memory.

Instruction for Verbal Information Learning

The external conditions for effective learning of verbal information can be reflected in instructional materials and procedures as summarized in Table 8.1. These examples are of necessity abbreviated, and the reader will probably be able to provide additional ones.

The role of previously acquired information, an internal condition for learning, needs to be taken into account in the design of instruction. Acquiring a new fact, or a new set of facts, will be easier for the learner who has a larger preexisting structure of knowledge in memory than for a learner with a small amount of prior knowledge. Thus, if one asks a young child to learn about howdahs, careful attention must be given to the kinds and amount of knowledge the child already has. For an older learner, a greater amount of preexisting knowledge about animals and animal seats may usually be assumed. The appropriate "advance organizer" would surely vary with age-correlated differences in learners.

The dependence of new learning of information on the existence of previously learned knowledge implies that the more people know, the easier it is for them to acquire new knowledge. This cumulative effect of learning seems to be a well-known fact that is readily observed in educational settings. The organization of previously learned verbal information into the form of schemata is a process that enables learners to anticipate some of the

TABLE 8.1 Instructional Procedures for Verbal Information Learning Using the Example "Howdah"

Learning Outcome	Procedure	Example
Name/Label	1. Providing a sentence context	1. Bow to the sultan in his HOWDAH!
	2. Using a keyword with image	2. Imagine the sultan saying "how-de-do" from his HOWDAH
	3. Furnishing distinctive cues	3. Picture of a howdah on an elephant; label HOWDAH in capitals
Facts and Organized Knowledge	1. Using an advance organizer	1. Orienting text on riding animals
	2. Activating a relevant schema	2. Information about seats on various animals, and the variety of their construction
	3. Review	3. Inserted questions, e.g., "How wide must a howdah be?"
	4. Furnishing distinctive cues, "deep processing"	4. (a) Picture of a HOWDAH on an elephant (b) Require learner to make inferences and to paraphrase

characteristics of new knowledge, and to incorporate it into the organized structures of their long-term memories.

GENERAL REFERENCES

Learning Names as Verbal Associates

Hall, J. F. *Verbal learning and retention.* Philadelphia: Lippincott, 1971.
Lorayne, H., and Lucas, J. *The memory book.* New York: Ballantine, 1974.
Paivio, A. *Imagery and verbal processes.* New York: Holt, Rinehart and Winston, 1971.

Meaningful Information Learning

Ausubel, D. P., Novak, J. D., and Hanesian, H. *Educational psychology: A cognitive view.* 2nd ed. New York: Holt, Rinehart and Winston, 1978.

Bartlett, F. C. *Remembering*. Cambridge: Cambridge University Press, 1932.

Cofer, C. N. *The structure of human memory*. San Francisco: Freeman, 1976.

Information Processing in Learning and Memory

Anderson, J. R. *Language, memory, and thought*. Hillsdale, N.J.: Erlbaum, 1976.

Anderson, R. C., Spiro, R. J., and Montague, W. E. (Eds.), *Schooling and the acquisition of knowledge*. Hillsdale, N.J.: Erlbaum, 1977.

Lindsay, P. H., and Norman, D. A. *Human information processing: An introduction to psychology*, 2nd ed. New York: Academic Press, 1977. Chapters 10, 11, and 12.

Klatzky, R. L. *Human memory: Structures and processes*, 2nd ed. San Francisco: Freeman, 1980.

Tulving, E., and Donaldson, W. (Eds.), *Organization of memory*. New York: Academic Press, 1972.

9

Problem Solving

The learning of rules and of domains of verbal information sets the stage for problem solving. In a sense, the activity of problem solving is a natural extension of both rule learning and schema learning. The solving of a problem is guided by the stored verbal knowledge possessed by the learner, which makes possible the interpretation of the problem.

The contents of memory that make problem solving possible are the rules that have previously been learned. Problem solving may be viewed as a process by which the learner discovers a combination of previously learned rules and plans their application so as to achieve a solution for a novel problem situation.

Problem solving is not simply a matter of applying previously learned rules, however. It is also a process that yields new learning. Learners are placed (or find themselves) in a problem situation. They recall previously acquired rules in the attempt to find a "solution." In carrying out such a thinking process, learners may try a number of hypotheses and test their applicability. When they find a particular combination of rules that fit the situation, they have not only "solved the problem" but have also learned something new. One newly learned entity is a "higher-order rule," which enables individuals to solve other problems of a similar type. The other aspect of new learning may be ways of solving problems in general—in other words, *cognitive strategies* that can guide learners' subsequent thinking behavior.

The sequence of events involved in problem solving is often referred to in the writings of Dewey (1910). The initial event is the *presentation of the problem*, which may be done by a verbal statement or some other means. The learner then *defines the problem*, or distinguishes the essential features of the situation. As a third step, the learner *formulates hypotheses* that may be applicable to a solution. Finally, *verification* of the hypothesis or successive ones is attempted until the learner finds one that achieves the solution. Relating these steps to our previous discussion, it may be noted that only the first step is an external event; the rest are internal. The hypotheses that are formed are often new rules; the successful one will be learned when its application has been tested and confirmed (see Gagné, 1964). In addition, in carrying out the steps learners practice using some cognitive strategies that govern their own thinking behavior.

This chapter is concerned with a description of both the external and internal events in problem solving. The phrase "problem solving" is used throughout to refer to the finding of solutions to *novel problems* and should be carefully distinguished from the routine substitution of numerical values in mathematical expressions of the same type (a kind of "drill"). We will see that problem solving depends upon previously learned *rules*. It also depends upon the type of intellectual skill that governs the individual's own thinking processes: *cognitive strategies*. First we shall examine the application of rules in problem solving. Later we shall describe the effects on the problem-solving process of organized verbal information in the form of schemata.

APPLYING RULES IN PROBLEM SOLVING

Situations that require problem solving are of great variety, yet they appear to have several formal characteristics in common. Someone may have the problem of parking a car in a spot that is close to work but at the same time free of parking restrictions. A student may have the problem of figuring out why the moon has phases. A scientist may have a problem of accounting for a discrepancy in the predicted and measured velocity of a nuclear particle. A fiction writer may have a problem of conveying a representation of sloth-fulness in describing the actions of one character. All these situations imply the existence of problems that are to be brought to some successful termination by thinking. All these problems are solved by the use of *rules*, simple or complex. Rules are the stuff of thinking.

One might be tempted to conclude, therefore, that problem solving is a set of events in which human beings *use rules to achieve some goal*. This is quite true; yet it is not the whole story. The results of using rules in problem solving are not confined to achieving a goal, satisfying as that may be to the thinker. When problem solution is achieved, something is also *learned*, in the sense that the individual's capability is more or less permanently changed. What emerges from problem solving is a *higher-order rule*, which becomes a part of the individual's repertoire. The same class of situation, when encountered again, may be responded to with great facility by means of recall and is no longer looked on as a "problem." Problem solving, then, must definitely be considered a form of learning.

Some Examples of Problem Solving

At some point in the study of modern algebra, students may be asked to demonstrate that the following statement, in which a and b are rational numbers, is true:

$$(a + b)21 = a \cdot 21 + b \cdot 21$$

If the students have acquired certain rules previously, they are able to do this in the following steps:

Step 1: $(a + b)21 = 21(a + b)$; by the commutative property of multiplication
Step 2: $(a + b)21 = 21 \cdot a + 21 \cdot b$; by the distributive property
Step 3: $(a + b)21 = a \cdot 21 + b \cdot 21$; by the commutative property

Of course, it is possible to instruct the students to take these specific steps, thus acquiring a rather lengthy verbal chain. But the intention here is to illustrate the instance in which they are not instructed by display of the steps (either in a text or on a chalkboard). Rather, they are simply given the problem: "Show that this statement is true: $(a + b)21 = a \cdot 21 + b \cdot 21$." The learners' problem is one of selecting and using certain number rules that they have previously learned in an order that will make it possible to arrive at a logically correct solution.

In considering this example of a set of events as problem solving, the reader should bear in mind that it is the *first encounter* of the students with this problem. Once these operations have been performed, of course, they may be repeated many times with any numbers belonging to the class concerned. Most adults naturally carry out these operations very rapidly, and in fact would be inclined to accept the given statement as true by inspection. But young students who meet this problem for the first time have no such recalled experience to fall back upon. All they know is that numbers can be manipulated in accordance with certain rules. To young learners the situation is a brand new one, and they must *supply* the steps in thinking that will achieve a solution. From the standpoint of such children, there are two notable points about the problem situation. First, instructions inform the learners of what they want to achieve, namely, a statement in which the product of two numbers is equal to the sum of two products. Second, the children obviously have to be able to recall from previous learning some particular rules.

As a second example, let us turn to a problem of a fairly simple and concrete sort used for the experimental study of problem solving. Here the students are presented with a set of square figures made from arrangements of wooden matches, examples of which are shown in Figure 9.1. In each case, the students are given the problem of transforming one pattern of matches into another in a stated number of moves. The object is for them to be able to make such transformations for a variety of match patterns they have never seen before, not simply to remember the particular patterns on which they have practiced. In the studies performed with such problems (Katona, 1940), the following results were obtained:

1. The least effective method of establishing the desired capability was showing the learner how to solve several problems by actually moving the matches until the learner could recall the correct moves.

Figure 9.1 Two matchstick problems, with their solutions. (Katona, G. *Organizing and memorizing.* New York: Columbia University Press, 1940).

2. Of considerably greater effectiveness was a method in which the learner was instructed in a *verbal proposition.* (Two different propositions were used, one called "arithmetic," which stated that the matches with double functions should be changed to have single functions; the other called "structural," which instructed the learner to proceed by creating holes and loosening the figures. Both statements were about equally effective.)
3. Most effective for solving new problems was a method that proceeded a step at a time to illustrate the changes that would be brought about by using a rule, without stating the rule verbally. Several examples were used to demonstrate the operation of the rule by shading drawings of the squares so as to create "holes" in the original figure. This was called "learning by help" and could equally well be termed "guided discovery." In other words, the performance of the learners subsequent to the presentation of these examples led to the inference that they had *discovered* the rule required for problem solving.

These conclusions throw considerable light on the events of problem solving. As in the previous example, the learners were instructed about the terminal achievement to be expected, the goal of their activity. Again, these results make clear that a higher-order rule is acquired when the problem is solved, and this rule may be immediately generalized to other new situations presenting problems of the same class. Presenting the *solutions* of problems to the learners was markedly ineffective for learning. Undoubtedly the reason is that such presentations did not require the acquisition of the higher-order rule; the solutions could be learned as simple chains. Using verbal cues to stimulate learning by stating the higher-order rule verbally brought about problem solving in some learners but not in others. The most dependable method of instruction used illustrations to stimulate the learners to discover the rule for themselves.

Figure 9.2 The solution to Maier's pendulum problem. (Maier, N. R. F. Reasoning in humans: 1. On direction. *Journal of Comparative Psychology*, 1930, *10*, 115–143).

A third example of problem solving is taken from a famous study by Maier (1930). The learner was first brought into a room about eighteen by twenty feet in size containing only a worktable. Each learner was provided with a set of materials, including some poles, lengths of wire, pieces of chalk, and several clamps. The problem as told to the learners was to construct two pendulums so that each would make a chalk mark at a designated point on the floor when swung over it. As shown in Figure 9.2, the correct solution to the pendulum construction problem was achieved by clamping two poles together and wedging them vertically against another pole, which they pressed horizontally against the ceiling. From the horizontal pole two wires were suspended, each weighted at its lower end by clamps that held the piece of chalk at the proper height so that it marked the floor when the pendulum was swung.

With some of the subjects in this experiment, Maier used an additional set of instructions that seem to have had the function of recalling certain previously learned rules (see Gagné, 1964). These included instruction on (1) how to make a plumb line by using a clamp, a pencil, and string; (2) how to make a long pole out of two short ones using a clamp; and (3) how to hold an object up against a wall with two poles by wedging them tightly. Another group of subjects received an additional instruction to the effect that the problem would be simple if one "could just hang the pendulums from a nail in the ceiling." (Nails were not among the materials provided.)

The results of this study showed that the added instructions that fostered recall brought about solution in a greater proportion of learners than did the simpler instructions stating the problem. The final additional set, which Maier called *direction*, improved the probabilities of solution still more. The proportion of college students solving the pendulum problem under each of these three conditions were 0 out of 15 (with statement of problem), 1 out of 18 (with added instructions), and 4 out of 10 (with instructions plus direction).

It is evident that the verbal instructions used in this experimental situation fulfilled a number of different functions. Briefly stated, they were as follows:

1. They informed the learner about the nature of the expected performance. In other words, they defined the learner's goal—two pendulums that could make chalk marks on the floor.
2. They were deliberately used to bring about the recall of certain subordinate rules.
3. They were employed to "channel," or "guide," the learner's thinking. They did this by emphasizing what was *not* a good direction for thought (for example, the table was not to be used in the construction, and no nails were available) as well as what *was* a good direction (hanging pendulums from the ceiling).

Although the pendulum problem seems simple when one knows the solution, this appearance is deceptive, since none of the college students was able to solve the problem when only the "problem-stating" instructions were given. To increase the probability of solution, additional resources were needed. These came from within the learner in the form of recalled rules applicable to the problem. They also came from the external situation in the form of verbal cues employed to guide thinking in the proper "direction."

Word Problems in Arithmetic

Some of the most familiar problems to generations of children and adults are word problems in arithmetic. At the same time, this is the kind of problem that clearly illustrates how rules are applied and some of the conditions that favor their correct application.

For the application of basic addition and subtraction facts, Riley, Greeno, and Heller (1983) have identified three types of word problems: those requiring "change," "combine," and "compare." (There are also subordinate types.)

A *change* problem might be the following:

John had 8 marbles
Then he gave some marbles to Ben
Now John has 3 marbles
How many marbles did he give to Ben?

A *combine* problem might read as follows:

John and Ben have 8 marbles together
John has 3 marbles
How many marbles does Ben have?

A *compare* problem has the following form:

John has 8 marbles
Ben has 5 marbles
How many more marbles does John have than Ben?

The difficulty of these types of problems varies considerably and differs with the school grade of the children. The *change* problem, for example, is performed correctly by at least three-quarters of children in grades K and 1 and by 100% of those in grades 2 and 3. The *combine* problem, in contrast, is done correctly by less than a quarter of the kindergartners, and reaches 100% performance only in grade 2. The *compare* problem shows a similar pattern of correct performance: 17% in kindergarten and increasing to 100% in grade 2.

What kinds of knowledge and skills must young students have in order to solve such word problems? Evidently, some intellectual skills are prerequisite to the performance of tasks such as these. (Riley, Greeno, and Heller call these skills "action schemata.") For instance, the children must already know such skills as (1) identifying a set of objects of specified amount, such as a set of eight objects belonging to John; (2) adding a given number of objects to an existing set; (3) removing a number of objects from a set; and (4) counting all the members of a set. In addition, there are some prerequisite *comparing skills*, such as (1) matching a set of objects with a subset of a different set; (2) separating a subset from a set of objects; and (3) identifying and counting a remainder.

Still another kind of component knowledge, however, is essential if successful solving of word problems is to be done. Evidence from a number of studies of children's problem solving (Riley, 1981; Siegler and Klahr, 1982) clearly shows that prerequisite skills, essential though they are, are not sufficient to assure successful solution. It appears that another necessary kind of knowledge is what is generally called "problem understanding." That is to say, students must have acquired a way of systematically representing the relations among the concepts and rules they know. A formal way of representing such understanding as a *schema* is shown in Figure 9.3. A way of reading this figure is as follows:

"If the Change causes an Event on the Quantity of an amount possessed by Joe, causing a decrease in Joe's amount, the result is a Quantity belonging to Joe which is a new amount."

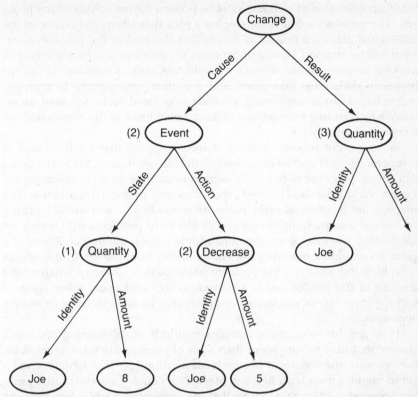

Figure 9.3 A schema on change in quantity. Joe's original amount of 8 is decreased by 5. (From Riley, M. S., Greeno, J. G., and Heller J. I. Development of children's problem-solving ability in arithmetic. In H. P. Ginsburg [ed.], *The development of mathematical thinking*. New York: Academic Press, 1983. Reproduced by permission of the copyright owner, Academic Press).

Several things may be noted about this "problem understanding." It conforms well to what is called a *schema* as an interrelated and interlinked set of concepts. The representation of Figure 9.3 is of a schema for "change in quantity of objects possessed by a designated person." A second point to be noted is this: The problem schema does not itself include the intellectual skills previously mentioned. It does not represent learner action in the sense that a rule does, although, to be sure, it includes concepts such as "quantity," "amount," and "increase." These concepts are interconnected in a syntactically meaningful fashion, that is to say, their relationships may be represented by propositions. This kind of knowledge is *verbal information*. It is clear, then, that solving problems requires learner competence not only in intellectual skills but also in the kind of verbal information that is organized in schemata that represent "problem understanding." Obviously, different kinds of problems, whether concerned with "change" or "combine" or "compare," must be represented by different problem schemata.

Still another kind of element must be present for the solving of any problem. The problem solver must employ a *plan* that allows the choice of the intellectual skills ("actions") to assure that the goal of the problem statement will be attained. Having understood the problem and having access in working memory to the necessary intellectual skills, a selection of the appropriate skills must take place, and also their arrangement in a proper order; for example, separating a subset may need to be followed in sequence by counting a remainder. Making a plan involves the employment of a *cognitive strategy*.

For successful problem solving, it would appear that a fourth kind of competence must also be possessed by the learner (Gagné, 1983). The problem solver who desires to insure success must have a way of *validating the answer*. Various kinds of learned capabilities may perform this function. The simplest are intellectual skills (rules), an example of which would be using an inverse operation. In the context of the word problems with which we are dealing, the inverse operation to adding a given number of objects to a given set would be removing the same number from the set. In this way of "checking the answer," the problem solver simply observes whether the amount of the original set is achieved. In this and many other kinds of arithmetic problems, validating the answer may be done by using an inverse operation.

There are, however, more complex methods of validating a problem's answer that may require more than a set of prerequisite intellectual skills. For example, the statement of a problem may indicate that John received a gift of marbles from both Ben and Mary. From such a statement, the problem solver should be able to infer that the number of marbles being sought as an answer is greater than those that Ben had and also greater than those that Mary had. Suppose that these latter quantities are 7 and 4. Then the problem solver should be able to reject immediately any trial answer such as "6." The conclusion of an invalid answer in this case is reached, not by applying the intellectual skill of an inverse operation, but by a crude sort of *estimation* procedure. Schemata that make estimation possible, then, provide other examples of learned capabilities that may be employed in validating the answer.

In summary, studies of children's behavior in solving word problems reveal important information about the kinds of learned capabilities that must be possessed by learners if they are to solve such problems successfully. Here is a list of these problem-solving essentials:

1. *Intellectual skills* in the form of rules for mathematical operations are required. In the simple kinds of problems we have discussed, examples are (1) removing a given number of objects from a set, (2) counting all the members of a set. It is usually assumed that these rules are possessed as prerequisite skills. Problems cannot be solved without them.

2. *Problem schemata* that represent understanding of problems (in the sense of interpretations of problem statements) are necessary. A different schema is appropriate for each kind of word problem, whether the latter type is "change," or "compare," or "combine." Generalizing to problems of greater complexity, one can suppose the need for schemata for problems of time and distance, for elapsed time, for cumulative hours of work, for discount purchases, and so on.
3. *Planning strategies*, obviously one kind of cognitive strategies, are needed to enable the problem solver to select and put in proper order the intellectual skills that will achieve the goal of the problem statement.
4. Another kind of schema, or sometimes *intellectual skills*, may be required to carry out a validation of the answer. This kind of activity surely has importance to problem solving if the learner is to be assured of success. The function of procedures based upon these capabilities is simply to eliminate wrong answers arrived at when the problem solver gets "off the track" in making use of the three previously listed intellectual resources. Validating the answer, in one way or another, is the kind of action that brings the problem-solving procedure to a close.

Knowledge and Strategies in Problem Solving

As these examples show, the solving of problems requires intellectual skills as a basic necessity. Beyond these, however, are (1) thinking processes called cognitive strategies, and (2) a set of schemata, or meaningfully connected elements of verbal information related to the problem.

Schemata: organized problem information.   The importance of verbal information that provides an understanding of the problem has been demonstrated many times. The kind of schema that enables a learner to relate the components of the problem in a meaningful manner to more general concepts appears to be the sort of knowledge that is important in the solution of problems of many types (Greeno, 1978a). The "task environment," which is the presentation of the problem itself, must be represented in what Simon (1978) refers to as a "problem space," the learner's own representation of the problem. Investigations of the solving of physics problems by experts and novices (Larkin, et al., 1980) show clearly that the former are able to bring to bear a large and complex body of knowledge in problem solving. In contrast, novices tend to deal with one narrow conception after another, abandoning each in turn when solutions are not achieved. Clearly, the difference between experts and novices does not lie in the quality of reasoning they exhibit; novices at physics are thinking well within the confines of their knowledge. The advantage to the expert physicist lies in the sets of rich schemata that are relevant to the problem and its interpretation.

Cognitive strategies.   The other kind of learned capability essential to successful problem solving is the cognitive strategy that makes possible the use of the appropriate techniques (intellectual skills) at the right time and in the right order. If the problems are word problems in arithmetic (Resnick and Ford, 1981), strategies must be employed to "translate" verbal statements into specific mathematical expressions. Other strategies (such as using the properties of the decimal system in multiplication) may be employed in computation. If the problems are in plane geometry (Greeno, 1978b), strategies may be used to advantage that help the learner determine the order in which axioms are to be employed. If the problem pertains to application of the laws of motion (Reif and Heller, 1982), strategies functioning as "heuristic rules" are appropriate. There are "description rules" for describing the problem situation, "decision rules" providing advice about when to use particular principles, and "implementation rules" about how to use the relevant knowledge.

Some investigators of human problem solving find evidence that cognitive strategies may be even more general in their applicability than those task-specific strategies mentioned in the previous paragraph. A number of suggestions about the *general* kind of cognitive strategy have been made. Examples are (1) analyzing the present state of the problem and comparing it with the goal, called "means-end analysis"; (2) decomposing the task into subtasks, called "subgoal decomposition"; and (3) solving by "working backward" from the goal. Other examples have been described in the previous chapter.

THE NATURE OF PROBLEM SOLVING

Research studies of problem solving have variously shown the importance of three kinds of learner capabilities in problem solving:

1. *Intellectual skills*, the rules, principles, and concepts that must be known in order for the problem to be solved;
2. *Organized verbal information* in the form of schemata that make possible understanding of the problem and assessment of the adequacy of solution; and
3. *Cognitive strategies* that enable the learner to select appropriate information and skills and to decide when and how to apply them in attempting to solve the problem.

Listing these as individual capabilities, however, doesn't answer the question as to how they operate together in an integrated fashion. Nor does such a list provide an impression of their relative priority as contributors to successful problem-solving performance. This is the aspect of problem solving that is still unknown and concerning which there is continuing discussion among those who study human problem solving. This group includes those who work with *artificial intelligence* as a computer capability as well as those whose interest centers on the problem solving of human beings.

Some notion of the range and variety of views of cognitive scientists may be gained from a discussion by Newell (1980). Among the ideas about how problem solving occurs are the following:

1. *Big switch.* The problem solver has a very large number of highly specific procedures. These are intellectual skills and task-specific cognitive strategies, and they number in the tens of thousands. The problem solver also has a "discrimination net" (the big switch) used to gain access to these procedures. By rapid searching, the ones that fit the problem are selected.
2. *Big memory.* The problem solver has a large web of facts, that is, verbal information in the form of schemata. These sets of organized information enable the problem solver quickly to have access to many ideas, some of which are found relevant to the problem at hand.
3. *Weak method.* This is Newell's name for the kind of cognitive strategies that have broad generalizability. These are such general strategies as "means-end analysis," "hill climbing," "subgoal decomposition," and "hypothesize and match." Newell calls them *weak*, because even though generally applicable, they do not have much power.
4. *Mapping.* The problem solver maps the problem situation into something known. The situation, for example, may be turned into a symbolic form in which analogy or metaphor are used. Or, general ideas ("treat it like a heat-loss problem") can be mapped onto the concrete situation of the problem.
5. *Planning.* The problem solver first constructs a plan in terms of abstract but simple concepts, then uses the plan (one kind of cognitive strategy) as a guide in solving the problem. By using a simplified, familiar situation, the problem solver is able to arrive at a solution by relatively simple means.

In these accounts of the problem-solving process, we see again the different emphases given to intellectual skills, to cognitive strategies, and to masses of organized verbal information. Perhaps problems are solved because the problem solver can "switch" among a large number of fairly specific intellectual skills. Or perhaps the switching that is done makes use of the generalizing properties of language through metaphor and analogy and thus depends upon the possession of organized masses of verbal information. Then there is still the third possibility that switching is a matter of selecting appropriate task strategies, and that these become increasingly generalizable executive strategies as the problem solver gains in experience. It is difficult to choose among these accounts at the present time, given our available scientific knowledge about problem solving. In fact, it seems probable that some elements of truth are contained in each one of them.

CONDITIONS FOR PROBLEM SOLVING

By recapitulating a number of points, we can now make a summary of the conditions of problem solving.

Conditions within the learner. In order to solve a problem, the learner must be able to recall relevant rules that have been previously learned. In the pendulum problem, rules of weighting a length of wire, clamping a marking tool, wedging poles to hold up an object, and clamping two poles to make a longer one must all be recalled if the problem is to be solved. For matchstick problems, some rules governing the construction of multiple patterns need to be recalled either in "arithmetical" or "structural" terms. For arithmetic word problems, the learner must possess the necessary computational rules and be able to recall them at the proper time. Thus, so far as the individual is concerned, a problem is never solved "in a vacuum." Problem solving always depends upon the learner's previous experience, specifically on the recall of previously learned rules.

Another important requirement for problem solving is the possession of verbal information organized in appropriate ways. Sets of knowledge relevant to particular kinds of problems (such as matchstick problems, money-changing problems, or problems of congruent triangles) are usually viewed as *schemata.* When the problem situation or problem statement provides a cue that links with some element of a schema, the entire set of knowledge within the schema becomes readily accessible in the learner's working memory. As a consequence, the learner can construct a problem space that gives essential help in "thinking out" the problem. As studies comparing experts and novices have shown, the possession of such schemata make it possible for the "expert" problem solver, as opposed to the "novice," to distinguish relevant aspects of the problem situation and thus to "define the problem" more readily.

The other important internal set of conditions is the activation and use of the cognitive strategies the learner possesses and may previously have learned. These strategies are likely to show themselves as individual differences in the rapidity and ease with which problems are solved. For example, some individuals may use strategies of *search* that are more efficient than those possessed by other people and thus be able to retrieve the necessary rules more rapidly. Also, there is the possibility that the *fluency of hypotheses* may distinguish one individual from another on the basis of the facility with which rules are combined into hypotheses. Intellectual fluency factors have been emphasized by investigators of "creativity," including C. W. Taylor (1958), Getzels and Jackson (1962), and Guilford (1967), among others. Finally, there may be differences in strategies of matching specific instances to a general class, an operation performed by the problem solver in verifying the solution.

Conditions in the learning situation.   The external conditions that support processes of problem solving often consist of verbal instructions. One function of such instructions is to ask the questions that stimulate recall of relevant rules. Thus, in the pendulum problem some learners were reminded that they knew the rule for weighting a string to make a plumb line and the rule of wedging sticks together to hold up an object. These rules were readily accessible for recall when the learners entered the problem situation.

Verbal instructions that are externally provided may also be used to "guide" or "channel" thinking in certain directions. (Such guidance may, of course, be provided by the learner in self-instructions). Guidance may vary in amount or completeness, always stopping short of describing the solution. As a minimum, guidance of thinking informs the learner of the goal of the activity, the general form of the solution; this amount of guidance appears to be required if learning is to occur at all. Greater amounts have the effect of limiting the range of hypotheses entertained by the learner in achieving solution. For example, the emphasis given in Maier's "direction" instructions limited consideration to the ceiling as a locus for the hanging of a pendulum while at the same time excluding hypotheses concerning the use of a nail as a device from which to suspend the pendulum.

Problem Solving and Discovery

As we have seen, one result of problem solving for the learner is the acquiring of a new and more complex rule that combines some simpler rules. The capability thus learned does not differ in a formal sense from the rules learned under conditions described in the previous chapter. What does differ is the *nature and amount of guidance* provided by verbal instructions, which are minimal in problem-solving situations. In rule learning, the instructions include a sentence or question that verbally cues the solution, but in problem solving they do not. For example, one group of learners of matchstick problems was told to "remove the matches that serve a double function," while another group was not given this instruction. The first group may be said to have engaged in rule learning, the second in problem solving. A higher percentage of the second group was successful in achieving the higher-order rule (Katona, 1940, pp. 88, 95). Retention of the rule was also superior in this group.

Problem solving as a method of learning requires that the learners *discover* the higher-order rule without specific help. Presumably, they thus construct the new rule in their own idiosyncratic manners and may or may not be able to verbalize it once it is constructed. A study by Worthen (1968) compared an instructional method emphasizing discovery with one emphasizing expository presentation in sixteen classes of students in the fifth and sixth grades who were studying mathematical concepts over a six-week period. This investigation found the expository method resulted in superior recall of rules learned when measured immediately following the learning period. The presentation of problems by means of a discovery method, however, led to greater transfer of the rules acquired. Since the latter is the more important practical outcome, it appears that the encouragement of discovery under conditions in which problem solving is appropriate to the instructional objectives can be of great value as a teaching technique. Worthen's study is of considerable significance in view of the uncertainty of interpretation of many studies of "discovery learning" (see Shulman and Keislar, 1966) whose findings are based upon relatively brief topics.

The evidence of experimental studies concerning the use of discovery in problem solving certainly does not demonstrate that higher-order rules *must* be learned by discovery. In much adult learning, for example, the guidance provided by verbal instructions is so complete that the rule to be learned is stated verbally during the course of learning. The key to achievement of a higher-order rule does not lie solely in the discovery method. Nevertheless, the evidence strongly suggests that achieving a higher-order rule by means of problem solving produces a highly effective capability that is well retained over considerable periods of time. For example, a study by J. T. Guthrie (1967) of problem solving in cryptograms showed a marked advantage of the discovery method of instruction for transfer to a task involving new rules. This finding suggests that exploratory strategies relevant to such new learning may have been engendered by the discovery method.

The discovery method is liable to gross misinterpretation in practical learning situations. Some writers and practitioners have treated problem solving as though it could be achieved with a *minimum* of instructions and prerequisite knowledge of rules. This is obviously an incorrect point of view, as the evidence shows. College students who tried to solve matchstick problems without prerequisite knowledge of rules and without guidance were markedly unsuccessful. Similarly, students who were told only the goal of problem solving for the pendulum problem without being reminded of subordinate rules and without "direction" were unable to solve the problem. Problem solving, or discovery, is only the final step in a sequence of learning that extends back through the many prerequisite learnings that must have preceded it. To be successful, problem solving must be based on the prior attainment and recall of the rules that are combined in the achievement of the solution—the higher-order rule. Of course, a problem may be set up that is "beyond" the individual learner in the sense that none of the subordinate rules have been acquired. Thus the learner must learn these rules in order to achieve a solution. Under such circumstances a problem may happen to be solved on certain occasions and in particular individuals; but to advocate such an approach as a practical learning method makes no sense.

To summarize, discovery or problem solving involves the combining of previously learned rules into a new higher-order rule that "solves" the problem and generalizes to an entire class of stimulus situations embodying other problems of the same type. Problem solving occurs when the instructions provided the learner do not include a verbally stated "solution" but require the construction of such a solution "on one's own." When this happens, the individually constructed higher-order rule is effective in generalizing to many situations and is, at the same time, highly resistant to forgetting. But the capability acquired by this means does not appear to differ in a fundamental sense from that acquired when instructions include the statement of a "solution" (unless, of course, the latter is learned simply as a verbal chain). What is learned in either case is a higher-order rule based upon some previously learned simpler rules.

Problem Solving and Creativity

No one can fail to stand in awed admiration of the great intellectual discoveries of history—Newton's laws of motion, Kepler's principles of planetary movement, Einstein's general theory of relativity. Equally awe-inspiring are artistic creations in painting, sculpture, music, and literature, which have also been generated by individual discovery. What do these remarkable achievements of genius have to do with problem solving as described here?

A great scientific discovery or a great work of art is surely the result of problem-solving activity. The solution to a problem, we are told, often comes to thinkers in a "flash of insight," although they may have been turning the problem over in their minds for some time. As problem-solving behavior, these creative acts are based on a tremendous amount of previously acquired knowledge, whether of the "public" sort known to science or the "private" sort known to the artist. Many creative thinkers testify that they have previously immersed themselves deeply in the subject matter of the problem, often over considerable periods. Indeed, it would be strange if they had not done this. Nothing in such testimony supports the idea that there is anything very different about problem solving that leads to discoveries of great social import. The act of discovery, even in the relatively predictable sense that it occurs in everyday learning, involves a "sudden insight" that transforms the problem situation into a solution situation. As we have seen, everyday discovery also requires that the learner have previous knowledge of the rules involved in the solution.

But the major discovery, in contrast to the common garden variety, involves a feat of generalizing far beyond what may be expected in the usual learning situation. There is an "inductive leap," a combining of ideas from widely separated knowledge systems, a bold use of analogy that transcends what is usually meant by generalizing within a class of problem situations. An excellent example of such inventiveness is provided by the kinetic theory of gases. What was known, on the one hand, was a set of principles concerning the behavior of gases; the relations among the variables of temperature, pressure, and volume. On the other hand, there were the laws of motion; the effects of force in imparting acceleration to objects of specified mass. The stroke of genius in this case was the hypothesis that the gas was composed of particles (molecules) that had mass and whose reactions to force could, therefore, be considered to obey the laws of motion. From this single new synthesizing idea—this remarkable higher-order rule—the consequences follow that permitted the confirmation of the theory. But the central idea was arrived at by putting together subordinate rules from two widely disparate systems of organized knowledge. A problem of this magnitude had to be solved by combining two sets of rules that originally seemed to have only the remotest connection with each other.

What has learning to do with creative discovery? The most obvious and dependable answer is that discoveries of great social importance have been made by people with a great store of intellectual skills. These persons have acquired many kinds of hierarchies of rules. They have been deeply immersed in the rules of the discipline within which they work and, often, in the rules of other disciplines. How did they learn these rules? Just as everyone else does: by combining sets of subordinate rules partly (perhaps) with the aid of verbal instruction and partly by making the "small" discoveries involved in the acquiring of the higher-order rules of any particular topic or system of intellectual skills.

Some scholars feel that this relation between learning and Discovery with a capital *D* is quite incomplete. Kestin (1970), for example, describes learning that involves discovery as a process of "bisociation," following Koestler (1964). In discovering solutions to problems, according to this conception, the learner's thoughts jump from one domain of rules to a second quite different domain, forming a link ("bisociation") between the two that leads to a new understanding. The instructional implication of this view is that in fostering creativity the teacher must create favorable grounds on which bisociations can flourish. Bruner (1966) appears to hold a similar view in his emphasis on varied and challenging problems as basic elements of a curriculum. Because this method is rich in reinforcement value, the solving of problems by students may well contribute to their love of learning and "thirst for knowledge." However, it is by no means certain that this kind of learning will predispose the learner to become a "creative" thinker capable of making a great contribution to science or art. As a method for acquiring the necessary skills and strategies, "practicing discovery" is not necessarily the antecedent variable involved in the production of genius (see Ausubel, Novak, and Hanesian, 1978, pp. 579–587).

SOME EDUCATIONAL IMPLICATIONS

Educational programs have the important ultimate purpose of teaching students to solve problems—mathematical and physical problems, health problems, social problems, and problems of personal adjustment. We have seen in this chapter that there are two primary sources of human capability that can contribute to problem solving. First, there are the intellectual skills, the concepts and rules, that form the fundamental structure of the individual's intellectual competence. Rules that have previously been learned are searched for in memory, retrieved, and brought to bear upon novel problems. Problem-solving activity results in the learning of new and more complex "higher-order" rules, which themselves are stored in memory for future application.

Much of the activity of problem solving is internally guided, and "learning by discovery" is typical of this form of human behavior. Accordingly, the teacher's task is mainly one of finding and organizing appropriate problem-solving situations. Problems for students are most effective when they are (1) novel, in the sense of presenting unfamiliar situations, and (2) within the students' capabilities, that is, their previously learned skills and knowledge.

Successful problem solving also depends upon the learner's possession of organized verbal information relevant to the problem being encountered. Most commonly, the useful set of information forms a schema, an interconnected and meaningfully related set of ideas specifically relevant to the type of problem presented. Often, several schemata may be related to the problem at hand, and the learner may have to choose among them, trying first one and then another. Knowledge in the form of a schema enables the learner to interpret the problem situation (or statement) and so to construct a "problem space" within which previously learned rules can be brought to bear.

A third and equally important category of human capability that makes problem solving possible is the internally organized skills that modify the learner's own processes of learning and thinking. These are *cognitive strategies*. In modern information-processing theories of learning and memory, they are called *executive control processes*. They serve to select, modify, and control the processing carried out by the learner in attending, perceiving, encoding, retrieving, generalizing, and organizing responses—all of the phases involved in a learning act. Many cognitive strategies have been identified that are "task specific." Thus, there are strategies that have particular application to arithmetic problems in time-distance-velocity; others that apply to problems in plane geometry; still others to physics problems of rotary motion. Beyond these particular types, investigators of human thinking continue to search for cognitive strategies that are highly general, in the sense that they are applicable to many different kinds of problems.

Of the three types of capability involved in problem solving, intellectual skills are of course indispensable, since the problem cannot be solved without the application of appropriate rules. Beyond this, it is not possible at present to give the different capabilities priority ranking in their contributions to problem-solving. It may be that a large number of specific intellectual skills are most characteristic of successful problem solvers. It may be that large and intricate masses of verbal information are most important. Or the possession of highly general cognitive strategies may confer the crucial advantage in the attainment of success in problem solving.

Educational programs are usually designed to teach all three types of capabilities: intellectual skills, verbal information, and cognitive strategies. The uncertainty that continues about the relative importance of these outcomes of learning for problem solving would appear to argue for balanced curricula and varied instructional content. It does not appear to be a wise course for schools or other educational programs to emphasize the learning of one of these types of capabilities at the expense of others, even though such action is not infrequently urged. Practice in solving problems of many kinds is bound to be helpful in producing good human thinkers. Such practice may probably best be conceived as making it possible for learners to bring to bear their entire repertoires of knowledge, skills, and strategies.

GENERAL REFERENCES

Problem Solving

Gagné, R. M. Problem solving. In A. W. Melton (Ed.), *Categories of human learning.* New York: Academic Press, 1964.

Johnson, D. M. *A systematic introduction to the psychology of thinking.* New York: Harper & Row, 1972.

Lawson, A. E. (Ed.), *The psychology of teaching for thinking and creativity.* 1980 AETS Yearbook. Columbus, Ohio: ERIC Clearinghouse for Science, Mathematics, and Environmental Education, 1979.

Newell, A., and Simon H. A. *Human problem solving.* Englewood Cliffs, N.J.: Prentice-Hall, 1972.

Tuma, D. T., and Reif, F. *Problem solving and education.* Hillsdale, N.J.: Erlbaum, 1980.

Wickelgren, W. A. *How to solve problems.* San Francisco: Freeman, 1974.

Knowledge and Skills in Thinking

Chipman, S. F., Segal, J. W., and Glaser, R. (Eds.), *Thinking and learning skills: Current research and open questions.* Hillsdale, N.J.: Erlbaum, 1984.

10

Motor Skills

Many important human activities require the coordination of muscular movements. Some acts of this nature—such as reaching, grasping, and following moving objects with the eyes—are acquired very early and appear to be determined largely by response patterns that are innate. Others, often incorporating these basic patterns of movement, must clearly be learned at early ages; examples are projectile throwing, using food utensils, shoelace tying, and the pronunciation of language sounds. Many motor performances, for instance, eating or dressing, are necessary for an individual's self-maintenance and survival. We learn a great many motor skills in early life and seldom think much about them thereafter. Yet they stay with us and are put to constant use throughout our lives.

By the time of kindergarten age, motor performances that children learn begin to have a definitely forward-looking purpose. The children need to learn to execute the motor acts that will serve them again and again in many future situations. Arrangements are made, therefore, for children to learn motor skills pertaining to clothing themselves: getting limbs into sleeves and legs, buttoning, zipping, typing, and so on. Children continue to learn the motor patterns of communicable speech. They learn the basic bodily control activities of balancing, running, jumping, throwing. And they begin to acquire some "fine" motor skills that involve manipulation of the tools of written communication, such as pencils and crayons.

Once the skills for these motor performances have been learned, the emphasis in school learning shifts progressively to tasks of a more intellectual cast. The student now uses these fundamental motor skills in the performance of other activities—singing songs, playing games, writing words and sentences and stories. The new motor skills to be learned are increasingly complex and require the integration of simpler motor acts. The child learns to print letters and numerals, to make simple written figures like circles and squares, and to write cursive letters and words. On the playground, children learn skills of great precision, such as yo-yo spinning, rope jumping, and ball pitching. Further, these and other precision skills are incorporated into the larger and more complex activities of games, which require the carrying out of comprehensive procedures according to rules of play. Meanwhile, in the schoolroom, the introduction of new kinds of motor performances becomes less and less frequent as the students devote attention to the learning of intellectual skills and information. Children continue to use the motor skills learned previously—they print letters, draw lines and figures, voice the sounds of language, move and carry objects—all as part of more comprehensive activities that are involved in their intellectual development.

Other kinds of motor skills, however, must be learned as the individual's education proceeds. Of course, games and athletic activities become progressively more demanding in their rule complexity and in their precision of bodily movement. Aside from the objectives of physical education, motor skills are involved in a variety of school learning. The student learns to use new kinds of tools—drawing instruments, microscopes, and the typing consoles of computers. The child studying a new language may need to acquire new skills involving mouth and tongue in the pronunciation of sounds that are foreign. And then, as activities that are vocationally useful begin to be learned, the student may undertake to learn motor skills of the great variety found in sewing, cooking, welding, materials construction, equipment repair, and so on.

Motor skills, then, have a certain importance for the individual. Basic varieties of motor skills useful throughout one's lifetime are learned in early life and become a seldom-thought-of part of the individual's repertoire. These skills are nonetheless essential to daily living and survival. Many motor skills involved in the pursuit of play, sport, and organized athletic activity are essential to the maintenance of physical and mental health. Here and there specialized motor skills, such as the use of scientific instruments, are intimately involved with the pursuit of learning in the intellectual sphere. And of great significance are the motor skills that underlie the performances of vocationally useful activities.

THE STRUCTURE OF MOTOR SKILLS

The extent and variety of motor acts may be contemplated by thinking of (1) executing a dive, (2) using a typewriter, and (3) adjusting an internal part of a watch. Motor performances have in common dependence on the precision and timing of muscular movement. The acquisition of these qualities of action, precision, and timing is the primary meaning of *motor skill learning*, since these characteristics are common to all varieties of such learning. It is of some usefulness, nevertheless, to consider some major dimensions that determine differences in motor performance.

Dimensions of Motor Performance

Investigators of motor skills have distinguished three important dimensions of the motor performances that result from motor skill learning: (1) fine versus gross; (2) continuous versus discrete; and (3) open loop versus closed loop.

Fine versus gross performance. The distinction between fine and gross refers to the amount of body musculature that is involved in the perform-ance. A "gross" motor act is one that uses the large muscles and often involves the whole body. Examples are skills of swimming, jumping, playing tennis, or lifting weights. Note that such activities may also require the de-velopment of muscular strength, but this is not what is meant by the learned motor skill. The latter is confined to the precision and timing of the performances. In contrast, at the other end of the continuum, are motor skills that are exhibited in movements of wrists and fingers; these are con-sidered "fine" because they appear to require extremes of precision. Exam-ples are threading a needle, printing letters, or operating a typewriter. Man-ual skills obviously constitute a large portion of the category of "fine" motor skills, although the term is not necessarily intended to exclude other mus-cle groups. Using the vocal cords in speech or singing must surely be classi-fied in the fine motor skill category, as would be wiggling the ears.

Individual differences apparently exist with respect to the ease with which different people acquire fine and gross motor skills (Hempel and Fleishman, 1955). Studies have shown low correlations between the two kinds of performances; and this small relationship constitutes one of the main reasons for believing that the gross-fine distinction is more than a superficial one. At the same time, the conditions for learning the two types of skills have much in common, as we shall see later in this chapter.

Continuous versus discrete. A discrete motor task is typically one in which a particular movement is made in response to a particular *external* stimulus. Of course, a total task may be composed of different movements, each of which is "set off " by a different external stimulus. Reduced to its simplest form, a "discrete" task is the movement of the hand and arm in a single direction, as in the measurement of reaction time. The Discrimina-tion Reaction Time Test, used in classifying aircrew trainees during World War II, is a good example of a discrete motor task and is shown in Figure 10.1. In performing, the individual was required to make four different dis-crete movements, one to each of four switches. Each movement was made to a different stimulus: a pattern of lights that appeared on the upright panel.

In contrast, a "continuous" task is one that requires the individual to make continuous adjustments and corrections to a combination of stimuli, some of which are internal (stimulus feedback from the muscles). The movement that results may be a continuous one, although this continuity may result from frequent adjustments in the correction of slight over- and underreactions (Poulton, 1957). An example of a continuous motor task is provided by another aircrew classification test called the Rotary Pursuit

Figure 10.1 The Discrimination Reaction Time Test, an example of a task requiring discrete motor performances. (Adapted from Fleishman, E. A. *A factorial study of psychomotor abilities.* Research Bulletin TR-54-15. Lackland Air Force Base, Tex.: Air Force Personnel and Training Research Center, 1954.)

Test. This task has been studied extensively in psychological laboratories for many years. It is shown in Figure 10.2.

The plastic disc with an inserted flush metal "target" rotates at 60 RPM. The performer follows the movement of the target with a stylus, attempting to maintain electrical contact between the metal tip of the stylus and the target. The resulting skill is a continuous, smooth movement of the arm and wrist, timed so as to correspond to the speed of the target in its revolution.

Figure 10.2   The Rotary Pursuit Test, an example of a task requiring continuous motor performance. (Adapted from Fleishman, E. A. *A factorial study of psychomotor abilities.* Research Bulletin TR-54-15. Lackland Air Force Base, Tex.: Air Force Personnel and Training Research Center, 1954.)

Closed-looped versus open-looped tasks.   A "closed-loop" skill is one that depends entirely upon internal feedback from the muscles as guiding stimuli. Such a task can be performed with the eyes closed. Making a smooth, continuous movement in a particular direction with the arm would be an example; performing the rotary movement of the Rotary Pursuit Test "in the air" while blindfolded would constitute a closed-loop skill. The rapid free-hand drawing of a large circle on the blackboard comes close to being a closed-loop skill, since the movement is not adjusted in response to the external appearance of the line as it is being drawn.

Most practically useful motor tasks have some open-loop characteristics, that is, their responses are influenced to a greater or lesser degree by external stimuli. The printing of letters is obviously largely influenced by the stimuli provided by the lines as they appear on the paper. Catching a ball, jumping a hurdle, making a dive are athletic skills that are obviously dependent upon the presence of external stimulation for their proper and precise performance.

Some kinds of open-looped skills are controlled in part by stimulation that must have the form of an intellectual plan distinct from muscular feedback. Such is the case with the skills of piano playing and typewriting. In these instances, the discrete individual movements occur with rapidity that is too great to allow for correction based upon feedback from the muscles. The attainment of skill in such activities can apparently not be accounted for on the basis of a simple "linking" of specific motor movements. Instead, it seems reasonable to suppose that the individual must acquire "executive routines" (Welford, 1968) or "motor programs" (Keele, 1968). A comparative review of theories of motor learning, containing a discussion of these issues, is provided by Singer (1980).

LEARNING MOTOR SKILLS

There are many kinds of human performances. They not only involve different portions of the body musculature but also bring into play a variety of internal processes. Since any performance is assessed (at least ultimately) in terms of *overt* action, some aspects of the performance are bound to be "motor." Yet we do not customarily consider that any action that results in muscular movement (such as recording the answer to a problem in addition) has involved the learning of a motor skill. It is necessary, therefore, to address the question of when and under what circumstances motor performances are to be considered as instances of *motor skill learning*.

Another related matter is that skilled motor performances often occur as parts of larger units of human action that may be given the general name of *procedures.* Putting an automobile into motion from a state of rest is a procedure. If we examine this procedure, or any procedure, as a sequence of actions, we find that some of the component actions may indeed require skilled motor performances and that one or more of these performances may require the learning of motor skills.

Focusing on the single motor skill, most investigators have become aware that learning typically progresses through certain *stages*. The performances exhibited by a novice and an expert differ most apparently in the observable degrees of precision, smoothness, and timing. In addition to this apparent change in the motor performance, however, are other evidences of changes in the quality of the skill as it is progressively mastered. These changes imply shifts in the kind of internal processes that control the motor performance. And these changes have definite implications for the learning of motor skills, which are reflected in the conditions of learning to be discussed later in this chapter.

Human Performance

Overt performances of human beings, often used as evidence of learning, take many forms. They may involve the entire body, as in running, jumping, swimming, or skating. They may require the movement of primarily one limb, as in turning a crank with one's arm. Very often, performances are executed with the primary involvement of a single hand and its fingers, as in writing, printing, or operating a small calculator. Other parts of the body may participate in a performance, as when the vocal cords and throat are used in forming language sounds.

It is evident that except for special purposes, we do not depend upon overt motor action for an identification of the type of human performance we wish to observe or examine. A student may be asked to "make a sentence using the word 'exemplary.' " The performance (if oral) obviously involves the use of mouth, tongue, and vocal cords in forming and uttering the speech sounds that make up a sentence. Yet we do not consider that the student's performance is "motor," or that it has involved the learning of a motor skill. Similarly, a student may use the hands and fingers to manipulate a pencil in recording the answer to the multiplication problem: 12 × 7 = ☐. We look upon this behavior as the exhibition of an intellectual skill but not as a motor skill.

Motor skill learning, then, cannot be identified simply by observing the overt motor performance of the learning. This means that it is of critical importance to observe what the learner is able to do *before* learning as well as afterward. In order to infer that a motor skill has been learned, we must first see what the learner's "entering behavior" is. The student who is learning to use the word "exemplary" in a sentence is *already* able to form the necessary words in speaking the sentence. The student who is performing multiplication already knows how to print the necessary numerals on a piece of paper. Although these performances are motor, the learning of a motor skill has not occurred. Of course, we know that at some time in their lives, perhaps much earlier, these students actually had to learn the motor skills that make possible the motor performances of speaking words and writing numerals. But the identification of newly learned motor skills must be done by considering the aspects of *motor* performance that are new and that were not present *before* learning began.

Even when tasks are deliberately designed to require motor action, the motor skills that must be learned may be minimal. This is the case, for example, with a task like the Discrimination Reaction Time Test (Figure 10.1). This test requires the learner to make rapid movements to any one of four switches. But to a considerable degree, the motor skills of pressing switches (forward, backward, to the left, or to the right) have already been learned and are well established. What, then, is being learned as the learner is given practice in responding to this device? The name of the task provides the answer—the learner is acquiring *discriminations* (or a *multiple discrimination,* since four stimuli and four responses are involved). Some degree of motor skill learning may take place in which the learner acquires greater precision and speed in pressing the switches of the device. But the amount of performance improvement attributable to this "motor learning" is minimal. The primary task is learning stimulus pattern 1 → response to switch 1, stimulus pattern 2 → response to switch 2, and so on.

Evidence that discrimination learning, rather than motor learning, is the primary component in such a task may be found in the results of an experiment by Gagné and Foster (1949). They used a four-switch task with switches and light patterns arranged somewhat differently from those of the Discrimination Reaction Time Test, but which was otherwise similar. Learners were given practice on the discrimination learning task before they attempted to learn the task with the actual device. Practice was provided in a paper-and-pencil form on a pictured representation of the lights and switches. The motor responses for this discrimination-learning task consisted simply of marking positions with a pencil on paper, a procedure very different from the responses required in pressing switches. Following practice in discrimination learning, the learning of the light-switch task was undertaken. The transfer of learning was very great, amounting to 80%. Only a few trials of practice were needed for these learners to achieve a degree of mastery on the final task comparable to that of skilled performers who had not learned the "pictured" task first. It is quite clear, therefore, that the major component learned on this device is not a motor skill but the simple intellectual skill called a multiple discrimination.

Similar conclusions can often be reached by analyzing more complex human performances. Running the bases of a baseball diamond is obviously a motor performance. Yet to a large extent, the motor skills involved are already present in the novice baseball player. They consist of running rapidly in an approximately straight path from one position to another, which the rookie already knows how to do. If additional motor skills are acquired, they must consist of touching bases with the foot, "rounding" a base, coming to a stop with foot on base, and other skills of this nature. Undoubtedly, these motor skills are learned as the player progresses from novice to expert status. The important point to be made, however, is that in identifying motor skills to be learned, one must first have a clear idea of what the "entering behavior" is—of what has already been learned. It would be best not to think of base running as a "motor skill," but as a total performance that involves the learning of several component motor skills.

Procedures

The running of bases is an example of one of many kinds of human performances that may be called *procedures*. While procedures that result in overt action are motor performances, they do not always require the learning of (new) motor skills. An order clerk, for example, may need to learn how to fill out a newly introduced order form, with coded symbols for the consignee, method of payment, stock numbers, and so on. The completion of this form may require that entries be made in a certain sequence and that various intellectual operations (subtraction, matching, and so forth) be carried out along the way. The overt actions required may include printing, making check-marks, filling blanks, or stamping with a rubber stamp. Obviously, though, motor skills do not have to be learned by the clerk, since the skills that make possible these performances have been learned long ago and practiced for many years.

What is learned when the capability of performing a procedure is acquired? A procedure is in fact an *intellectual skill*, often a *rule* determining sequence (a *sequential rule*), with which certain subordinate rules are also associated. In filling out a form, the sequential rule controls the order in which actions are taken—the date is entered first, the name of the consignee next, the code for the type of goods next, and so on. The total procedure may also require the use of subordinate rules, for example, when a step requires that a subtraction rule be applied to "current balance" to find "amount due." Sequential rules are not new or strange entities; for example, the intellectual skill of long division obviously involves a sequence-governing rule along with other subordinate rules for factoring, subtraction, and so on (see Chapter 6).

What is new at this point is our consideration of procedures made up of steps involving different motor performances that in turn may or may not require the learning of new motor skills. An example is provided by the procedure of parking an automobile parallel to a curb. An analysis of this procedure is presented in Figure 10.3.

The procedure itself is seen to consist of a *sequence of rules:* first, the car must take a position about a foot away from, and in line with, the vehicle in

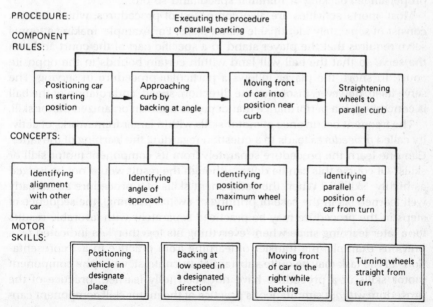

Figure 10.3 The procedure of parallel parking, analyzed to show the major component rules, concepts, and the motor skills on which it depends.

the next forward parking space. As a next step in the sequence, the car must be backed at an angle of 35 to 40 degrees, at low speed. Then the front wheel must be turned sharply so that the car will approach a position near the curb. And as a final step, the front wheels must be straightened so that they are parallel to the curb, while backing the car at minimal speed is maintained. The rules that constitute the procedural sequence can be seen to require certain subordinate concrete concepts to be identified (position of the car, for example). Most importantly, though, the execution of the procedure requires the possession of certain *motor skills*, indicated in the bottom row of Figure 10.3.

Evidently, then, the procedure of parallel parking is one that includes a number of component skills, some of which are intellectual skills (such as identifying the "lined-up" position of the front of the car), whereas others are motor skills (such as backing the vehicle at minimal speed). Shall we call the whole procedure a "motor skill"? That would be only approximately correct, although it is often done. Preferably, it should be identified as a procedure. It is sometimes called a motor skill because, in contrast with certain other procedures, the major new components to be learned are motor skills. In this case, the procedural components that are intellectual skills (lining up the car, estimating a backing angle, and so on) are likely to already have been fairly well learned. The skills to be learned and brought to a stage of reasonable mastery are the motor skills—turning the car to a proper angle, backing at minimal speed, and so on.

Most sports activities are also composed of procedures, which in turn consist of separately identifiable motor skills. For example, making a tennis serve requires that the player stand in a specific part of the court and aim the serve so that the ball will land within certain bounds in the opposite court. In short, the player follows a particular procedure in serving. The serve itself, however, insofar as the direction, speed, and rotation of the ball is concerned, is a performance that depends upon an organized motor skill.

The frequent occurrence of motor skills within larger frameworks of activity called *procedures* leads to a question regarding the learning of the latter. Can one learn the procedure separately from its component motor skill or skills? Of course this can be done, although the result would not be judged as highly "skillful." When the component skills of a procedure are already well learned (as in the case of printing or switch pushing), the sequence of steps in the procedure may be practiced separately, with favorable results for a later learning stage when "everything fits together." As indicated by a previous example, the transfer of learning from practice in a "representation" of the task may be quite substantial. In contrast, when the component motor skills of a procedure have not been fully learned, practice of the procedure *without* simultaneous practice of the motor skill component cannot be expected to contribute very much to the learning of the total activity.

These various examples lead to a number of conclusions about the learning that underlies human activities of a motor sort. Many practical motor performances involve separately identifiable *action steps*. Sometimes, these action steps are arranged sequentially (as in parking a car); sometimes, the individual steps are chosen as alternatives (as in the choice of which switch to press). Each action step may be a motor performance previously well learned, or it may be a performance for which a motor skill must be newly learned. The total performance is often spoken of as a *total skill*. It is noteworthy that a total skill has the characteristics of a *procedure* and that its components may be called *part-skills*. The learning of the procedural aspect of a performance results in the acquisition of what is sometimes called a *movement plan* (Singer, 1980) or an *executive subroutine* (Fitts and Posner, 1967). Part-skills may be learned and practiced separately as motor skills, but integrating them into practice for the total skill is essential.

The Acquisition of Skill

The course of learning for a motor skill depends, among other things, upon the task to be learned: the nature and length of the procedure, the type and number of part-skills that compose the total skill. If the component motor acts of a total skill have been previously well learned, a minimal amount of time may have to be spent in "putting them together" in a procedural sequence. Conversely, if the component motor skills have not been learned to the point at which they exhibit adequate precision and timing characteristics, further practice on the procedure by itself will not yield added proficiency. In the latter case, additional periods of learning devoted to part-skills, to the total skill, or to both will be required.

Practice.   Surely, the most obvious feature of motor skills is that they improve with practice. That is, the movements that make up the desired performance attain greater precision and more appropriate timing characteristics as the performance is practiced. By "practice" is meant the repetition of the procedure (1) with intent on the part of the learner to achieve an improved performance, and (2) with "feedback," which provides information to the learner. Repetition of the motor act without these two conditions is not normally meant by the word "practice"; learning under such negative conditions is essentially nil.

The effects of systematic practice on the acquisition of motor skill are shown in performance on the Rotary Pursuit Test (previously described), in Figure 10.4. In fifteen practice trials, a steady improvement in learning is shown, with a gradual decrease in amount of improvement from trial to trial. It is notable, however, that small variations in this general trend occur, even when the curve is based upon the average performance of 403 learners, which is the case with Figure 10.4. After fifteen 20-second practice periods, learning is still going on, and it appears that performance improvement would not slow appreciably for many practice trials.

Typically, the *learning curve* for a motor skill exhibits a rapid rise in proficiency during its early portion, with a gradual tapering off of improvement as practice proceeds. The curve is a negatively accelerated one, which appears to approach an asymptotic limit. Sometimes, the learning curve for a motor skill has an initial portion of gradual improvement before the period of rapid acceleration. This initial portion can usually be attributed to the necessity for learning the procedure before the effect of practice in increased motor precision can show itself.

Why is practice necessary for the learning of a motor skill? We have seen that practice is not a factor that considerably affects the learning of rules or of factual information. Yet we do not expect that shooting baskets or print-

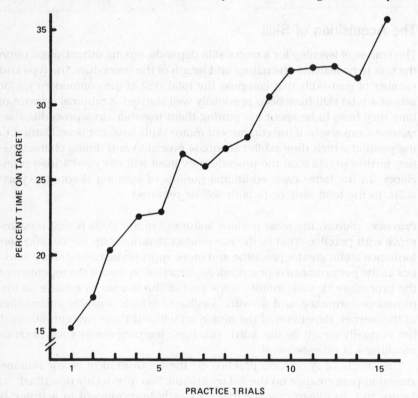

PRACTICE TRIALS

Figure 10.4   A learning curve for the Rotary Pursuit Test, showing the change in average performance of 403 learners during fifteen practice trials each of 20 seconds duration, with 10 seconds rest between trials. (Data from Melton, A. W. [Ed.], *Apparatus tests.* Army Air Forces Aviation Psychology Program Research Report No. 4. Washington, D.C.: 1947.)

ing letters or turning stock in a lathe can be adequately achieved without practice. The reason appears to lie in the nature of *stimulus control* for motor skills. The desired movements must be cued by stimuli that are only partly outside the learner. Some very important stimuli (cues) are internal to the learner and arise as feedback from the muscles. As we have seen, this is true when the motor skill to be learned is of the open-loop sort as well as when a closed-loop skill is to be learned. By repeating the essential movements in successive trials of practice, the learner is discovering the kinesthetic cues that signal the difference between error and error-free performance. In addition to the external cues, these internal cues come to control and regulate the performance and thus lead to increasing degrees of precision and timing accuracy. Practice is necessary, then, because only by repeating the essential movements can the learner be provided with the cues that regulate the motor performance. As practice proceeds (with suitable feedback), internal cues leading to error are progressively rejected, and internal cues associated with performance smoothness and precision become established and retained as regulators of skilled performance.

Improvement of motor skills with practice is often gradual, and the more difficult it is for the learner to detect the "correct" internal kinesthetic cues, the slower learning occurs. A *New Yorker* cartoon once depicted a golfer who had just completed a drive that placed the ball inches from the cup. Her remark was, "I wish I knew what I did right!" Thus a golfer may be aware of her difficulty in detecting the exact set of cues to posture and swing that have resulted in an excellent performance. The likelihood is that many more trials of practice, some good and some bad, will be needed before the internal stimuli that control the good performance are established as regulating cues.

There is much evidence to indicate that improvement of motor skill can proceed with continued practice for very long periods of time (Fitts and Posner, 1967). For example, Crossman (1959) made a study of the speed with which cigar-makers completed the manufacture of a cigar on a hand-operated machine. The workers had varying amounts of experience, some as much as seven years. Gradual increases in skill occurred for at least four years or during the time workers were producing an estimated two million cigars. Similar findings concerning continued gradual improvement in motor skills over long periods of practice have been obtained with a variety of practical and laboratory tasks (Stevens and Savin, 1962).

Feedback in Motor Skill Learning

Several kinds of feedback of information are available to learners of motor skills through their various senses. Of particular importance in the learning of skills are the two types that come to the learner as a result of his or her own efforts (Singer, 1980).

When an individual shoots a ball at a basket, one type of feedback is provided by the kinesthetic sense—the "feel" provided by receptors in the muscles when the response is executed. This is the kind of feedback whose timing is such that the learner can modify the action while it is occurring. The total performance occurs slowly enough to allow the feedback to be processed before the motor act is completed. In other words, this kind of feedback is used to accomplish smoothness of the performance.

A second form of feedback arises from the observation of the learner that the ball has either reached the basket or has missed by some distance. Obviously, this kind of feedback is also effective in modifying the muscular movement, but this must happen to a subsequent action and not to the one that produced the observed result. Some motor skills (such as swatting a fly with the hand) are performed so rapidly that response-produced information cannot influence the performance while it is occurring. In those cases, the learner uses the feedback from visual observation of the results to detect and correct errors and thus to influence a subsequent performance of the skill.

A third kind of feedback is called *augmented feedback* and is provided by a source other than those arising from the learner's own efforts. Such feedback is often referred to as *knowledge of results*, to imply that the information is usually given by an outside source (Singer, 1980). This source may be a teacher or coach who is providing information to the learner about incorrect or partially incorrect responses. In certain games (for example, bowling or darts) automatic devices may be used to provide precise augmented feedback. In general, this kind of feedback tends to improve the performance during the time it is supplied. In some situations, it has also been shown that performance can be maintained when the "extra" knowledge of results is removed. Of course, the augmented feedback must be taken away at an appropriate time in order for the skill to be properly executed and to "stand on its own feet."

An interesting practical example is provided by a device known as a Golf-Lite, described by Mathews and McDaniel (1962). A small light attached to the shaft of a golf club is powered by a battery in the player's pocket. The light projects a bright spot on the ground, and permits the golfer to receive visual feedback on the direction and accuracy of a swing, with reported improvement in the acquisition of skill. Smode (1958) studied the performance of learners on a tracking task that required keeping a moving needle centered on a scale by rotating a dial. One group of learners was provided after each practice trial with information about their time on target. The other group was given augmented feedback by viewing a counter that accumulated the time on target as it occurred during each trial. This second group attained considerably higher proficiency scores than did the first group. The time-on-target scores were 63% versus 51% after eleven practice trials. Furthermore, the advantage for the augmented-feedback group was retained as greater skill; the group's performance remained better on a second day, when it was tested without the presence of the counter.

School learning tasks may also take advantage of augmented feedback to speed the learning of motor skills. An example is the use of specially prepared guides to the printing of letters. When the child's hand movement departs from the form of the desired letter, a carbon impression shows the nature and extent of the "error." Thus, immediate feedback is given during the practice trial as opposed to after the total letter is completed. Such a device appears particularly useful during the early stages of acquiring the skill.

Combining Part-Skills into Skilled Procedures

We have seen that individual motor skills often occur within larger units of activity called procedures. Learning motor skills, in a general sense, often means combining part-skills into these larger units. Procedures to be executed in a particular order are often considered to require the learning of *behavioral chains.*

When one says to a novice driver, "Now start the engine," one is asking for the execution of a learned behavior chain containing several component skills. If the training of the driver has been successful, what will take place is the reinstatement of a sequence something like this: S ("Start the engine") → R (looking forward and to the rear) . . . S (sight of clear road) → R (testing for gear in neutral) . . . S (gear in neutral) → R (turning key to activate starter) . . . S (sound of motor catching) → R (release of key) . . . S (key released) → R (depressing accelerator). Each of the individual acts in the chain is something that the learner knows how to do. What must be learned is to get them done in the proper order.

There are many varieties of sequential procedures. Sometimes the linked components are intellectual skills, as in the operations of long division; sometimes the components are entirely motor skills; but most often, both are involved. T. F. Gilbert (1962) describes the analysis of several varieties of procedural chains. He indicates how such an analysis can simplify the requirement for learning a procedure such as multiplication with the slide rule. Gilbert's derivation of learning principles from these analyses emphasizes several points. One is the desirability of learning a chain by beginning with the final "link" and working backward in order to ensure that each newly learned act is optimally reinforced. Another is the importance of making each link as distinctive as possible in order to reduce the tendency for "competition" (or interference) to occur among them. When tendencies to interference exist, preference in learning practice should be given to links most prone to competition. Verbal mediators (that is, extra verbal cues) also have the effect of reducing competition by increasing the distinctiveness of the component links of a chain.

CONDITIONS FOR LEARNING MOTOR SKILLS

Motor skills that are practically useful are frequently complex. They may be composed of a number of unitary part-skills, which themselves are made up of different body and limb movements. Single motor skills often occur as components of procedures such as parking a car, making a tennis serve, or drawing a square.

As a consequence of this complex structure, the learning of motor skills during periods of practice appears to emphasize the establishment of different aspects of skilled capability in several *phases*. Fitts and Posner (1967) distinguish three main phases of learning:

1. *Early, or Cognitive, Phase.* The beginning learner attempts to "understand" the task and what it demands. The instructor provides verbal guidance directing the learner's attention to the proper sequence of actions and also to the external cues that signal the start of each subordinate movement. During this stage, previously acquired part-skills (subroutines) are selected by the learner and put together into the required procedure. The primary consequence of this phase is the learning of an *executive routine*; in other words, the *procedure*. Fitts and Posner (1967) identify this learning of a procedure as "cognitive." The intellectual skill guides the entire complex of subordinate movements.
2. *Intermediate, or Associative, Phase.* During the intermediate phase of learning practice, two kinds of change typically take place. First, part-skills not previously brought to high degrees of smoothness and timing are achieving these qualities. Second, unitary subskills are being integrated into the total skill in the sense that competing responses (interference) are being eliminated. Actually, separate practice is sometimes given to achieve these two learning effects. Part-skills may be practiced separately, before or alternately with the total skill. An example is the crawl swimmer's separate practice of the kick and the head movements associated with breathing, alternating with practice of the total skill. For some skills, part-skill practice may be advantageous in terms of total-skill learning. This seems particularly true when the components of the skill are independent (Fitts and Posner, 1967). When part-skills must be coordinated to achieve the total performance, however, practice in the total skill is usually a more efficient learning procedure.
3. *Final, or Autonomous, Phase.* During the final phase of learning, the motor skill becomes less subject to interference from other ongoing activities. The procedural steps no longer need to be initiated by cues supplied by the learner; that is, the learner no longer needs to "think of what to do next." The skill becomes *autonomous*, which means that it can be executed while the individual is engaged in other activities (such as conversing or solving intellectual puzzles). Improvements in smoothness

and precision of the skill continue to take place as practice continues, although at a continually decreasing rate.

This account of motor skill learning, derived from observations of learners during practice, and also from interviews with skill instructors (Fitts, 1964), implies that the conditions for learning motor skills must take cognizance of the *different* primary outcomes of these three phases of learning.

Following our general plan, we proceed here to describe the internal and external conditions that lead optimally to the learning of motor skills.

Internal Conditions

Recall of part-skills.   A new motor skill is typically assembled from part-skills, some of which have been previously learned. Even the execution of a "simple" skill such as the drawing of a square by a child requires that the part-skills of holding the pencil and making directional marks on paper be employed. For an adult learner, a skilled procedure such as removing the wheel from an automobile involves the part-skills of fitting a wrench to a nut, loosening a nut by turning, and so on. Often, part-skills have been learned and practiced over many years. In order that a total skill be learned, these component skills must be recalled. That is to say, the internal cues that set each part-skill into motion must be retrieved and made accessible in the working (short-term) memory. Of course, some of the part-skills of a total motor skill may have to be newly learned. As we have said, this new learning may be done by separate practice of a novel part-skill or as a part of the practice provided for the total skill.

It is important to note that previously learned part-skills, depending on their nature, may actually interfere with the learning of new skills. Thus a previously well-learned relationship such as that between a light located on the *left* of a panel and a response to the *left* may have a low degree of "compatibility" with a new skill that requires a response to the *right* to the same left-located light. Considerable variations in the difficulty of learning new skills of varying degrees of compatibility with old part-skills were demonstrated by Fitts and Seeger (1953). Previously learned part-skills are completely incompatible with new skills when all of the relationships between stimuli and response movements are reversed; and this condition results in *negative transfer* (Lewis, Shephard, and Adams, 1949).

Recall of executive routine.   The execution of a motor skill involves a pattern of movements, often a sequence of movements. This *procedure* must be recalled as a movement plan during the second phase of motor skill learning when increasing smoothness and precision are being acquired. For example, a bowler who is practicing a skill follows a procedure of positioning the ball, approaching the release line, selecting an aiming point, imparting a twist to the ball, and so on. This executive routine must be learned by a novice during an early phase of motor skill learning, as Fitts and Posner (1967) suggest. It is actively retrieved and employed in the working memory during the intermediate phase of learning. The learner must continue to "think of what is being done."

External Conditions

Verbal instructions.   Verbal instructions have an important but limited role in the learning of motor skills. In the early phase of learning, when the executive routine (movement plan) must be acquired, verbal instructions can provide the cues for procedural steps. The instructor tells the novice driver to "line the front of your car with the front of the forward car," "turn your wheels so that the car will back at a 40-degree angle," and so on. As learning proceeds, the learner may rehearse these verbal instructions in short-term memory. They are stimuli, initially external, that guide the learner as to "what to do next."

Verbal instructions have a second function that is sometimes of considerable importance: they can operate to increase the distinctiveness of external cues (Ellis, 1965). Thus, in responding to the light patterns of the Discrimination Reaction Time Test (Figure 10.1) or similar tasks, the learner is aided by verbalizing the relationships between patterns of lights and response directions (as in saying to oneself "red-left, green-right" or similar appropriate word phrases). This effect may be conceived as a *mediational* function of verbal self-instructions (T. F. Gilbert, 1962). Of course, these instructions may originally have been provided by the instructor as part of the external conditions of learning.

Pictures.   Pictures of the movement involved in a motor performance, whether still or moving, may serve functions similar to those of verbal instructions. Often pictures can accomplish these purposes more effectively than words can. Diagrams that depict for children the separate steps in the procedure of printing an *E* may be more effective than a verbal instructional sequence, which they may have some difficulty retaining in their short-term memories. In motor tasks undertaken by adults, pictures may provide an effective medium for the presentation of procedural sequences to be learned and remembered, as in knot tying (Roshal, 1949) and operating a cutting press (Lindahl, 1945).

Pictures can also aid the learning of motor skills by directing the learner's attention the the external cues for the control of motor responses. This function is served, for example, by training in the identification of the "correct sighting picture" in rifle firing at a target (Gagné and Fleishman, 1959, p.

249). During the intermediate stage of motor skill learning, the selection of appropriate external cues is an event of considerable significance to the attainment of increased performance precision (Singer, 1980).

Demonstrations. Actual demonstrations of the execution of a motor performance, when observed by learners, can serve functions similar to those of pictures. The "motor plan" (Singer, 1980) or the steps in the sequence of movements comprising the executive routine (Fitts and Posner, 1967) can be acquired by learners as they observe the act of a skilled performer.

Interestingly, learners may accomplish a substantial amount of motor skill learning by engaging in *mental practice* after watching a demonstration of the motor performance. Usually, such practice in actively imagining the movements involved is most effective when the learners have had some initial experience with the motor act, followed by mental rehearsal For example, Clark (1960) found that mental practice of basketball foul shots was nearly as effective as physical practice in producing a moderate amount of skill. Mental practice has been found to have some effectiveness when employed in connection with the learning of many different types of motor skills (Richardson, 1967).

Practice. An essential part of externally arranged conditions for the learning of a motor skill is provision for repeated *practice* of the motor performance. As we have seen in previous sections, a motor skill is typically acquired in a gradual fashion; and increasing degrees of smoothness, timing, and precision of movement are acquired in successive practice periods. The effects of practice are presumably a result of the progressively greater precision with which stimuli, both external and internal, come to exert control over the responses of the learner.

Periods of practice naturally alternate with periods of no practice, or "rest." Thus practice may be *distributed* or *massed*. *Continuous*, or *massed*, practice typically has the effect of depressing the level of performance, which then recovers during any subsequent rest period. The effect of massing seems to be confined to this phenomenon of "performance inhibition." So far as learning is concerned, massed practice has not been shown to be inferior to distributed practice. A number of studies (for example, Whiteley, 1970) have shown that the performance of learners under massed-practice conditions recovers, following a rest, to the level of performance of learners given distributed practice. It appears, then, that the amount of practice, rather than its "distribution," is the important variable in determining the level of learning achieved. Of course, practical considerations such as avoiding learner fatigue and lowered motivation need to be considered in planning practice sessions. Reasons such as these may favor the "distribution" of occasions for practice or at least the avoidance of extreme "massing."

Feedback. Practice in the sense of repeated movement contributes to learning only when learners receive feedback from their performance or its results. Thus, one of the most important external conditions for the learning of a motor skill is the provision of *informative feedback* that provides reinforcement for the motor performance. It is evident that some feedback is *intrinsic* to the motor performance, when the "feel" of the movement is right. Feedback may also come from direct observation, as when the archer sees the arrow hit the target or when the basketball player sees the ball going into or out of the net.

Informative feedback may also be furnished externally in a supplementary form as *augmented feedback* supplied by a device or by an external observer. Generally, it has been found that augmented feedback that adds to the precision or improves the immediacy of knowledge of results is beneficial to motor skill learning (Singer, 1980, pp. 455–458).

EDUCATIONAL IMPLICATIONS

Although not the most highly visible part of the curriculum of schools, the learning of various kinds of motor skills nevertheless has a definite part to play in education. In the primary grades, motor skills are involved in many personal and social activities as the child learns to manipulate clothing, articles of furniture and equipment, and other physical objects. In addition, basic tool skills such as printing, cursive writing, drawing, and the pronunciation of language are essential motor skills that have long-term uses and implications for further school learning. In grades beyond the elementary, motor skills occupy a less important place in the curriculum, but they are present in the manipulation of the implements of science, in the playing of musical instruments, and in many activities of a vocational nature such as mechanical drawing, and wood and metal working. And, of course, motor skills are prominent in all physical education and sports activities.

In designing instruction for motor skills, it is of considerable importance to recognize that they are more than merely "muscular" in nature. Very often, even usually, motor skills occur as components of *procedures*, involving either choices of alternative movements or sequences of movements. In its totality, a procedure is an intellectual skill, since it is a complex combination of rules. Executing the procedure may be a matter of using these rules in a certain order; and in doing so, the individual must employ the motor skills that comprise the desired activities. For this reason, the learning of a complex procedure requires that a *motor plan*, or *executive routine*, be acquired at an early stage. Children do not learn to print an *E* simply by seeing the model of an *E* or by practicing random movements with a pencil. Somehow, they must acquire the executive routine that organizes the individual vertical and horizontal pencil-strokes that make a printed *E*.

Various kinds of external stimulation may be employed to guide the learning of a motor skill. Verbal instructions may be given; pictures or actual demonstrations may be used. By means of such "guidance," two functions are accomplished. First, the executive routine may be learned and "internalized" either as an image or as a verbal sequence. Second, pictures or demonstrations serve to highlight the external cues that partially control the desired motor responses. The model of an *E*, for example, shows the middle bar to be shorter than the top and bottom bars and thus provides an external stimulus that guides the learner's performance. The model of the correctly spoken French word *rue* provides guidance for the performance of the motor skill of pronouncing words containing the "u" sound.

External stimuli play an important (but limited) role in the learning of motor skills. Crucial stimulation is provided by internal feedback from the muscular movement itself. This internal stimulation makes possible the attainment of precision, smoothness, and timing that characterize high levels of skill in motor performances. To obtain and utilize the control of this internal stimulation, the learner must engage in *practice*. By this word is meant repeated attempts to execute the correct movements, followed in each case by *informative feedback*. Periods of practice, interspersed with periods of "rest," bring about continued improvement in the motor performance; and the improvement may go on for long periods of time as the practice continues.

The essentiality of practice to motor skill learning should not be generalized to other activities. "Practice makes perfect" is not a bad principle so far as motor skills are concerned. But the same requirements for practice do not apply to the learning of other capabilities such as intellectual skills, information, and attitudes. For these types of performances, practice does not have the meaning of "repetition of a set (or sequence) of overt responses." Nor is their learning characterized by the gradual improvement that is so typical of motor skills. The teacher, therefore, must think of arranging suitable periods of practice when motor skills are to be learned; but quite a different set of conditions are implied by "practice" in the learning of other capabilities.

GENERAL REFERENCES

Motor Skill Learning

Cratty, B. J. *Movement behavior and motor learning.* Englewood Cliffs, N.J.: Prentice-Hall, 1973.

Fitts, P. M., and Posner, M. I. *Human performance.* Monterey, Calif.: Brooks/Cole, 1967.

Keele, S. W. *Attention and human performance.* Pacific Palisades, Calif.: Goodyear Publishing Co., 1973.

Singer, R. N. (Ed.), *Readings in motor learning.* Philadelphia: Lea & Febiger, 1972.
Singer, R. N. *Motor learning and human performance,* 3rd ed. New York: Macmillan, 1980.
Stelmach, G. E. (Ed.), *Motor control: Issues and trends.* New York: Academic Press, 1976.

Motor Learning and Physical Education

Cratty, B. J. *Teaching motor skills.* Englewood Cliffs, N.J.: Prentice-Hall, 1973.
Lawther, J. D. *The learning and performance of physical skills,* 2nd ed. Englewood Cliffs, N.J.: Prentice-Hall, 1977.
Singer, R. N., and Dick, W. *Teaching physical education.* Boston: Houghton Mifflin, 1974.

11

Attitudes

In addition to the capabilities that underlie various kinds of performance, learning also results in the establishment of internal states that influence the individual's *choices of personal action*. These outcomes of learning are called *attitudes*. Their relation to the behavior of the individual is somewhat less direct than is the case with capabilities like intellectual or motor skills. Attitudes do not determine particular actions; rather, they make certain classes of individual action more or less probable. For this reason, attitudes have often been described as "response tendencies" or as states characterized by "readiness to respond." A valuable definition which has withstood the test of time is Allport's (1935, p. 810): "An attitude is a mental and neural state of readiness, organized through experience, exerting a directive or dynamic influence upon the individual's response to all objects and situations with which it is related."

The indirect (or complex) relation that attitudes have with human action means that their attainment and their modification pose difficulties for assessment. It is not easy, in other words, to be sure that one is measuring a change in attitude as a result of learning rather than of something else. In addition, it appears that the conditions for learning attitudes are more complex than the conditions pertaining to other kinds of learned internal states. Nevertheless, there can be little doubt, as Allport's definition suggests, that attitudes are established and "organized" by learning.

Historically, attitudes have been considered to constitute the basic core of the discipline of social psychology. Consequently, they are often exemplified with a "social" orientation—as in "attitude toward religion," "attitude toward marriage," or "attitude toward Jews." In the very extensive research literature on attitudes, social themes are prominent; that is, the "situation" in which the attitude is detected and the "object" at which it is directed are often defined in social terms. Regardless of this focus, however, it is generally recognized that the meaning of attitudes is quite broad and need not be restricted to the social realm. A lathe operator, for example, may display an "attitude of precision" toward a task, in which the object of the attitude is a steel rod. An "attitude of carefulness" toward situations not directly involving other human beings may be possessed by a farmer, a hunter, or a housepainter. Attitudes need not be social in their orientation, although many of them are.

Most of our attitudes are learned incidentally rather than as a result of preplanned instruction. Conditions that form and modify attitudes surround the individual constantly, from birth onward. As a young child, a person acquires attitudes toward parents, brothers and sisters, other children, and adults. The child's experiences lead to attitudes toward animals, such as cats, dogs, snakes, spiders, and insects. Some of the attitudes acquired early in life are remarkably persistent and resistant to change. Usually as a result of family living, the young child also acquires attitudes related to sharing possessions, keeping promises, helping people, and making truthful statements. From association with playmates, the child may also acquire attitudes of cooperation, competition, compromise, and "fair play," as well as combativeness and vengeance.

Social institutions conduct various kinds of activities primarily aimed at the establishment of attitudes. Families may be very deliberate about the instruction of children in the "virtues" of trustworthiness, promptness, cleanliness, politeness, and helpfulness. In carrying out family chores or work tasks, the individual may encounter intentional feedback supporting attitudes of "good workmanship" and "perseverance." Religious organizations, of course, spend a great deal of time and effort on planned educational programs designed to establish desirable social attitudes such as those embodied in the Ten Commandments and the Golden Rule. And the attitudes that various manufacturers wish us to learn are very apparent from the product advertisements we see and hear.

Although many different attitudes are acquired in the home, in the church, and in the neighborhood, there is a definite expectation that some attitudes will be learned or strengthened in the school as a result of deliberate planning (Gagné, 1984). Actually, it has always been considered appropriate for the school to undertake the establishment of attitudes. If there has been a change in recent times, it consists in the *kinds* of attitudes that are thought to be appropriate or inappropriate as objectives of the curriculum. In an earlier age, "reverence toward God" was considered an appropriate attitudinal goal of the school as well as the home and the church. But this objective is no longer deemed appropriate by some for the public school curriculum. In an earlier age, education in "manners" (attitudes of courtesy) was thought to be primarily a responsibility of the family; nowadays a great deal more dependence is placed upon school education for the establishment of such attitudes.

Planned objectives of attitude learning, whatever their specific nature, are definite components of educational programs for children and adults. The curriculum is said to include an *affective domain* (Krathwohl, Bloom, and Masia, 1964); this term emphasizes the "feeling tone" of these learned internal states. The kinds of attitudes to be established sometimes become the subject of controversy between school and community or even within the community itself. At the same time, many attitudes appropriate for school learning would hardly be controversial. Here, for example, is a list of such attitudes, many of which are suggested by Klausmeier (1975, p. 375):

Respect for the individuality of others
Acceptance of responsibility for one's own actions
Positive liking for a given subject matter
Positive attitude toward classmates
Positive attitude toward the teacher
Enthusiasm for work
Promptness in beginning schoolwork
Taking care of own and others' property
Cooperation in working with others
Courtesy to others
Carefulness in observing safety rules

Despite differences in opinions about which attitudes are legitimate and which are of high priority to adopt as curriculum objectives, educators seem in substantial agreement about the importance of attitudes in educational programs of all sorts. They generally recognize that attitudes of a social nature, such as those pertaining to personal violence or the use of harmful drugs, play a critical role in the operation of our modern society and affect the quality of life for all individuals in that society. If desirable attitudes could be identified, agreed upon by the community, and taught as part of educational programs, a better quality of life would presumably be insured. The major hitch in such a plan involves that difficult objective, "community agreement."

THE NATURE OF ATTITUDES

There is much disagreement about the nature of attitudes. We shall be unable here to resolve these differences in points of view and can only describe them in general terms. It will be apparent from this discussion that we are not so concerned with what attitudes *are* as with what they *do* in the lives of the individuals who possess them. In addition, our discussion naturally emphasizes how attitudes are acquired and changed by the processes of learning.

Three Aspects of Attitudes

Attitudes are generally agreed to encompass three different aspects, which may be investigated separately or together (Triandis, 1971). These features are (1) a *cognitive* aspect, pertaining to the ideas or propositions that express the relation between situations and attitudinal objects (as in "automobiles use too much gasoline"); (2) an *affective* aspect, pertaining to the emotion or feeling that accompanies the idea; and (3) a *behavioral* aspect, pertaining to the predisposition or readiness for action (such as the action of purchasing an automobile having a high miles-per-gallon rating).

Generally speaking, these aspects are considered to characterize the internal states that are the learned attitudes. In other words, each such state has an affective, or emotional, component; a cognitive component; and an "action-tendency," or behavioral, component (Rosenberg and Hovland, 1960). Differences among theories of attitudes pertain to questions about which of these components is primary or which is a cause of the others. Many theorists hold that discrepancies in "beliefs" (cognitive component) result in attitude change (for example, Festinger, 1957). Others emphasize the learning of emotional (affective) responses to stimulus objects by conditioning (Staats and Staats, 1958). A third and different view maintains that attitudes follow from the individual's self-perception of behavior (Bem, 1970). Actually, there is evidence to support each of these viewpoints, and it is difficult to choose among them. For purposes of considering how attitudes function, such a choice may not even be necessary.

The cognitive component.   Most theoretical accounts of the origins of the cognitive component of attitudes adopt the basic premise of the "need for consistency." It is postulated that human individuals strive for consistency in their own thoughts, beliefs, attitudes, and behavior. Various forms of this theory, including those emphasizing "balance" (Heider, 1958), "symmetry" (Newcomb, 1961), and "dissonance" (Festinger, 1957) have been given critical reviews by Kiesler, Collins, and Miller (1969). The basic idea is that when an inconsistency or dissonance among beliefs is encountered, the individual strives to achieve consistency and in this process may undergo a change in attitude.

In a well-known study (Kelman, 1953), whose results can be interpreted in accordance with this principle, children were offered prizes for writing essays favoring a particular type of comic book, which they actually did not prefer. When the essays had been written and the prizes received, it was found that the comic books they had praised in the essays were rated higher in attractiveness by the children. One way of viewing these results is to say that the children experienced dissonance (inconsistency) when they undertook to praise comic books they did not originally favor. Several ways of achieving consistency can be imagined—for example, the provision of some large external reward, or approval from the teacher. These justifications for writing favorable essays were not available to the children in this study. Consequently, consistency was achieved by a change in attitude in favor of the comic books they praised in their essays.

The affective component.   Evidence that attitudes are accompanied by positive and negative "feelings" derives largely from introspective accounts. A few studies, however, have shown changes in emotional states to accompany changes in attitudes, as revealed by physiological measures. For example, Rankin and Campbell (1955) measured changes in the galvanic skin response of experimental subjects when an experimenter entered the room to adjust the apparatus. The experimenter was either black or white. Changes in skin resistance (a typical emotional measure) were shown to be related to measures of racial attitudes obtained from a questionnaire. Other studies that have found relationships between physiological measures and reported attitudes include those of Westie and de Fleur (1959), Staats, Staats, and Crawford (1962), and Porier and Lott (1967).

Attitudes vary from "positive" to "negative." According to Triandis (1971), these positive and negative tendencies represent *two* dimensions rather than only one. The most obvious quality is the behavioral tendency of *seeking* versus *avoiding* contact (with the person or other object of the attitude). The second dimension pertains to "affect," to *liking* and *disliking*. Thus an attitude may reflect seeking contact, when the individual is willing to pay money to attain the contact; such an attitude is "positive" in both the seeking and the affective dimensions. Suppose, though, that the attitude is positive in seeking contact but seeks this in a wish to *destroy* the object. The latter represents a negative value of the affective component of the attitude.

The behavioral component.   An attitude is defined as a disposition or readiness for some kind of action. What is the relation between the attitude and the actual behavior of the individual possessing that attitude?

The classic study of this question was done by La Piere (1934). He traveled through the United States with a Chinese couple, stopping at 66 different hotels and motels and dining at 184 restaurants. Service was refused only once during this entire trip. Six months later, letters were sent to the hotels and restaurants visited and the same letters to a similar "control" group, which had not been visited. Of the replies received, 92% indicated that they would not furnish service to Chinese guests. Thus the result showed a marked discrepancy between attitudes expressed in the letter replies and the actual behavior exhibited.

Many other studies have been performed that illustrate the same basic trend: an absence of any high degree of relationship between attitudes as reported by responses to questions and actual behavior (Triandis, 1971). There are several possible reasons for this finding. The first is that attitudes, as customarily measured, are simply not the same as behavior; and such a relationship should not be expected. The situation of responding to a letter about Chinese guests contains many elements that differ from the situation of being confronted with an actual Chinese couple seeking accommodations. The two situations involve very different response thresholds, as Campbell (1963) has pointed out. Another way to say this is to state that social behavior is largely *situationally determined,* and attitudes play only a limited role in regulating behavioral outcomes.

A second reason for a small degree of relationship between measured attitudes and behavior derives from the methods used to assess attitudes and pertains to the *validity* of such measures. Very often, attitudes are assessed by asking people to respond to verbal statements on scales that indicate dimensions of like-dislike or favorable-unfavorable. The statements themselves, however, may refer to *other people's* behavior rather than to the behavior of the individual whose attitude is being tested. For example, it is not uncommon to find statements such as the following on a questionnaire assessing attitude toward religion:

A person who goes to church is likely to have a good moral character.

Agree __ __ __ __ __ Disagree

Conflicting doctrines of the church make religion confusing to the average person.

Agree __ __ __ __ __ Disagree

Statements such as these, and others like them, are commonly used to assess attitudes—the attitude "score" is obtained by accumulating values of responses indicating degree of agreement with each statement. Obviously, such measures are indeed indirect so far as the individual's *own choices* of action are concerned. Scores based on such instruments can tell us an individual's opinions about other people's behavior, but not about his or her own. Part of the reason, then, for the lack of correspondence found between attitude measures and behavior may well be the lack of validity of the attitude measures.

As a first step to achieving validity in attitude measures, efforts may be made to insure that the printed statements used for assessment describe *choices of personal action.* Items of this sort were used originally by Bogardus (1925) to assess attitudes toward people of different nationalities, yielding a measure of what he called "social distance." The questions used asked people to indicate, with reference to different nationalities, whether they would (1) marry a member of the group, (2) have members of the group as close friends, (3) work in the same office as a member of the group, (4) have members of the group as speaking acquaintances, (5) exclude members of the group from the nation. The development of scales of social distance was pursued further by Triandis and Triandis (1960), and led to the development of the Behavioral Differential (Triandis, 1964), which measures the "behavioral intentions" of people toward any person or category of persons. This method employs items that first give a description of the person to be judged (the attitudinal object). A series of scales describing choices of personal action follows, each of which is to be checked as to likelihood of choice. For example:

A 50-year-old black minister

would __ __ __ __ __ __ __ __ __ would not
obey this person

would not __ __ __ __ __ __ __ __ __ would
ask this person for advice

would __ __ __ __ __ __ __ __ __ would not
invite this person to dinner

Informative studies concerning attitudes toward persons of various nationalities have been carried out by Triandis and his associates using this method (see Triandis, 1967). Factor analyses of these results have indicated the existence of certain *dimensions* of attitude, which have been named as Respect, Marital, Friendship, Social Distance, and Superordination. Perhaps the most important point of this research, however, is the possibility of making a more or less direct assessment of behavioral intentions. In other words, the method provides *content validity* for the assessment of *choices of personal action*. The same kind of assessment could readily be applied to "objects" other than people of various nationalities. For example, attitudes toward chemistry as a college subject might be assessed by a number of items, including:

would __ __ __ __ __ __ __ __ __ would not
elect this subject as a major

would not __ __ __ __ __ __ __ __ __ would
drop the course if I could without penalty

The Scope of Attitudes

The objects of attitudes, as we have seen, may be classes of persons (such as Asians), or events (such as parades), or physical objects (such as auto trailers). Such object classes may be large and inclusive or small enough to contain only a single member. Does this variability in the scope of attitudes give us any clue as to how to delimit them? And if not, is there a way of conceptualizing how large or small an entity an attitude is?

Personal action.   A clue to the problem of attitude scope may be provided by the results of the factor-analysis study of Triandis (1964), based upon assessments of choices of statements describing *personal action* toward certain nationalities. It is notable that the items of this attitude measure that tended to be highly correlated were those that pertained to certain classes of personal action, which were given names such as Respect, Friendship, and Superordination. Friendship, for example, was indicated by items that asked about (1) being partners in an athletic game, (2) eating with the person, (3) gossiping with the person, (4) accepting the person as an intimate friend. Superordination, as a distinct class, pertained to (1) treating the person as a subordinate, (2) commanding the person, (3) obeying the person, and (4) criticizing the work of the person.

Thus it appears that, regardless of the size of the class of objects to which the attitude refers, the kind of personal action delimits the scope of an attitude in the sense of defining a *consistent unit*. A unitary attitude is one defined by a *class of personal action* toward some category of objects, persons, or events.

The implication is that one cannot legitimately conceive of single attitudes such as "attitude toward Mexicans" or "attitude toward school" or even "attitude toward Calvin Coolidge." The size of the object class does not determine the unity of the attitude; instead, the singleness of an attitude is determined by the class of personal action that it influences. An instrument that purports to measure "attitude toward school" can be analyzed to reveal several different unitary attitudes: personal actions of *traveling* to school, of *associating with* schoolmates, of *interacting with* the teacher, of *doing* school assignments. Thus, an assessment instrument that includes all of these types of personal action actually measures a *collection of attitudes*.

Of course, it may be the case that what is wanted in assessing the outcomes of an instructional program aimed at changing attitudes is a measure of change in a collection of attitudes rather than in a single attitude. An attitude questionnaire that measures such a collection would then be perfectly appropriate. If one is concerned, however, with the question of *validity* (that is, with what has actually been learned), the recognition that single attitudes are definable in terms of classes of personal action is an important one.

Attitudes and Values

Values are often spoken about in the same breath with attitudes. Some investigators make no distinction between these two words, and this is perhaps the simplest point of view to adopt at the present moment. Others consider that *value* is a name given to a social attitude that enjoys widespread societal acceptance. Examples of such attitudes would be "respect for the law," "reverence toward God," and the Golden Rule. Different societies, of course, exhibit and reward different choices of personal action reflected in such values (Ringness, 1975).

Internalization of values. A widely held view of the relationship of attitudes and values is that the former may be arranged on a continuum that represents increasing degrees of *internalization* ranging from those that are lightly held to those that are strongly valued (and therefore highly resistant to change). This is the view described by Krathwohl, Bloom, and Masia in the *Taxonomy of Educational Objectives, Handbook II: Affective Domain* (1964).

The most lightly held attitudes, according to this conception, fall into the general category of personal action called Receiving. An example of *willingness to receive* is "accepting differences of race and culture, among people known." Increasingly greater degrees of internalization of attitudes are indicated by the categories of Responding and Valuing. *Preference for a value*, for example, is indicated by the kinds of action reflected in the descriptions "assumes an active role in current literary activities" and "writes letters to the press on issues he feels strongly about."

Still greater degrees of internalization of attitudes are indicated by the categories of Organization and Characterization by a Value Complex. Since more than one value may be relevant to a situation, values become organized, first, by being conceptualized and later by being formed into a value system in which some are more dominant than others. At the peak of the internalization process a generalized set and a characterization of values is attained that is reflected in the development of conscience, codes of behavior, and a philosophy of life.

During the course of individual development, different kinds of values, perhaps exhibiting differing degrees of "internalization," may become evident from the individuals' choices of personal action. Kohlberg (1966) has described six stages of moral development covering ages from childhood to adulthood. A brief summary of these stages, categorized in three levels, is as follows:

I   *Preconventional level.* Stage 1 is "the punishment and obedience orientation," in which choices of action depend upon the physical consequences of the action. Stage 2 is called "the instrumental relativist orientation"; choices are made that satisfy the child's own needs and occasionally the needs of others.

II *Conventional level.* In stage 3, attitudes are characterized by "the interpersonal concordance or 'good boy-nice girl' orientation"; a tendency to act in ways that please or help others and bring their approval. Stage 4 is "the 'law and order' orientation," leading to choices in accordance with authority and fixed rules.

III *Post-conventional, autonomous, or principled level.* Stage 5 is described as "the social-contract legalistic orientation, generally with utilitarian overtones"; in this stage, there is consideration of general individual rights and accepted societal standards. Stage 6 is "the universal ethical principle orientation," in which right actions are chosen in accord with self-selected ethical principles (the conscience).

While Kohlberg considers that such stages represent increasing degrees of maturity, he points out that moral development is not automatically achieved, and that some adults do not attain the highest level. It follows, therefore, that the more mature attitudes need to be a part of what is learned as children grow into adults.

Moral education.   Education in the realm of morality aims at the development of *moral character* rather than simply a change in attitude in a narrow or temporary sense. A number of dimensions of character have been identified by Hogan (1973). The latter are as follows:

1. Socialization, as shown by behavior conforming to the established moral code.
2. Empathy, indicated by an understanding of other people's behavior and an appreciation of their feelings.
3. Autonomy, the tendency of the individual to make moral choices consistent with his or her integrity as a person.
4. The ethics of personal conscience, or the ethics of personal responsibility.

Presumably, then, it is stable individual characteristics like these that represent the aim of "character education" in educational systems. It is difficult to identify the social forces, institutions, and experiences that affect such development in the human individual, for they are many. One can realize, however, that the foundations for these stable character dimensions begin with the instruction for the young child in the family environment and in the early school grades. Relatively simple, commonly occurring social situations can establish the attitudes that, when reinforced over a period of time, eventually become part of the individual's character. For example, the parent or teacher can exhibit the action choices of a human model in conforming to a prevailing moral code when the child is confronted with the question of respecting another child's property or "turn" in a game. Likewise, the influence of the human model on an attitude of empathy can be exhibited in a social situation such as the hitting or kicking of another child Of course, as the individual grows older, the moral decisions to be made become more difficult. Their basis, however, remains in the concrete situations in which a variety of human models are seen to make choices of action.

Beliefs, Emotions, or Behavior?

The functionally important conceptions that may be derived from the voluminous literature on attitudes appear to be those of a *learned internal state* that influences *choices of personal action* toward some class of objects, events, or persons. Such a state possesses "affective," or emotional, components that have not figured largely in the characterization of the attitude except in the generally recognized accompaniments of "good or bad feeling." An attitude also has a cognitive component, reflected in the conceptualization of principles that guide or influence action choices.

Some investigators conceive of attitudes almost entirely in cognitive terms, as "systems of beliefs" (Rokeach, 1969) or categories of concepts and their attributes (Kelly, 1955) or ideas arising from dissonances in other ideas (Festinger, 1964; Zajonc, 1960). Different communications of ideas that convey partially conflicting information are evidently integrated by an "averaging" process, as shown in a study by N. H. Anderson (1973). Surely the cognitive organization of attitudes is an important problem. It is a problem most readily approached by using systematic variations in the kinds of *verbal statements* people are asked to select or respond to when attempts are made to assess their attitudes. But the widespread use of the questionnaire with its propositional statements should not mislead us to conclude that these propositions are themselves attitudes.

Beliefs and ideas and the conflicts among them may be convenient descriptions of the cognitive components of the internal states called attitudes. They do not seem to be adequate, however, to account for the dynamic effects that attitudes have in their influence on the choices of action made by the individual. This latter characteristic of attitudes (sometimes called "behavioral") is their most illuminating feature.

An operational definition.   In terms of the operations of an external observer, an attitude is a state that influences or modifies the individual's choices of personal action. Such influence can sometimes be observed in actual choices exhibited in overt behavior. Acts of kindness to other children may be taken to indicate an "attitude of kindliness"; the borrowing of books from the library can be used as an indicator of "preference for reading." However, the effects of attitudes on overt behavior cannot always be observed, given a limited period of time and limited access to individuals and all their situations. As is well known, attitudes are most commonly assessed by means of responses to verbal statements contained in questionnaires, rating scales, and other instruments of this general sort (M. E. Shaw and Wright, 1967).

How should an attitude be defined in operational terms when responses to verbal statements are used as measures? Obviously, with the use of such instruments, one wishes to make the inference of an *internal state*—just as one would if overt behavior choices were being made. Assume that the individual responds to statements by indicating the "degree of agreement" or the "degree of likelihood of choice" for each one. Then a cumulative score for each attitude measured could be described as *the degree of commitment expressed to statements describing choices of personal action (of a designated type)* toward some class of objects, persons, or events. Is the inference of the internal state, using such verbal instruments, as valid as the inference made from our behavior? This would seem to depend primarily on the comprehension of the verbal statements and their meaningfulness to the individuals whose attitudes are being assessed. For most adults, the inference appears a justifiable one; for young children, it does not.

ATTITUDE CHANGE

Many of our attitudes are learned as a result of a series of interactions with other people—with parents, friends, and associates. Attitudes may be acquired or changed rather suddenly as the result of a single experience. Or they may undergo gradual change over a period of years, presumably as the result of a cumulative series of experiences.

Three major kinds of learning situations have been extensively studied as producing attitude learning. We shall describe these here as (1) classical conditioning, (2) perception of success in behavior, and (3) human modeling.

Classical Conditioning

It has long been known that conditioning of the classical (Pavlovian) sort can produce learned emotional reactions to stimuli. The study of Watson and Rayner (1920) showed that an unconditioned stimulus for "fear" (sound of striking a metal bar), when paired with a conditioned stimulus (a white rat), quickly produced a newly conditioned response (withdrawing from the rat) in a child. This fear response, with its apparent "affect," might reasonably be taken as evidence of the establishment of an attitude toward the animal. It is generally believed that certain irrational fears of childhood, such as those toward snakes, spiders, or other animals, probably arise through the accidental pairing of stimuli as in classical conditioning. Sometimes these attitudes persist for many years and are changed only with difficulty.

The establishment of attitudes by means of classical conditioning methods has been studied in experimental settings. For example, Razran (1940) showed that the presentation of a set of political slogans along with a free lunch resulted in a change to positive acceptance of these slogans, whereas presenting another set of slogans accompanied by unpleasant odors brought about a change in the opposite direction. The participants could not recall, when they were asked, which slogans went with which condition. (This control is used to demonstrate that conditioning, and not deliberate choice, was the causal factor.)

Staats (1967) considers that attitudes are acquired by classical conditioning in the sense that an object takes on an emotional meaning by this means. A laboratory study by Staats, Staats, and Crawford (1962) demonstrated that words paired with shocks or with loud sounds (unconditioned stimuli) came to evoke the galvanic skin response (an emotional indicator) and also to exhibit changes in their ratings. In another study (Staats and Staats, 1958) "favorable" words like "beauty," "sweet," and "gift" were presented together with one set of male first names ("Tom," "Bill," "Jack," and so forth), whereas "unfavorable" words such as "bitter," "ugly," and "sad" were presented together with another set of male first names. The first condition resulted in an increased positive rating of the names, the second in a decrease in positive attitude.

Reinforcement

Operant conditioning, involving the manipulation of contingencies of reinforcement, has also been used as a method for the learning of attitudes. For example, Insko (1965) reinforced students over the telephone, using the word "good" when they agreed or disagreed with particular statements of opinion. A week later the same students were asked to respond to these opinion statements presented in questionnaire form. The reinforcement was found to influence their attitudes in the predicted direction. In a study by Scott (1957) attitudes of students engaged in a debate were shown to change in the direction in which they had argued when they won the debate and in the opposite direction when they lost. The reinforcement provided by letter grades (A versus D) has been shown by Bostrom, Vlandis, and Rosenbaum (1961) to alter the attitudes of students who were required to write essays advocating a position inconsistent with their original attitudes; in this case, A was a more effective reinforcer than D.

Studies such as these appear to show that favorable attitudes may be established by suitable arrangement of reinforcement contingencies. They also appear to be interpretable in a somewhat different way, which is that favorable attitudes arise from the *experience of success* (which is itself dependent upon reinforcement). Many incidents of everyday life attest to the importance of success in an activity in attaining a positive attitude. The child who has not yet become successful at skating tends not to "like to skate"; but attitudes change rapidly to the positive once success is achieved in this performance. Schoolwork, of course, exhibits the same phenomenon. Positive attitudes toward mathematics or English composition or public speaking follow one or more experiences of success in these activities. Conversely, attitudes of dislike result from repeated instances of failure. Practical methods of establishing attitudes, based on reinforcement principles, are the subject of a book by Mager (1968).

Bem (1970) marshals evidence that "attitudes follow behavior." This is the case, he says, because individuals infer their own inner states on the basis of clues that come from their own behavior; they engage in *self-perception*. It is

not unreasonable to suppose that individuals' perception of successful behavior provides them with one of the strongest clues to their own "feelings"
toward some external object. It may be, then, that reinforcement contingencies affect attitudes not simply because the reinforcement occurs but more
importantly because such occasions produce success. The perception of
success (in some activity) leads to the establishment of a positive attitude.
The perception of lack of success may accordingly be expected to change
the attitude (toward some particular activity) in the negative direction.

Self-reinforcement.   Since reinforcement works so well to maintain attitudes, it is not surprising that the application of reinforcement can be done
by individuals themselves. Children are able to learn techniques of self-control that gain them reinforcement from parents or other adults. If these
attitudes are continually practiced over a period of years, self-control may
work without the need for external reinforcement. Self-reinforcement processes are put into play, and one may say that the individuals have acquired
an attitude called "self-respect" (Bandura, 1977).

Attitudes underlying self-control require that standards of behavior are
acquired through human modeling by respected persons. Children, for example, can acquire standards of ethical and moral behavior from parents
and teachers. Once standards are communicated, individuals must monitor
their own action choices and apply self-reinforcement when the standard
has been attained. In this manner the practice of self-reinforcement and the
attitude of self-respect can become a lasting feature of the individual's
makeup.

Human Modeling

One of the most dependable sets of events that has been found to produce
changes in attitudes is the phenomenon of *human modeling*. In these circumstances, learning results in imitation of the model's behavior, or more
precisely, in imitation of action choices. When suitably designed learning
conditions are present, the learner acquires an attitude reflecting that expressed or demonstrated by the human model. The process of human modeling has been extensively studied by Bandura and his associates (Bandura,
1969).

The basic design for human modeling is as follows. A person who is
admired, respected, or perceived as having "credibility" is observed (by one
or more learners) to exhibit certain behaviors or to make certain choices of
personal action. For purposes of study, the model may exhibit choices of
undesirable behavior (such as aggressiveness) or desirable choices (such as
making objective moral judgments). The demonstration may take the form
of acting out the behavior concerned and may or may not be accompanied

by appropriate verbal remarks. Or the model may use only verbal descriptions of the behavior choices being modeled. As part of the demonstration, the impression is usually conveyed that the action choices exhibited are either "good" (when socially desirable) or "bad" (when undesirable). This may be done when the learners observe the model being rewarded or being punished, whichever is appropriate.

In one study (Bandura, 1965), nursery school children observed a model (an adult male) exhibiting several sorts of aggressive behavior toward an adult-sized Bobo doll. Following this demonstration, another adult praised the performance and rewarded the model with soft drinks and candy. For another group of children, this second adult scolded and punished the model for his aggressive behavior. A third group of children saw the demonstration with no following consequences. Then the children were led (individually) to a room containing toys including a Bobo doll, and their behavior was observed and recorded during a 10-minute period. The results showed that the observation of reinforcement to the model had a significant effect on the amount of aggressive behavior exhibited by the children. That is to say, the children who observed positive reinforcement of the model tended to increase their aggressive behavior; those who observed punishment of the model tended to show decreased amounts of aggression. This phenomenon is called *vicarious reinforcement* by Bandura.

A study by Chittenden (1942) undertook to test the effectiveness of dramatic presentations in changing choices of personal actions in a set of preschool children who were domineering and hyperaggressive when frustrated in their activities. These children observed and discussed a series of eleven 15-minute plays in which dolls (representing children) displayed aggressive solutions to interpersonal conflict and alternative solutions that were cooperative. The children's behavior in their nursery school environment was observed before they saw and discussed the plays, immediately afterwards, and again a month later. Increases in cooperative behavior and decreases in domination behavior were observed on both post-play occasions, as illustrated in Figure 11.1.

The many studies of behavior modeling and attitude change through human modeling suggest that human beings play an essential role in the conditions for effective learning of attitudes. Presumably, the learners acquire a "conception" or "image" of the human model. Since the model is in some sense an admired person, the affective component of this image is distinctly positive. The learners then "imitate" the model in choosing identical or similar courses of personal action. As a consequence, they may themselves receive positive reinforcement (see Baer, Peterson, and Sherman, 1967). Often, though, the attitude is established following observation of rewards to the model, that is, by means of vicarious reinforcement (Bandura, 1965). The attitude acquired by this means is not limited to the spe-

Figure 11.1 Amount of cooperative and domineering behavior exhibited by a group of hyperaggressive preschool children before and after seeing and discussing plays in which the desirable choices of behavior were modeled. Drawn from data of Chittenden (1942). (Reprinted from Figure 3-7, in A. Bandura, *Principles of behavior modification*. Copyright 1969 by Holt, Rinehart and Winston. Reproduced by permission of Holt, Rinehart and Winston.)

cific behavior exhibited by the model, but generalizes broadly to other behavior and situations (Bandura and McDonald, 1963; Bandura and Mischel, 1965).

Human modeling may occur in many learning situations. The model may be presented to the learner in pictures, movies, or TV scenes and need not appear in person. Presumably, modeling can occur in older children and adults when the model is merely described, as in a biography, a history text, or a novel. Thus, the ways of introducing conditions of learning for attitude change by modeling are many.

Most probably, parents are the primary human models for the transmission of attitudes in the young child. As Thornburg (1975) points out, the family is the locus of the child's initial social learning. In the early years, the teacher, as well as the parent, can serve as a human model for the child's learning of desirable attitudes such as consideration for others, completion of tasks, and fairness. As adolescence is approached, the typical rejection of adult models may herald the period when peer models become predominant, conflicts occur between values and behavior, and many new attitudes are acquired from admired schoolmates. When adulthood is reached, the "selection" or acceptance of models becomes related to the adoption of the individual's own social role (Thornburg, 1975), and the model's credibility is a dominant factor in the changing of attitudes.

Message Content and Attitude Change

Research on the attitude-changing effects of various kinds of communication has been conducted for many years by investigators at Yale University. Studies of "communication and persuasion" were begun during World War II, when the effects of various communications in motion picture form were investigated (Hovland, Lumsdaine, and Sheffield, 1949). Subsequent results of the program have been reported in several volumes, beginning with that of Hovland, Janis, and Kelley (1953).

Perhaps the most important findings obtained in this program of research pertain to the effects of the *kind of communication*. What kind of message is most effective in changing attitudes? The most interesting generalization of the research findings is this: most variations in type of message make no appreciable difference in attitude change. No dependable effectiveness has been found for verbal communications that (1) present rational arguments, (2) give both sides of a question, (3) appeal to emotion, (4) contain fear-arousing stimuli, or (5) draw specific conclusions. While single adjurations such as "Drive safely!" have long been known to be ineffective in changing attitudes, these studies found that various elaborations on the basic message theme also are not effective.

The source of the message.   In contrast with the findings concerning the *content* of the communication, the Yale investigators early discovered that the "communicator," or "source," of the message made a considerable difference in determining its effectiveness for attitude change. A variety of studies have confirmed the importance of the source as an important determiner of attitudes. The relationship between the characteristics of the source and those of the learners is naturally a critical matter. Triandis (1971) has summarized findings about these characteristics as including (1) physical attractiveness; (2) clothes and speech as indicators of status; (3) demographic qualities such as age, race, nationality; (4) the source's attitudes; and (5) evidence that the source's past behavior relates in a rewarding (or punishing) way to the learners.

Attitude theorists generally emphasize the importance of the communicator to the process of attitude change. Kelman (1958), for example, has proposed that effective attitude change requires that the source deliver a "compliance communication," indicating the possession of a means of control (as would be the case with a police officer, a college dean, or the manager of a baseball team). A second kind of message is an "identification communication," which conveys to the listeners the attractiveness of the communicator (as would be the case with an admired sports figure or a student class president). Still a third kind of communication pertaining to the source is called the "internalization combination," which conveys the idea of the communicator's high degree of credibility (as would be the case with an expert in art criticism, race relations, or whatever).

It is evident, then, that whatever aspects of the communication may be found to be effective, a great mass of evidence indicates that these effects are overwhelmed by the influence of the *source*. Obviously, the source is simply another name for the *human model*. Thus it is most illuminating that two or more different lines of evidence, beginning with separate problem definitions and approaches, converge in their agreement that the *human agent* is one of the critically important conditions for attitude learning and change.

CONDITIONS OF LEARNING: ATTITUDES

Having discussed the major theoretical positions concerning the nature of attitudes and some relevant evidence regarding attitude change, we should now be able to describe the conditions that are optimal for attitude learning. It will be recalled that we view an attitude as a learned internal state whose function is to influence choices of personal action. We are ready now to examine the internal and external conditions that need to be present when the learning of an attitude takes place. Such learning, of course, may establish an attitude that was not previously present in the learner, or it may change an existing attitude in either the positive or negative direction.

Internal Conditions

As is the case with other kinds of learned capabilities, attitudes require that certain *prerequisite* capabilities be present in the learner. Primarily, these are intellectual skills of the *concept variety* and a certain amount of relevant *information*.

Concepts.   First, it is evident that the learner must possess the concept of the class of object, event, or person to which the new (or newly changed) attitude will be directed. For example, if the attitude is directed at people of the nationality called Estonian, the meaning of Estonian people must be present in the learner's memory. Otherwise, instruction must establish this concept prior to the delivery of the "attitudinal message." Similarly, if attitude is directed at a harmful drug such as cocaine, this concept must be present internally.

Of major importance, as we have seen, is the concept of the "source," or human model. The characteristics that insure the learner's identification with the human model must have been previously acquired, or "internalized." For best effects, the model needs to be conceived as attractive, powerful (in the sense of being capable of control), and highly credible. When the concept of the model is already present (as might be the case with a student leader or a popular sports figure), the designer of instruction may simply *select* the model who has appropriate characteristics. When the model is not already known, his or her appealing characteristics may need to be established as prerequisite to the communication of the attitude itself.

A third necessary internal condition is a set of concepts pertaining to the personal action to which the attitude relates. In the case of harmful drugs, for example, concepts are necessary of the *situations* in which such drugs are likely to be encountered as well as of the *actions* likely to be involved in using them (smoking, sniffing, injecting, and so on). As another example, consider the concepts required as prerequisites in the establishment of a consumer attitude of price comparison of packaged foods. If comparison of cost per unit is to be established as an attitude, the learner must possess the concepts of pounds, ounces, dollars, and cents, as well as the rules that permit ratios to be made and compared (see Gagné and Briggs, 1979).

Information.   Relevant information is also an important prerequisite to the learning of attitudes. In particular, such information is likely to pertain to the *situations* in which choices of action are likely to be made. Thus in the case of attitude toward harmful drugs, the learner may need to know the "street names" of the common drugs as well as the social situations in which they are likely to be available. If the target attitude is one of refusing to drink alcoholic beverages before driving, information concerning the situations in which such drinking is likely to occur (or to be rejected) is necessary as a background for attitude learning.

It is not uncommon for teachers who wish to establish positive attitudes to place undue dependence upon concept learning and information learning. These kinds of learning outcomes constitute *essential prerequisites* for the acquiring of attitudes, and they may, of course, be learned within the same unit of instruction that contains the attitude communication. Their learning, however, does not in itself produce attitude learning or attitude change. The learner may acquire many new concepts about ethnic characteristics, for example, or obtain masses of information about ethnic customs; but it is perfectly possible for these to be learned without any attitudinal change. Concepts and information are merely prerequisite internal conditions. They are not the crucial events that bring about attitude learning.

External Conditions

The conditions external to the learner that are favorable to the establishment of attitudes may take a number of different forms, depending upon what model of attitude change is favored. Thus, it is possible to employ classical conditioning techniques for some kinds of attitude change, but this method would hardly be applicable to the broad range of attitudes with which schools or other educational establishments might be concerned. Reinforcement contingencies for a great variety of attitudes may be suitably arranged to provide the perception of success on the part of the learner. It would seem by all odds, however, that the method employing human modeling is the most generally applicable and quite possibly the most effective approach to attitude learning.

Observation of the human model's choices.   The events that result in learning from human modeling occur in approximately the following order:

1. *The model's appeal and credibility is established.* If the model (such as a teacher, parent, or prominent person) is already known to the learners, this step is assumed. If the model is unknown, information is provided to the learner with the purpose of bringing about "identification" and belief in the model's credibility.
2. *The learner's recall of the object of the attitude and the situations to which it is applicable is stimulated.* The learner recalls relevant intellectual skills and information previously described as internal conditions for learning. For example, to impart the attitude of refraining from drinking before driving, situations are recalled in which drinks are offered, followed by situations involving automobile driving.
3. *The model demonstrates or communicates the desired choice of personal action.* For example, the human model indicates that he or she refuses alcohol in anticipation of driving.
4. *A demonstration or communication indicates a reinforcing state of affairs for the model.* For example, the model may be shown keeping a cool head in a difficult driving situation. Further (if appropriate), the model may be seen receiving a "safe driving" award. Or a model who happens to be a professional automobile driver may be seen receiving an award for skillful driving on a difficult course.

The presentation of these steps may be more or less elaborate, depending upon the attitude to be imparted and the nature of the learners. One can see that the steps occur in fairly simple form when a teacher of first-grade children undertakes to teach an attitude of helpfulness. In this case, the teacher is the model. For step 2, the teacher reminds the children what "helping" means and in what kinds of situations it occurs. The choice of personal action by actually helping a child with a task (such as lifting a piece of furniture) is then demonstrated. The task is seen to be accomplished readily with "helping." The child who is helped is pleased. The teacher shows satisfaction in the pleasure of another person (the child who is helped). The children also experience pleasure, that is, they are vicariously reinforced. By this means, the children's attitudes are changed in the positive direction toward "helping others."

Variations on the human modeling theme.   The effects of human modeling on attitudes are considered to occur widely in many kinds of situations. Obviously, the basic events of human modeling occur when dramatic presentations are employed, as in actual plays and in television programs. Another form that human modeling can take is *role playing,* in which the actor is influenced by the role of an imagined person rather than by an actual person. Fictional characters encountered in reading can be human models, and often are. Presumably, human modeling represents the basic psychological process involved in the acquisition of values from the reading of history and literature.

Particular mention may be made of the way in which the factors in human modeling come into play in class discussion. The class may be presented with a problem, perhaps one involving moral values. The students' discussion leads to the presentation of various and sometimes conflicting attitudes. Each person who presents a point of view (toward the choice of personal action) is, for the moment, behaving as a model. The discussion typically leads to the rejection of extreme attitudes that are unacceptable to the group as a whole. More importantly, the communications of attitudes are progressively expressed with greater precision. The teacher or discussion leader (again, acting as a model) may help in the process of reasonable expression of attitudes. Some consensus emerges from the discussion, which is satisfying to most or all of the members; there is, then, reinforcement of both direct and vicarious sorts. Socially acceptable attitudes and changes in attitudes emerge from events of this nature. Note the effectiveness of group discussion in changing attitudes, as contrasted, say, with the ineffectiveness of a verbal communication delivered to the learner without the presence of other human beings.

Reinforcement of action choice.   Whether or not the attitude has been initially conveyed to the learner by a human model, its establishment is aided by direct reinforcement of the choice of personal action concerned. If a child has learned an attitude of "helping others," the probability of choice of this class of personal action is increased when the child receives direct reinforcement. Having heard about helping, a young child may choose to help another in some task requiring cooperation. When such an act is followed by indications of pleasure or thanks or a returned favor, the conditions of reinforcement are present. In such circumstances, the helping attitude is strengthened, that is, the choice of "helping" actions is made more probable in the child's future behavior.

Reinforcement works equally well at all age levels. Adults who have acquired attitudes against cigarette smoking have their attitudes strengthened when they receive social approval for not smoking and perhaps also when they see "No Smoking" signs in public buildings. People who have learned to be skillful at certain activities (typing, diving, or mountain climbing) acquire strong positive attitudes toward these activities. The experience of success, or in other words, the fulfillment of an expectation, is a powerful factor in the establishment of positive attitudes. Conversely, the absence of success often leads to negative attitudes toward an activity.

EDUCATIONAL IMPLICATIONS

The learning and modification of attitudes, referred to by some as the affective domain of objectives, is surely of great importance to educational programs of almost every kind. It is customarily desired that students acquire positive attitudes toward any subject they are studying and more broadly toward the activities of learning in general. Practical training programs usually incorporate objectives that represent attitudes toward work, toward performance standards, and toward safety measures. School programs are expected to produce in their students attitudes useful for social living, such as consideration for others, cooperativeness, and tolerance of cultural and ethnic differences. In addition, many school programs are concerned with teaching attitudes favoring protection of the environment, avoidance of harmful drugs, and exercise of citizenship responsibilities.

Although many kinds of attitude education are deliberately instituted, human individuals acquire a host of attitudes as a result of their experiences in the larger social and physical environment. Family influences are particularly important in establishing attitudes affecting personal conduct and interpersonal behavior as well as precision of language and thought. The church, the labor union, the social club, the peer group, and other social organizations and groups to which the individual holds allegiance likewise have strong effects in determining attitudes. Then, too, the various media from which the individual seeks information or entertainment are often powerful sources of attitude change.

Attitudes have both cognitive and affective components. That is to say, they are internally mediated, in part, by propositions that incorporate the category of "object" (events, persons, or things) to which the attitude is directed. Usually, they appear also to be mediated, in part, by feelings that give them their "affective" nature. These characteristics, however important they may be in understanding the essential nature of attitudes, give few clues regarding the *function* of attitudes. It is this latter aspect of attitudes that is of central importance to educational programs. If attitudes are to be established or changed, they must be identified as *learning outcomes* and as instructional objectives. For such purposes, a useful definition of attitude is a *learned internal state that influences choices of personal action toward some category of persons, objects, or events*. The aim of instruction in this domain is to establish or to strengthen particular internal states that perform this function.

Although attitudes may be formed and changed in several ways, the principles of *reinforcement contingencies* can usually be readily recognized as playing an important part in attitude learning. However an attitude is originally introduced or communicated, its establishment (as is true of other kinds of behavior) depends upon the occurrence of reinforcement to complete the act of learning. It is also true that people like what they do well. The kinds of personal action that lead to *success* are most likely to be those toward which the individual displays a positive attitude. In many educational situations a desired positive attitude may most readily be assured by making it possible for the student to achieve success.

One of the most dependable methods of establishing attitudes is by means of a set of learning conditions that includes *human modeling*. In brief, this method involves the demonstration or communication of the desired choice of personal action (the attitude) by a respected or admired person. Such a person may be a parent, a teacher, a prominent or popular figure, or any individual who inspires confidence and trust (see Gagné, 1973). The human model may present the "message" in person or via a medium like television or the printed page; the model does not have to be "real," as is illustrated by the example of a fictional hero. The learner then perceives that the model is reinforced, or rewarded, for the action choice he or she has made, an event called "vicarious reinforcement."

The effectiveness of human modeling for attitude change contrasts markedly with the ineffectiveness of anonymously delivered messages conveying information, or verbal commands. Adjurations such as "Be a safe driver" are, according to the evidence, almost entirely ineffective for attitude learning. They remain similarly ineffective even when placed in larger contexts of emotional appeals and rational arguments. While information may need to be acquired by the learner as a *prerequisite* to attitude change, its learning does not in and of itself produce the desired change. Students may need to know what a *prothonotary* is before they acquire an attitude toward this class of persons. But such knowledge does not establish or change the students' attitude to an appreciable degree—it only makes such change possible. Similarly, drug education, if it is designed to establish attitudes of rejection of harmful drugs, cannot be effective if it simply conveys to the students additional knowledge about drugs.

GENERAL REFERENCES

Attitudes and Attitude Change

Bandura, A. *Principles of behavior modification*. New York: Holt, Rinehart and Winston, 1969.

Bem, D. J. *Beliefs, attitudes, and human affairs*. Monterey, Calif.: Brooks/Cole, 1970.

242   Attitudes

Kiesler, C. A., Collins, B. E., and Miller, N. *Attitude change*. New York: Wiley, 1969

Kohlberg, L., and Turiel, E. (Eds.), *Recent research in moral development*. New York Holt, Rinehart and Winston, 1973.

Krathwohl, D. R., Bloom, B. S., and Masia, B. B. *Taxonomy of educational objectives Handbook II: Affective domain*. New York: McKay, 1964.

Ringness, T. A. *The affective domain in education*. Boston: Little, Brown, 1975.

Rokeach, M. *Beliefs, attitudes and values*. San Francisco: Jossey-Bass, 1969.

Thornburg, H. D. *Development in adolescence*. Monterey, Calif.: Brooks/Cole, 1975.

Triandis, H. C. *Attitude and attitude change*. New York: Wiley, 1971.

Attitude Measurement

Shaw, M. E., and Wright, J. M. *Scales for the measurement of attitudes*. New York: McGraw-Hill, 1967.

12

A Theory of Instruction

If the various kinds of learning outcomes and the ways of analyzing learning requirements are combined in a rational and systematic manner, it is possible to describe a total set of ideas that constitute a *theory of instruction*. The idea of calling such an integrated account a "theory" is of rather recent origin and has been influenced largely by the writings of Simon (1969) on "sciences of the artificial." The ideas described in previous chapters of this book provide the content of a theory of instruction. We have by now reviewed the essential features of what is known about the outcomes of learning (Chapters 5 through 11). In order to weave the fabric of a theory of instruction, we must review briefly the *processes* of learning that were discussed in Chapter 4.

Learning as a Set of Processes

Human beings are engaged in learning, in its broadest sense, during most of their waking hours. Much of the time, of course, the learning that occurs is of strictly temporary value, such as "I left my wristwatch on the living-room table," or "Independence Day falls on Wednesday this year." But the kinds of things that are learned cover a range of capabilities that are of considerably more lasting value to the individual and ultimately to society. These include the learned capabilities we have categorized as intellectual skills, cognitive strategies, verbal information, attitudes, and motor skills.

Learning processes, then, are going on all the time people are awake (and possibly when they are asleep). As depicted in the information-processing model (Chapter 4), previously learned material in long-term memory is continually being retrieved to the working memory and to consciousness. There it may be rehearsed, not only in the sense of being repeated, but also *re-encoded* before being again returned to long-term memory. The process of encoding as it occurs in the working memory is continually influenced by inputs whose origins are external to the learner. These inputs have been processed initially by the sensory registers and by the kind of transformation we call selective perception.

Thus, the processes suggested by the information-processing model of human learning and memory are considered to be going on more or less all the time. While the temporal sequence suggested by the model proceeds from the external environment to the internal stores of the individual's brain, the model does not necessarily imply that learning invariably proceeds in that sequence. The processes implied by the model (Figure 4.2) may indeed occur sequentially, and often do. However, some of the processes of learning may take place in a simultaneous fashion, or "in parallel." For example, in the performance of reading, selective perception of the features of a word as a set of printed symbols may be occurring in parallel with the retrieval of the meaning of a word that in a semantically meaningful sense could "fit" the sentence being read. This kind of "parallel processing" is considered a likely possibility by those who espouse an *interactive theory* of reading (Lesgold and Perfetti, 1981). If a match is found between perceptual features and semantic meaning, reading proceeds; a mismatch becomes a signal for the skilled reader to initiate a different kind of processing of the word and perhaps also the sentence.

The originating "spark" that sets off a learning event may arise from a number of different sources. It may come from a cognitive strategy (a "plan") that has been guiding the individual's thoughts over a period of time. It may come from an item of verbal knowledge retrieved from long-term memory. And, of course, the originating stimulus for learning may come from the learner's environment. When one is concerned with instruction, one deals with the deliberate arrangement of events in the learner's environment for the purpose of making learning happen, but also to make it effective. As we have seen in Chapter 4, this is a matter of selecting and arranging *events of instruction* that provide support to the internal processes of learning.

THEORY: DIFFERENTIAL INSTRUCTION FOR DIFFERENT LEARNING OUTCOMES

A theory of instruction should attempt to relate the external events of instruction to the outcomes of learning by showing how these events lead to appropriate support or enhancement of internal learning processes. It may be noted that an instructional theory does not in itself try to state what the processes of learning are or how they work. An instructional theory is not a learning theory; rather, it adopts and uses what appear to be the principal aspects of learning theories that are based upon contemporary research (for example, Estes, 1976, 1978; Bower and Hilgard, 1981). The province of an instructional theory is to propose a rationally based relationship between instructional events, their effects on learning processes, and the learning outcomes that are produced as a result of these processes.

In order to describe our ideas as instructional theory, therefore, we must review the *events of instruction*, those external events that are designed to help learning occur. Since first defining these events in Chapter 4, a great deal of detailed information about them has been covered in the intervening chapters. Accordingly, it will be possible to view them as components of theory with the enhanced meaning they have gathered along the way.

The major themes of the instructional theory to be described here may be stated as follows:

1. Learning is best conceived as a set of processes, internal to the individual, that transform stimulation from the individual's environment into a number a forms of information leading progressively to the establishment of long-term memory states; such states (learning outcomes) provide the individual with capabilities for various human performances.

2. The capabilities for performance that are learning outcomes may be categorized in several ways, some practically oriented, others theoretically based. For the purpose of designing instruction, we consider five categories: intellectual skills, cognitive strategies, verbal information, attitudes, and motor skills. These categories of human capability underlie distinctively different classes of human performance, which means that the effectiveness of the learning which produced them can be differentially assessed (Gagné, 1984).

3. While the events of instruction that support learning processes fall into common categories irrespective of the learning outcome expected, the *specific operations* that constitute these events are *different* for each of the five learning outcomes. Learning intellectual skills requires a different design of instructional events from those required for learning verbal information or for those required for learning motor skills, and so on. This theme is surely the most important "core" statement of the instructional theory described in these pages.

It will now be possible to fill in the details of instructional theory by reviewing what we have learned about the conditions of learning in previous chapters. As a prelude to those chapters, we introduced in Chapter 4 the idea of external support for internal processes of learning, as displayed in Figure 4.2. In the account to follow, these external events are called the *events of instruction*. Under headings naming these events, we shall examine what this instructional theory has to say about how instructional events may be specifically designed to achieve each of the five different learning outcomes in an optimal fashion. By way of an overview, Table 12.1 shows the *internal processes* of learning (as in Figure 4.2), the *instructional event* corresponding to each, and an *action example* to suggest how the event of instruction might be specifically carried out. For convenience as well as correspondence with a previous work (Gagné and Briggs, 1979), the instructional events are numbered from one to nine, indicating an approximate typical sequential order. As for the action examples, they can only be stated in somewhat general terms in the table but will be described specifically in the sections to follow.

TABLE 12.1   Internal Processes and Their Corresponding Instructional Events, with Action Examples

Internal Process	Instructional Event	Action Example
Reception	1. Gaining attention	Use abrupt stimulus change
Expectancy	2. Informing learners of the objective	Tell learners what they will be able to do after learning
Retrieval to Working Memory	3. Stimulating recall of prior learning	Ask for recall of previously learned knowledge or skills
Selective Perception	4. Presenting the stimulus	Display the content with distinctive features
Semantic Encoding	5. Providing "learning guidance"	Suggest a meaningful organization
Responding	6. Eliciting performance	Ask learner to perform
Reinforcement	7. Providing feedback	Give informative feedback
Retrieval and Reinforcement	8. Assessing performance	Require additional learner performance, with feedback
Retrieval and Generalization	9. Enhancing retention and transfer	Provide varied practice and spaced reviews

1. Gaining Attention

The attention of students, in the sense of alertness for reception of stimuli, is gained by introducing rapid stimulus change. Instructors may do this by gesturing, or by suddenly changing the loudness of their speech. Alertness also may be stimulated by visual or auditory stimuli related to the content of a lesson to be taught. For example, a science lesson on the oxidation of metals might begin with the instructor igniting a strip of magnesium. A lesson in foreign language learning might begin with a sharply stated question in that language, having mainly the function of commanding attention. It is clear that there is no particular advantage to an attempt to make an attention-getting stimulus different for the various types of learning outcomes. In the case of this initial instructional event, whatever changing stimulus is chosen is likely to work equally well for intellectual skills, verbal information, or any other outcome. Matching the stimulus with content to be learned, however, has some small advantage in achieving lesson coherence. A lesson on driving safety, for example, might begin with a scene of a shocking accident.

2. Informing Learners of the Objective

When learners comprehend the objective of instruction, they will acquire an expectancy that normally persists throughout the time learning is taking place and that will be confirmed by the feedback given when learning is complete. Unless the basis for the expectancy is already associated with learner motivation, an important phase of instruction may be to establish (or reactivate) this association. For example, learning the skill of making proper sentences should surely be associated with a student's desire to be a TV sports announcer.

Surely the differences among types of objectives become exceedingly clear as these objectives are transmitted to, and comprehended by, the student. Table 12.2 illustrates a summary account of the different instructional techniques that inform the learner of the objective for each of the five learning outcomes.

TABLE 12.2   Differential Instruction for Five Learning Outcomes: Informing the Learner of the Objective

Learning Outcome	Instructional Technique
Intellectual Skill	Demonstrate the activity to which the concept, rule, or procedure applies
Cognitive Strategy	Describe or demonstrate the strategy
Verbal Information	Describe what the learner will be expected to state
Attitude	(Learner is to be informed later)
Motor Skill	Demonstrate the expected performance

Intellectual skills. *Demonstrating an example* of the procedure is required to convey the objective of an *intellectual skill*. For instance, if the skill to be taught is finding the length of the hypotenuse of a right triangle, the instructional event might take this form: Present a right triangle with the lengths of sides indicated; then show the length of the hypotenuse as the square root of a number (the correct number). If the rule pertains to the nominative case of pronouns, an incomplete sentence such as: _____ and I have a secret" may be presented to indicate the problem of choosing between "she" and "her." The objective is conveyed by the question, "How do you choose the proper pronoun?"

Cognitive strategies. Communicating *cognitive strategies* as objectives may be done in a variety of ways. The most straightforward (and often most efficient) method of informing the learner about cognitive strategies is to use a *verbal communication*. As we saw in Chapter 7, even young children can acquire strategies for remembering the names of objects shown in pictures by being given oral directions to (1) think of the objects in familiar categories, or (2) say them over and over to themselves ("rehearsal"). For older children and adults, verbal communication of strategies is doubtless a most efficient procedure in many learning situations. Since cognitive strategies have the basic nature of skills, the additional use of *demonstration* is seldom out of place. Thus, the strategy of "chunking" strings of letters might be demonstrated by means of the triplets in ERAFTCNSF.

Strategies applicable to the solving of problems are most readily derived from the content of these problems. For example, a strategy of mental multiplication calls for the use of the properties of decimal numbers, as when the problem 19 × 7 is transformed and solved as 20 × 7 = 140 minus 7 = 133. Obviously this strategy has considerable generality, since it can be used efficiently with a great many different multiplication examples. At the same time, it is notable that it is a *task strategy* and does not have sufficient generality to apply, say, to such a problem as writing a sonnet.

Verbal information. The objective of verbal information may be communicated to the learners by informing them what they will be expected to be able to *state*. Since a greater or lesser amount of detail may be considered adequate as a criterion of learning, the degree of this detail, as well as its nature, is an important piece of information for learners to have. In studying American history, for example, it would be possible for a teacher to require statements about the dates of significant events within an era, although another instructor might prefer to ask students to tell how such events related to each other. Both objectives require stating, either orally or in writing. Obviously, though, they are in other respects quite different. As might be expected, students' performance in learning and remembering verbal information is strongly influenced by their knowledge of the objective (Gagné and Rothkopf, 1975).

Attitudes. If an attitude is to be established or changed, the objective is seldom announced beforehand, for that might defeat the purpose of the instruction. Typically, the objective of *choosing a course of personal action* is made evident during the event called *providing learning guidance*, to be described later on as event 5.

Motor skills. The objective of learning a motor skill must be communicated clearly to the student, and is done usually by means of a demonstration. A first-grader may be shown how the teacher makes a printed R; the student of tennis can watch the instructor demonstrate a backhand stroke.

3. Stimulating Recall of Prior Learning

The learner is next asked to recall some things previously learned. The best kind of recall is somehow related naturally to what has been chosen as a task to be newly learned. The kinds of relationship this previously learned material needs to have with the new learning is different for different learning outcomes.

The instructional techniques appropriate for each type of learning outcome are briefly described in Table 12.3.

TABLE 12.3 Differential Instruction for Five Learning Outcomes: Stimulating Recall of Prior Learning

Learning Outcome	Instructional Technique
Intellectual skill	Recall prerequisite rules and concepts
Cognitive strategy	Recall simple prerequisite rules and concepts
Verbal information	Recall well-organized bodies of knowledge
Attitude	Recall the situation and action involved in personal choice. Remind learner of the human model and the model's characteristics
Motor skill	Recall the "executive subroutine," and part-skills, if appropriate

Intellectual skills. The relevant prior learning, or at least the most important part of it, consists of simpler intellectual skills that are components of the skill to be learned. Thus, if the addition of fractions with unlike denominators is the rule to be learned, the three simpler rules for recall are (1) making equivalent fractions by multiplying numerator and denominator by the same number, (2) multiplying whole numbers, and (3) adding whole numbers. In the learning of language skills, if what is to be learned is the use of the objective case of pronouns following prepositions (after *her*, before *him*), evidently the learner should recall the concepts (1) preposition and (2) objective-case pronouns. As a third example, suppose the task to be learned is the procedure of using a voltmeter to measure the voltage in a circuit of electrical equipment. Analysis of this task would reveal such prerequisite skills (which may have been previously learned) as (1) identifying continuity in an electrical circuit, (2) using the metallic terminals of a voltmeter as probes, and (3) reading a graduated instrument scale. These, then, would be the previously learned items to be recalled by the learner as the new task of learning is undertaken.

Cognitive strategies. The prior learning to be recalled as an early stage of acquiring a cognitive strategy, just as in the case of intellectual skills, consists of previously learned concepts and rules. If there is a difference, it lies in the fact that the rules that are components of cognitive strategies are usually *very simple and highly familiar.* For instance, a commonly learned strategy for learning from printed text is "first identify the main points, then read the passage in detail." Acquiring such a strategy requires the learner to recall, as prerequisites, (1) how to identify the main points in a passage, and (2) how to process the details. Such skills are likely to have been practiced in school from the second grade on and are therefore likely to be highly familiar. General strategies of problem solving often imply even simpler learned prerequisites. For example, a commonly suggested problem-solving strategy is "subgoal decomposition" (Newell, 1980), which means, simply, decompose the problem into a set of subtasks. The main prerequisite skill, in this case, is also the simple one of "identifying parts (subtasks) of a task." It appears to be characteristic of cognitive strategies that the component skills involved are either very simple, very familiar, or both. Thus, it may be that instruction needs to pay little attention to this event, so long as the necessary prerequisites can be assumed to be already known.

Verbal information.   Effective instruction must include stimulation of the recall of previously learned verbal information. In practical terms, this may be done by using an *advance organizer* (Ausubel, 1960), by means of *adjunct questions* (Rothkopf, 1970), or by such devices as outlines and summaries of prior knowledge presented before the material to be learned. Of course, if teachers believe that previously acquired knowledge has been well learned and can be readily recalled they may simply remind the learners of the prior knowledge. For instance, a teacher might say "you remember that we have discussed the 'fair use' provisions of the copyright law" and expect these ideas to be retrieved to the students' working memories.

The demands of prior knowledge in this domain of verbal information contrast markedly with those applicable to intellectual skills. Prior knowledge for newly learned verbal information is *not a specific component* of that information, as is the case with intellectual skills. Quite the contrary; the prior knowledge to be recalled is a *larger complex of organized knowledge.* When a law student learns about a particular "case," or even a Supreme Court decision, what must be recalled is as much of an entire body of knowledge related to the specific issue as is possible. Thus, for instruction of verbal information, the precise details to be recalled by the student are not determinable. Instead, what must be identified for recall is the large body of organized knowledge that is available from prior learning. The larger and more well organized this previously learned knowledge is, the better.

Attitudes.   As an instructional event for attitude learning, stimulating recall has the effect of making available to the learner the information and skills involved in the "action" implied by the phrase "choice of personal action." Thus, if an attitude toward rejection of harmful drugs is to be established, students must have knowledge of the "street names" of such drugs and of the various situations in which they are likely to be made available. Sometimes, intellectual skills may make up the needed prior knowledge, as would be the case if an attitude of consumer caution were the objective, and the action to be chosen were a matter of distinguishing between 14 oz. at $1.53 and 1 lb. 3 oz. at $1.79. The particular knowledges and skills that may be relevant for recall, then, tend to have specific relations to the attitude being established.

If human modeling is to be employed as a means for teaching or modifying an attitude, one other item must be recalled from prior learning. This is the model himself or herself, together with the perception of the model as admirable, credible, and powerful (Triandis, 1971). If the model has been previously known to the students (for example, a national sports figure) they may be reminded by means of a name, a picture, or by a brief statement of the model's status and achievements. Of course, there are situations in which the model must be introduced only just prior to the attitudinal message. A surprise visit by a school alumna who has become president of a well-known college may be the occasion for a laudatory introduction to an assembly speech, with the intention of establishing credibility of this person as a human model.

Motor skills.   Perhaps the most obvious candidate for recall of prior learning in motor skills is what Fitts and Posner (1967) called the "executive subroutine." This is the procedure that constitutes the active framework within which the motor skill is executed, practiced, and refined. For the skill of "using a stapler," for example, the executive subroutine consists in (1) positioning the papers under the striking element; (2) holding the paper steady while raising the other hand; (3) pressing down the head of the stapler rapidly and with sufficient force; (4) releasing the head by raising the hand; and (5) removing the stapled papers. In this relatively simple skill, students may be able to learn the subroutine after a single demonstration. The procedure is nonetheless an essential one for the skill. A more complex example is that involved in parking an automobile (see Chapter 10).

Other possible items of prior learning are part-skills. In the skill of archery, for example, the part-skills of stance, aiming, and stretching the bow may have been practiced separately. An instructor may ask for them to be separately recalled and demonstrated before asking the student to "put them together" in the total act of aiming and shooting at a target.

4. Presenting the Stimulus

A fourth event of instruction calls for the presentation of the essential stimulus to the learner. Table 12.4 outlines the relevant instructional techniques. If verbal information is to be learned, the stimulus may be printed prose in the form of a chapter in a textbook or oral discourse from an audio tape. If learning of an intellectual skill is to be undertaken, the object or the symbols (or both) that must be formed into a concept or rule, or the problem to be solved, may be displayed. In the case of a cognitive strategy, the procedure of the strategy itself may be described to the learner or shown by the instructor in a demonstration. For a motor skill, the stimulus presented is usually the situation existing at the point of initiation of the skill. For instance, the tennis stroke begins with the presentation of the court, ball, and racquet. In the case of an attitude, the stimulus consists of the human model and the general nature of the message or demonstration that the model will deliver (such as "What do you do with paper trash?").

TABLE 12.4   Differential Instruction for Five Learning Outcomes: Presenting the Stimulus

Learning Outcome	Instructional Technique
Intellectual skill	Delineate features of objects and symbols to be formed into the concept or rule
Cognitive strategy	Describe problem and show what the strategy accomplishes
Verbal information	Display printed or auditorially delivered verbal statements, with distinctive features
Motor skill	Display situation in existence at initiation of skilled performance; demonstrate executive subroutine
Attitude	Human model describes the general nature of the choice to be presented

Obviously, the stimulus presented as an instructional event depends specifically on what is to be learned. The content is specific to the category of capability that is the objective, whether verbal information, intellectual skill, or any of the other varieties. Since the stimulus must be perceived as an initial phase of learning, clear delineation of stimulus *features* is desirable. For a picture or diagram, significant features may be highlighted, pointed to, or traced in heavy outlines (Dwyer, 1970). When text in prose form is the stimulus, techniques of making features distinctive include underlining or using bold print and topic headings (Anderson and Faust, 1974). When speech is delivered orally, the lecturer gives emphasis to distinctive features by variations in loudness and pitch of voice.

5. Providing "Learning Guidance"

This event of instruction supports the internal process usually called *semantic encoding*. In familiar language, the instructional technique may be described as follows: Make the stimulus as meaningful as possible. There are several ways of achieving augmented meaningfulness, and these differ from each other depending upon the learning outcome expected. In general, meaningfulness may be enhanced by (1) using concrete examples of abstract terms and concepts, and (2) elaborating each idea by relating it to others already in memory. Summary versions of this event as it relates to the five major kinds of learned capabilities (learning outcomes) are given in Table 12.5.

Intellectual skills.   For concepts and rules, follow the display of the stimulus with one or more concrete examples. Specifically, a concrete concept requires showing several instances and noninstances. For a defined concept, the definition of the concept is followed by the identification of several

TABLE 12.5   Differential Instruction for Five Learning Outcomes: Providing "Learning Guidance"

Learning Outcome	Instructional Technique
Intellectual skill	Give varied concrete examples of concept or rule
Cognitive strategy	Provide verbal description of strategy, followed by example
Verbal information	Elaborate content by relating to larger bodies of knowledge; use images, mnemonics
Attitude	Human model describes or demonstrates action choice, followed by observation of reinforcement of model's behavior
Motor skill	Continue practice

concrete instances. A rule is usually presented as a verbal statement and is followed by several concrete examples (applications). Other meaningful relations in the form of "elaborations" may be established, although the limits of their effects cannot currently be assessed (Gagné and White, 1978).

Cognitive strategies.   Strategies that are specific to the content being learned may readily be communicated to learners by means of a verbal statement. Examples are "use each word in a sentence," or "look for the topic sentence of each paragraph." Essentially the same method is used in conveying general problem-solving strategies, for example, "break the problem down into subordinate parts." As with intellectual skills, such statements may be followed by one or more concrete examples.

Verbal information.   The encoding process is supported by added meaningfulness, using the ideas of (1) concrete examples and (2) elaboration. Both of these principles imply that the content to be learned (declarative knowledge) should be deliberately related to a larger body of knowledge already in the learner's memory. Presumably, such prior knowledge is stored as a network of associated propositions. A newly learned idea or set of ideas is incorporated in this network by means of a phenomenon known as *spreading activation* (Anderson, 1980). Other techniques of external support for semantic encoding include the use of images and sentences in learning foreign vocabularies, as in the *key-word method* (Pressley, Levin, and Delaney, 1982). The encoding of isolated facts may be aided by placing them in the categories of a table or in the "boxes" of a spatial array.

Attitudes.   The learning guidance provided for attitude learning is the demonstration of action choice made by the human model (see Chapter 11). For example, the model may state "I always keep gum wrappers in my pocket until I come to a trash container" and actually demonstrate the action referred to. Additional behavior of the human model may also be viewed by the learner, such as an incident of reward that functions as "vicarious reinforcement" (Bandura, 1969). Presumably, the learner encodes this entire episode, including the human model, the statement of the action choice, the demonstration, and the consequences to the model. Obviously, some rather complex processing occurs when an attitude is established or changed, with a good deal of involvement of previously stored outcomes of learning.

Motor skills. Provided that previously described instructional events have been adequately done, guidance for the learning of motor skills is quite simple. It consists of practice, direct and continued.

6. Eliciting Performance

The instructional events so far described are designed to assure that learning "takes hold." The new capability reflected in the objective, whether verbal information, intellectual skill, cognitive strategy, attitude, or motor skill, has been encoded into a form for storage in long-term memory. It is then time for the learner to demonstrate the newly learned capability.

Very simply, the learner of verbal information is asked to "tell" it, or at least some part of it. The learner of a new concept or rule is asked to demonstrate its applicability to a particular instance not previously encountered during the learning. The learner of a cognitive strategy of problem solving is given the challenge of an unfamiliar problem whose solution may use the strategy. The learner of a motor skill takes another turn to exhibit the learned performance. As for the newly acquired attitude, it is shown by the choices made by the learner in a previously unencountered situation (or, practically, by the choices revealed in a questionnaire).

7. Providing Feedback

Following the performance which shows that learning has occurred, there must be a communication to the learner about the correctness and the degree of correctness of the performance. This event may be carried out in a number of different ways. In the case of a motor skill such as throwing darts at a target, the feedback may be said to be "built in" and immediate. For many varieties of performance, however, feedback about correctness of performance may need to be separately delivered by a teacher or another agent. Some valuable kinds of feedback can be provided in computer-aided instruction. However, judgments of the quality of a written composition are examples of the precision of feedback that depends upon a human teacher.

8. Assessing Performance

The performance that accompanies the learning of a new capability is simply a verification that learning has occurred. Since performance is typically a single act of the learner, it indicates only some reasonable probability that the capability has been stored in a reliable (i.e., stable) manner. In order to assure that such stability is indeed present, it is necessary to require additional instances of the performance. If verbal information has been learned, paraphrased versions of the statements, or elaborations of them, may be asked for. If a rule has been learned, application to a number of additional novel examples may be called for.

Assessing performance in this manner is what is meant usually by "giving a test." The functions served by such a test are (1) establishing that the newly learned capability has reasonable stability, and (2) providing additional practice that serves to consolidate what has been learned.

9. Enhancing Retention and Transfer

What kind of event will increase the probability that what has been learned will (1) be retained over long periods of time, and (2) be capable of being employed as a performance in new situations, with new problems? It may be hoped that much more knowledge will be forthcoming about this question than is currently known.

Increased amounts of practice constitute a fairly dependable factor for affecting amount of retention. This generalization appears to apply to the remembering of verbal information, intellectual skills, and motor skills. Although specific evidence is not readily available, it might be expected that practice has similar effects on the retention of cognitive strategies and attitudes. As noted in Chapter 6, arrangements of practice in the form of spaced reviews have been shown to be advantageous for the retention of intellectual skills.

Transfer of knowledge, skills, and strategies to new problems and new situations is a matter on which evidence continues to be sought. It would appear that a certain amount of practice *variety* favors transfer of intellectual skills to new situations. Another way to view the problem of learning transfer is as a circumstance influenced by the *number of cues* in common between the learning situation and the new situation requiring transfer. This view implies that newly learned rules, for example, may be enhanced in transferability when they are linked to networks of other concepts and propositions (Gagné and White, 1978). Embedding a newly learned intellectual skill in a larger meaningful context, such as a *schema* (Rumelhart and Ortony, 1977) or as a component of a *work model* (Bunderson et al., 1981) may be viewed as a way of increasing the cues available in the situation in which transfer is called for.

OTHER VARIABLES IN INSTRUCTION

The instructional theory represented in this work and summarized in the present chapter identifies the variables affecting learning as embodied in the events of instruction. The theory states that learning will occur in an optimal fashion if each of these events takes a form indicated by research to be most effective. By this is meant the form that has been shown to provide greatest support to the internal processes involved in learning. A further point made by the theory is that the optimal form for some of these events (particularly those numbered 3, 4, 5, and 9) is distinctly different for each of the five kinds of learning outcome.

It is important to note that not every one of the nine events of instruction is always present in the learning situation. For young children, it is usually advantageous for the teacher to use the entire set. As learners gain experience, however, they are increasingly able to practice *self-instruction*. This means that the events are supplied by the learners themselves, in the form of learning strategies. A high-school student, for example, may have a strategy for making features of a history lesson distinctive, another strategy for encoding the facts to be learned, and still another for enhancing retention. The instructional events are still present in this instance, but they come from the student rather than from the teacher. Obviously, truly mature learners will have learned to supply most or all of these supporting events on their own initiative.

Conditions Affecting Instruction

Other theories, such as those of Carroll (1963) and Bloom (1976), attempt to account for the influence of a larger set of variables, including those that arise beyond the instructional situation (defined in a narrow sense) or those that may pertain to the administration of instructional programs. A brief word needs to be added about several of these variables in order to make clear their relation to the theory described here.

Time. The amount of time devoted to learning may be expected to affect the amount of learning. As a number of empirical studies have shown, the time students spend in actual learning ("time on task") is a particularly potent variable in the determination of what is learned, as indicated by student proficiency in school subjects. The present theory simply makes the assumption that time devoted to learning will have this expected effect; otherwise, the theory makes no attempt to deal with time as an instructional factor. Obviously, the favorable effects on achievement of time on task are not in conflict with the theory or with predictions from it.

Motivation. Another assumption made by the present theory is the presence of favorable motivation on the part of the learner. The event of instruction concerned with informing the learner of the objective intends to deal with motivation by relating the performance made possible by learning to some pre-existing motivation of the learner. For example, if the objective of a unit of instruction pertains to mathematical operations on fractions, this might be related to a learner's desire to evaluate stocks listed on the New York Stock Exchange in terms of their price-earnings ratios.

Additional considerations relating motivation to learning are discussed in Chapter 14.

Individual differences. The factors identified in the current theory are proposed as applying to every human learner, regardless of level of intellegence or other academic ability. Naturally, individual differences in the rate at which various learning objectives are achieved will be apparent.

In making practical applications of the theory to the design of instruction, two kinds of individual differences may be particularly noted and taken into account.

1. *Prior knowledge.* This factor is reflected directly in instructional event number 3, "stimulating recall of prior learning." As previously indicated, this particular variety of differences among individual learners is expected to have a substantial effect upon the ease with which learning of new material occurs. When educational programs are designed to be adaptive to individual differences, assessing the kind and extent of prior knowledge of students is the most important step to take at the beginning of each new unit of instruction.

   The kind of knowledge to be assessed in adaptive instructional programs depends upon the type of learning outcome anticipated. For example, prior knowledge for the learning of a new intellectual skill are the *particular* rules and concepts that are prerequisite to the learning of that skill. In contrast, prior knowledge for the learning of verbal information consists of *any* large body of knowledge (network of propositions) that is relevant to the information to be learned.

2. *Discourse comprehension.* This factor is reflected in instructional event 4, "presenting the stimulus." Very often, material to be learned is in the form of printed text, in which case one would be concerned with *reading comprehension.* Should the stimulus material be presented auditorially, individual scores pertaining to the comprehension of such content would presumably be more highly related to learning success, although they are still likely to correlate highly with reading comprehension scores. This variable affects the ease of learning of individuals because it influences how readily they comprehend the communication of the substance to be learned. Naturally, its effects are not as great when the learn-

ing tasks are of a visual-spatial nature, or when they partake strongly of precision in motor performance.

GENERAL REFERENCES

Events of Instruction

See references for Chapters 5 through 11.

Instructional Theories

Ausubel, D. P., Novak, J. D., and Hanesian, H. *Educational psychology: A cognitive view*, 2nd ed. New York: Holt, Rinehart and Winston, 1978.

Bruner, J. S. *Toward a theory of instruction*. Cambridge, Mass: Harvard University Press, 1966.

Case, R. A developmentally based theory and technology of instruction. *Review of Educational Research*, 1978, 48, 439–463.

Gagné, R. M., and Briggs, L. J. *Principles of instructional design*, 2nd ed. New York: Holt, Rinehart and Winston, 1979.

Gagné, R. M., and Dick, W. Instructional psychology. *Annual Review of Psychology*, 1983, 34, 261–295.

Reigeluth, C. M., Merrill, M. D., and Bunderson, C. V. The structure of subject-matter content and its instructional design implications. *Instructional Science*, 1978, 7, 107–126.

13

Analyzing the Requirements for Learning

Previous chapters have described the conditions of learning that are optimal for the five varieties of learning outcomes: intellectual skills, cognitive strategies, verbal information, motor skills, and attitudes. The principles and generalizations we have been able to assemble from learning research and theory are those that make possible the selection and design of conditions for effective human learning. Events that facilitate learning can accordingly be planned to activate and support the processes of learning, as has been indicated in our description of instructional theory in the previous chapter. Planning of instructional events in accordance with the latter theory can take account of *internal* conditions (the contents of long-term memory accessible to the learner) and of *external* conditions (the relevant stimulation from the learner's environment).

Proper usage of the principles of learning to achieve effectiveness of outcome requires, first, that the *class of learning outcome* be identified for any specific learning task that the learner undertakes. Once this is done, steps can be taken to discover what internal conditions are applicable to the learning task, and further, to arrange the external conditions so that the expected outcome will be achieved.

Evidently, then, when an instructional plan for learning is to be made, an initial step is to conduct a *learning analysis* of the particular learning outcome to be expected. In this chapter, we shall consider how such a learning analysis, or *learning task analysis*, may best be done.

TASK DESCRIPTION

Human beings undertake many sorts of tasks. Most of them are learned. They range from the apparently simple actions of a young child in locomotion and object manipulation to the most complex intellectual ratiocinations that may enter into the invention of a scientific theory. The description of human tasks may also be done in various ways, to meet different needs. Describing a task for purposes of classifying a job, for example, requires a different approach than does describing a task in order to reveal what is necessary for its learning. We need to consider here the kind of description that is most appropriate for revealing the requirements of planning for the internal and external conditions of learning.

Describing Job Tasks

Tasks can be described with differing degrees of specificity. One can describe a performance in general terms as "installing a shingle roof," its components in more specific terms as "nailing a shingle to a roofing board," or in even more detail as "striking a roofing nail with a hammer." The problem of choosing a degree of specificity for the description of human tasks has been a puzzling one. It appears to be best solved by considering the *communication purpose* of the description (see Gagné, 1965.) That is to say, the degree of specificity of description should be determined by consideration of the question, "*What* is being communicated to *whom?*"

Tasks described as job components (job tasks) may be thought of as "activities that are the smallest a supervisor would normally ask a job incumbent to perform." The following are examples:

> For an office clerk:
> File incoming correspondence in folder by name, arranged by date of receipt.
> For someone who repairs small appliances:
> Remove and replace defective heating element in electric toaster.

The basic notion of "job task" need not be confined to tasks that are parts of identifiable occupations. Job tasks occur much more generally; there is no reason why this basic conception should not be applied to all aspects of life—to performances that make up one's roles as a citizen, family member, social being, and as one who seeks enjoyment in living. Job tasks in this general sense might reasonably be called *life tasks* and include descriptions of such activities as the following:

> Reading and understanding accounts of events printed in daily newspaper
> Recording deposits and withdrawals to maintain an accurate balance in a personal checking account
> Seeking enjoyment in watching a variety of sports events and dramatic shows
> Feeding a baby with a bottled formula
> Selecting fresh vegetables for family meals in a supermarket
> Orally expressing opinions and communicating information in meetings as a member of a neighborhood council
> Seeking opportunities to go scuba diving

The significance of a general meaning for the concept of "life task" is that human activities described at this level of specificity often correspond to *educational goals.* When one attempts to achieve greater specificity in educational planning than exists in the "Seven Cardinal Principles" (Commission on the Reorganization of Secondary Education, 1918), the result is typically a list of human tasks that can reasonably be called "life tasks" if the broad meaning of that phrase is accepted. In this sense, a *life task is any task that a human being would reasonably be asked to do while in the course of fulfilling one or more purposes understood as contributing to his or her life goals.*

TASK ANALYSIS FOR INSTRUCTIONAL DESIGN

With this broadened definition of job task, the degree of specificity intended becomes apparent. One would not ask an individual to perform a task so insignificant in purpose, and at the same time so general in its occurrence, that its particular relation to one or more life goals could not be perceived. "Lifting an arm," "sitting in a chair," and "holding a pencil" are not life tasks, whereas those given in the previous list do qualify. However, tasks such as "reading a daily newspaper with comprehension" and others in the list of life tasks still do not have the level of specificity needed for the planning of learning conditions. In order to reveal learning requirements, these tasks must be analyzed further. Educational programs designed to insure optimal learning conditions cannot be planned by dealing only with tasks that express educational goals. Such statements must be subjected to additional analysis to make clear the components of what is to be learned.

Clarifying principles of the analysis of tasks for purposes of instructional planning have been greatly augmented by the work of R. B. Miller (1963; see also Gagné, 1965). Miller made a careful distinction between "job-task description" and "learning task description" in terms of their different communication purposes. In general, the level of specificity needed for describing the tasks that make up a job is not as detailed as the level needed for describing what has to be learned. In communicating the job task of an electronic equipment technician, for example, it may be sufficient to state that the technician "adjusts the gain of amplifier MP-32 to a prescribed standard." In terms of the total job, this may be one fairly "small" specific performance out of many. However, if one asks what the electronic technician has to learn in order to adjust the gain of amplifier MP-32, one gets an entirely different answer. It is likely to be found that the adjustment task requires the technician to use a voltmeter, and that this is something that must be learned. Thus, the job task identified as "adjusts an amplifier gain" needs further analysis to reveal such tasks (subtasks?) as "identifies contact positions for voltage measurement in a designated circuit" and "reads value of voltage from voltmeter scale." It may be necessary for the analysis to proceed still farther to reveal the "supporting knowledge" or "supporting skills" that are prerequisites for the learning of the subtasks that make up the amplifier gain adjustment task.

Human Tasks as Procedures

The first analysis of tasks is likely to reveal that a set of different actions must be performed in a sequential or steplike fashion. That is to say, the task goal is achieved by following a *procedure*, as described in Chapter 10. T. F. Gilbert's (1962) account of procedures includes analyses of long division, reading color-coded electrical resistors, multiplying with the slide rule, and balancing tellers' accounts. A simple procedure—changing a tire on an automobile—is illustrated in Figure 13.1.

Steplike procedures may also be involved in what appear to be very simple tasks, such as those learned by preschool children. Examples of procedures of this sort are described by Resnick, Wang, and Kaplan (1970), and one illustration is shown in Figure 13.2.

Procedures often require that decisions be made about alternative steps. That is, the outcome of one step gives a clue to the choice of the next step. Such procedures are sometimes called *conditional procedures*, and they are frequently described in more complicated flow charts, an example of which is shown in Figure 13.3. This distinguishes the *inputs* to the procedure (trapezoidal boxes), the *decision points* (diagonal boxes), and the *action* (rectangular boxes). Some of the steps taken are conditional upon the decision that must be made, whereas others simply follow in a regular order.

It is evident that this kind of analysis of a human task results in a step-by-step description of the performance that the task represents. Since some of these steps may be internal to the learner, rather than overt behavior, this kind of analysis is sometimes called an "information-processing" task analysis. As Merrill (1978) points out, it stands in contrast to the *learning analysis* to be described in the next section and should be conducted prior to that kind of analysis (Gagné, 1977). Other examples of information-processing analysis of children's problem solving are described by Siegler and Klahr (1982).

Figure 13.1 Analysis and description of the procedure of changing a tire.

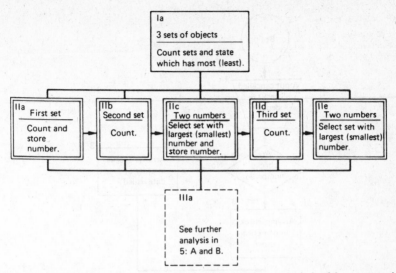

Figure 13.2 Procedure for a mathematics task to be accomplished by young children: Identifying which of three sets of objects has most (least). (Adapted from L. B. Resnick, M. C. Wang, and J. Kaplan, *Behavior analysis in curriculum design: A hierarchically sequenced introductory mathematics curriculum.* Pittsburgh, Pa.: University of Pittsburgh, Learning Research and Development Center, 1970, Figure 27.)

The analysis of tasks to reveal their procedural characteristics has two major implications for learning. First, it is evident that each step, or "link," in the procedure must be a capability of the learner. Sometimes the step is highly familiar (such as removing a jack from the trunk of a car); sometimes it is not familiar and must be newly learned (such as operating the jack to raise the car). In order to institute the entire procedure, the learner must have learned to perform each step, including the steps that require a decision about which action is appropriate next.

The second implication for learning is equally important: the learner must acquire the *executive routine* that governs the procedure as a whole. The learner must be able, in other words, to institute the steps of the procedure in the proper order so that one follows another in a sequence that will accomplish the task goal. As we have seen in Chapter 10, learning the routine may constitute a separate event from learning the individual steps in the procedure. Even so, the entire task can sometimes be learned "as a whole." The latter circumstance most frequently occurs when the procedure is a short one and its component steps are mostly familiar. The learning of executive routines for longer procedures is often aided by the mediation of verbal sequences, which provide cues to the ordering of the steps.

The results of analysis of tasks (job tasks) in terms of their procedures reveal (1) the executive routine that must be learned in order for the learner to carry out the task, and (2) the individual steps, or "links," of the proce-

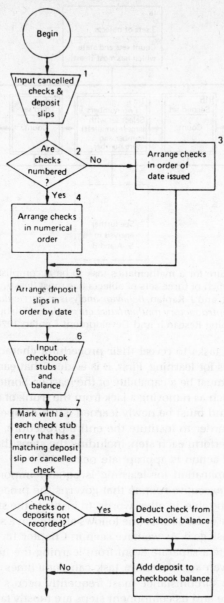

Figure 13.3 A vertically arranged flow chart showing initial steps in the procedure of reconciling a bank statement with checkbook records. In such a chart, diagonal boxes indicate decision points for choice of alternative steps. (From Merrill, P. F., *Task analysis: An information processing approach*. Technical Memo No. 27. Tallahassee: Florida State University, CAI Center, 1971, Figure 2.)

dure, each of which must be recalled from previous learning or learned newly. The latter steps may be motor skills (as we have seen in Chapter 10) or they may be intellectual skills, that is, concepts or rules. For example, the steps in long division (using the algorithm most widely known) include the intellectual skills of (1) multiplying several-place numbers by single-place numbers, (2) subtracting one several-place number from another, and (3) estimating single-place quotients of several-place divisors. These individual skills, as well as the executive routine for the procedure, become *instructional objectives* for learning the task as a whole.

LEARNING ANALYSIS

It might be supposed that the analysis of human tasks into their procedural steps is all that is needed to discover the requirements for learning; but this is not the case. Consider what is revealed by the methods of analysis described up to this point. A broad educational goal, such as "maintaining health" is broken down into parts called job tasks, an example of which is "brushing teeth to remove accumulated food particles." When analyzed as a procedure, this task is seen to consist of a sequence of several steps, some of which are familiar ("grasping the toothbrush"), while others may need to be learned by a child ("identifying crevices between inner surfaces of teeth"). When completed, this analysis results in a detailed *task description.*

Viewed broadly, a task description of a human activity has a number of applications. It may be used, for example, to construct a detailed guide to the actions required, in printed or pictorial form. When a task forms a part of a job or occupation, a task description may be of value for describing the job to applicants, for classifying the job within a career ladder, or for developing standards of performances to be used by a job incumbent (see R. B. Miller, 1963). From the standpoint of learning, a task description represents a description of "terminal" or "targeted" learning outcomes; that is, it describes the performances that a program of learning is designed to insure the learner acquires as a result of completing the program.

A detailed task description of a useful activity, however, does not tell us all we need to know about how to arrange optimal conditions for learning. Two additional operations are needed. First, the task must be *categorized* as a learning outcome into one of the five categories described—intellectual skill, cognitive strategy, information, motor skill, or attitude. This classification is necessary in order to plan the internal and external conditions of learning differentially for each type of learning outcome, as discussed in previous chapters. Second, each procedural component of the task must be further analyzed to reveal its *prerequisites.* This procedure has the purpose of specifying the internal conditions of learning that pertain to the *recall of previously learned entities* from the long-term memory. These substantive components are recalled so that they can become a part of what is to be newly learned.

Categorizing Learning Outcomes

A human task described at the level of specificity of a job task may be categorized in terms of the type of learning outcome it represents. Examples of such tasks, including some from the previous list of life tasks, are displayed in Table 13.1. It may be noted that the kind of *action* described by the task does not provide a certain clue to its nature as a learning outcome. The individual who performs the task may be standing or sitting, may be alone or in a social group, or may be using hands, feet, or head. The learning outcome must be *inferred* from the kind of *mental processing* required. The mental processing that is to be learned as an internal state is what we have called a *capability*.

Describing Tasks as Learning Objectives

The necessity for making an inference about capabilities to be learned has led to the suggestion (Gagné and Briggs, 1979) that tasks be described by statements using *standard verbs*. Of course, capabilities do not have to be described in that fashion. The important point is simply that a correct inference be made about category of learning outcome. Nevertheless, standard verbs can provide an automatic clue to the type of capability to be inferred.

The description of tasks as learning objectives has been the subject of

TABLE 13.1 Examples of Useful Human Tasks and the Categories of Learning Outcomes They Represent

Task	Category of Learning Outcome
Reading with comprehension accounts of events printed in daily newspaper	*Intellectual skills*—applying rules for the decoding of words and the comprehension of language
Seeking enjoyment in watching a variety of sports events and dramatic shows	*Attitudes*—choosing courses of personal action toward particular kinds of entertainment
Communicating the precautions necessary in installing fiberglass ceiling insulation	*Information*—stating information so that its propositional meaning is preserved
Manually lowering the needle onto a phonograph record so as to engage the initial groove	*Motor skill*—executing a smoothly timed motor performance
Originating a game of "Ecology," to be played on family outings in an automobile	*Cognitive strategy*—solving a novel problem by invention

many books and articles (for example, Bloom, Hastings, and Madaus, 1971; Mager, 1975; Popham and Baker, 1970). A fundamental necessity for good description proposed by Mager (1975) is the use of verbs that are unambiguous. Examples of ambiguous verbs are "knows," "appreciates," "understands," as opposed to verbs denoting definite action such as "selects," "calculates," or "writes." However, although action verbs are clearly useful in describing the tasks that are the objects of learning, they do not always provide the necessary clues for inferring the human capabilities to be learned. For example, one task may require "writing" the answer to an arithmetic problem (an intellectual skill), whereas another may require "writing" a sentence to express a fact (verbal information).

The suggestion made by Gagné and Briggs (1979) is that standard verbs be used in statements of human tasks to imply the type of capability (learning outcome) that they involve. Examples of such descriptive statements are reprinted from that source in Table 13.2. It will be evident that each of the learning outcomes described in this book, and their subvarieties, is repre-

TABLE 13.2 Verbs to Describe Human Capabilities, with Examples of Phrases Incorporating Them

Capability	Verb	Example
Intellectual Skill Discrimination	DISCRIMINATES	Discriminates, by matching, the French sounds of "u" and "ou"
Concrete Concept	IDENTIFIES	Identifies, by naming, the root, leaf, and stem of representative plants
Defined Concept	CLASSIFIES	Classifies, by using a definition, the concept "family"
Rule	DEMONSTRATES	Demonstrates, by solving verbally stated examples, the addition of positive and negative numbers.
Higher-order Rule (Problem Solving)	GENERATES	Generates, by synthesizing applicable rules, a paragraph describing a person's actions in a situation of fear
Cognitive Strategy	ORIGINATES	Originates a solution to the reduction of air pollution, by applying model of gaseous diffusion
Information	STATES	States orally the major issues in the presidential campaign of 1932
Motor Skill	EXECUTES	Executes backing a car into driveway
Attitude	CHOOSES	Chooses playing golf as a leisure activity

From R. M Gagné, and L. J. Briggs, *Principles of Instructional Design*, 2nd ed., p. 125, Table 7–1. Copyright 1979 by Holt, Rinehart and Winston. Reproduced by permission of Holt, Rinehart and Winston.

sented in Table 13.2. The *major verb* in each task statement, listed in the middle column, immediately suggests the kind of human capability to be learned. Most of the statements also employ *action verbs* in the form of gerunds, as in the phrases "by matching," or "by naming."

Analyzing Tasks for Prerequisites

When tasks representing learning outcomes have been adequately described and categorized, it then becomes possible to conduct a further step, which constitutes *learning analysis*. This step identifies the prerequisites for the learning of the capability represented by the task description.

Most investigators of the process of instruction acknowledge the importance for planning of finding out what the learner *brings to* the learning situation. Glaser (1967, 1979), for example, has often emphasized the importance of *entering behavior* as a critical element in instructional design. The point of view elaborated here is that certain previously learned capabilities need to be retrieved from the long-term memory and need to be readily accessible in the working memory whenever a new capability is learned. These resultants of prior learning may *support* the new learning; an example is the retrieval of a cognitive strategy that permits the encoding of information to be learned. At least an equally important function of retrieval of previously learned entities, however, is their *incorporation* into new learning. When the intellectual skill of adding integers is learned, the previously acquired skill of subtracting whole numbers is incorporated as a part of the new capability. Similarly, when the intellectual skill of making the subject of a clause agree in number with its verb, the previously learned skills of identifying subject and verb are incorporated into the newly learned skill.

Prior learning as support for new learning. A case can be made for the idea that certain previously learned capabilities provide necessary *support* for new learning, regardless of what is being learned. For example, cognitive strategies of one kind or another must be brought to bear upon the phases of the learning process—attending, perceiving, encoding, retrieving, and problem solving. Whatever strategies are available to the learner as a result of prior learning must be retrieved and activated as executive control processes for the new learning. Although these strategies may be refined by the learning exercise, they do not themselves become a part of what is learned— which may be a new intellectual skill, a new motor skill, a new set of information, or an attitude.

In a similar sense, certain intellectual skills, often those learned years ago, may be seen to give *support* to the learning of any or all kinds of capabilities. The learner who is acquiring new information or a new attitude from reading must be able to use the intellectual skills needed in the decoding of words and the comprehension of printed prose. Attitudes provide another source of support for learning in that they engender choices of action toward particular subject matter to be learned and preferences for achievement in the attainment of expected goals.

Prerequisites as components of what is learned.   While previously learned capabilities may facilitate learning in a number of different ways, the true meaning of *prerequisite* is a *capability of prior learning that is incorporated into new learning*. The previously learned entity actually enters into the newly learned capability and becomes and remains a part of the behavior that results from the events of learning.

The most obvious examples of prerequisites as components of new learning occur in the domain of intellectual skills, some examples of which have already been mentioned. When the new skill of pronouncing printed words having a final "e" and a medial "a" is learned, this skill *incorporates* the prerequisite skills of (1) identifying a final "e," (2) identifying a medial "a," and (3) naming the long "a" sound. When the new skill of subtracting multiple-place numbers is acquired, it incorporates the prerequisite skills of (1) subtracting single-place numbers, (2) subtracting zero from a number, and (3) "borrowing" (or another operation having this purpose). As pointed out in Chapter 6, these prerequisites may be considered *subordinate* skills to the new and more complex skill that is being learned. A complex rule may actually be composed of simpler rules and concepts. The latter may be learned as prerequisites immediately prior to the new skill, or they may have been learned some time ago. When the new and more complex skill is being learned, they must be accessible in the working memory of the learner.

Incorporated prerequisites also become involved in the learning of other kinds of capabilities. In the case of motor skills, prerequisites are often the *part-skills* that compose the total skill; the skill of handwriting, for example, includes the part-skills of forming each of the letters. Attitudes, too, have prerequisites incorporated into their learning. Intellectual skills in the form of *concepts* of the categories of objects toward which the attitudes are directed are essential to the learning of attitudes. Thus, to acquire a positive attitude toward the maintenance of health, the learner must have prerequisite concepts that provide meaning to "good health" in terms of the functioning of various parts and organ systems of the body. Another kind of prerequisite for the learning of attitudes, as described in Chapter 11, is information about the situations in which the attitude will operate. An attitude toward "obeying the speed limit" in automobile driving incorporates prerequisite knowledge about the range of speed limits and the situations in which they are posted (highways, urban streets, school zones, and so on).

Does the learning of cognitive strategies, such as those of productive thinking, require prerequisites that are incorporated into the newly acquired (or newly refined) strategy? As indicated in Chapter 7, this is a matter of theoretical controversy and cannot be given a final answer at the moment. According to the views of Piaget (1970) and others, cognitive strategies require prerequisite intellectual growth in the sense of the maturation of capabilities of logical thought. Learned intellectual skills *support* this intellectual growth, since they make possible the variety of specific performances required in the practice of the cognitive strategies. A contrasting view (Gagné, 1968a) is that intellectual skills (rules and concepts) are incorporated into cognitive strategies by cumulative generalization and thus are true prerequisites in the learning of problem-solving strategies (see the discussion of learning hierarchies, Chapter 6).

What prerequisites are required for verbal information learning? Let us suppose that the fact being learned is "Jack captured a squirrel." Evidently, the concepts represented by each word must be known as prerequisites if the sentence is to be learned as a meaningful fact. However, we noted in Chapter 8 that a proposition can be acquired and stored even when word meaning is not known, as in the sentence "Turlop glavered renstil." Another essential prerequisite, then, is the basic skill of identifying the *syntactic relations* in strings of words. By this is meant the identification (not by name, of course) of *agent-action-object* and their transformation into *subject-predicate*. The sentence "Turlop glavered renstil" is learned as a proposition because "turlop" appears to be a subject, "glavered" appears to be a verb, and "renstil" appears to be the object of the verb. It is reasonable to conclude, then, that the specific intellectual skill of "taking in" a sentence as a set of words having subject-predicate relations with each other is an essential prerequisite for information learning. The identification of subject and predicate is *incorporated* into what is learned.

Enabling Objectives for Learning

We have seen that job-tasks may be analyzed as procedures into the individual steps that compose them. Each of these action steps may be considered a prerequisite to the total performance, since each must be learned before the whole performance can be exhibited. Then again, each step may have its own prerequisites, not in the sense of comprising a sequence but as entities of prior learning that are incorporated into the new learning.

Sometimes, the prerequisites of learning make sense as separate job tasks, each of which a human learner might perform in and by itself. Sometimes, however, the prerequisite capabilities are not of this sort, but are useful *only* because they enter into the learning of a new capability. Learning outcomes that are prerequisites to other learning objectives are called *enabling objectives*. It is important to recognize, though, that although some enabling objectives may stand by themselves as useful human tasks (life tasks), others have *only* the enabling function.

For the task of subtracting multiple-place numbers, one of the enabling objectives is subtracting single-place numbers. But this is by itself a useful task, which may be required in identifying innings in a baseball game, in making up shortages of goods, and in many other situations. In contrast, the enabling objective of "borrowing" (or whatever operation takes its place) is *only* enabling for the operation of subtracting multiple-place numbers and is not useful for other purposes. Nevertheless, it is an *essential prerequisite* and therefore deserves to be called an enabling objective. In the reading of words with final "e," the identification of a final "e" is an essential enabling objective, even though it fails to stand by itself as a useful human task.

The importance of this distinction among learning prerequisites is simply this: in order to discover the requirements for learning, *the capability to be learned must be analyzed into enabling objectives*, including those that serve *only* this purpose. Some enabling objectives that are themselves life tasks will be found by analysis. Others will be found that are not life tasks but are equally essential as learning prerequisites. A teacher might report to a parent that a child has learned to subtract single-place numbers but would probably not report that the child had learned "borrowing." Reporting the former makes sense because it is in itself a useful human task. Yet the latter, although not reported, is an equally essential enabling objective for learning to subtract multiple-place numbers.

The Results of Learning Analysis

Analyzing human tasks with the goal of learning in mind results in the identification of prerequisites for learning. Along the way, prior learning that *supports* the new learning, such as the possession of certain cognitive strategies and attitudes, may be noted. True prerequisites, however, are the previously learned entities that deserve to be called *enabling objectives*, because they are *incorporated* into the new learning. These may have been learned long ago or only a few minutes ago. At the time the new learning is to occur, they must be retrieved from the learner's long-term memory to the working (short-term) memory, to be accessible for involvement in the new learning (Gagné, 1980).

A summary of learning prerequisites that constitute necessary "entering behavior" of the learner is given in Table 13.3. From the example shown, the prerequisites of a newly learned intellectual skill are clearly other intellectual skills (rules, concepts). Notable, however, is the frequency with which intellectual skills appear as prerequisites for other kinds of learning outcomes, such as the learning of information and attitudes. As we have noted, in the case of motor skill, the executive routine that is an essential component is an intellectual skill in the form of a procedural rule. As for the cognitive strategy described in Table 13.3, we propose that this strategy is derived by the learner from a number of previously learned specific rules of categorizing.

Learning hierarchies as statements of prerequisites. As we recall the topic of learning hierarchies in Chapter 6, a special word needs to be said about their representation of prerequisites. As our discussion of rules and concepts has indicated, these intellectual skills can be readily analyzed to reveal subordinate skills that are either simpler rules or concepts. Such subordinate skills are true prerequisites; that is, they are *incorporated* into a newly learned skill that is more complex. The subordinate "boxes" of a learning hierarchy are intended to represent only these kinds of essential prerequisites. The process of analysis may be continued on each of the prerequisite skills so as to reveal rules or concepts that are in turn subordinate to these. In general, the analysis is conducted by asking the following question about each skill: "What [skill] should the learner already know how to do and be able to recall when faced with the task of learning the new rule, the absence of which would make it impossible for him to learn the new rule?" (see Gagné, 1968b).

By means of such an analysis, successively carried out for each intellectual skill and for its subordinates, a learning hierarchy is defined. It is clear,

TABLE 13.3 Prerequisites of Learning for Five Kinds of Learning Outcome, with Examples

Type of Learning Outcome	Example	Prerequisites
Intellectual skill	Finding the hypotenuse of a right triangle	Subordinate intellectual skills: rules for square roots, concepts of right triangle, adjacent sides, and so on.
Cognitive strategy	Originating a novel set of categories for a group of nonfiction books	Rules for classifying and constructing superordinate categories
Verbal information	Stating "The capital of Missouri is Jefferson City"	Concepts of things and relations; syntactic rules of subject-verb-object; previously organized information
Motor skill	Punting a football	Part-skills of holding ball, dropping ball, aiming kick; executive routine for total action
Attitude	Choosing "careful" actions in automobile approach to stoplights	Rules pertaining to customary stoplight operation; information about traffic situations in which stoplights occur

however, that the prerequisites so derived are only *minimal essentials* for learning any new intellectual skill.

A learning hierarchy represents only the prerequisites that must be available to the learner because they are to be incorporated in the newly learned skill. The previously learned entities that simply *support* the new learning are not represented. There are, of course, a number of possible supports that may be available to the learner—previously learned information, for example, or previously learned cognitive strategies. A considerably more complex diagram would be needed to represent learning prerequisites in this broader meaning of the term.

A learning hierarchy that has been the subject of several research studies (Linke, 1974; Trembath and White, 1979; White, 1973, 1974; White and Gagné, 1978) is shown in Figure 13.4. The target task may be stated as follows: Given a straight-line graph relating position and time, and given either a specified value for position (of a body) or a specified value for time, demonstrate the determination of velocity. The hierarchy of Figure 13.4 was a part of a larger one formulated in White's (1974) original study and was subjected by White and Gagné (1978) to a formative evaluation. Students in grades 10 and 11 of three different secondary schools participated in the study. There were 148 in all, about half of each gender. These students had been taught the skills of the hierarchy as part of their courses in mathematics and science. Their performance of each of the skills was assessed by a proficiency test containing three items representing each skill. Scoring of the test was by skill, two or more items correct was graded *pass* for that particular skill. From these results a table of *prerequisite relations* was constructed to provide evidence of the dependence of each higher-level skill on the lower-level skill specifically related to it. According to the theory of prerequisite intellectual skills, no students should be able to learn a higher-level skill unless they had mastered the related lower-level skill. The study assumed that this kind of prerequisite relation would become evident from a test that measured retention of these skills.

In general, the results verified the prerequisite relations posited by the proposed hierarchy. No students (or in some instances a very small number assumed to represent test error) were able to perform a higher-level skill who had not mastered the related lower-level skill. For example, only one student out of 148 was able to pass skill 2 after apparently failing skill 1. For one strand of the proposed hierarchy, however, these results did not apply. This is the strand represented by skills 9, 8, and 7, and this notable exception is instructive. For instance, 22% of the students who failed to perform on skill 7 showed that they had learned skill 8; as many as 25% who failed on skill 9 were able to perform target skill 12.

When most of the prerequisite relations of Figure 13.4 turn out to be as predicted by theory, why are those marked with an X found to be invalid? In several studies of learning hierarchies (Beeson, 1977; Trembath and White,

Figure 13.4 A learning hierarchy showing relationships of prerequisite skills to the task: Calculating velocity from a straight-line graph of position (vertical axis) and time (horizontal axis). x = relationships found invalid. (Based on a description in White, R. T., and Gagné, R. M. Formative evaluation applied to a learning hierarchy. *Contemporary Educational Psychology*, 1978, 3, 87–94.)

1979; White, 1974), the same answer to this general question has been obtained. Performances that are *invalid* are items of *verbal information* and do not behave as do typical intellectual skills. For example, proposed skill 7 is obviously a verbal statement, as is also skill 9. It is these particular performances that turn out *not* to be prerequisites for intellectual skills. Results of this sort add to the evidence for distinctive conditions of learning applicable to "declarative" and "procedural" knowledge (Anderson, 1976). The validated hierarchy derived from that shown in Figure 13.4 would eliminate the strand shown as 7-8-9-12.

Prerequisite relations in the form of learning hierarchies have been applied to intellectual skills of many different content types. Beeson (1977) developed and evaluated a hierarchy on the determination of quantities in electric circuits. Ozsogomonyan (1979) has described the use of a learning hierarchy for instruction in chemical combination by molecular weights (stoichiometry). Prerequisite relations have been employed successfully in programs of remedial education, particularly for basic skills. In the Canadian province of Ontario, computer-aided instruction has been developed for thirty of the most important topics in intermediate mathematics, including arithmetic, algebra, probability, and measurement (Gershman and Sakamoto, 1980). Learning hierarchies have also served as a basis for training of basic skills related to initial job training programs in the U.S. Navy (Harding, Mogford, Melching, and Showel, 1981).

While the idea of learning hierarchies does not illuminate the organization of instructional content composed of verbal information (such as the events of history), applicability to the field of social studies is not entirely lacking. For example, Deming (1974) has proposed several learning hierarchies for social studies topics, including one for predicting the location of cities on a map, shown in Figure 13.5. Other suggestions for the use of learning hierarchies in curriculum design and instructional planning are made by Cook and Walbesser (1973). Cook (1976) suggests expanding the meaning of learning hierarchy to include *topic hierarchies* applicable to the design of courses in such fields as art, history, and literature.

The uses of learning prerequisite analyses. When a learning analysis has been completed, the information about prerequisite relations (as suggested by the final column of Table 13.3) may be used for the planning of conditions for learning, that is, for the *design of instruction.* Depending on other factors in the situation, two alternatives are available to the designer. One way of using prerequisites in planning is to select learners who have acquired the necessary capabilities through prior learning, and proceed with the design of learning conditions on that assumption. This method is sometimes used in vocational or industrial training programs. For public education, however, a second alternative is usually followed: the conditions of instruction are planned so that students who have not acquired the prerequisites may learn them before undertaking the "new" learning. Essential to optimal effectiveness for the latter method is careful identification of prerequisite learning for each student or for groups of students having common capabilities. Various educational arrangement, including "homogeneous grouping" and programs called "compensatory" or "remedial," may be

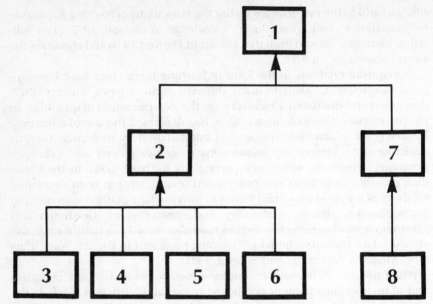

Figure 13.5 A learning hierarchy of prerequisite skills for the problem of predicting locations of cities on a map. 1. Predict the locations of cities on a map. 2. Order by importance the prerequisites for city growth. 3. Demonstrate the relation of waterways to development. 4. Demonstrate the relation of natural resources to development. 5. Demonstrate the relation of terrain to development. 6. Demonstrate the relation of climate to development. 7. Classify map symbols by definition. 8. Identify key symbols and map features. (Suggested by the work of Deming, B. S., A learning hierarchies approach to social studies instruction. *Journal of Curriculum Studies*, 1974, 7, 155–159.)

used to accomplish this purpose. In programs of *individualized instruction*, the progress of each individual student is assessed and made dependent upon the learning of necessary prerequisites (Gagné and Briggs, 1979).

DERIVING EXTERNAL CONDITIONS FOR LEARNING

Analysis of human tasks to reveal the prerequisites of learning yields a large portion of the information needed for design of optimal learning conditions. The other major part, the external conditions, is also implied by the classification of human tasks in terms of the categories of learning outcomes to which they belong. Previous chapters have been devoted to discussions of the ways in which external events can be used to *activate* and *support* internal processes of learning, and these ideas have been brought together as a theory of instruction in Chapter 12.

Some of the external conditions for effective learning are common to all kinds of expected learning outcomes. External provisions made to stimulate the learner's *alertness*, or *attention*, for example, may be very similar regardless of the capability being learned. Likewise, whatever *performance* is associated with the learned capability—whether a motor act, a verbal statement, or the application of a rule—must be elicited as one essential event in learning. Some external conditions, however, are *specific* to the nature of what is being learned and differ with the learning outcome expected. For example, the kind of event that supports the encoding process for a motor skill is quite different from that which facilitates the learning of verbal information. As we have seen in previous chapters, the encoding of a motor skill is affected critically by stimulation arising in the muscles and resulting from performance of muscular movement. In contrast, encoding verbal information does not depend upon the act of "stating" but is affected by the contextual meaning to which it can be related.

Differential External Conditions for Learning

In line with the instructional theory presented in Chapter 12, it is clear that some of the external conditions of learning differ from each other depending on the outcome expected. It will be worthwhile to review briefly the critical conditions for each category of learned capability in terms of the kind of instructional event these conditions represent.

Stimulating recall of prerequisites. The condition of stimulating recall of prerequisites is common to all kinds of learning outcomes. As we have seen in Chapter 4, stimuli for recall have the purpose of activating retrieval of previously learned entities to the working (short-term) memory so that they can be incorporated into the new learning. However, the nature of *what* must be retrieved obviously differs among learning outcomes. The basic requirements are described in Table 12.2.

It should be noted also that other kinds of previously learned material may support learning differentially, depending upon what the learner has in store. For example, the "larger meaningful context" for (new) information learning often comes mainly from the store of organized (old) information in the learner's memory. Different degrees of learning support can be expected from this organized knowledge, depending upon its amount, its degree of organization, and its relevance to the new learning. Likewise, the nature of previously stored information available to the learner may be expected to affect the ease of learning intellectual skills and to facilitate the processes of problem solving and thinking.

Providing learning guidance (encoding). External conditions exhibit critical differences for different learning outcomes when they pertain to the guidance provided to support the encoding process. A summary of these conditions is presented in Table 12.4. Despite a number of other features common to the learning situation (such as presentation of the stimulus, eliciting learner performance, providing reinforcement), it is evident that the conditions of learning that relate to the encoding process are indeed very different. These critical differences in encoding, in fact, most clearly distinguish the five kinds of learned capabilities and argue against the idea that "all learning is the same."

Enhancing retention and transfer. The internal process supported by these external conditions is *retrieval*. This process is activated by external *cues*, and the more that can be provided, the better. Thus the condition that best supports retrieval of what is learned is a variety of external cues. In practice, this means that in addition to the essential stimuli for learning, the surrounding context of stimulation helps retrieval by providing additional cues. Since recall (and also transfer of learning) takes place in situations different from that of original learning, *variety* of contextual cues raises the probability of effective performance in these new situations.

For intellectual skills, variety is provided by requiring the learner to apply a newly learned rule or definition to several kinds of examples. For cognitive strategies, problems varying in their content are used to enhance retention and transfer. Motor skills may be practiced in a variety of surrounding conditions, including noise and distractions, to aid their transfer to situations in which they will be used.

Variety in the cueing function can also be provided by requiring the learner to reinstate the learned capability at various times following initial learning. This is done in the technique of *spaced review*. Even a "next-day" recall and review of a learned rule or concept, for example, may greatly enhance its retention over longer periods. By reviewing after a period of time, the learner must utilize new cues not present at the time of original learning. Thus the variety of cues for retrieval is increased by such reviews. Deliberate introduction of varied contextual cues during review likewise serves to enhance the transferability of what is learned.

Learning Conditions and Instructional Design

In the manner indicated in the previous section, learning analysis leads to the identification of external conditions that are critically related to the attainment of different types of human capabilities. These conditions can be incorporated into the planning and *design* of instruction intended to bring about any of these learning outcomes. Techniques for accomplishing instructional design based upon these principles have been described by Gagné and Briggs (1979). A similar account, abbreviated in scope, is contained in Chapter 15. There we shall show how instruction having various purposes can be designed for optimal effectiveness by using knowledge of learning conditions, internal and external.

EDUCATIONAL IMPLICATIONS

Programs of education are typically designed or selected with certain broad goals in mind. Sometimes these goals are specifically formulated, sometimes not. Their further analysis is always necessary if one wishes to answer the question, "What is required of human learning in attaining these goals?" The purpose of analysis is to make possible the detailed specification of what must be learned, in other words, the human tasks that the learner will be able to accomplish when a period of learning has been completed.

Several degrees of specificity are possible in the description of human tasks. This state of affairs is not inherently deplorable, for task descriptions serve many different purposes. For educational planning to be based on sound learning principles, description must begin with a fairly specific level of detail for human performance, sometimes called the *job task*. A job task is the kind one might reasonably ask another person to do as a single act, as a part of a larger human undertaking (such as a job). Examples of job tasks are "typing a letter," "writing a descriptive report," or "constructing an alphabetical file." Acts too specific to be so classified are "striking an *e* on the typewriter," "stating a sentence," or "finding a folder labeled M."

The human task at this level of description is equally meaningful when *life task* is substituted for job task. Such a substitution makes the concept applicable to human activities that are not solely vocationally oriented. Reading the newspaper, feeding the baby, and watching a football game are examples of life tasks described at a level of specificity comparable to the tasks that comprise a job. They are human tasks that one expects other human beings (depending on their ages) to do, and to be able to do. Specific goals of educational programs are often expressed at the level of specificity of life tasks (Gagné, 1975).

Beginning at this point, it is possible to proceed with analyses having the purpose of designing educational programs that take account of the conditions for learning. Job tasks or life tasks usually involve *procedures* in which one action (or step) precedes another. Some procedures are quite short, others are quite long. Procedures may involve fixed sequences of steps, or, more often, steps contingent upon the outcomes of previous steps. Analysis that identifies individual human actions, their dependencies, and their sequence is a desirable and often essential first step in the specification of the required outcomes of learning. Whether the human task to be accomplished is long division or parallel parking an automobile, the delineation of its "steps" and their sequence provides the initial revelation of what must be learned. Usually, this turns out to be two things: (1) the procedure itself, or more specifically, *the executive routine* that enables the learner to perform the procedure; and (2) the component steps of the task (sometimes called *subtasks*).

In contrast to the analysis of tasks into procedural steps, a *learning analysis* seeks to identify the *prerequisites* for the learning of the total task and any of its subtasks that are not already well established. This kind of analysis asks of each component of the total task, "What must the learner have acquired by previous learning, and be able to recall, when the new learning is undertaken?" Some prerequisites are merely *supportive* of the new learning. The learner may be able to use certain previously learned cognitive strategies to advantage or may be able to recall a useful set of organized information. Other prerequisites, however, are *essential* in that they actually become incorporated into the newly learned capability. Clearest examples of these are intellectual skills; the learning of a complex rule involves the combining of simpler rules or concepts. When successively applied to prerequisites of intellectual skills and their subordinate skills, learning analysis results in a description called a *learning hierarchy*.

Learning hierarchies indicate the essential prerequisites for the learning of new rules and concepts and may for this reason be useful in the planning of sequences of instruction. Several precautions, however, should be noted. First, rational methods have not been devised to develop learning hierarchies for the four other kinds of learning outcomes (for example, information and motor skills); nor have valid hierarchies been demonstrated in these areas of human capability. Thus, methods of describing and diagramming *essential* prerequisites for these other capabilities, if feasible, have yet to be developed. Second, learning hierarchies for intellectual skills are intended to indicate *only* essential subskills; they do not depict supportive prerequisites such as information, attitudes, and cognitive strategies. For this reason, they do not contain all the information needed for the planning of instructional sequence.

Learning hierarchies, however, are not the only method for analyzing prerequisite knowledges and skills. Instructional theory tells us that each of the different kinds of learned capability has its own type of prerequisite, established by prior learning. One of the important results of a learning analysis is the identification of prerequisites for all five kinds of learning outcomes. Prerequisites are kinds of learning outcomes that an "entering" learner is expected to possess as a result of prior learning. Once these are identified, the planning of instruction may proceed in one of two ways. An instructional program may be designed for learners who are *selected* to have the essential (and supportive) prerequisite capabilities. Alternatively, the program may be designed to teach the prerequisites in a sequential fashion before teaching of the "target" capabilities is attempted. In practice, all educational programs incorporate some combination of these two alternatives.

A second result of learning analysis is the identification of critical *external* conditions for the learning of different kinds of human capabilities. In particular, the classification of the type of capability to be learned makes it possible to specify the external events that are *differentially effective* for each kind of learning outcome. In this way, the conditions of learning described in previous chapters can be applied to the design of programs of instruction on any topic.

GENERAL REFERENCES

Educational Goals

Boyer, E. L. *High school: A report on secondary education in America.* New York: Harper & Row, 1983.

Commission on the Reorganization of Secondary Education. *Cardinal principles of secondary education.* Department of the Interior, Bureau of Education. Bulletin No. 35. Washington, D.C.: GPO, 1918.

Gagné, R. M. Taxonomic problems of educational systems. In W. T. Singleton and P. Spurgeon (Eds.), *Measurement of human resources.* London: Taylor and Francis, 1975.

Kaufman, R., and English, F. W. *Needs assessment: Concept and application.* Englewood Cliffs, N.J.: Educational Technology Publications, 1979.

National Commission on Excellence in Education. *A nation at risk: The imperative for educational reform.* Washington, D.C.: U.S. Department of Education, 1983.

Tyler, R. W. *Basic principles of curriculum and instruction.* Chicago: University of Chicago Press, 1949.

Task Description and Analysis

Miller, R. B. Task description and analysis. In R. M. Gagné (Ed.), *Psychological principles in system development.* New York: Holt, Rinehart and Winston, 1963.

Learning Analysis

Briggs, L. J., and Wager, W. W. *Handbook of procedures for the design of instruction*, 2nd ed. Englewood Cliffs, N.J.: Educational Technology Publications, 1981. Chapter 2.

Dick, W., and Carey, L. *The systematic design of instruction.* Glenview, Ill.: Scott, Foresman, 1978. Chapters 3 and 4.

Gagné, R. M., and Briggs, L. J. *Principles of instructional design*, 2nd ed. New York: Holt, Rinehart and Winston, 1979.

Merrill, P. F. Hierarchical and informational processing task analysis: A comparison. *Journal of Instructional Development*, 1978, *1*, 35–40.

14

Selecting Media for Instruction

Instruction designed for effective learning may be delivered in a number of ways and may use a variety of media. The term *media*, when employed in an educational context, means whatever combination of things or systems of things used to deliver communications or other instructional stimuli to the learner. Media do not design or formulate these communications; they simply deliver them. The content and scheduling of the communications delivered by media may be relatively simple matters, like a set of familiar quotations written on a chalkboard; or they may be quite complex, as in the case of feedback to the learner from a computer screen. The content and its scheduling have been created by an instructional designer, a teacher, or instructor. Delivery of what has been designed is the function of a medium or combination of media.

In this chapter, the attempt is made to show how the ideas of this book, and particularly the instructional theory described in Chapter 12, can be applied to an educational problem of considerable scope and complexity. This undertaking extends way beyond the settings of elementary and secondary school classrooms, which have often been sources of instructional examples in previous chapters. In considering media and their selection, the intention here is to encompass such settings for instruction as the professional education of adults and programs of training for jobs and occupations as well as various "informal" programs of instruction that occur beyond the bounds of schools. The reader should realize that schoolchildren are by no means being abandoned in this chapter; rather, their requirements for instruction are being shown as part of a larger picture.

Some media are widely and frequently used and therefore highly familiar, such as books or TV programs. In order to encompass the entire range of "things that communicate," one must include at one end of the spectrum the instructor's voice and toward the other end an interactive system including the computer and video disc. Sometimes the choice of media is done almost unthinkingly, as when an instructor decides "of course" to use the printed pages of a book to present a lesson on the poetry of Wordsworth. In other circumstances, however, several different choices are possible. For example, to give instruction in the principles of aerodynamics, should one use a printed text with mathematical equations, a set of air flow drawings on a chalkboard, a motion picture of an airplane wing in a wind tunnel, or perhaps all three?

When instruction is planned to result in effective learning, choices about the nature of the communication to the learner are likely to involve at the same time choices of media. Both decisions are affected by conditions that support learning processes. Both may be viewed in the light of instructional theory as described in previous chapters and summarized in Chapter 12. Thus, even when the selection of media depends on local circumstances such as ready availability, it is desirable for instructors to be aware of the appropriateness of the media to be employed in terms of their ability to deliver the communications desired.

THE INSTRUCTIONAL SITUATION

The choice of media must be undertaken within the context of the prevailing or intended instructional situation. By introducing this idea, we wish to imply that our discussion is by no means restricted to the situation of a teacher with a classroom of students. While that setting undoubtedly allows for choices of many different media, it carries at the same time its own limitations. In viewing education broadly, it will be desirable to consider a variety of instructional situations that include (1) individuals completing a correspondence course in accounting, (2) persons in remote areas served by radio, (3) individuals learning critical skills such as those required in a nuclear power plant or in piloting an aircraft, and (4) home viewers of television documentary programs. The place of instruction can be a public school classroom, a learning center, a military or industrial workplace, or the living room of a home. In all these places and situations, instruction may be delivered and may utilize one or another set of media.

Limitations Imposed by the Instructional Situation

Most systems of media selection propose that decisions be made on the basis of media characteristics—the kinds of properties the media have that influence the nature of the instructional communication (Braby, 1973; Reiser and Gagné, 1982). However, it must be recognized that the *instructional situation* within which media are to be employed is an even more broadly limiting factor affecting media choice. The nature of the instructional situation is a factor that at one end of the spectrum limits media choice to a mere couple of options, while at the other end a score or more of possibilities are available. The following paragraphs describe the reasons for these limitations.

Required fault-free performance.   Sometimes, the instructional situation is designed to produce fault-free performance as soon as training is completed or from the first moment performance is called for "on the job." The consequences of inadequate performance or error may even be life-threatening. One expects such characteristics in certain of the tasks performed by physicians, dentists, and other health professionals; in those performed by people who operate vehicles such as aircraft; and in those who monitor potentially dangerous systems such as nuclear power plants.

When the consequences of error are serious, the instructional situation must be designed to produce dependable fault-free performance. Some obviously desirable media characteristics follow from this aim. The individuals being instructed must learn and practice (as many times as feasible) the particular procedural skills that are critical to error-free performance. It will be necessary, for example, that an aircraft pilot practice the skills involved in landing in a real plane, on an actual landing strip, or in a situation as close to such reality as possible. One cannot consider media such as an instructor's lecture, a textbook, or a motion picture as adequate to bring about the degree of competence needed for error-free performance. While it is reasonable to suppose that such media may be useful in some aspects of pilot training, none of them is adequate to produce the degree of skill required for critical tasks like landing. As further examples, similar considerations would apply to the critical procedures of a surgeon, an explosives handler, or a nuclear power-plant technician.

When fault-free performance is required as an outcome of instruction, the medium employed must be either the *real equipment* used in the job or profession or a highly faithful *simulation* of the task or tasks to be performed with the use of this real equipment. Perhaps the best-known examples of the latter option are the simulators used for the training of aircraft pilots. While pilots practice many aspects of their job in actual aircraft, tasks such as landing, crash landing, and a number of emergency procedures can be represented by using a simulator. In general, it may be said that the requirement of fault-free performance limits media choice to these two possibilities: *real equipment* or *real task simulation.*

Central broadcast.   Another kind of limitation on media choice arises when the instruction requires broadcast to several receiving points from a central station. This kind of situation is likely to occur in parts of the world where populations are sparse and widely scattered. Of course, broadcast may be employed in highly populated areas as well, as evidenced by the popular success of public television programs in the United States.

The limits of choice for central broadcast of instruction (if one excludes the notion of periodically delivered printed pages) are radio and television. Both media have been employed with a reasonable amount of success. As will be noted later on, their limiting characteristic so far as learning is concerned is the absence of provision for learner interaction. Communication to the learner is adequate, but receipt of feedback from the learner is lacking.

Self-instruction. Many forms of instruction make the assumption that learners will receive communications from a medium and will react to such communications in an individual manner without the directions or guidance of an instructor. Homework in school subjects has this form. In addition, topics or courses may be planned to utilize self-instruction throughout, as is true, for example, for a variety of courses using computer-based instruction.

The self-instruction mode imposes some limitations on the choice of media. That is to say, there are certain instructor functions that cannot, so far as is known, be adequately performed by a medium by itself. For one thing, the provision of individual feedback to the learner cannot be provided in a "personalized" form. Also, the function of human modeling, frequently essential to instructional goals, often cannot be adequately provided by a medium by itself. Deciding to use media for self-instruction, then, is to choose an instructional situation that has distinctly different characteristics from a situation that includes the instructor.

Learner characteristics. Still another set of circumstances affecting the nature of the instructional situation consists of the characteristics of the students who are to receive the communications of instruction. One thinks of student age, or "amount of educational experience" in this connection. Obviously the medium employed for six-year-olds may not be entirely appropriate for twenty-year-olds or for students over sixty. Much has yet to be learned concerning the proper "matching" of learner characteristics and media properties.

One quality of learners, however, is prominent in its effects on media choice and applicable regardless of learner age. This is the *ability to read*. The range of media possibilities available for students who read is virtually limitless. In contrast, media for nonreaders are severely limited, beginning with the exclusion of printed texts or chalkboard writing. It is possible that research like that of Olson (1974) and Salomon (1979) will reveal other kinds of learner characteristics to be taken into account in choosing media. Meanwhile, ability to read remains a strongly limiting factor.

If instructional theory is to be brought to bear upon the choice of media for instruction, consideration must first be given to features of the *instructional situation*, as described in preceding paragraphs. The requirement that instruction produce error-free performance imposes the most severe limitations on the possibilities for media choice, since real equipment, or something close to it, must serve as the instructional medium. Other situations that influence the range of media choices are the decision to employ broadcast (radio or TV) for instruction, the extent to which self-instruction will be employed, and the effect of different learner characteristics, particularly ability to read, on the instructional situation.

Media selection "models" (R. H. Anderson, 1976; Heidt, 1978; Kemp, 1980; Romiszowski, 1974) make various provisions for taking aspects of the instructional situation into account. A model proposed by Reiser and Gagné (1983) uses the instructional theory described in this book as a basis for arriving at media choices that will assure effective learning. This model employs a procedure of "progressive rejection" of inadequate media. It is noteworthy that this procedure worked *within* five different instructional situations: (1) job competence critical, (2) central broadcast, (3) self-instruction with readers, (4) instructor with readers, and (5) instructor with nonreaders. Obviously, these five different situations reflect the factors previously discussed in this section. If one sets out deliberately to choose an effective medium or set of media, the instructional situation must first be known or decided upon.

Media for Instruction

What are the possible media from which choices can be made for instruction? They are listed in Table 14.1. (When some particular meanings of media names are intended, defining comments are also given.) The intention in this table is to present a list that is complete, containing media designated by their commonly understood names. Obviously, some are highly familiar and frequently used, such as "printed text" and "motion picture." Others tend to be used only in special contexts, such as military and industrial training. "Simulators and training devices" fall in this category. A balanced view of the question of learning effectiveness can best be gained by considering the entire range of possibilities.

MEDIA AND LEARNING EFFECTIVENESS

When the nature of the instructional situation is known, instructional theory may be brought to bear on the choice of media to assure learning effectiveness. This involves consideration, first, of the nature of the learning outcome expected, whether intellectual skill, verbal information, cognitive strategy, attitude, or motor skill. With this goal (or goals) in mind, an instructor or instructional designer can then proceed to determine how instructional events can best be delivered. The tables of the previous chapter indicate the critical decisions that need to be made, in accord with instructional theory.

Bringing theoretical requirements to bear on media choices can be done

TABLE 14.1   Media from Which Choices for Learning Effectiveness Can Be Made, with Defining Comments

Media	Defining Comments
Real equipment	Large, nonportable equipment; *example:* aircraft, power plant
Simulator; simulation	Equipment that incorporates the operating characteristics of real equipment or a real system; *example:* flight simulator
TV broadcast	Broadcast to several points from a central station
Radio broadcast	Broadcast to several points from a central station
Portable equipment	Real and portable equipment; *example:* rifle, circular saw
Training device	Reproduces essential human performance of real equipment but not its appearance or operating characteristics
Computer	Displays printed text and diagrams on CRT; may have type keyboard, joystick, or light pen; program can adapt to student response
Programmed text	Printed frames of text, providing frequent feedback
Interactive TV	TV display that adapts to student response; requires video disc for fast response
Motion picture	Visual display, accompanying sound; nonreactive to student response
Slide/tape	
TV cassette	Visual display, accompanying sound; nonreactive to student response
Filmstrip	
Printed text	
Training aid	Displays appearance of equipment system without provision for student performance; *example:* cutaway display of auto engine block and cylinder
Audio	Audio cassette
Chart	Diagram; includes chalkboard drawing
Overhead projection	
Slides	
Instructor	Specifically, audio instruction via instructor's voice; also, demonstration with other media

in a number of ways (Reiser and Gagné, 1982). A frequently used method is to display in a *matrix* rows representing media and columns denoting the characteristics of these media relating to learning effectiveness and to other factors related to use. This method is employed by Briggs and Wager (1981). Another approach is the progressive narrowing of media choices by means of a flowchart. This is a method employed by Anderson (1976) and by Romiszowski (1974) as well as by Reiser and Gagné (1983) in an approach to be described here.

Chart C. Self-Instruction with Readers

Explanation of Questions · Chart C

7. Self-Instruction? Are students expected to learn by self-instruction, without an instructor?
8. Readers? Can the students, with reasonable efficiency, gain information from printed text?
9. Either an Attitude or Verbal Information? Is the aim either to influence the student's values (attitudes) or to have the student learn to 'state' (rather than 'do') something?
10. Motor Practice Necessary? Does the skill to be learned require smooth timing of muscular movements (a "motor skill")?
11. Attitude? Does instruction aim to influence the student's values or opinions?
12. Will Visuals Help Recall? Is it likely that the use of visuals will help the student establish images that will aid recall of verbal information?

Figure 14.1 A portion of a flowchart leading to the narrowing of media options, under the assumed instructional situation of self-instruction with readers. (From Reiser, R., and Gagné, R. M. *Selecting media for instruction.* Copyright, Educational Technology Publications, 1983. Reproduced by permission of the copyright owner.)

An example of progressive narrowing of media choices may be illustrated by "Chart C, Self-Instruction with Readers," reproduced from the work of Reiser and Gagné (1983) in Figure 14.1. In this figure, the possible media "candidates" are shown in a box at the left. It may be noted that "real equipment" and "simulator" are not included in the list, since it does not appear possible for these to be used in a self-instructional mode; some means must be provided, perhaps via an instructor, to describe the operation of such media. Likewise, radio and TV broadcast are omitted, since the learning situation requiring these media has not been assumed. Steps 7 and 8 of the flowchart identify the initial decisions reflecting the instructional situation being assumed in this chart.

The first question relating to learning effectiveness is number 9, "Is it a skill (mental or motor)?" The identification of these categories amounts to a division of the five learning outcomes into two sets: (1) intellectual skills, cognitive strategies, and motor skills as one set, and (2) verbal information and attitudes as another. The first of these sets shares a quality in common that differentiates them from the other set. This quality is *precision of feedback*. When an intellectual skill is being learned and practiced, it is best for the medium to receive the learner's responses and to provide precise feedback. For an intellectual skill, the latter is typically in the form of showing the correct answer, and when a wrong answer has been given, the way of arriving at the correct answer; similar requirements hold for cognitive strategies. For a motor skill, the practice situation typically shows whether the learner's movements are "on target" or how far off the responses are. Thus, question 9 of Chart C identifies the categories of learning outcomes that require an "interactive" medium providing precise feedback to the learner.

The motor skill option. Question 10 proceeds to make the critical division among this set of human skills. It asks whether the muscular movements involved in the skill require practice in order to attain the timing and smoothness recognized as characteristic of a *motor skill*. Thus, if the skill requires, let us say, tracking a moving target with a cursor, it is likely to show improvement in proficiency with practice of the movements that make up the skill. Other examples of motor skills would be the use of a typewriter, or of a motorized weed cutter.

If the answer to question 10 is affirmative, the chart sends us to a box indicating the two media that are appropriate. One is the *portable equipment* itself (the typewriter or weed cutter). Motor skill learning requires this degree of "realism" because, as noted in Chapter 10, the actual movements that are part of the skill must be practiced. Should large equipment be involved (as in following a target on a CRT screen responding to an industrial operation), a training device may be chosen as the medium. Obviously, such a device need not have the exact appearance or operating characteristics of the real equipment; but it must permit practice of the movements that make up the motor skill.

One other point may be noted about the box to which a positive answer to question 10 sent us. A plus sign appended to each of the media indicates that they may be accompanied by printed text. Since we are dealing with students who are readers, initial directions about how to react to, or otherwise use, the particular medium may be given by means of print. A weed cutter, for example, may come to its purchaser with a set of printed instructions about its use. While these do not substitute for the actual motor practice in cutting weeds, they do serve the purpose of giving instruction in the executive subroutine (Chapter 10).

The intellectual skill option.   Should the answer to question 10 be in the negative, the implication is that an intellectual skill (or cognitive strategy) has been identified as the instructional objective. The critical requirement for a medium in this case is its ability to be "interactive" with the learner. Specifically, this means that the medium must provide *precise* feedback to responses made by the learner. For example, if finding the length of the hypotenuse of a right triangle is the rule being learned, the exact correct answer must be confirmed or a correction of a wrong answer suggested. Given as an example a right triangle with sides 6 and 8, the answer 10 would be confirmed. An answer such as 9.2 might yield the feedback: "Did you remember to square the lengths of both sides?" An answer such as 50 might result in the response: "Did you take the square root of the sum?"

A text designed to deliver *programmed instruction* has the interactive quality needed for learning intellectual skills. Sometimes, to be sure, such texts provide feedback that simply gives the correct answer. Other texts are designed to give differential feedback matched to the kinds of typical errors learners are inclined to make. In either case, it is clear that the feedback has the quality of precision in its attempt to deal with an exact learner response and particular deviations from that response.

The degree of feedback precision is likely to have greater possibilities when the medium chosen is the *computer* or *interactive TV* (possibly involving the video disc). While the report of the correct answer is not increased in precision with these media, either one may provide greatly enhanced possibilities of corrective feedback for wrong answers. Suitable programs can be designed for the computer to give corrections for a considerable variety of learner responses. Likewise, rapid access to a number of corrective displays is possible with the video disc or other TV equipment having similar properties. These characteristics of media, which make possible the precise feedback necessary for intellectual skill learning, bring the media choices down to three possibilities. None of the other candidate media (excepting, of course, the instructor) has this important property. Thus, a large reduction in media possibilities can be achieved by the negative answer to question 10, identifying intellectual skill as the category of outcome expected. Similarly, it may be seen that a positive answer to question 9 has led to the identification of no more than five possible media options, all of which are candidates for the instruction of skills, intellectual or motor.

In further following the logic of Figure 14.1, we need next to suppose that question 9 has had a negative answer. This would mean that the expected outcome is not a skill. One or more of the remaining two types of learning outcome must be foreseen—either verbal information or attitude or both. Thus, the next set of possibilities to be considered are these "nonskill" categories of learned capabilities.

The attitude option. Question 11 asks whether the design of instruction deals with an attitude. Is the expected outcome of instruction an internal state that will influence the learner's choice of personal action toward some object, person, or event (Chapter 11)? A positive answer to this question identifies attitude as the type of outcome expected. The media options are motion picture, TV cassette, and slide/tape. Each of these makes possible a communication including human beings and human action, and this characteristic is considered to be the critical one. Attitudes are best taught by means of a communication or demonstration made by a human model. The most appropriate media options are therefore the three that make possible realistic showing and talking by human beings. The footnote acknowledges the fact that slide/tape doesn't communicate human action as well as the other two media. By rapid sequencing of slides, of course, action can be strongly conveyed, and that means that the slide/tape medium can be appropriately employed for attitude instruction.

The verbal information option. When question 11 is answered with a "no" for attitudes, the remaining possibility of learning outcome is verbal information ("declarative knowledge"). The designer of instruction is led to question 12, "Will visuals help recall?" Were we dealing with nonreaders rather than readers, this would be an easier question to answer. As it is, the designer is faced with the problem of deciding whether pictures and diagrams will help learners who generally learn both well and rapidly from meaningful, logically connected verbal statements. Evidence reviewed by Gagné and White (1978) suggests that pictures that evoke images improve the retention of verbal materials. This effect is particularly strong when combined with a mnemonic technique for remembering verbal lists or word pairs, as in the keyword technique (Pressley, 1981; Pressley, Levin, and Delaney, 1982) employed in the learning of foreign words. The evidence is weaker that images derived from pictures help the retention of meaningfully connected verbal material. Nevertheless, there remains some likelihood that pictures aid in the encoding and retrieval of expository prose texts.

Appropriately designed visuals thus may be judged capable of aiding recall, and this is the decision called for as an answer to question 12. When an affirmative answer can be given, a number of media options become candidates for use. These include filmstrip, motion picture, printed text (including pictures or diagrams), slide/tape, training aid, and TV cassette. In other words, when the students are readers, media that include both print and pictures cannot be differentiated on learning effectiveness grounds. All of them may be equally effective, depending upon their particular instructional content. The choice of media must then be based upon other criteria— practical considerations such as cost, availability, and appeal to students.

The question about inclusion of visuals (question 12) may be answered negatively. Does it make sense to consider the alternative of communications (oral or printed) that are not accompanied by pictures or diagrams? Of course it does, for two different reasons. One reason is that pictures cost money to make and to reproduce. A second reason is that highly skilled readers may actually prefer to be instructed by means of printed text and may not be helped by pictures at all.

With students who are readers, then, it is entirely possible that instruction can most effectively be delivered in the form of logically connected sentences and paragraphs. These may be delivered as oral speech from cassette recorders or other types of audio devices. Refresher topics and new professional techniques may be learned via cassette recorders in automobiles, for example, by the physician, lawyer, or other professional person while driving to work. There are learning situations, in other words, in which the inexpensive audio medium is an excellent choice. However, the more frequently appropriate and more widely used medium for the learning situation "self-Instruction with readers" is the printed text. Some further instructional implications of this medium are discussed in the next section.

The flowchart method of media selection illustrated in Figure 14.1 makes possible a highly systematic procedure requiring only a few minutes to accomplish (Reiser and Gagné, 1983). Based upon the instructional theory of Chapter 12, the flowchart method makes use of the idea of differentially effective conditions for the learning of intellectual skills, cognitive strategies, verbal information, attitudes, and motor skills. In particular, this method takes account of the different requirements for the instructional event called "learning guidance." For example, the decision that separates motor skills from intellectual skills recognizes the necessity for motor practice of a movement sequence in the former case. The decision that differentiates attitude instruction from verbal information instruction pertains to the use of a human model's behavior in communication attitudes. The aim of the flowchart is to display how these different learning conditions came to be represented by different media. In some cases, the media options remain relatively numerous, while in others they are reduced to only one or two. Following such reduction in terms of learning effectiveness, final media choices can be appropriately based upon practical factors.

LANGUAGE AND PICTURES IN MEDIA

One of the general themes running through the activity of instructional design as it focuses on media is the mode of *language*, oral or printed.

Whether one thinks of a medium like the recording of an instructor's voice or a highly sophisticated computer-based program displaying printed text on a screen, it is evident that language provides the basic vehicle for instructional delivery. Language in its propositional form can be employed to direct the learner's behavior and thus to bring about any or all of the conditions needed to activate and support internal processes as provided by instructional theory. Language communications can channel learners' motivation, inform them of learning objectives, stimulate (by questions) the retrieval of prerequisites, provide guidance for encoding and cues for retrieval, ask for the relevant performance, and provide feedback. Oral or printed language, however presented, is therefore the most universal and versatile form for the delivery of instruction.

Of course, instructional events *can* be designed without the use of language, and they may be so designed for nonreaders, including young children. The flowcharts presented by Reiser and Gagné (1983), for example, include panels pertaining to the instructional situations "self-instruction with nonreaders" and "instructor with nonreaders." In the delivery of such instruction, language in oral form is usually combined with, and supplemented by, pictures and objects. In terms of the media named in Table 14.1, these include such items as portable equipment, training devices, training aids, filmstrips, charts, and slides. Actual objects like blocks and beads may accompany oral instruction when number concepts are being taught to children.

The range of nonlanguage media for instruction is enormously extended by representations in the form of *pictures* and *diagrams*. In these forms, concrete objects and events—which would otherwise be expensive, difficult, or even impossible to introduce in their actual form—can be presented (or "represented") to the learner. Mount Everest can be shown to students who cannot travel to see it; the internal parts of cells can be shown to those who cannot use a microscope; the flow of blood to the capillaries can be shown to students who have no opportunity to observe the actual event.

In choosing media, then, the instructional designer has first to select the kind of *language medium* that will be able to perform all of the functions required in establishing the events called for by instructional theory to support learning processes. The basic choices, beyond that of employing instructor-led as opposed to self-instruction media, pertain to the delivery of oral language, printed language, or some combination of these. It will be worthwhile to look more closely at the kinds of instructional events both oral and printed language can bring about.

Oral Communication

All of the events of instruction can be performed by oral communication, provided that objects or pictures are included when required by the learning task. Typically, oral communication is given by an instructor and in that form achieves greatest versatility and flexibility in its adaptation to particular requirements of students and situations. Instruction may also be delivered orally by means of tape recorders, which have many valuable uses. Oral language is, of course, the major instructional component of television programs, whether broadcast or recorded. Oral instruction may also be delivered by radio, and this medium has been shown to have great effectiveness in situations involving students who are widely dispersed, for example, over sparsely settled areas.

Oral communications can be used to good effect in channeling motivation toward instructional aims. A teacher or another person in the role of a human model can perform this instructional function effectively. In *informing the learner of the expected learning outcome*, oral communication sometimes needs to be supplemented by printing or pictures. For example, if the objective is "computing the normality of chemical solutions," the printed example ".5 N" is evidently a good model for the kind of performance required. Oral communication may suffice, however, when the learned performance is an oral one, for example, in constructing sentences in a foreign language or in making a speech.

The *guidance of learning*, including the suggestion of encoding schemes, can often be accomplished by means of oral language. Procedural steps involved in children's printing or writing of letters may be prompted by a teacher's oral directions, for example, "First a long line down," "Next, a line across the top," and so on. Guidance in the form of questions may be used in the discovery of new rules, as in the following example. Asked to demonstrate the truth of the statement

$$8 \times 3 + 16 = 5 \times 8$$

the students' thinking may be guided by such questions as, "Can you think of another name for 16?"—and others as needed—to enable them to arrive at the expression

$$8 \times 5 = 8 \times 5.$$

For the more mature learner, adequate learning guidance can often be given in oral form. The earth's orbit around the sun can be described rather than being directly observed. The passage of a bill through Congress can be verbally described. But oral communications are often more effective when supplemented by pictures or by actual objects. The science teacher would feel grossly handicapped if the concept of wave motion could not be pictured. The description of a town meeting may not be as satisfactory for encoding purposes as the direct observation or a filmed record of a town meeting.

Questions designed to enhance *retention* and *transfer* can be presented orally. If students have learned information and concepts pertaining to the distribution of powers among the legislative, executive, and judicial branches of government, a question such as the following can be asked: "What possible means could there be of legislative restraint on judicial powers?" When actual objects and events are used in instruction (as in simulation games), they set the stage for transfer of learning, a process that is continued by oral discussion.

Teachers often employ oral questions to *elicit the performance* of the learner and oral statements to *provide feedback.* For young children, a good deal of the teacher's conversation may consist in statements of "Yes," "Good!," "That's right," as the pupils attain successive goals of instruction. At later ages, the necessity for such "oral reinforcement" is greatly reduced, since students are able to match their performances with external standards or with those they themselves supply.

All of these functions, then, *can* be performed by oral communication. Perhaps this is the reason why the model of the teacher and student talking to each other from two ends of a log seems so appropriate for the instructional situation. But many of these functions can be more readily and more efficiently accomplished when pictures or actual objects are added to the stimulus situation for learning. And, of course, the same instructional events can be carried out by the use of printed media.

Printed Media

Books, pamphlets, and leaflets are a traditional part of many instructional situations. For the later years of formal education, dependence on books as media of instruction is very high relative to dependence on other media. To be sure, it is sometimes suggested that this situation may undergo change with the increased adoption of such media as the video disc–computer combination and interactive TV. It is noteworthy, however, that oral discussion still has an instructional function at the level of postgraduate education. The instruction of an experienced university scholar may be derived mostly from the printed media of books and learned journals; yet the scholar still finds it necessary to discuss with colleagues the ideas so obtained. At the other extreme of the educational scale, printed communication can accomplish very little; the presentation of actual objects accompanied by oral communication is the typical mode of instruction for children in the elementary grades. Accordingly, learning the skill of reading is still the crucial event that determines the increasing dependence on printed media from the early grades of school onward.

Assuming that the student possesses the necessary prerequisite skills, instruction by means of a book is usually a remarkably rapid and efficient process. Although no figures are available, the time required for oral communication must surely be three or four times as much as that needed for instruction by means of a book. For the vast range of subject matters taught following the primary school years, printed communication can certainly be the major medium of instruction, and often is. When pictures and diagrams are combined with printed text (as, for example, in a good high school physics text), the dangers of excessive verbalism can largely be overcome, and the book can impart a great deal of instruction in a relatively short time when used by a suitably prepared student. At this level of schooling, in fact, whatever ineffectiveness books possess as instructional media may often be attributed to difficulties not inherent in the medium: the student has not acquired the necessary background knowledge or has not learned how to read or both.

The printed medium, however, does have other limitations. These have to do with the ways in which the sentences on the printed page function in the instructional situation. Textbooks, after all, are not always well written in terms of properly supporting the processes involved in each learning phase. For example, does the printed text introducing a topic direct attention to the proper stimuli? Does it inform the learner of the nature of the performance expected from learning? Does it supply or suggest useful schemes for encoding? Does it require the learner to exhibit what has been learned and provide corrective feedback for this performance? Many printed texts would score quite low in their accomplishment of these necessary instructional functions. What happens, usually, is that learners carry out these functions themselves by the time they have as much experience as a college student. But it is perhaps too much to expect that fifth-graders will have acquired this much sophistication about self-instruction through reading.

The potentialities of printed texts for instruction are very great, and it is doubtful that they are always well exploited. Designing a printed text that will efficiently instruct ten-year-olds is not simply a matter of matching their vocabulary. Primarily, it is a matter of organizing the statements in such a way that they will perform the functions prescribed by instructional theory. Unless one is simply "telling a story" (that is, seeking to have learners acquire meaningfully organized verbal information), it is doubtful that the proper sequence of printed statements is much like a story. Each sentence or question is likely to have a distinct purpose in supporting a particular internal learning process. The reader will be able to identify the events of instruction represented by the propositions in the following list, which refers to Figure 14.2.

1. Look at the pictures.
2. How is the pressure at the bottom of a vessel full of liquid related to the shape of the vessel?
3. Remember that pressure is the ratio of a force to (what)?
4. In a vessel whose walls flare outward (B), where is the force of the central cylindrical portion of water exerted?

Figure 14.2 Vessels of different shapes, each containing a liquid.

5. The areas of the bottoms of the vessels are equal.
6. What can you say about the pressure at the bottom of vessels A and B?
7. State the relationship in general terms. (*Answer:* The pressure of the bottom of the vessel of liquid is not affected by the shape of the vessel.)
8. Now look at the other vessel, with walls flaring inward (C).
9. (And so forth.)

Nonverbal Media

As we have seen, oral or printed language is seldom employed by itself to accomplish all instructional functions. Typically, verbal communications are accompanied by actual objects (such as portable equipment or training devices) or by representations of objects in the form of pictures or diagrams (for example, charts or slides). One primary reason for the use of objects in instruction is that they are *directly involved* in the performance expected as a result of learning. In terms of the chart depicted in Figure 14.1, the answer to question 9 ("Is it a skill?") is "yes." For example, if the expected outcome is skill in using a microscope, an actual microscope should be employed in the instruction; if the outcome pertains to map reading, actual maps should be used in the instruction.

A second and much broader reason for the use of objects or pictures in instruction is that they are the means by which the learner can acquire the *visual images* that are presumed to be a very important type of memory encoding and storage. Thus, objects and pictures are frequently used to perform the function of learning guidance by providing *encoding images*. This is true even when the performance expected as an outcome of learning does not itself require reaction to these objects or pictures. Image encoding appears to be a prominent feature in the instructional use of (1) motion pictures, (2) slide/tape presentations, and (3) instructional TV programs.

What does a picture contribute? A picture contributes an *image*. As an encoding scheme, this image has certain important properties. First, it is an image of a *specific* object, person, or event. If the picture shows a tree, for example, the image generated in the learner is not that of a "generalized" tree, but of the tree depicted. Of course, the process of perceiving this particular tree may be selective, and as a result the image may not exactly match the picture in all its features. Some features may be omitted from the image, while others may be added from previously stored memories. Nevertheless, the image derived from the picture is of a specific tree. Similarly, if a diagram is pictured, the image generated is of the specific diagram.

The image that is formed and stored as a result of viewing a picture can presumably be *retrieved* in its specific form. That is, it is not the same as the prototype or generalized concept that would result from the instruction "Imagine a tree." Instead, the image of the tree derived from viewing a picture is retrieved with the features and form it took when originally perceived. This is not to deny that certain minor changes or losses of detail may occur in the process of retrieval; nevertheless, what is retrieved is the same specific object or scene shown in the picture. In sum, then, the addition of a picture to verbal instruction makes it possible for the learner to encode the objects or events as *specific, retrievable images.*

When an intellectual skill is being learned, an image may first of all aid the retrieval of prerequisite skills. For example, if the skill being learned is the construction of an equilateral triangle with a compass, an image that includes the intersecting arcs at the apex of the triangle will serve to recall to the learner the procedure for drawing these arcs. At the same time, the image of the equilateral triangle with arcs at its apex also aids in retrieval of the procedure for constructing the figure.

Suppose that a cognitive strategy of problem solving is being learned, such as "waiting until all the evidence is in." Various problem situations to which this strategy is applicable may be presented in pictorial form (as in television scenes). These pictures generate an equal variety of images that, when retrieved by the learner, provide cues for the transfer of the strategy to new situations in which it may be employed.

When verbal information is being learned, a great deal of added meaningful material may be contributed in a short time as a context for the encoding of the newly learned propositions. For example, if new facts are being learned about a state's agricultural products, a considerable variety of scenes depicting the growing of these products can be shown. The specific images formed from such pictures are capable of adding a great many additional cues for the retrieval of the new information.

In the case of a motor skill, pictures often depict the sequence of actions and the movements involved in them. Essentially, this amounts to a display of the executive subroutine. The image formed from such a picture can probably not be derived in any better way.

Pictures are particularly supportive of attitude learning and attitude change. They can establish images that aid the learner's retrieval of the variety of situations in which the attitude may be displayed. And they produce images of the human model's behavior in choosing a course of action within these situations, as well as the reinforcement that follows such choice. Suppose an attitude toward "disposing of personal trash" is the aim of instruction. Pictures (shown in television scenes, in movies, or on slides or filmstrips) can display situations in which personal trash must be disposed of, including when walking on a sidewalk and traveling in an automobile. Pictures can show a respected human model behaving in desirable ways in disposing of trash: saving aluminum cans, depositing gum wrappers in trash receptacles, and so on. The reinforcing events for the model, also shown in pictures, could be views of clean streets and of unspoiled forest trails. The images thus established contribute features to the encoding and retrieval of the attitude.

It is apparent that the features of media that combine pictures with oral or printed verbal instruction are able to support encoding and retrieval processes involved in various learning outcomes. The same combination, as embodied in television programs, for example, has many other valuable characteristics for the support of learning. In this combination, rapid changes of scenes and unusual visual stimulation are highly effective in controlling attention. Many techniques of pictorial emphasis are available to direct selective perception. Motion and sequences of action can be portrayed in ways that make possible specific retrievable images of these events. The implications of these characteristics of the oral instruction–picture combination have been explored by a number of writers (see, for example, Gropper, 1963; Levie and Dickie, 1973; Olson, 1974; Salomon, 1979).

EDUCATIONAL IMPLICATIONS

Delivering planned instruction requires that selection be made of one or more media having the function of communicating to learners. The great variety of instructional goals that exist in schools, in industry, in the military services, and in the home means that many different media are possible, ranging from the simple chart on a chalkboard to the highly sophisticated simulator of aircraft operation. In making media choices for effective learning, one must first identify some general characteristics of the instructional situation.

The range of choices of media is limited by the situations intended for instruction. There may be a requirement that the instruction lead to fault-free performance, because the consequences of error are serious. The intended recipients of instruction may be widely dispersed, necessitating the use of broadcast media. It may have been decided that self-instruction will be employed, or, alternatively, that an instructor will teach assembled students. The characteristics of learners also determine the instructional situation, particularly with respect to their ability to read. All of these conditions of instruction impose different limitations on the variety of media available for use. For example, various printed media are ruled out if one is attempting to design self-instruction for nonreaders.

The learning effectiveness of media for the delivery of instruction can be assured when consideration is given to the prescriptions of instructional theory. Specifically, the differential requirements of learning outcomes can be matched with media characteristics. Using a flowchart method of progressive narrowing of media options, the usefulness of media for the learning of skills (intellectual or motor) may first be distinguished from employment of media for other learning outcomes. Practice of motor skills makes different demands on media than does the learning of intellectual skills. The latter, in turn, require media qualities that are different from those necessary for instruction in organized verbal information. Finally, the use of human models in the teaching of attitudes implies a need for a medium that can display human communication and action.

As the word "media" is generally understood, most vehicles for the delivery of instruction include both verbal communication and the representation of objects by means of pictures and diagrams. When they are appropriate and available, actual objects may be used in preference to pictures. Pictures add many valuable features to instructional events when employed in combination with either printed or oral communications. Their function in supporting *encoding* and *retrieval* functions is considered critical. Their operation is conceived as one of generating *specific retrievable images* in the learner, which in turn constitute a means of encoding and memory storage and a source of cues for retrieval of what has been learned. The planning of these functions in media such as television requires the instructional designer to take account of the particular category of learning outcome intended, in order to achieve optimal effectiveness of the pictures' role in learning support.

GENERAL REFERENCES

Media in Instruction

Dale, E. *Audiovisual methods in teaching*, 3rd ed. New York: Holt, Rinehart and Winston, 1969.

Reiser, R. A., and Gagné, R. M. *Selecting media for instruction*. Englewood Cliffs, N.J.: Educational Technology Publications, 1983.

Heidt, E. U. *Instructional media and the individual learner*. London: Kogan Page, 1978.

Levie, W. H., and Dickie, K. E. The analysis and application of media. In R. M. W. Travers (Ed.), *Handbook of research on teaching,* 2nd ed. Skokie, Ill.: Rand-McNally, 1973.

Romiszowski, A. J. *The selection and use of instructional media.* London: Kogan Page, 1974.

Learning from Television and Related Media

Olson, D. R. (Ed.), *Media and symbols: The forms of expression, communication, and education.* 73d Yearbook, National Society for the Study of Education. Chicago: University of Chicago Press, 1974.

Salomon, G. *Interaction of media, cognition, and learning.* San Francisco: Jossey-Bass, 1979.

Schramm, W. *Big media, little media.* Beverly Hills, Calif.: SAGE Publications, 1977.

15

Designing Instruction for Learning

Knowledge of the learning process combined with analysis of the tasks for learning in accordance with instructional theory finds a direct application to the *design of instruction*. In this chapter, we take the viewpoint of an instructional designer, who may be an instructor, a course planner, or a writer of instructional texts, computer courseware, or other materials. This is, of course, a different viewpoint from that of a person who is examining the process of learning in order to understand it. The reader will need to keep in mind this shift in orientation. We shall need to mention many of the conditions of learning described in previous chapters as well as the analysis of learning requirements and the selection of media. All of these ideas will be put here into a framework of application.

The analysis of human tasks described in Chapter 13 makes possible their classification into types of capabilities to be learned. These classes, in turn, imply different conditions for effective learning that depend upon differential characteristics of the categories of learning outcomes. We have seen that optimal conditions differ particularly in relation to the *prerequisites* appropriate to the different types, and in relation to the provisions made for the activation and support of *encoding* processes.

The results of learning analyses provide essential information for the design of instruction relevant to any kinds of learning outcomes. In this chapter, we intend to examine how such results can be applied practically to instructional design. To do this systematically, we shall need to recall the learning processes involved in the information-processing model described in Chapter 4 and the implications these have for the instructional theory of Chapter 12. We intend to describe how instructional events can be planned to support learning processes. In doing this, we shall be dealing with the external conditions (such as gaining attention, establishing motivation, and giving feedback) generally applicable to all learning outcomes as well as with the conditions that must be different for each variety of outcome.

PLANNING FOR PHASES OF LEARNING

The model of learning and memory described in Chapter 4 implies a succession of phases of learning corresponding to different processes. Thus a very brief phase of learning occurring early in the total sequence is the *selective perception* that transforms output from the sensory register to the input as features to the short-term memory. *Encoding* for storage in the long-term memory is a succeeding phase, and *storage* is still another. Relations between the phases of learning implied by the model, and the *events of instruction* implied by them, are shown in Figure 15.1. The right-hand column of the figure indicates the instructional events that need to be designed for each learning phase.

The kinds of instructional events listed in the right-hand column of Figure 15.1 can perhaps best be understood with the help of an example. Suppose that what is to be learned is an intellectual skill described by the rule "In a written sentence, a singular indefinite pronoun ('any,' 'each,' 'someone,' etc.) as subject requires a singular verb." As the figure indicates, an *expectancy* first needs to be established by activating the learners' motivation and informing them of the objective to be achieved by the learning. This may be done by telling the learners of the personal advantages of correct, as opposed to incorrect, writing. Further, the teacher would probably indicate which kind of sentence "sounds right" (such as the sentence "Someone has to go") and which "sounds wrong" (such as "Someone have to go"). Next, events need to be planned for directing attention to features so as to accomplish *selective perception*. In terms of the example, attention must be drawn to the indefinite pronoun as a subject and to the verb that follows it. Several sentences with these parts printed in bold type, and with other nondistracting parts, might be employed.

The process of *encoding* calls upon external events that stimulate the recall of prerequisites. In the example employed here, what this amounts to is reminding the learner of the previously learned concepts *subject*, *verb*, *pronoun*, and *singular*. The next step in encoding suggests one or more schemes to the learner; these schemes should preferably add distinctiveness to the concepts being learned. Each indefinite pronoun, for example, might be contrasted with a plural noun or pronoun, as "each" may be contrasted with "all," and "something" with "some things." *Retrieval* is facilitated by events that provide cues for the enhancement of *recall* and *transfer of learning* by contextual variety in external stimulation. Typically, such events take the form of a variety of examples, using a number of different sentences for each of the indefinite pronouns to which the rule applies.

The remainder of instructional events appear straightforward. The learners must *respond* with the performance that reflects their newly learned

LEARNING PROCESS   INSTRUCTIONAL EVENT

LEARNING PROCESS	INSTRUCTIONAL EVENT
ATTENTION: ALERTNESS	1. Gaining attention
EXPECTANCY	2. Informing learner of the objective; activating motivation
RETRIEVAL TO WORKING MEMORY	3. Stimulating recall of prior knowledge
SELECTIVE PERCEPTION	4. Presenting the stimulus material
ENCODING: ENTRY TO LTM STORAGE	5. Providing learning guidance
RESPONDING	6. Eliciting performance
REINFORCEMENT	7. Providing feedback 8. Assessing performance
CUEING RETRIEVAL	9. Enhancing retention and transfer

Figure 15.1 Relations between phases of learning and events of instruction. The latter events represent the functions performed by instruction which support internal learning processes.

capability. In practice, learners are given several sentences containing indefinite pronouns and asked to supply the missing verb. Alternatively, they may be given sentences containing indefinite pronoun subjects, some correct and some incorrect, and asked to make them all correct in agreement of subject and verb. Following such an exercise, corrective feedback is given to provide *reinforcement* to the learners.

This example serves to make the point that properly designed instruction does not necessarily have to be unconventional. On the contrary, what is done in instruction is probably what any good teacher has learned to do. However, a teacher or instructional designer who is intent on "adequate coverage" of the subject may easily lose sight of one or more of the events that support learning processes. This is particularly true of the events that pertain to coding, storage, and retrieval (the external conditions of learning) as they have been described in preceding chapters. The reasons for careful design of these events of instruction can now be seen to be clearly related to the internal processes of learning and memory, as identified by information-processing theories of learning.

A Broad View of Instructional Events

By referring again to the structures and processes of learning described in Chapter 4, we will now present a broad view of the influences of external events on learning. We have described the conditions of learning that are distinctive for each general class of learning outcome. We now ask the question, "What are *all* the circumstances that must be considered as composing what is called instruction?" The answer is a more inclusive one than is suggested by the individual chapters.

The following sections of this chapter take the point of view of a designer who is engaged in planning instruction for an educational enterprise—a program of training for a vocation, a school program, or perhaps an adult education program. In a comprehensive sense, what must such a designer plan and what general specifications can be given for the arrangement of instructional events? The plan for instruction, perhaps not surprisingly, begins with the problem of motivating the learner.

MOTIVATION

The motivation of human behavior is a large and complex subject, a small portion of which can be treated here. Of course it is of great interest to try to know what varieties of motives exist, how they originate and develop within the individual, and how they determine the "force" and direction of human behavior. Psychologists continue to study these matters intensively. Many investigations of motivation have been and are being made, and there are many books on the topic (Cofer and Appley, 1964; Hall, 1961; McClelland, Atkinson, Clark, and Lowell, 1953).

Given the fact of multiple kinds and sources of motivation, the task of the instructional designer is one of *identifying* the motives of students and of *channeling* them into activities that accomplish educational goals. Three ways of viewing the approach of harnessing existing motivation are described as incentive motivation, task motivation, and achievement motivation.

Incentive Motivation

Essentially, the use of incentives to change the directions of motivated behavior is a matter of employing *reinforcement contingencies* wisely (Skinner, 1968, pp. 160–168). In the elementary grades, for example, the young child may receive reinforcement for *social* activities: working with other children and relating appropriately to the teacher become essential for effective learning. The child comes to be motivated by a desire to gain the approval of others, to avoid their disapproval, and to establish a position of social esteem among peers (see Hewett, 1968). Beyond this, there is the acquisition of motivation for *mastery*, involving the learning of intellectual skills that enable the child to function independently. Reinforcement for such learning is provided by accuracy and completeness of accomplishment of tasks the child undertakes. Higher in a developmental sequence is motivation for *achievement*. This calls for the development of true self-motivation, in which the successful mastery of more and more difficult tasks becomes a source of self-satisfaction and generates a desire for greater improvement. When students attain this level of functioning, they possess the motivation required to become true "self-learners."

Practical motivational programs utilizing incentive motivation have been described by Bereiter and Engelmann (1966, pp. 81–91) and by Mager (1968), among others. Rather than waiting until exactly the correct response is made, emphasis is on the reinforcement of behavior that initially approximates the desired behavior. Providing students with information that enables them to judge their own success and failure is another suggestion commonly put forth. And finally, the idea of proceeding in steps, or "stages," from very concrete rewards to those that require a sense of satisfaction derived from self-imposed standards is frequently recommended. None of these techniques, of course, provides a magic key that will guarantee student interest in learning. However, if they are understood as contributing to the establishment of states of expectancy, themselves acquired according to principles of reinforcement contingencies, these techniques can be of great value in establishing the necessary preconditions for school learning.

Task Motivation

Although motives of a social nature, sometimes called *affiliative needs*, are a part of the individual's makeup, some writers consider them of less importance to programs of instruction than the motivation of *task mastery and achievement*. Ausubel (1968, pp. 363–433) has reviewed the evidence concerning various forms of social motivation and points out that these do not always constitute a dependable basis for learning readiness. In contrast, he believes the advantages of achievement motivation for learning lie, first, in the fact that such motives are intrinsic to the task, and hence the reward (the attainment of new knowledge or skill) is capable of wholly satisfying the underlying motive. Second, achievement is ego-enhancing, because the status achieved by individuals is in proportion to their achievement or competence level, affecting directly their self-esteem and feelings of adequacy.

This view of motivation also emphasizes the power of intrinsic and positive motives, including curiosity and exploration as well as mastery. Such "cognitive" motives may be the most important kind of motivation in school learning. Consideration of their potential effects leads Ausubel (1968) to make the following statement:

> The causal relationship between motivation and learning is typically reciprocal rather than unidirectional. Both for this reason, and because motivation is not an indispensable condition of learning, it is unnecessary to postpone learning activities until appropriate interests and motivations have been developed. Frequently, the best way of teaching an unmotivated student is to ignore his motivational state for the time being, and to concentrate on teaching him as effectively as possible. Some degree of learning will ensue in any case, despite the lack of motivation; and from the initial satisfaction of learning he will, hopefully, develop the motivation to learn more. In some circumstances, therefore, the most appropriate way of arousing motivation to learn is to focus on the cognitive rather than on the motivational aspects of learning, and to rely on the motivation that is developed from successful educational achievement to energize further learning [pp. 365–366].

It is interesting to note that despite great differences from Ausubel in his theoretical point of view toward school learning, Skinner (1968, pp. 145–168) holds an essentially similar view about the importance of motivation intrinsic to the performance of the task. Skinner states that the problem of motivation for the schools is not a matter of imparting motivation but of arranging conditions for study and learning so that they will be reinforcing. The teacher must often invent and use "contrived proximate reinforcers," to aid not only in the imparting of knowledge but also in getting the student to acquire diligent behavior of the learning-readiness variety ("precurrent management behaviors").

Achievement Motivation

Motivation to achieve is carried far beyond the idea of "task mastery" by some theorists. These writers propose that individuals may acquire, to a greater or lesser degree, a persisting trait of striving to achieve that provides motivation for a great many of their activities, including those pertaining to school learning.

McClelland (1965) describes twelve propositions, derived from a variety of sources, that have been employed in studies designed to heighten the achievement motivation of groups of business people and, more recently, groups of disadvantaged students. It is McClelland's view that a combination of techniques—including those leading to clear definition of individual goals, perception of self-improvement, an increasing trend toward the assumption of responsibility for one's performance, and a supportive social environment—can lead to the acquisition of persisting motivation for achievement. It appears a distinct possibility that beneficial effects may be obtained by a program designed to increase this "general" form of achievement motivation in certain categories of students, for example, high school dropouts.

Another theory about achievement as a general motivational state is that of R. W. White (1959), who describes the concept of *competence*. In White's view, competence motivation has a broadly based biological origin, related to such sources as exploration, activity, and manipulation, as they have been studied in animal behavior. Many investigators of motivation have expressed the need to identify a similar source of positive motivation, variously termed *mastery, ego-development, a sense of industry,* and *dealing with the environment.* White maintains that many human activities must be explained not through the operation of need satisfactions (for example, hunger, thirst, and sex) but through the persistence of activities that constitute effective interaction with the environment and are accompanied by a "feeling of efficacy." In other words, human individuals have a need to master their environment, in some small or large way, throughout their lives.

Competence motivation can obviously be put to use in the educational process. According to this conception, when the situation is properly arranged for learning, mastering the problem of multiplying two-place numbers or of constructing passive forms of sentences or of producing a white precipitate from a mixture of chemical solutions will provide a rewarding experience to the learner. The problem is not primarily one of "acquiring" new motivation, according to this view. Rather, it is one of cleverly arranging situations for learning in such a way that competence will be displayed and the feeling of efficacy experienced.

It can be seen from this discussion that several possible ways have been proposed to account for the operation of motivation that is either intrinsic or closely related to performance resulting from learning. Despite differences in language, these approaches have practical implications that are very similar: the learners can be rewarded and their subsequent learning can be enhanced by the accomplishment of learning tasks within their capabilities. Achievement, successful interaction within the learning environment, and mastery of the objectives of an educational program can themselves lead to persisting satisfaction on the part of the learner and can therefore become a most dependable source of continuing motivation. Even beyond this, evidence reported by Kifer (1975) strongly suggests that continued success in achievement over several years of schooling leads to the establishment of positive self-concepts and attitudes of self-esteem that become stable aspects of the individual's personality.

Informing the Learner of the Objective

If incentive motivation is to be used effectively for instructional design, the learner must be informed of the nature of the achievement expected as an outcome of learning. In terms of the learning model being followed here, the purpose of such a communication to the learner is to establish an expectancy of the performance to be achieved as a result of learning. If the learner is to acquire information about the process of reproduction, for example, such verbal directions as these may be used: "There are several different ways in which living organisms reproduce themselves. What you will be learning is how to describe each of these ways and to give some actual examples of them." Or, if someone is to learn the intellectual skill of adding decimals, instructions may say, "What you will learn is how to add numbers such as 124.27 and 16.743 to obtain the sum 141.013."

The primary effect of providing learners with an expectancy of the learning outcome is to enable them to match their own performances with a class of performance they expect to be "correct." Thus the reinforcement, in the form of informative feedback, confirms the learners' expectancy. For example, the performance expected in adding decimals, learners know, must be an expression that contains a decimal point and otherwise has the general form 141.013. It cannot be of the form 141013 or 141 1/77. Sometimes, the objective of learning is perfectly obvious to the learner and does not have to be explicitly stated. For this reason, studies that contrast "telling" with "not telling" the objective may fail to indicate an advantage for the former procedure (see Duchastel and Merrill, 1973). When there are alternatives to be chosen, however, the effects of informing the learner about the objective can be clearly shown in resulting achievement (Rothkopf and Kaplan, 1972).

Under many circumstances, the clearest directions about expected performance following learning may be those that actually show the learners, before learning begins, what such a performance looks like. Is this "telling the learners the answer"? Obviously, the answer is not really being supplied, because learners are expected to learn a whole class of performances, not just the single one used to illustrate the class. However, if in fact learners can acquire all they are supposed to learn by simply being told about this class (not a rare occurrence), surely this is economical learning! Presumably, keeping learners in the dark in such instances serves no useful function.

DIRECTING ATTENTION

Among the first steps to be taken in designing instruction is making provision for directing attention. It is commonly recognized that there are two kinds of attention, two separate meanings for this term. The first is a general *alerting* function, by means of which the learners' posture and general muscular tone assume a state of readiness to receive stimulation. In addition, they may turn their heads and direct their sense organs so as to be in line with the source of stimulation. Alerting is accomplished by many different means—by sounds, by light changes, and in general by sudden changes in stimulation. Teachers use various techniques—for example, the introduction of novel stimuli or changes in voice pitch—to bring about alertness on the part of students. In television programs, the sudden changes in pictures produced by rapid "cutting" of successive scenes are used to maintain alertness on the part of student viewers.

The second meaning of attention is *selective perception*. The stimulation delivered to the learner is arranged to give emphasis to the distinctive features of the presentation, that is, to the features to be stored and processed in the *short-term memory*. Again, this function is accomplished in various ways. In a printed text, words and phrases may be underlined, italicized, or printed in bold type. Pictures and diagrams may use heavy outlining, arrows, circled portions, or different colors in order to highlight the features to be selectively perceived. When auditory communications are being employed, the use of meter and rhyme are often effective means of directing attention. Animated techniques in motion pictures and television provide many additional ways of insuring selective perception of the material to be learned.

The designer of instruction needs to be highly aware of the variety of ways that can be employed to give selective emphasis to stimulus presentations for learning. The "information" that is processed in learning is a *selected set* from the total stimulation presented to the learner. Using techniques of highlighting components and features of the communication to the learner—whether verbal, pictorial, auditory, or whatever—can be an important early step in laying the foundation for what is learned.

LEARNING GUIDANCE FOR ENCODING

The next phase of learning for which instruction may be planned consists of the encoding process that transforms the information into the form in which it is stored in long-term memory. The guidance of learning may present actual schemes for encoding (such as tables, graphs, or pictures), or it may simply suggest such schemes. Often, learning guidance consists of verbal communications to the learner, which may be given the general name *verbal directions.* Their function is not "instruction," in a strict sense (since this word is used to apply to the total set of events accompanying learning), but telling the learner what to do at any given time. Directions are not themselves a part of the content to be learned, but have a *mathemagenic* function (Gagné, 1974b; Rothkopf, 1970). Of course, learning guidance *can* be given without verbal directions, as happens when the learner is a young child who does not understand words. Verbal communication is, however, a frequently used mode for most instruction.

As indicated in Figure 15.1, two aspects of learning guidance affect the encoding process. One consists in the stimulation of recall of necessary prerequisites and other supportive material from the learner's long-term memory. The process involved is retrieval from the long-term memory to the working (short-term) memory. The second function for learning guidance is the presentation or suggestion of an encoding scheme, which affects the form in which the newly learned material will be stored in the long-term memory.

Stimulating Recall of Relevant Prerequisites

If a new intellectual skill is being learned, subordinate skills must be retrieved so that they can be recoded as parts of the new skill. If verbal information is being learned, previously learned organized knowledge may need to be retrieved to become a part of the larger meaningful context for the newly acquired information. The various prerequisites that must be recalled for the five different types of learning outcomes have been described in a previous chapter (see Table 13.3).

Two different kinds of verbal directions can be used to induce retrieval of previously learned entities, and each may be preferable in particular instances. When a relatively simple concept definition is being learned, it may be sufficient for directions to stimulate *recognition* of what has previously been learned. For example, in connection with the learning of a definition for "sodium," the directions might say, "You remember what sodium looks like; you also remember what a metal is." When more complex rules are being acquired, it may be desirable for directions to require *recall* (reinstatement) of the subordinate intellectual skills. Thus, if the learner is acquiring a rule about the hypotenuse of a right triangle, it may be desirable to require the *recall* of subordinate rules by saying, "Draw a right triangle," and asking "Which sides enclose the right angle?" The learning of the new rule can then proceed satisfactorily with the assurance that the necessary subordinate concepts are accessible in the working memory.

Guidance for Encoding

Guidance for the encoding of material to be stored in long-term memory may take a number of forms, depending to a large extent on the learning outcome expected. The essential functions to be performed by such learning guidance have been summarized in Chapter 13.

Suggesting schemes for encoding.   The learning of procedures is often accompanied by a form of learning guidance called *prompting*. For example, if a child is learning to spell words having the common suffix "—ate," the suffix may be initially suggested by the stimulus "a__e," as in the word "infla__e." Subsequently, the cues may be reduced ("faded") as in the word "summa____," and finally eliminated for the word "dict____." This example illustrates a form of learning guidance that uses extra cues—cues which are eliminated in a step-by-step fashion.

Verbal directions are often employed in learning guidance to *suggest* rather than specify the form of encoding to be used by the learner. When this is done, instruction is said to be using the technique of *guided discovery*. Many rules are learned by providing verbal cueing. For example, one can make the verbal statement, "Current flows in the direction of higher to lower electric potential." In contrast, when discovery of an encoding scheme is being suggested to the learner, a statement such as the following may be made: "Remember that a given point in a circuit may have a greater potential than another point. In which direction would you expect current to flow?" The first of these statements is designed to stimulate retrieval. The second is a question asking the student to *discover* the rule governing the flow of electric current. It is an example, then, of a verbal instruction of *guiding* discovery.

Directions that guide the learner's discovery of encoding schemes are very often in the form of questions. Of course, more than one question may be needed, in contrast to the rather simple example just given. In general, questions used for this purpose do not include all the language needed in the "answer" but are designed to suggest the answer required. Guidance provided by this kind of verbal communication is a method familiar to every teacher. It has been found to be effective in experimental studies of rule learning (Gagné and Brown, 1961; Gagné, Mayor, Garstens, and Paradise, 1962), although the question of how much or how little guidance is most effective has not yet received a satisfactory answer. Presumably, the effect of such verbal questioning is to channel the thinking of the learner away from the extreme incorrect hypotheses that would otherwise be tried. The effect of such guidance may be, therefore, to speed up the learning, since the learner does not waste time on discovered rules that are wildly wrong. Questions are also effective in suggesting encoding schemes for information learning, as the work of Rothkopf (1970) and Frase (1970) suggests.

Coding in terms of images.   The process of encoding may utilize images as well as words and propositions. Diagrams and graphs, for example, may be presented to the learner to represent rules and definitions, procedures, or collections of information. Many learning theorists who operate within the information-processing model are inclined to favor a *dual-process* model of long-term memory, which acknowledges the possibilities of encoding in terms of both verbal propositions and images (J. R. Anderson and Bower, 1973; Paivio, 1971). Pictures and diagrams may be used in instruction to provide concrete visual images to serve an encoding function. Alternatively, the use of images as coding schemes can simply be suggested to learners, who then form their own.

The use of pictures in instruction serves the important function of support for the encoding process. Pictures are used in still or moving forms in various instructional media, which will be further discussed in a later portion of this chapter.

ENHANCING RETENTION AND TRANSFER OF LEARNING

Instructional design provides for retention of what is learned and for transfer of the learning to new situations. Various techniques may be employed to insure that *cues for retrieval* are available to the learner. The organization of material to be learned into categories or in the form of tables, graphs, and diagrams provides a source of cues that serve to enhance later retention. Such cues may be a part of what is initially learned, as when lists of words are categorized and later retrieved with the cues of their category names (Tulving and Osler, 1968). Cues may also have their origin in previously learned associations (Bahrick, 1970) or in the organized cognitive structures that Ausubel (1968) describes. The employment of pictures and diagrams in presentations for learning often constitutes an effective part of instructional design for the provision of cues to be used by the learner in recall.

Cues that favor transfer of learning to new tasks and new situations are taken into account in instructional design by providing a *variety* of features of the learning task as well as a variety of contexts in which the learning occurs. The more broadly based a learned capability, the better chance it will have to transfer to new and different situations. Accordingly, the usefulness of any learned capability will be increased if it is practiced in as wide a variety of situations as possible. The learning of the intellectual skill of finding a cosine of an angle, for example, has a greater probability of being transferable if it is practiced in situations that are widely different from each other. The transferability of foreign words and phrases will be increased if they are practiced in a wide variety of contexts. The transferability of the scientific skill of "formulating operational definitions" will be increased if the skill is practiced in connection with a wide variety of natural phenomena. The implication for instructional design is quite clear: provision needs to be made for encouraging the learner to apply the learning in as great a variety of new situations as can be devised.

LEARNER PERFORMANCE AND FEEDBACK

Instruction designed to achieve a learning objective begins with the establishment of a state of expectancy in the learner. Each single act of learning, having involved a number of intervening processes, is completed when the performance of the learner is followed by a *reinforcing event*. In theory, such an event provides learners with information concerning the correctness, and often with the *degree* of correctness, of their performances.

The Learner's Performance

The elicitation of the performance that reflects the newly learned capability seems a reasonably natural event. The learner who has acquired the motor skill of tracing a figure eight on ice skates exhibits this performance readily. If the student of algebra has learned to transform terms from one side of an equation to another, provision is made to demonstrate the skill by application to a new example. The principle of requiring a performance in one or more instances is equally applicable to other kinds of learning outcomes— cognitive strategies, attitudes, and information learning, for example. The situations for eliciting performance may not be quite so clear-cut for these latter capabilities, but the importance of provisions for the relevant performing is not diminished. Performances to exhibit what has been learned provide evidence to an instructor and learner that learning has attained its objective.

In addition to the exhibition of a performance in one or two instances following learning, performance of the learner may be appraised in a more formal way by means of a test. Usually, a test is designed to appraise the learning of several instructional objectives over an extended period. It there-fore gives an indication of the retention of what has been learned as well as the immediate outcome of instruction. Techniques of assessment by means of tests have been thoroughly described in such volumes as Bloom, Hast-ings, and Madaus (1971) and Popham (1975). It may be noted here that while tests have several important functions in programs of instruction, they are not substitutes for the elicitation of performance that occurs as an end-point in the learning act. The immediate performance of the learner can best be observed by an instructor (or even by the learner) on an occasion that permits the natural and smooth completion of a sequence of learning processes.

Feedback

Closely associated with the elicitation of a performance that exhibits the new learning is the provision of feedback to the learner. In the most typical instance, the learner exhibits a performance that reflects the newly learned capability and then is "told" whether he or she is right or wrong. However, this does not mean that the words *right, wrong, correct,* or *incorrect* have to be used. In the classroom, a correct performance may be indicated by the teacher's going on to the next point in the lesson. Many other subtle cues may be employed—a nod, a smile, or a glance. There is no need to specify all the possibilities. Presumably, the learner must have previously learned that these events signify a correct performance. This can be assumed under most circumstances, since such knowledge is probably learned quite early in life. For some learning outcomes, such as motor skills and cognitive strat-egies, feedback must convey the *degree* to which the learner's performance approaches some standard.

The usefulness of frequent feedback during the acquisition of newly learned capabilities should not be overlooked. This is particularly the case when sequences or interrelated sets of components are being learned (for example, procedures, and information in connected discourse). The design-ers of programmed instruction frequently emphasize the importance of confirming responses for each "frame" of the program (Skinner, 1968). Many instructional programs are composed of single sentences containing blanks to be filled by the learner and a printed answer that may then be checked against the filled-in response. When entire topics are being learned, feed-back for the correct accomplishment of each subtopic can be of considera-ble value in increasing the efficiency of learning. The use of feedback in the form of "correction procedures" is a way of adapting instruction to the needs of the individual student. Several procedures having this purpose are discussed by R. C. Anderson and Faust (1974).

Feedback need not always come from the external situation but may arise from concepts or rules previously acquired and recalled by the learner.

There are many instances in which learners know they are right because of an internal check they can apply to their own performances. For example, in completing the chemical equation the compounds on the right are (let it be assumed) familiar ones, with previously learned chemical compositions.

$$HCL + NaOH \rightarrow H_2O + NaCl$$

Furthermore, the number of atoms of each element in the equation is the same on the right as on the left. Thus a learner who discovered how to complete this equation would be pretty confident of its correctness without being told. Of course, the learner might like further verification at a later time, but would be able to use recalled rules to supply self-reinforcement immediately after completing the performance.

THE PROCEDURES OF INSTRUCTION

The instructional process as a whole may be thought of as a set of procedures designed to support learning in each of the phases just described. Once the learning task has been analyzed and classified (as described in Chapter 13), planning instruction becomes a matter of arranging the external situation for optimal support of each learning phase, beginning with the establishment of motivation and a specific expectancy and ending with feedback for the learner's performance. The order in which these instructional events takes place is not precisely fixed, although some must obviously come before others. Each of the functions is essential; however, it should be noted that a greater or lesser amount of self-instruction can be assumed, depending on the learner's sophistication (see Gagné, 1974a, pp. 131–138).

How do these procedures fit together in a typical instructional exercise? This can be illustrated by an analysis of an instructional sequence in elementary science, entitled "Inferring the Presence of Water Vapor in Air" (AAAS Commission on Science Education, 1963). This exercise has the objective of teaching the child to identify an inference, namely, that the liquid accumulating on a cold surface exposed to the air comes from the air. From the instruction provided, the child is expected to be able not only to state the inferred rule but also to demonstrate the operations that make possible the checking of the inference. The analysis of instruction for this exercise is given in Table 15.1.

Table 15.1 makes it clear that each step in the instructional procedure can be accounted for as an event designed to activate and support internal learning processes. First, it is apparent that a state of *motivation* is aroused and made specific as an *expectancy* of the outcome of learning. *Attention* and *selective perception* are directed by verbal communications from the instructor. A number of previously learned rules and concepts, prerequisite to the new learning, are *recalled*. Schemes for *encoding* the concepts and rules are suggested, although there is considerable dependence on discovery of these by the learner. *Performance* of the learner is called for and

TABLE 15.1   Instructional Procedure for an Exercise on "Inferring the Presence of Water Vapor in Air"

Instructional Event	Function
1. Teacher directs attention to clouding of windows on a cold day, the ring of water left by a glass of ice water, the cloud left by breathing on a mirror. Questions students about why these events happen.	1. Establishment of *achievement* motivation based on curiosity and the desire to display knowledge to other children and to parents.
2. Children are given tin cans and ice cubes.	2. Providing *stimulus objects*.
3. Students are told to put the ice cubes in the cans and to watch what happens to the outside of the cans.	3. Completion of stimulus situation. Directions to focus *attention, selective perception*.
4. Students are asked to describe what they see. "Fog"; "drops of water"; "large drops running down"; "ring of water at base of can."	4. Verbal directions to stimulate *recall* of previously learned concepts.
5. Students are asked what they can infer from their observations. "Liquid is water from the air."	5. Learning of a rule by discovery; for some students, this may be *recall*. Feedback provided.
6. Other alternatives are pointed out to students. Could it be some other liquid? Could it come from the metal of the can? *How can one test an inference?*	6. Verbal directions to inform the learners of the expected outcome of instruction (how to test this inference). Establishing an *expectancy*.
7. "How can we tell whether this liquid is water?" ("Taste it.")	7. Requiring *recall* of previously learned rule.
8. "If the water comes out of the metal, what should happen when it is wiped off?" ("Can should weigh less.")	8. Requiring *recall* of previously learned rule.
9. Students are asked, "If the water comes from the air, what should happen to the weight of the can after the water collects on it?" ("Can should increase in weight.") Direct observation is made of increase in weight of can by ice by weighing on an equal-arm balance.	9. Requiring *recall* of previously learned rules.

TABLE 15.1   Instructional Procedure for an Exercise on "Inferring the Presence of Water Vapor in Air" (continued)

Instructional Event	Function
10. Students are asked to recall that steam consists of water droplets and water vapor (an invisible gas). Air can contain water vapor.	10. Requiring *recall* of previously learned rules.
11. Students are asked to state (a) what they observed; (b) what they inferred; and (c) how they checked their inference.	11. Verbal guidance to suggest *encoding* for concepts of observation and inference and of rules for checking inferences. *Feedback* provided.
12. Students are asked to make and test inferences in two or three other new situations and to describe the operations and reasoning involved. These might be (a) water evaporation; (b) the extinguishing of a candle in a closed cylinder; (c) the displacement of water by gas in an inverted cylinder.	12. Additional *examples* of the concepts and rules learned for the purpose of insuring *retention* and *learning transfer.*
13. Another new situation is presented to the students and they are asked to describe it in terms of (a) what they observed; (b) what they inferred; (c) how they checked their inference.	13. *Appraisal* providing *feedback.*

Based on an exercise of the same name occurring in AAAS Commission on Science Education. *Science: A Process Approach, Part 4.* Washington, D.C.: American Association for the Advancement of Science, 1963.

followed by *reinforcement.* The *transferability* of the newly learned skills is tested, again with suitable feedback informing the learner of success in achieving a new capability.

Instructional procedures for adult learners take account of the same learning phases. However, those who are used to learning will undoubtedly have developed strategies of self-instruction. Mature learners are likely to approach the learning situation with motivation already well established. They may be able to realize immediately what the expected outcome of learning should be (although information about objectives is often helpful in confirming their expectancy). They have learned to perceive the stimulus selectively. They have a variety of encoding schemes and cues for retrieval at their command. They make provision for their own performances and are able to provide their own feedback. External events of instruction are frequently helpful but evidently not essential for the learning of these "truly sophisticated" learners. As a result, such learners are able to acquire many new capabilities simply from reading. The important point for the instructional designer, however, is that not all learners can do all these things, whether they are children or adults. Hence there is a need for insuring that external means are available to actively support the internal transformations required in each learning phase.

PLANNING INSTRUCTIONAL DELIVERY

The design of instruction must take into account the way in which the instruction is going to be delivered. Not only is the choice of media influenced by the "learning situation," as we have seen in the previous chapter, but other aspects of instructional design are also affected by the anticipated *delivery system* for instruction.

At one end of the spectrum, instruction may be delivered directly from a medium such as the printed page to the individual learner. This is quite a common mode for instructional delivery for the adult learner. Individuals may learn from books, from watching television programs, and by interacting with computer-based programs. Once an individual having "instructor" functions is introduced into the learning situation, several different systems of delivery become possible (Gagné and Briggs, 1979). There is, first, the arrangement of one-to-one interaction called *tutoring*. Then, as one moves to a consideration of group instruction, there are the *small group with recitation* and the *small group with discussion*. While no exact definition is available, a small group is considered to number up to eight students. (Some teachers believe successful classes involving recitation or discussion can be conducted with as many as fifteen students.) Increased numbers lead to a consideration of the *large group*, which may also employ *recitation*, and very often uses the mode of *lecturing*, a system characterized by one-way communication from instructor to students. Of course, a lecture may allow for scheduled periods of recitation or questioning.

Tutoring

The system of instructor-student interaction called *tutoring* occurs perhaps most commonly in the teaching of youngsters, although tutoring for adults may be employed in the learning of specialized skills such as foreign-language speaking and musical performance. With children, the tutor may typically be an adult. However, it is notable that many successful tutoring programs have been conducted by "children teaching children" (Gartner, Kohler, and Riessman, 1971). Both cross-age and peer tutoring have been used to good advantage. Of course, a critical factor in the success of such programs is the careful and conscientious training of tutors in the techniques of effective instruction.

Events of instruction in tutoring. This mode of instructional delivery typically makes possible the execution of the nine events of instruction (Figure 15.1) in a flexible manner. That is to say, the tutor is able not only to deliver instruction that takes each of the events of instruction fully into account, but also to *adapt* them to the learner's responses at each phase of the instructional process. Having gained the learner's attention, the tutor proceeds to inform the learner of the lesson's objective. In doing this, the tutor takes care to insure that "what the learner will be able to do" is fully understood, but also that some likely motivation of the learner has been "captured." For instance, the tutor might use a mispronounced-word in the student's native language in order to provide an understanding of the objective "identifies accurate German pronunciation of words with umlauted vowels."

Next, the tutor attends to the matter of stimulating the student's recall of relevant prior knowledge. If the relationship has extended over some time, the tutor is likely to be aware of what prior knowledge the student is likely to possess and can take full advantage of such knowledge. If the tutor is new, then a variety of probes can be employed to assess the "entering capabilities" of the student. In presenting the stimulus material for instruction, the tutor is able to use either oral or visual cues to emphasize relevant features that will aid the student's perception. Thus, instruction in gender of the definite article in French might have the tutor saying "la" and "le" with increased vocal amplitude, or pointing to these articles in a printed passage, or both. Furthermore, the tutor carefully observes the student as stimuli are being presented and is thus able to redirect the student's attention at any moment when the perception of stimulus features is required.

In selecting and planning the event called learning guidance, the tutor can use both expert judgment and knowledge of the student's past performance. Suppose that a new intellectual skill is being taught, and preparations have been made for the ready accessibility (in working memory) of the prerequisite skills. The merest "hint" from the tutor as to how subordinate skills are to be put together is often enough to bring about an insightful experience and a reinforcing accomplishment on the part of the learner. Should more than a hint be required, the tutor can of course tell the student how the new concept or rule is composed, and in the extreme, show how it is done. For verbal information in the form of connected prose, learning guidance typically takes the form of questioning by the tutor. The questions should be such as to require expression of the verbal information in the student's own words and perhaps encourage "deeper processing" and elaboration of the content of the verbal passage. In dealing with attitudes, an older tutor can conceivably play the part of the human model for a younger student. Otherwise, the tutor may call upon a knowledge of the student's interests to identify a suitable human model from real life or from other sources such as television, the theater, or fiction. Again, the great flexibility of choice available to the tutor in this mode of delivery is apparent.

The Recitation Class

Groups of students assembled in classes are often given instruction by way of a delivery system of *recitation*. This is carried out in a sequence of activities beginning with a question by the instructor, who then "calls upon" one of the students to recite or give an answer. Other students are then called upon one by one in some unpredictable order until the objective of the session is attained.

Actually, recitation methods can be used to bring about the initial instructional events for the learning of intellectual skills or cognitive strategies (Gagné and Briggs, 1979). With a class of bright and well-prepared students, a teacher can derive an enormous amount of reinforcement from observing students "discover" one by one the successive phases of learning processing, or the prerequisites of a complex intellectual skill. A more frequent use of the recitation method, however, is one that partakes of the instructional events that follow initial acquisition—assessment of performance, corrective feedback, and provisions for enhancing retention and the transfer of learning.

Events of instruction in recitation. In a typical recitation class, an assignment has been made on which the students are to come prepared to be called upon to recite. Let us suppose that this assignment has been made to a class of immigrant adults learning in the English language to use the objective case following prepositions. Either in a previous learning session or in homework with a workbook students have learned the objective-case form of the pronouns and been reminded of the most common prepositions. This means that the events of instruction applicable to initial acquisition of these grammatical rules have been utilized (by the instructor or the student, or both).

Presumably, the initial performances of such phrases as "for me," "with him," "between us," "to her," or "above you and me," have been made by the students to their own satisfaction. In the recitation class, the instructor presents new sentences containing new pronoun phrases and calls upon students individually to supply missing pronouns to complete the meaning of sentences. What occurs is a combination of eliciting performance, providing feedback, and assessing the performance. Each student called upon to supply the proper form of pronoun is given feedback that informs about the correctness of the response or else tells what can be done to correct it. As the recitation proceeds, the instructor is gaining an impression about how well students have learned—in other words, an informal assessment of students' performance is taking place.

Of course, the risk in this method of delivery, so far as instruction is concerned, resides in the question as to whether *all* students are equally able to perform, since the instructor can observe only one at a time. In the middle grades of school, it is not uncommon for students to "play the game" of avoiding being called upon to recite. When a large portion of students' attention is devoted to such an activity, the instructor can expect that little learning is going to occur. Accordingly, the instructor also often resorts to games, such as finding and calling upon ill-prepared students or springing a quiz on the entire class. The aim, of course, is to reestablish the events of instruction that support learning.

The Discussion Group

Discussion is a valuable mode of delivery for instruction. It can be done with fairly large groups, but its typically effective form occurs in small groups of ten or less. Instruction in such groups may be thought of as "interactive communication" (Gall and Gall, 1976). The instructor may serve as a leader of the discussion and introduce the topic by means of a question. One student speaks at a time, while the others listen. Other students respond to the speaker's remarks, again one at a time and not in any predetermined order. The instructor introduces questions or other remarks when appropriate, and on occasion calls upon particular students to speak. It is common for discussion groups to pursue instructional objectives in one or more of three areas: subject-matter review, attitude formation, and problem solving (Gall and Gall, 1976).

Events of instruction in discussion groups.   In discussions of social or political issues, the instructor typically introduces the topic by citing an example, often one that has already received the attention of students. Censorship by a school of an item in the school newspaper might be an example of known student interest. Expectancy of the learning outcome would thereby be engendered. Next, the instructor would take the time to ask all students in the group to recall what they know about the censorship of news, the provisions of the First Amendment to the U.S. Constitution, and about legal precedents in cases of censorship. The recall of this background of knowledge is essential for a successful discussion.

It would be appropriate for the instructor, at this juncture, to point out the distinctive features of the issue, such as the matter of ownership of the school newspaper, the question concerning its classification as "the press," and others. In so doing, the instructor is "presenting the stimulus" in the clearest possible way.

In a discussion group of this sort, it is not immediately predictable who will serve as a human model. The instructor may, of course, but one or more students may serve this function as well. As the discussion proceeds, the arguments put forward by various members of the group will be perceived as having greater or lesser credibility. These will doubtless be the views that prevail and that will be acquired as attitudes by members of the group. In this way the choices of personal action described by members who put forward the most credible views become a kind of group consensus and are encoded as the "acceptable" attitude. Discussion in such instances might be brought to a close following the provision of additional examples of personal action choices reflecting the attitude by various group members.

The Lecture

The lecture is an exceedingly common form for delivery of instruction, particularly when a large group must be taught at the same time. The instructor delivers an oral communication to a group of assembled students. This communication may also make use of demonstrations, pictures, slides, writing on a chalkboard, or other media. The students listen to the communication of the lecturer and observe the demonstration or other message. Some students take notes, and these may later be used for review or as a basis for their own elaborations.

The lecture can fulfill some desirable instructional purposes (McLeish, 1976). It is possible for a lecturer to (1) convey an enthusiasm to a student audience, (2) point out the relation between the special field being taught and the more general interests of students, and (3) explain how theory and research findings relate to practical problems.

A good lecturer utilizes the organization of instructional events as a way of ordering communication. However, the lecturer's cues for the timing of these events come not from a single student but from many different students. As a consequence, although the lecturer may be employing an effective organization, there can be no certainty that the remarks are having the same effect on each and every student. The result of this circumstance is a *loss of precision* in the employment of instructional events (Gagné and Briggs, 1979). There is a contrast here with the flexibility of the tutor in being able to adapt both the timing and content of instructional events to the student's reactions. The lecturer can only count on the *probable* effects of these events on the many individual students.

Events of instruction in the lecture. Following the gaining of student attention, the lecturer may typically proceed by informing students of the lecture's objective. For example, if the topic is the political effects of choice of the vice-presidential nominee in presidential elections, a reasonable objective of the lecture might be "predicting the probable choices of vice-presidential candidates in the next presidential election." Having gotten across the objective, the lecturer turns next to the task of stimulating recall of prior knowledge. Since this objective falls in the category of verbal information, the precise nature of the prior knowledge recalled by learners is not important. The lecturer may ask students to recall how vice-presidential candidates were chosen in the most recent election. Alternatively, if the students have been studying the era of Franklin D. Roosevelt, they might be asked to recall the succession of vice-presidential candidates who were chosen in those elections. The significant purpose of this instructional event is to assure that a "network" of relevant knowledge is readily accessible to each student.

The lecturer then proceeds to the "body" of the lecture, in which the "stimulus material is presented" with suitable emphasis on its distinctive features. These might be the vice-presidential candidate's appeal to regional interests, ethnic qualities, liberal or conservative philosophies, and other politically prominent aspects. Proceeding to the "provision of learning guidance," the lecturer may decide to use several different and contrasting examples of vice-presidential choices in order to assure effective encoding of the procedure and of the political factors that influence it. As mentioned in the previous chapter, material in slide form may be introduced, suggesting images that will serve to provide elaborative cues.

The lecturer has no ready means to "elicit the performance" of an entire group of students. Typically, this event will have to wait until a quiz can be given to assess performance. However, the lecturer can use questions that have the effect of eliciting covert performance of attentive students. Such questions might be of the "problem-solving" type. For example, if the lecture has proceeded to the point of describing the vice-presidential candidates in the election of 1968 without giving their names, the question of who was actually chosen might be presented as a problem to the class. Several different answers to the problem might lead to a brief discussion but would in any case have the effect of bringing out student responses. The lecture might then be brought to a close with a brief review of the several examples described along with their distinguishing features and some suggested cues for later recall.

It is evident, then, that the events of instruction can be followed in the planning of a lecture, just as they are for other modes of delivery such as the discussion class or the tutoring session. Since the lecture is not an interactive mode, instructional events cannot be adapted to the moment-to-moment needs of every individual student. Their expected effects in supporting learning processes are not certain, only probable, in terms of the total membership of the lecture audience. From the students' point of view, it is they on whom greatest responsibility rests in learning from a lecture. For well-prepared and suitably motivated students, learning from lectures can be both effective and pleasurable. This is the state of affairs that university lecturers hope will prevail.

EVALUATION OF INSTRUCTIONAL DESIGN

When the principles of instructional theory are employed in the design of instruction, activities that include analysis of learning requirements (Chapter 13) and selection of media (Chapter 14), as well as those described in the current chapter, are involved. Good instructional design, though, is seldom perfect, or even as good as it can be on the first try. Instructional designers are inclined to derive much of their confidence in an instructional product from *empirical results* of tryouts with one or more sets of typical learners. Designing instruction is a creative process requiring the designer to keep in mind the many variables that influence effectiveness. It is not unusual for mistakes and omissions to occur. Even relatively gross errors may crop up in instructional material of generally excellent quality. It is not surprising, therefore, to find experienced instructional designers giving special emphasis to the importance of results from tryouts of material they have originated.

The procedures used in trying out and thus testing the worth of products of instructional design are called *formative evaluation*. Literally, this phrase implies that instructional material is to be evaluated while it is being formed. Of course, this means that the evaluation must be carried out at certain stages; it can scarcely be done continuously. A first "draft" of instructional material, cast in a form that uses some particular media, represents a stage at which a first formative evaluation can occur. The results of this trial yield information, qualitative or quantitative, that may be used to make a revision of the material. Subsequent revisions are undertaken on the basis of results obtained with a second tryout and again with a third. Each of these evaluation-revision cycles is expected to yield an instructional product that is improved in acceptability, feasibility of use, and effectiveness for learning.

Three Phases of Formative Evaluation

In describing the process of formative evaluation, Dick and Carey (1978) identify three phases. The first is *one-to-one evaluation*, and the following phases are called *small-group evaluation* and *field evaluation*. Each yields information used to revise and improve instructional materials. We shall note later that an evaluation conducted on a product that has been put into use is called a *summative evaluation*. The primary purpose of this latter type of evaluation is to make possible a decision about use, such as is reflected in the question, "Has this instruction made a difference in student learning—a difference that accomplishes a worthwhile purpose?" At this point, though, we return to the procedures for tryout and revision: formative evaluation.

One-to-one evaluation. As its name implies, this kind of evaluation is conducted by the instructional developer with one student at a time. Of course, the students who participate should be as nearly typical as possible to those for whom the instruction is intended. Each student's reactions to the instructional material is solicited, with the stated aim of finding particular deficiencies, errors, and omissions. At the same time, the designer observes hesitations and misunderstandings of the material on the part of the student. An assessment of the student's performance is also carried out by means of a quiz or test; however, the results are interpreted cautiously in the light of the procedure employed.

The one-to-one evaluation is capable of yielding a variety of information important to the revision process. First of all, it can tell the designer whether the instructional material is comprehensible to the student or whether there are portions that are not. Related to this feature is the question of whether the instruction is teaching what was intended to be taught. In addition, "small" mistakes such as typographical errors, omissions, and the like, can be caught at this phase and corrected in a revision.

Small-group evaluation. This phase of evaluation is normally done with a set of students numbering between ten and twenty (Dick and Carey, 1978). In this case, the selection of the students is a critical matter, because they should be *representative* of the students for whom the instruction is intended. This means that a randomization procedure might be used in selection, or that individuals are chosen who specifically represent portions of the intended population of students.

Once the small group has been selected, the evaluation can proceed, using environmental surroundings as close as possible to those expected to prevail when instruction is given "in earnest." Both the learning situation for which the instruction has been designed and the medium or media selected for its delivery (Chapter 14) should correspond to intended usage to the maximum possible extent. In contrast to the one-to-one evaluation, the designer does not interact with individual students. Instead, the instruction is given as planned using the materials that embody it. For example, if the instruction is intended for instructor use with students who read, the designer observes the delivery of the instruction with an assembled small group. As an alternative, if the instruction has been designed for TV broadcast to a home viewing audience of adults, observations must then be made on ten to twenty individual adults.

The primary results of this type of evaluation pertain to the effectiveness of the learning and accordingly are derived from a test or other performance assessment administered as a final activity. In addition, however, other features of the instruction may be evaluated that pertain to the feasibility of use of the instructional "package." The participants in this phase of evaluation, for instance, may be asked questions about (1) their comprehension of and interest in the material; (2) whether sufficient feedback was provided during learning; and (3) the appropriateness of examples and practice exercises. Student attitudes toward the materials as a whole also may be assessed.

Obviously, the results of the small-group evaluation provide a rich source of information for the revision process. Portions that fail to bring about the intended learning can be replaced. Portions found dull can be improved to heighten student interest. The test or other means used for learning assessment can be revised to include items that are most clearly "content valid." And in particular, the entire set of instructional materials can be checked and modified with the aim of assuring that it accomplishes its learning objective.

Field evaluation.   A group of thirty or more students, representative of those for whom the instruction is intended, may be used as participants in a field evaluation. In this case, the designer is attempting to assess the entire "package" of instructional materials. A setting typical of that intended for continued use of the materials is employed. If classroom usage is expected, a representative classroom is selected; if individual interaction with the instruction is intended, an appropriate example of that mode of delivery is chosen. The medium or media for delivery match those planned for ultimate use. The entire set of instructional materials, including such things as instructor's manuals, tests, and other accompanying instructional aids, forms a part of field evaluation.

The results of field evaluation provide more precise indicators of learning effectiveness, acceptability, and interest than do those of the small-group evaluation. Accordingly, field-study data form the basis for revision and refinement of the instructional product. Although design may have followed closely the procedures implied by instructional theory, the empirical data yielded by evaluation studies are likely to bring about revisions that are highly valuable for meeting learning goals.

When a suitably designed instructional "package" shows signs of being successful in bringing about the desired learning, it is likely to be evaluated not just once, but again and again. Field evaluations therefore may come to be seen not simply as formative, but as *summative evaluations*. Studies of this sort make possible the drawing of conclusions about how well the instruction has worked. They also lead to decisions on the part of the educational agency about the adoption and continued use of the designed instruction, whether it be in the form of a single lesson, a course, or an entire system (Dick, 1977; Gagné and Briggs, 1979).

Procedures for summative evaluation of courses of education and training involve consideration of many factors affecting design and administration. These are given more complete coverage in volumes that deal comprehensively with instructional design and development (Briggs, 1977; Dick and Carey, 1978; Gagné and Briggs, 1979) and also in books that address the problems of evaluation directly (Popham, 1975; Struening and Guttentag, 1975; Worthen and Sanders, 1973).

EDUCATIONAL IMPLICATIONS

This chapter has attempted to draw together the implications of our description of *varieties of learned capabilities* and of the *phases of processing during learning* as incorporated in Chapter 12 on *instructional theory*. The application of these ideas has been to the *design of instruction*.

The sources of knowledge about learning and its conditions may be put to use in the process of instructional design. To be carried out effectively, such a process must include attention to the details as well as to the general characteristics of human learning. Instructional design generally requires that two major questions be answered as bases for design procedures. The first is, "What kinds of capabilities are to be learned?" And the second is, "What kinds of stimulation external to the learner will best support the internal processing necessary for learning?"

Having identified the intended learning outcome, the instructional designer undertakes to specify the external conditions of learning and to embody them in a series of events given the general name of *instruction* (Chapter 13). The events of instruction are planned as stimulation to the learner during successive phases of learning, as indicated in Figure 15.1 and exemplified in Table 15.1. The purpose of these external events is to activate, support, and maintain the internal processes of learning (Chapter 12; Gagné, 1974a; Gagné and Briggs, 1979). With the learning situation in mind, the designer makes a choice of media to perform the function of communicating the content of instruction (Chapter 14).

Instructional design draws the specifications for events that support the processes of (a) motivation channeling and the establishment of expectancies, (b) attention and selective perception, (c) encoding, (d) retrieval and recall, (e) learning transfer, and (f) performance reflecting the learned capability. Finally, the event of reinforcement serves to complete the learning act by confirming the learner's expectancy. Each of these events requires a specific design. Some (such as the direction of attention) have common features that are applicable in the learning of any or all types of capabilities. Others (such as encoding and provisions for retrieval) require different arrangements of events for each kind of learning outcome. Naturally, these events take many forms, as determined by the learning task and also by the characteristics of the learner. The *functions* of these events in support of learning processes are the critical features that determine their planning and selection.

Having been designed, an instructional module, topic, or course along with its chosen media will be compatible with a *system of delivery*. How the instruction will be delivered involves planning that affects the "instructional situation" and therefore such design considerations as the choice of media and the manner of executing the events of instruction required for effective learning. The precision with which these events can be controlled is greatest with tutoring, least with the lecture. In the lecture, then, responsibility for many of the events of instruction devolves upon the students.

When instructional materials are carefully designed according to the principles of instructional theory, one expects them to be of high quality. However, additional assurance of quality comes from the systematic gathering of *empirical* evidence obtained from tryouts of the instruction with students. Such evidence is collected in procedures of *formative evaluation*. It is used to interpret the effectiveness, acceptability, and feasibility of use of the instructional package and so to revise the instructional content with the aim of improving its quality. As use of the instructional product continues, additional efforts are made to obtain evidences of usefulness and cost; these procedures are called *summative evaluation*.

GENERAL REFERENCES

Foundations of Instructional Design

Anderson, R. C., and Faust, G. W. *Educational psychology: The science of instruction and learning.* New York: Dodd, Mead, 1974.

Farley, F. H., and Gordon, N. J. (Eds.), *Psychology and education: The state of the union.* Berkeley, Calif.: McCutchan, 1981.

Levin, J. R., and Allen, V. L. *Cognitive learning in children.* New York: Academic Press, 1976.

Designing Instruction

Briggs, L. J. (Ed.), *Instructional design.* Englewood Cliffs, N.J.: Educational Technology, 1977.

Briggs, L. J., and Wager, W. W. *Handbook of procedures for the design of instruction,* 2nd ed. Englewood Cliffs, N.J.: Educational Technology, 1981.

Dick, W., and Carey, L. *The systematic design of instruction.* Glenview, Ill.: Scott, Foresman, 1978.

Gagné, R. M., and Briggs, L. J. *Principles of instructional design,* 2nd ed. New York: Holt, Rinehart and Winston, 1979.

Romiszowski, A. J. *Designing instructional systems.* London: Kogan Page, 1981; New York: Nichols, 1981.

Delivery Systems

Block, J. H., and Anderson, L. W. *Mastery learning in classroom instruction.* New York: Macmillan, 1975.

Hudgins, B. B. *Learning and thinking.* Itasca, Ill.: Peacock, 1977.
Joyce, B., and Weil, M. *Models of teaching.* Englewood Cliffs, N.J.: Prentice-Hall, 1972.

Formative Evaluation

Berk, R. A. (Ed.), *Criterion-referenced measurement: The state of the art.* Baltimore, Md.: Johns Hopkins University Press, 1980.
Briggs, L. J. (Ed.), *Instructional design: Principles and applications.* Englewood Cliffs, N.J.: Educational Technology, 1977. Chapters 6, 10, 11.
Popham, W. J. (Ed.), *Evaluation in Education.* Berkeley, Calif.: McCutchan, 1974.

References

AAAS Commission on Science Education. *Science: A process approach, part 4.* Washington, D.C.: American Association for the Advancement of Science, 1963.

Adams, J. A. *Human memory.* New York: McGraw-Hill, 1967.

Allport, G. W. Attitudes. In C. Murchison (Ed.), *Handbook of social psychology.* Worcester, Mass.: Clark University Press, 1935.

Anderson, J. R. *Language, memory, and thought.* Hillsdale, N.J.: Erlbaum, 1976.

Anderson, J. R. *Cognitive psychology and its implications.* San Francisco: Freeman, 1980.

Anderson, J. R., and Bower, G. H. Recognition and retrieval processes in free recall. *Psychological Review,* 1972, 79, 97–123.

Anderson, J. R., and Bower, G. H. *Human associative memory.* Washington, D.C.: V. H. Winston, 1973.

Anderson, N. H. Information integration theory applied to attitudes about U.S. presidents. *Journal of Educational Psychology,* 1973, 64, 1–8.

Anderson, R. C. The notion of schemata and the educational enterprise: General discussion of the conference. In R. C. Anderson, R. J. Spiro, and W. E. Montague (Eds.), *Schooling and the acquisition of knowledge.* Hillsdale, N.J.: Erlbaum, 1977.

Anderson, R. C., and Faust, G. W. *Educational psychology: The science of instruction and learning..* New York: Dodd, Mead, 1974.

Anderson, R. C., and Kulhavy, R. W. Learning concepts from definitions. *American Educational Research Journal,* 1972, 9, 385–390.

Anderson, R. C., and Myrow, D. L. Retroactive inhibition of meaningful discourse. *Journal of Educational Psychology Monograph,* 1971, 62, 81–94.

Anderson, R. C., and Pichert, J. W. Recall of previously unrecallable information following a shift in perspective. *Journal of Verbal Learning and Verbal Behavior,* 1978, 17, 1–12.

Anderson, R. C., Spiro, R. J., and Montague, W.. E. (Eds.). *Schooling and the acquisition of knowledge.* Hillsdale, N.J.: Erlbaum, 1977.

Anderson, R. H. *Selecting and developing media for instruction.* New York: Van Nostrand Reinhold, 1976.

Atkinson, R. C., and Shiffrin, R. M. Human memory: A proposed system and its control processes. In K. W. Spence and J. T. Spence (Eds.), *The psychology of learning and motivation,* Vol. 2. New York: Academic Press, 1968.

Ausubel, D. P. The use of advance organizers in the learning and retention of meaningful verbal material. *Journal of Educational Psychology,* 1960, 51, 267–272.

Ausubel, D. P. *Educational psychology: A cognitive view.* New York: Holt, Rinehart and Winston, 1968.

Ausubel, D. P. In defense of advance organizers: A reply to the critics. *Review of Educational Research*, 1978, 48, 251–257.

Ausubel, D. P., and Blake, E. Proactive inhibition in the forgetting of meaningful school materials. *Journal of Educational Research*, 1958, 52, 145–149.

Ausubel, D. P., and Fitzgerald, D. Organizer, general background, and antecedent learning variables in sequential verbal learning. *Journal of Educational Psychology*, 1962, 53, 243–249.

Ausubel, D. P., Novak, J. D., and Hanesian, H. *Educational psychology: A cognitive view*, 2nd ed. New York: Holt, Rinehart and Winston, 1978.

Ausubel, D. P., Robbins, L. C., and Blake, E. Retroactive inhibition and facilitation in the learning of school materials. *Journal of Educational Psychology*, 1957, 48, 334–343.

Ausubel, D. P., and Youssef, M. The effects of spaced repetition on meaningful retention. *Journal of General Psychology*, 1965, 73, 147–150.

Baer, D. M., Peterson, R. F., and Sherman, J. A. The development of imitation by reinforcing behavioral similarity to a model. *Journal of the Experimental Analysis of Behavior*, 1967, 10, 405–416.

Bahrick, H. P. Two-phase model for prompted recall. *Psychological Review*, 1970, 77, 215–222.

Bandura, A. Influence of model's reinforcement contingencies on the acquisition of imitative responses. *Journal of Personality and Social Psychology*. 1965, 1, 589–595.

Bandura, A. *Principles of behavior modification*. New York: Holt, Rinehart and Winston, 1969.

Bandura, A. Vicarious and self-reinforcement processes. In R. Glaser (Ed.), *The nature of reinforcement*. New York: Academic Press, 1971.

Bandura, A. *Social learning theory*. Englewood Cliffs, N.J.: Prentice-Hall, 1977.

Bandura, A., and McDonald, F. J. The influence of social reinforcement and the behavior of models in shaping children's moral judgments. *Journal of Abnormal and Social Psychology*, 1963, 67, 274–281.

Bandura, A., and Mischel, W. The influence of models in modifying delay of gratification patterns. *Journal of Personality and Social Psychology*, 1965, 2, 698–705.

Bartlett, F. C. *Remembering*. New York: Cambridge University Press, 1932.

Battig, W. F. Paired-associate learning. In T. R. Dixon and D. L. Horton (Eds.), *Verbal behavior and general behavior theory*. Englewood Cliffs, N.J.: Prentice-Hall, 1968.

Beeson, G. W. Hierarchical learning in electrical science. *Journal of Research in Science Teaching*, 1977, 14, 117–127.

Belmont, J. M., and Butterfield, E. C. What the development of short-term memory is. *Human Development*, 1971, 14, 236–248.

Bem, D. J. *Beliefs, attitudes and human affairs*. Monterey, Calif.: Brooks/Cole, 1970.

Bereiter, C., and Engelmann, S. *Teaching disadvantaged children in the pre-school*. Englewood Cliffs, N.J.: Prentice-Hall, 1966.

Berk, R. A. (Ed.). *Criterion-referenced measurement: The state of the art*. Baltimore, Md.: Johns Hopkins University Press, 1980.

Block, J. H., and Anderson, L. W. *Mastery learning in classroom instruction*. New York: Macmillan, 1975.

Bloom, B. S. *Human characteristics and school learning*. New York: McGraw-Hill, 1976.

Bloom, B. S., Hastings, J. T., and Madaus, G. F. *Handbook on formative and summative evaluation of student learning*. New York: McGraw-Hill, 1971.

Bogardus, E. S. Measuring social distance. *Journal of Applied Sociology*, 1925, *9*, 299–308.

Bostrom, R., Vlandis, J., and Rosenbaum, M. Grades as reinforcing contingencies and attitude change. *Journal of Educational Psychology*, 1961, *52*, 112–115.

Bourne, L. E., Jr. *Human conceptual behavior*. Boston: Allyn and Bacon, 1966.

Bousfield, W. A. The occurrence of clustering in the recall of randomly arranged associates. *Journal of General Psychology*. 1953, *49*, 229–249.

Bower, G. H. Mental imagery and associative learning. In L. Gregg (Ed.), *Cognition in learning and memory*. New York: Wiley, 1969.

Bower, G. H. Imagery as a relational organizer in associative learning. *Journal of Verbal Learning and Verbal Behavior*, 1970, *9*, 529–533.

Bower, G. H. A selective review of organizational factors in memory. In E. T. Tulving and W. Donaldson (Eds.), *Organization of memory*. New York: Academic Press, 1972.

Bower, G. H. Cognitive psychology: An introduction. In W. K. Estes (Ed.), *Handbook of learning and cognitive processes*, Vol. 1. *Introduction to concepts and issues*. Hillsdale, N.J.: Erlbaum, 1975.

Bower, G. H., and Hilgard, E. R. *Theories of learning*, 5th ed. Englewood Cliffs, N.J.: Prentice-Hall, 1981.

Bower, G. H., and Winzenz, D. Comparison of associative learning strategies. *Psychonomic Science*, 1970, *20*, 119–120.

Boyer, E. L. *High school: A report on secondary education in America*. New York: Harper & Row, 1983.

Braby, R. *An evaluation of ten techniques for choosing instructional media*. TAEG Report No. 8. Orlando, Fla.: USN Training Analysis and Evaluation Group, 1973.

Briggs, L. J. (Ed.). *Instructional design: Principles and applications*. Englewood Cliffs, N.J.: Educational Technology, 1977.

Briggs, L. J., and Reed, H. B. The curve of retention for substance material. *Journal of Experimental Psychology*, 1943, *32*, 513–517.

Briggs, L. J., and Wager, W. W. *Handbook of procedures for the design of instruction*, 2nd ed. Englewood Cliffs, N.J.: Educational Technology, 1981.

Brooks, L. Nonanalytic concept formation and memory for instances. In E. Rosch and B. B. Lloyd (Eds.), *Cognition and categorization*. Hillsdale, N.J.: Erlbaum, 1978.

Brown, A. L. Knowing when, where, and how to remember: A problem of metacognition. In R. Glaser (Ed.), *Advances in instructional psychology*, Vol. I. Hillsdale, N.J.: Erlbaum, 1978.

Bruner, J. S. The act of discovery. *Harvard Educational Review*, 1961, *31*, 21–32.

Bruner, J. S. *Toward a theory of instruction*. Cambridge, Mass.: Harvard University Press, 1966.

Bruner, J. S. *The relevance of education*. New York: Norton, 1971.

Bruner, J. S., Goodnow, J. J., and Austin, G. A. *A study of thinking*. New York: Wiley, 1956.

Bunderson, C. V., Gibbons, A. S., Olsen, J. B., and Kearsley, G. P. Work models: Beyond instructional objectives. *Instructional Science*, 1981, *10*, 205–215.

Campbell, D. T. Social attitudes and other acquired behavioral dispositions. In S. Koch (Ed.), *Psychology: A study of a science*, Vol. 6. New York: McGraw-Hill, 1963.

Carroll, J. B. A model of school learning. *Teachers College Record*, 1963, *64*, 723–733.

Case, R. A developmentally based theory and technology of instruction. *Review of Educational Research*, 1978, *48*, 439–463.

Chipman, S. F., Segal, J. W., and Glaser, R. (Eds.). *Thinking and learning skills: Current research and open questions.* Hillsdale, N.J.: Erlbaum, 1984.

Chittenden, G. E. An experimental study in modifying assertive behavior in young children. *Monographs of the Society for Research in Child Development,* 1942, 7 (Serial No. 31).

Clark, L. V. Effect of mental practice on the development of a certain motor skill. *Research Quarterly,* 1960, *31,* 560–569.

Cofer, C. N. (Ed.). *Verbal learning and verbal behavior.* New York: McGraw-Hill, 1961.

Cofer, C. N. (Ed.). *The structure of human memory.* San Francisco: Freeman, 1976.

Cofer, C. N., and Appley, M. H. *Motivation: Theory and research.* New York: Wiley, 1964.

Cofer, C. N., and Musgrave, B. S. (Eds.). *Verbal behavior and learning: Problems and processes.* New York: McGraw-Hill, 1963.

Collins, A. M., and Quillian, M. R. How to make a language user. In E. Tulving and W. Donaldson (Eds.), *Organization of memory.* New York: Academic Press, 1972.

Commission on the Reorganization of Secondary Education. *Cardinal principles of secondary education.* Department of the Interior, Bureau of Education Bulletin No. 35. Washington, D.C.: GPO, 1918.

Cook, J. W. *A classroom guide for the successful teacher.* Columbia, Md.: Globe Publishers, 1976.

Cook, J. W., and Walbesser, H. H. *How to meet accountability with behavioral objectives and learning hierarchies.* College Park, Md.: University of Maryland, Bureau of Educational Research and Field Services, 1973.

Covington, M. V., Crutchfield, R. S., Davies, L. B., and Olton, R. M. *The productive thinking program.* Columbus, Ohio: Merrill, 1973.

Craik, F. I. M., and Lockhart, R. S. Levels of processing: A framework for memory research. *Journal of Verbal Learning and Verbal Behavior,* 1972, *11,* 671–684.

Cratty, B. J. *Movement behavior and motor learning.* Englewood Cliffs, N.J.: Prentice-Hall, 1973.

Cratty, B. J. *Teaching motor skills.* Englewood Cliffs, N.J.: Prentice-Hall, 1973.

Crossman, E. R. F. W. A theory of the acquisition of speed-skill. *Ergonomics,* 1959, *2,* 153–166.

Crothers, E. J. Memory structure and the recall of discourse. In J. B. Carroll and R. O. Freedle (Eds.), *Language comprehension and the acquisition of knowledge.* Washington, D.C.: V. H. Winston, 1972.

Crouse, J. H. Retroactive interference in reading prose materials. *Journal of Educational Psychology,* 1971, *62,* 39–44.

Crovitz, H. F. *Galton's walk.* New York: Harper & Row, 1970.

Crowder, R. G., and Morton, J. Precategorical acoustic storage (PAS). *Perception and Psychophysics,* 1969, *5,* 365–373.

Crutchfield, R. S., and Covington, M. V. Facilitation of creative problem solving. *Programmed Instruction,* 1965, *4,* 3–10.

Dale, E. *Audiovisual methods in teaching,* 3rd ed. New York: Holt, Rinehart and Winston, 1969.

Deese, J. *The structure of associations in language and thought.* Baltimore: Johns Hopkins Press, 1965.

Deming, B. S. A learning hierarchies approach to social studies instruction. *Journal of Curriculum Studies,* 1974, *7,* 155–159.

Dewey, J. *How we think.* Boston: Heath, 1910.

Dick, W. Formative evaluation. In L. J. Briggs (Ed.), *Instructional design: Principles and applications.* Englewood Cliffs, N.J.: Educational Technology Publications, 1977.

Dick, W., and Carey, L. *The systematic design of instruction.* Glenview, Ill.: Scott, Foresman, 1978.

Dixon, T. R., and Horton, D. L. (Eds.). *Verbal behavior and general behavior theory.* Englewood Cliffs, N.J.: Prentice-Hall, 1968.

Dong, T., and Kintsch, W. Subjective retrieval cues in free recall. *Journal of Verbal Learning and Verbal Behavior,* 1968, *7,* 813–816.

Duchastel, P. C., and Merrill, P. F. The effects of behavioral objectives on learning: A review of empirical studies. *Review of Educational Research,* 1973, *43,* 53–70.

Dwyer, F. M. Exploratory studies in the effectiveness of visual illustrations. *AV Communication Review,* 1970, *18,* 235–249.

Ebbinghaus, H. *Memory: A contribution to experimental psychology.* (Transl. by H. A. Ruger.) New York: Teachers College, 1913.

Ellis, H. C. *The transfer of learning.* New York: Macmillan, 1965.

English, H. B., Welborn, E. L., and Killian, C. D. Studies in substance memorization. *Journal of General Psychology,* 1934, *11,* 233–260.

Estes, W. K. The statistical approach to learning theory. In S. Koch (Ed.), *Psychology: A study of a science,* Vol. 2. *General systematic formulations, learning, and special processes.* New York: McGraw-Hill, 1959.

Estes, W. K. Reinforcement in human behavior. *American Scientist,* 1972, *60,* 723–729.

Estes, W. K. (Ed.). *Handbook of learning and cognitive processes,* Vol. 1, *Introduction to concepts and issues.* Hillsdale, N.J.: Erlbaum, 1975.

Estes, W. K. (Ed.). *Handbook of learning and cognitive processes,* Vol. 4, *Attention and memory.* Hillsdale, N.J.: Erlbaum, 1976. Especially Introduction.

Estes, W. K. (Ed.). *Handbook of learning and cognitive processes,* Vol. 5, *Human information processing.* Hillsdale, N.J.: Erlbaum, 1978.

Farley, F. H., and Gordon, N. J. (Eds.). *Psychology and education: The state of the union.* Berkeley, Calif.: McCutchan, 1981.

Festinger, L. *A theory of cognitive dissonance.* Stanford, Calif.: Stanford University Press, 1957.

Festinger, L. *Conflict, decision, and dissonance.* Stanford, Calif.: Stanford University Press, 1964.

Fishbein, M. (Ed.). *Attitude theory and measurement.* New York: Wiley, 1967.

Fitts, P. M. Perceptual-motor skill learning. In A. W. Melton (Ed.), *Categories of human learning.* New York: Academic Press, 1964.

Fitts, P. M., and Posner, M. I. *Human performance.* Monterey, Calif.: Brooks/Cole, 1967.

Fitts, P. M., and Seeger, C. M. S-R compatibility: Spatial characteristics of stimulus and response codes. *Journal of Experimental Psychology,* 1953, *46,* 199–210.

Flavell, J. H. *The developmental psychology of Jean Piaget.* New York: Van Nostrand, 1963.

Flavell, J. H. Metacognitive aspects of problem solving. In L. B. Resnick (Ed.), *The nature of intelligence.* Hillsdale, N.J.: Erlbaum, 1976.

Fleishman, E. A. *A factorial study of psychomotor abilities.* Research Bulletin TR-54-15. Lackland Air Force Base, Tex.: Air Force Personnel and Training Research Center, 1954.

Frase, L. T. Paragraph organization of written materials: The influence of conceptual clustering upon the level and organization of recall. *Journal of Educational Psychology*, 1969, *60*, 394–401.

Frase, L. T. Boundary conditions for mathemagenic behavior. *Review of Educational Research*, 1970, *40*, 337–347.

Gagné, E. D. Long-term retention of information following learning from prose. *Review of Educational Research*, 1978, *48*, 629–665.

Gagné, E. D., and Rothkopf, E. Z. Text organization and learning goals. *Journal of Educational Psychology*, 1975, *67*, 445–450.

Gagné, R. M. Problem solving. In A. W. Melton (Ed.), *Categories of human learning*. New York: Academic Press, 1964.

Gagné, R. M. The analysis of instructional objectives for the design of instruction. In R. Glaser (Ed.), *Teaching machines and programmed learning. II: Data and directions*. Washington, D.C.: National Education Association, 1965.

Gagné, R. M. Contributions of learning to human development. *Psychological Review*, 1968, *75*, 177–191. (a)

Gagné, R. M. Learning hierarchies. *Educational Psychologist*, 1968, 6, 1–9. (b)

Gagné, R. M. *Expectations for school learning*. Phi Delta Kappa Monograph. Bloomington, Ind.: Phi Delta Kappa, 1973.

Gagné, R. M. *Essentials of learning for instruction*. New York: Holt, Rinehart and Winston, 1974. (a)

Gagné, R. M. Task analysis—its relation to content analysis. *Educational Psychologist*, 1974, *11*, 19–28. (b)

Gagné, R. M. Taxonomic problems of educational systems. In W. T. Singleton and P. Spurgeon (Eds.), *Measurement of human resources*. London: Taylor and Francis, 1975.

Gagné, R. M. The learning basis of teaching methods. In N. L. Gage (Ed.), *The psychology of teaching methods*. 75th Yearbook, National Society for the Study of Education. Chicago: University of Chicago Press, 1976.

Gagné, R. M. Task analysis. In L. J. Briggs (Ed.), *Instructional design: Principles and applications*. Englewood Cliffs, N.J.: Educational Technology Publications, 1977.

Gagné, R. M. Preparing the learner for new learning. *Theory into Practice*, 1980, *19*, No. 1, 6–9.

Gagné, R. M. Some issues in the psychology of mathematics instruction. *Journal for Research in Mathematics Education*, 1983, *14*, 7–18.

Gagné, R. M. Learning outcomes and their effects. *American Psychologist*, 1984, *39*, 377–385.

Gagné, R. M., and Bassler, O. C. Study of retention of some topics of elementary non-metric geometry. *Journal of Educational Psychology*, 1963, *54*, 123–131.

Gagné, R. M., and Briggs, L. J. *Principles of instructional design*, 2nd ed. New York: Holt, Rinehart and Winston, 1979.

Gagné, R. M., and Brown, L. T. Some factors in the programming of conceptual learning. *Journal of Experimental Psychology*, 1961, *62*, 313–321.

Gagné, R. M., and Dick, W. Instructional psychology. *Annual Review of Psychology*, 1983, *34*, 261–295.

Gagné, R. M., and Fleishman, E. A. *Psychology and human performance*. New York: Holt, Rinehart and Winston, 1959.

Gagné, R. M., and Foster, H. Transfer to a motor skill from practice on a pictured representation. *Journal of Experimental Psychology*, 1949, *39*, 342–355.

Gagné, R. M., Mayor, J. R., Garstens, H. L., and Paradise, N. E. Factors in acquiring knowledge of a mathematics task. *Psychological Monographs*, 1962, *76*, No. 7 (Whole No. 526).

Gagné, R. M., Wager, W., and Rojas, A. Planning and authoring computer-assisted instruction lessons. *Educational Technology*, 1981, 17–26.

Gagné, R. M., and White, R. T. Memory structures and learning outcomes. *Review of Educational Research*, 1978, *48*, 187–222.

Gall, M. D., and Gall, J. P. The discussion method. In N. T. Gage (Ed.), *The psychology of teaching methods*. 75th Yearbook, National Society for the Study of Education. Chicago: University of Chicago Press, 1976.

Gartner, A., Kohler, M., and Riessman, F. *Children teach children*. New York: Harper & Row, 1971.

Gates, A. I. Recitation as a factor in memorizing. *Archives of Psychology*, 1917, *26* (Whole No. 40).

Gershman, J. S., and Sakamoto, E. J. *Intermediate mathematics: CARE Ontario Assessment Instrument Pool*. Toronto: Ontario Institute for Studies in Education, 1980.

Getzels, J. W., and Jackson, P. W. *Creativity and intelligence*. New York: Wiley, 1962.

Gibson, E. J. A systematic application of the concepts of generalization and differentiation to verbal learning. *Psychological Review*, 1940, *47*, 196–229.

Gibson, E. J. Retroactive inhibition as a function of degree of generalization between tasks. *Journal of Experimental Psychology*, 1941, *28*, 93–115.

Gibson, E. J. Intra-list generalization as a factor in verbal learning. *Journal of Experimental Psychology*, 1942, *30*, 185–200.

Gibson, E. J. *Principles of perceptual learning and development*. New York: Appleton, 1969.

Gibson, J. J. *The perception of the visual world*. Boston: Houghton Mifflin, 1950.

Gilbert, T. F. Mathetics: The technology of education. *Journal of Mathetics*, 1962, *1*, 7–73.

Gilbert, T. H. Overlearning and the retention of meaningful prose. *Journal of General Psychology*, 1957, *56*, 281–289.

Glaser, R. Some implications of previous work on learning and individual differences. In R. M. Gagné (Ed.), *Learning and individual differences*. Columbus, Ohio: Merrill, 1967.

Glaser, R. Concept learning and concept teaching. In R. M. Gagné and W. J. Gephart (Eds.), *Learning research and school subjects*. Itasca, Ill.: Peacock, 1968.

Glaser, R. Educational psychology and education. *American Psychologist*, 1973, *28*, 557–566.

Glaser, R. Trends and research questions in psychological research on learning and schooling. *Educational Researcher*, 1979, *8*, 6–13.

Glover, J. A., Plake, B. S., and Roberts, B. Distinctiveness of encoding: The effects of paraphrasing and drawing inferences on memory from prose. *Journal of Educational Psychology*, 1981, *73*, 736–744.

Goss, A. E. Comments on Professor Noble's paper. In C. N. Cofer and B. S. Musgrave (Eds.), *Verbal behavior and learning: Problems and processes*. New York: McGraw-Hill, 1963.

Greeno, J. G. Natures of problem-solving abilities. In W. K. Estes (Ed.), *Handbook of learning and cognitive processes*, Vol. 5. *Human information processing*. Hillsdale, N.J.: Erlbaum, 1978.(a)

Greeno, J. G. A study of problem solving. In R. Glaser (Ed.), *Advances in instructional psychology*, Vol. 1. Hillsdale, N.J.: Erlbaum, 1978.(b)

Greeno, J. G., and Bjork, R. A. Mathematical learning theory and the new "mental forestry." *Annual Review of Psychology*, 1973, *24*, 81–116.

Gropper, G. L. Why is a picture worth a thousand words? *AV Communication Review*, 1963, *11*, 75–95.

Guilford, J. P. *The nature of human intelligence*. New York: McGraw-Hill, 1967.

Guthrie, E. R. *The psychology of learning*. New York: Harper & Row, 1935.

Guthrie, J. T. Instruction versus a discovery method. *Journal of Educational Psychology*, 1967, *58*, 45–49.

Guttman, N., and Kalish, H. I. Discriminability and stimulus generalization. *Journal of Experimental Psychology*, 1956, *51*, 79–88.

Hall, J. F. Retroactive inhibition in meaningful material. *Journal of Educational Psychology*, 1955, *46*, 47–52.

Hall, J. F. *Psychology of motivation*. Philadelphia: Lippincott, 1961.

Hall, J. F. *The psychology of learning*. Philadelphia: Lippincott, 1966.

Hall, J. F. *Verbal learning and retention*. Philadelphia: Lippincott, 1971.

Harding, S. R., Mogford, B., Melching, W. H., and Showel, M. *The development of four job-oriented basic skills (JOBS) programs*. San Diego, Calif.: Navy Personnel Research and Development Center, 1981. Technical Report 81–24.

Harlow, H. F. The development of learning sets. *Psychological Review*, 1949, *56*, 51–65.

Harlow, H. F., and Harlow, M. K. Learning to think. *Scientific American*, 1949, *181*, 36–39.

Hartshorne, H. and May, M. A. *Studies in deceit*. New York: Macmillan, 1928.

Hayes, J. R. It's the thought that counts: New approaches to educational theory. In D. Klahr (Ed.), *Cognition and instruction*. Hillsdale, N.J.: Erlbaum, 1976.

Hebb, D. O. *A textbook of psychology*, 2nd ed. Philadelphia; Saunders, 1966.

Heider, F. *The psychology of interpersonal relations*. New York: Wiley, 1958.

Heidt, E. U. *Instructional media and individual learner*. London: Kogan Page, 1978.

Hempel, W. E., Jr., and Fleishman, E. A. A factor analysis of physical proficiency and manipulative skill. *Journal of Applied Psychology*, 1955, *39*, 12–16.

Hewett, F. M. *The emotionally disturbed child in the classroom*. Boston: Allyn and Bacon, 1968.

Hill, W. F. *Principles of learning: A handbook of applications*. Palo Alto, Calif.: Mayfield, 1981.

Hinton, A. E., and Anderson, J. R. (Eds.). *Parallel models of associative memory*. Hillsdale, N.J.: Erlbaum, 1981.

Hogan, R. Moral conduct and moral character: A psychological perspective. *Psychological Bulletin*, 1973, *79*, 217–232.

Hovland, C. I. "Inhibition of reinforcement" and phenomena of experimental extinction. *Proceedings of the National Academy of Sciences*, 1936, *22*, 430–433.

Hovland, C. I. The generalization of conditioned responses. I. The sensory generalization of conditioned responses with varying frequencies of tone. *Journal of General Psychology*, 1937, *17*, 125–148.

Hovland, C. I., Janis, I. L., and Kelley, H. H. *Communication and persuasion*. New Haven, Conn.: Yale University Press, 1953.

Hovland, C. I., Lumsdaine, A. A., and Sheffield, F. D. *Experiments in mass communication*. Princeton, N.J.: Princeton University Press, 1949.

Hudgins, B. B. *Learning and thinking*. Itasca, Ill.: Peacock, 1977.

Hull, C. L. *Principles of behavior*. New York: Appleton, 1943.

Hulse, S. H., Egeth, H., and Deese, J. *The psychology of learning*, 5th ed. New York: McGraw-Hill, 1980.

Inhelder, B., and Piaget, J. *The growth of logical thinking from childhood to adolescence*. New York: Basic Books, 1958.

Insko, C. A. Verbal reinforcement of attitudes. *Journal of Personality and Social Psychology*, 1965, *2*, 621–623.

James, W. *Principles of psychology*. New York: Holt, Rinehart and Winston, 1890.

Jenkins, J. J. Mediated associations: Paradigms and situations. In C. N. Cofer and B. S. Musgrave (Eds.), *Verbal behavior and learning*. New York: McGraw-Hill, 1963.

Johnson, D. M. *A systematic introduction to the psychology of thinking*. New York: Harper & Row, 1972.

Jones, H. E., and English, H. B. Notional vs. rote memory. *American Journal of Psychology*, 1926, *37*, 602–603.

Joyce, B., and Weil, M. *Models of teaching*. Englewood Cliffs, N.J.: Prentice-Hall, 1972.

Katona, G. *Organizing and memorizing*. New York: Columbia University Press, 1940.

Kaufman, R., and English, F. W. *Needs assessment: Concept and application*. Englewood Cliffs, N.J.: Educational Technology Publications, 1979.

Kausler, D. H. *Psychology of verbal learning and memory*. New York: Academic Press, 1974.

Keele, S. W. Movement control in skilled motor performance. *Psychological Bulletin*, 1968, *70*, 387–403.

Keele, S. W. *Attention and human performance*. Pacific Palisades, Calif.: Goodyear Publishing Co., 1973.

Keller, F. S., and Schoenfeld, W. N. *Principles of psychology*. New York: Appleton, 1950.

Kelly, G. A. *The psychology of personal constructs*, Vol. 1. New York: Norton, 1955.

Kelman, H. C. Attitude change as a function of response restriction. *Human Relations*, 1953, *6*, 185–214.

Kelman, H. C. Compliance, identification, and internalization: Three processes of attitude change. *Journal of Conflict Resolution*, 1958, *2*, 51–60.

Kemp, J. E. *Planning and producing audiovisual materials*, 4th ed. New York: Harper & Row, 1980.

Kendler, H. H., and Kendler, T. S. Effect of verbalization on reversal shifts in children, *Science*, 1961, *141*, 1619–1620.

Keppel, G. Retroactive and proactive inhibition. In T. R. Dixon and D. L. Horton (Eds.), *Verbal behavior and general behavior theory*. Englewood Cliffs, N.J.: Prentice-Hall, 1968.

Kestin, J. Creativity in teaching and learning. *American Scientist*, 1970, *58*, 250–257.

Kiesler, C. A., Collins, B. E., and Miller, N. *Attitude change*. New York: Wiley, 1969.

Kifer, E. Relationships between academic achievement and personality characteristics: A quasi-longitudinal study. *American Educational Research Journal*, 1975, *12*, 191–210.

Kimble, G. A. *Hilgard and Marquis' "Conditioning and learning,"* New York: Appleton, 1961.

Kimble, G. A. *Foundations of conditioning and learning*. New York: Appleton, 1967.

Kintsch, W. Notes on the structure of semantic memory. In E. Tulving and W. Donaldson (Eds.), *Organization of memory.* New York: Academic Press, 1972.

Klahr, D. (Ed.). *Cognition and instruction.* Hillsdale, N.J.: Erlbaum, 1976.

Klatzky, R. L. *Human memory: Structures and processes,* 2nd ed. San Francisco: Freeman, 1980.

Klausmeier, H. J. Cognitive operations in concept learning. *Educational Psychologist,* 1971, *9,* 1, 3–8.

Klausmeier, H. J. *Learning and human abilities: Educational psychology,* 4th ed. New York: Harper & Row, 1975.

Klausmeier, H. J. Conceptual development during the school years. In J. R. Levin and V. L. Allen (Eds.), *Cognitive learning in children.* New York: Academic Press, 1976.

Klausmeier, H. J. *Learning and teaching concepts.* New York: Academic Press, 1980.

Klausmeier, H. J., and Allen, P. S. *Cognitive development of children and youth: A longitudinal study.* New York: Academic Press, 1978.

Klausmeier, H. J., Ghatala, E. S., and Frayer, D. A. *Conceptual learning and development: A cognitive view.* New York: Academic Press, 1974.

Koestler, A. *The act of creation.* London: Hutchinson, 1964.

Kohlberg, L. Moral education in the schools: a developmental view. *School Review,* 1966, *74,* 1–30.

Kohlberg, L. The contribution of developmental psychology to education: Examples from moral education. *Educational Psychologist,* 1973, *10,* 2–14.

Kohlberg, L., and Turiel, E. (Eds.). *Recent research in moral development.* New York: Holt, Rinehart and Winston, 1973.

Köhler, W. *The mentality of apes.* New York: Harcourt, 1927.

Köhler, W. *Gestalt psychology.* New York: Liveright, 1929.

Krathwohl, D. R., Bloom, B. S., and Masia, B. B. *Taxonomy of educational objectives. Handbook II: Affective domain.* New York: McKay, 1964.

Lachman, R., Lachman, J. L., and Butterfield, E. C. *Cognitive psychology and information processing: An introduction.* Hillsdale, N.J.: Erlbaum, 1979.

La Piere, R. I. Attitudes vs. actions. *Social Forces,* 1934, *13,* 230–237.

Larkin, J., McDermott, J., Simon, D. P., and Simon, H. A. Expert and novice performance in solving physics problems. *Science,* 1980, *208,* 1335–1342.

Lawson, A. E. (Ed.). *The psychology of teaching for thinking and creativity.* 1980 AETS Yearbook. Columbus, Ohio: ERIC Clearinghouse for Science, Mathematics, and Environmental Education, 1979.

Lawther, J. D. *The learning and performance of physical skills,* 2nd ed. Englewood Cliffs, N.J.: Prentice-Hall, 1977.

Lesgold, A. M., and Perfetti, C. A. (Eds.). *Interactive processes in reading.* Hillsdale, N.J.: Erlbaum, 1981.

Levie, W. H., and Dickie, K. E. The analysis and application of media. In R. M. W. Travers (Ed.), *Handbook of research on teaching,* 2nd ed. Skokie, Ill.: Rand-McNally, 1973.

Levin, J. R., and Allen, V. L. (Eds.). *Cognitive learning in children: Theories and strategies.* New York: Academic Press, 1976.

Lewis, D., Shephard, A. H., and Adams, J. A. Evidences of associative interference in psychomotor performance. *Science,* 1949, *110,* 271–273.

Lindahl, L. G. Movement analysis as an industrial training method. *Journal of Applied Psychology,* 1945, *29,* 420–436.

Lindsay, P. H., and Norman, D. A. *Human information processing: An introduction to psychology,* 2nd ed. New York: Academic Press, 1977.

Lindsley, D. B. The reticular system and perceptual discrimination. In H. H. Jasper (Ed.), *Reticular formation of the brain.* Boston: Little, Brown, 1958.

Linke, R. D. Influence of cultural background on hierarchical learning. *Journal of Educational Psychology,* 1974, *66,* 911–918.

Loftus, E. F., and Loftus, G. R. On the performance of stored information in the human brain. *American Psychologist,* 1980, *35,* 409–420.

Lorayne, H., and Lucas, J. *The memory book.* New York: Ballantine, 1974.

Mager, R. F. *Developing attitude toward learning.* Belmont, Calif.: Fearon, 1968.

Mager, R. F. *Preparing objectives for instruction,* 2nd ed. Belmont, Calif.: Fearon, 1975.

Maier, N. R. F. Reasoning in humans. I. On direction. *Journal of Comparative Psychology,* 1930, *10,* 115–143.

Markle, S. M., and Tiemann, P. W. *Really understanding concepts.* Champaign, Ill.: Stipes, 1969.

Markle, S. M., and Tiemann, P. W. Some principles of instructional design at higher cognitive levels. In R. Ulrich, T. Stachnik, and T. Mabry (Eds.), *Control of human behavior,* Vol. 13. Glenview, Ill.: Scott-Foresman, 1974.

Marx, M. H., and Bunch, M. E. (Eds.). *Fundamentals and applications of learning.* New York: Macmillan, 1977.

Masur, E. F., McIntyre, C. W., and Flavell, J. H. Developmental changes in apportionment of study time among items in a multitrial free recall task. *Journal of Experimental Child Psychology,* 1973, *15,* 237–246.

Mathews, D. K., and McDaniel, J. Effectiveness of using Golf-Lite in learning the golf swing. *Research Quarterly,* 1962, *33,* 488–491.

May, M. A., and Lumsdaine, A. A. *Learning from films.* New Haven, Conn.: Yale University Press, 1958.

Mayer, G. R. *Applying behavior analysis procedures with children and youth.* New York: Holt, Rinehart and Winston, 1977.

Mayer, R. E. Some conditions of meaningful learning of computer programming: Advance organizers and subject control of frame sequencing. *Journal of Educational Psychology,* 1976, *68,* 143–150.

Mayer, R. E. Advance organizers that compensate for the organization of text. *Journal of Educational Psychology,* 1978, *70,* 880–886.

Mayer, R. E. Can advance organizers influence meaningful learning? *Review of Educational Research,* 1979, *49,* 371–383.

McClelland, D. C. Toward a theory of motive acquisition. *American Psychologist,* 1965, *20,* 321–333.

McClelland, D. C., Atkinson, J. W., Clark, R. A., and Lowell, E. L. *The achievement motive.* New York: Appleton, 1953.

McGeoch, J. A., and Irion, A. L. *The psychology of human learning,* 2nd ed. New York: McKay, 1952.

McLeish, J. The lecture method. In N. L. Gage (Ed.), *The psychology of teaching methods.* 75th Yearbook, National Society for the Study of Education. Chicago: University of Chicago Press, 1976.

Mechner, F. Behavioral analysis and instructional sequencing. In P. C. Lange (Ed.), *Programmed instruction.* Chicago: National Society for the Study of Education, 1967.

Melton, A. W. Learning. In W. S. Monroe (Ed.), *Encyclopedia of educational research.* New York: Macmillan, 1940.

Melton, A. W. (Ed.) *Apparatus tests.* Army Air Forces Aviation Psychology Program Research Report No. 4. Washington, D.C.: GPO, 1947.

Melton, A. W. (Ed.). *Categories of human learning.* New York: Academic Press, 1964.

Melton, A. W., and Martin, E. (Eds.). *Coding processes in human memory.* Washington D.C.: V. H. Winston, 1972.

Merrill, P. F. *Task analysis: An information processing approach.* Technical Memo No. 27. Tallahassee: Florida State University, CAI Center, 1971.

Merrill, P. F. Hierarchial and information processing task analysis: A comparison. *Journal of Instructional Development,* 1978, *1,* 35–40.

Meunier, C. F., Ritz, D., and Meunier, J. A. Rehearsal of individual items in short-term memory. *Journal of Experimental Psychology,* 1972, *95,* 465–467.

Meyer, B. J. F., and McConkie, G. W. What is recalled after hearing a passage? *Journal of Educational Psychology,* 1973, *65,* 109–117.

Mill, J. *Analysis of the phenomena of the human mind.* (Ed. by A. Bain, A. Findlater, and G. Grote; ed. with additional notes by J. S. Mill.) London: Longmans, 1869.

Miller, G. A. *Language and communication.* New York: McGraw-Hill, 1951.

Miller, G. A. The magical number seven, plus or minus two: Some limits on our capacity for processing information. *Psychological Review,* 1956, *63,* 81–97.

Miller, N. E. Liberalization of S-R concepts. Extensions to conflict behavior, motivation, and social learning. In S. Koch (Ed.), *Psychology: A study of a science,* Vol. 2. New York: McGraw-Hill, 1959.

Miller, N. E. Laws of learning relevant to its biological basis. *Proceedings of the American Philosophical Society,* 1967, *111,* 315–325.

Miller, R. B. Task description and analysis. In R. M. Gagné (Ed.), *Psychological principles in system development.* New York: Holt, Rinehart and Winston, 1963.

Murdock, B. B. *Human memory: Theory and data.* Hillsdale, N. J.: Erlbaum, 1974.

National Commission on Excellence in Education. *A nation at risk: The imperative for educational reform.* Washington, D.C.: U.S. Department of Education, 1983.

Neisser, U. *Memory observed: Remembering in natural contexts.* San Francisco: Freeman, 1982.

Neves, D. M., and Anderson, J. R. Knowledge compilation: Mechanisms for the automatization of cognitive skills. In J. R. Anderson (Ed.), *Cognitive skills and their acquisition.* Hillsdale, N.J.: Erlbaum, 1981.

Newcomb, T. M. *The acquaintance process.* New York: Holt, Rinehart and Winston, 1961.

Newell, A. One final word. In D. T. Tuma and F. Reif (Eds.), *Problem solving and education.* Hillsdale, N.J.: Erlbaum, 1980.

Newell, A., and Simon, H. A. *Human problem solving.* Englewood Cliffs, N.J.: Prentice-Hall, 1972.

Newman, E. B. Forgetting of meaningful material during sleep and waking. *American Journal of Psychology,* 1939, *52,* 65–71.

Newman, S. E. A mediation model for paired-association learning. In J. P. DeCecco (Ed.), *Educational technology.* New York: Holt, Rinehart and Winston, 1964.

Noble, C. E. Meaningfulness and familiarity. In C. N. Cofer and B. S. Musgrave (Eds.), *Verbal behavior and learning.* New York: McGraw-Hill, 1963.

Norman, D. A., and Rumelhart, D. E. (Eds.). *Explorations in cognition.* San Francisco: Freeman, 1975.

Olson, D. R. (Ed.). *Media and symbols: The forms of expression, communication, and education.* 73rd Yearbook, National Society for the Study of Education. Chicago: University of Chicago Press, 1974.

Olton, R. M., and Crutchfield, R. S. Developing the skills of productive thinking. In P. Mussen, J. Langer, and M. Covington (Eds.), *Trends and issues in developmental psychology.* New York: Holt, Rinehart and Winston, 1969.

Olton, R. M., Wardrop, J. L., Covington, M. V., Goodwin, W. L. Crutchfield, R. S., Klausmeier, H. J., and Ronda, T. *The development of productive thinking skills in fifth-grade children.* Technical Report No. 34. Madison, Wis.: University of Wisconsin, Center for Cognitive Learning, 1967.

O'Neil, H. F., Jr. *Learning strategies.* New York: Academic Press, 1978.

Orlando, R., and Bijou, S. W. Single and multiple schedules of reinforcement in developmentally retarded children. *Journal of the Experimental Analysis of Behavior,* 1960, *3,* 339–348.

Ozsogomonyan, A. An application of Gagné's principles of instructional design. *Journal of Chemical Education,* 1979, *56,* 799–801.

Paivio, A. *Imagery and verbal processes.* New York: Holt, Rinehart and Winston, 1971.

Paivio, A., and Yuille, J. C. Changes in associative strategies and paired-associate learning over trials as a function of word imagery and type of learning set. *Journal of Experimental Psychology,* 1969, *79,* 458–463.

Palmer, S. E. Visual perception and world knowledge. Notes on a model of sensory-cognitive interaction. In D. A. Norman and D. E. Rumelhart (Eds.), *Explorations in cognition.* San Francisco: Freeman, 1975.

Pavlov, I. P. *Conditioned reflexes.* (Transl. by G. V. Anrep.) New York: Oxford, 1927.

Penfield, W. Memory mechanisms. *Transactions of the American Neurological Association,* 1951, *76,* 15–31.

Piaget, J. *The construction of reality in the child.* New York: Basic Books, 1954.

Piaget, J. Piaget's theory. In P. H. Mussen (Ed.), *Carmichael's manual of child psychology.* New York: Wiley, 1970.

Piaget, J., and Inhelder, B. *The early growth of logic in the child.* New York: Harper & Row, 1964.

Popham, W. J. (Ed.). *Evaluation in education.* Berkeley, Calif.: McCutchan, 1974.

Popham, W. J. *Educational evaluation.* Englewood Cliffs, N.J.: Prentice-Hall, 1975.

Popham, W. J., and Baker, E. L. *Establishing instructional goals.* Englewood Cliffs, N.J.: Prentice-Hall, 1970.

Porier, G. W., and Lott, A. J. Galvanic skin responses and prejudice. *Journal of Personality and Social Psychology,* 1967, *5,* 253–259.

Postman, L. The present status of interference theory. In C. N. Cofer (Ed.), *Verbal learning and verbal behavior.* New York: McGraw-Hill, 1961.

Poulton, E. C. On prediction in skilled movements. *Psychological Bulletin,* 1957, *54,* 467–478.

Pressley, M. Use of a mnemonic technique to teach young children foreign language vocabulary. *Contemporary Educational Psychology,* 1981, *6,* 110–116.

Pressley, M., Levin, J. R., and Delaney, H. D. The mnemonic keyword method. *Review of Educational Research,* 1982, *52,* 61–91.

Quillian, M. R. Semantic memory. In M. Minsky (Ed.), *Semantic information processing.* Cambridge, Mass.: MIT Press, 1968.

Rankin, R. E., and Campbell, D. T. Galvanic skin response to Negro and white experimenters. *Journal of Abnormal and Social Psychology,* 1955, *51,* 30–33.

Razran, G. Conditioned response changes in rating and appraising sociopolitical slogans. *Psychological Bulletin*, 1940, *37*, 481.

Reif, F., and Heller, J.I. Knowledge structure and problem solving in physics. *Educational Psychologist*, 1982, *17*, 102–127.

Reigeluth, C. M., Merrill, M. D., and Bunderson, C.V. The structure of subject-matter content and its instructional design implications. *Instructional Science*, 1978, *7*, 107–126.

Reiser, R. A., and Gagné, R. M. Characteristics of media selection models. *Review of Educational Research*, 1982, *52*, 499–512.

Reiser, R. A., and Gagné, R. M. *Selecting media for instruction*. Englewood Cliffs, N.J.: Educational Technology Publications, 1983.

Resnick, L. B. *Design of an early learning curriculum*. Working Paper No. 16. Pittsburgh, Pa.: University of Pittsburgh, Learning Research and Development Center, 1967.

Resnick, L. B., and Ford, W. W. *The psychology of mathematics for instruction*. Hillsdale, N.J.: Erlbaum, 1981.

Resnick, L. B., Wang, M. C., and Kaplan, J. *Behavior analysis in curriculum design: A hierarchically sequenced introductory mathematics curriculum*. Pittsburgh, Pa.: University of Pittsburgh, Learning Research and Development Center, 1970.

Reynolds, J. H., and Glaser, R. Effects of repetition and spaced review upon retention of a complex learning task. *Journal of Educational Psychology*, 1964, *55*, 297–308.

Richardson, A. Mental Practice: A review and discussion, Parts I and II. *Research Quarterly*, 1967, *38*, 95–107, 263.

Riley, D. A. *Discrimination learning*. Englewood Cliffs, N.J.: Prentice-Hall, 1968.

Riley, D. A. Discrimination learning. In M. H. Marx and M. E. Bunch (Eds.), *Fundamentals and applications of learning*. New York: Macmillan, 1977.

Riley, M. S. Conceptual and procedural knowledge in development. Master's thesis, University of Pittsburgh, 1981.

Riley, M. S., Greeno, J. G., and Heller, J. I. Development of children's problem-solving ability in arithmetic. In H. P. Ginsburg (Ed.), *The development of mathematical thinking*. New York: Academic Press, 1983.

Ringness, T. A. *The affective domain in education*. Boston: Little, Brown, 1975.

Robinson, E. S. *Association theory today*. New York: Appleton, 1932.

Rohwer, W. D., Jr. Constraint, syntax and meaning in paired associate learning. *Journal of Verbal Learning and Verbal Behavior*, 1966, *5*, 541–547.

Rohwer, W. D., Jr. Images and pictures in children's learning. *Psychological Bulletin*, 1970, *73*, 393–403.

Rohwer, W. D., Jr. Elaboration and learning in childhood and adolescence. In H. W. Reese (Ed.), *Advances in child development and behavior*. New York: Academic Press, 1975.

Rohwer, W. D. Jr., and Lynch, S. Semantic constraint in paired-associate learning. *Journal of Educational Psychology*, 1966, *57*, 271–278.

Rokeach, M. *Beliefs, attitudes and values*. San Francisco: Jossey-Bass, 1969.

Romiszowski, A. J. *The selection and use of instructional media*. London: Kogan Page, 1974.

Romiszowski, A. J. *Designing instructional systems*. London: Kogan Page, 1981; New York: Nichols, 1981.

Rosch, E. Principles of categorization. In E. Rosch and B. B. Lloyd (Eds.), *Cognition and categorization*. Hillsdale, N.J.: Erlbaum, 1978.

Rosch, E., and Lloyd, B. B. (Eds.). *Cognition and categorization*. Hillsdale, N. J.: Erlbaum, 1978.

Rosenberg, M. J., and Hovland, C. I. Cognitive, affective and behavioral components of attitudes. In C. I. Hovland and M. J. Rosenberg, *Attitude organization and change*. New Haven: Yale University Press, 1960.

Roshal, S. M. *Effects of learner representation in film-mediated perceptual-motor learning*. State College, Pa.: Pennsylvania State College Instructional Film Research Program, 1949.

Rothkopf, E. Z. The concept of mathemagenic activities. *Review of Educational Research*, 1970, *40*, 325–336.

Rothkopf, E. Z. Experiments on mathemagenic behavior and the technology of written instruction. In E. Z. Rothkopf and P. E. Johnson (Eds.), *Verbal learning research and the technology of written instruction*. New York: Teachers College, 1971.

Rothkopf, E. Z. Writing to teach and reading to learn: A perspective on the psychology of written instruction. In N. L. Gage (Ed.), *The psychology of teaching methods*. Seventy-fifth Yearbook, NSSE. Chicago: University Press, 1976.

Rothkopf, E. Z., and Bisbicos, E. E. Selective facilitative effects of interspersed questions on learning from written material. *Journal of Educational Psychology*, 1967, *58*, 56–61.

Rothkopf, E. Z., and Kaplan, R. Exploration of the effect of density and specificity of instructional objectives in learning from text. *Journal of Educational Psychology*, 1972, *68*, 295–302.

Rumelhart, D. E., Lindsay, P. H., and Norman, D. A. A process model for long-term memory. In E. Tulving and W. Donaldson (Eds.), *Organization of memory*. New York: Academic Press, 1972.

Rumelhart, D. E., and Ortony, A. The representation of knowledge in memory. In R. C. Anderson, R. J. Spiro, and W. E. Montague (Eds.), *Schooling and the acquisition of knowledge*. Hillsdale, N.J.: Erlbaum, 1977.

Salatas, H., and Flavell, J. H. Behavioral and metamnemonic indicators of strategic behaviors under remember instructions in first grade. *Child Development*, 1976, *47*, 81–89.

Salomon, G. *Interaction of media, cognition, and learning*. San Francisco: Jossey-Bass, 1979.

Saltz, E. Compound stimuli in verbal learning: Cognitive and sensory differentiation versus stimulus selection. *Journal of Experimental Psychology*, 1963, *66*, 1–5.

Schank, R., and Abelson, R. *Scripts, plans, goals and understanding*. Hillsdale, N.J.: Erlbaum, 1977.

Schramm, W. *Big media, little media*. Beverly Hills, Calif.: SAGE Publications, 1977.

Scott, W. A. Attitude change through reward of verbal behavior. *Journal of Abnormal and Social Psychology*, 1957, *55*, 72–75.

Shaw, G. B. *Adventures of the black girl in her search for God*. New York: Putnam, 1959.

Shaw, M. E., and Wright, J. M. *Scales for the measurement of attitudes*. New York: McGraw-Hill, 1967.

Shiffrin, R. M. Capacity limitations in information processing, attention, and memory. In W. K. Estes (Ed.), *Handbook of learning and cognitive processes*, Vol. 4, *Attention and memory*. Hillsdale, N.J.: Erlbaum, 1976.

Shulman, L. S., and Keislar, E. R. *Learning by discovery: a critical appraisal*. Chicago: Rand-McNally, 1966.

Siegler, R. S. (Ed.). *Children's thinking: What develops?* Hillsdale, N.J.: Erlbaum, 1978.

Siegler, R. S., and Klahr, D. When do children learn? The relationship between existing knowledge and the acquisition of new knowledge. In R. Glaser (Ed.), *Advances in instructional psychology*, Vol. 2. Hillsdale, N.J.: Erlbaum, 1982.

Sigel, I. E., and Hooper, F. H. *Logical thinking in children.* New York: Holt, Rinehart and Winston, 1968.

Simon, D. P., and Simon, H. A. Individual differences in solving physics problems. In R. S. Siegler (Ed.), *Children's thinking: What develops?* Hillsdale, N.J.: Erlbaum, 1978.

Simon, H. A. *The sciences of the artificial.* Cambridge, Mass.: MIT Press, 1969.

Simon, H. A. Information-processing theory of human problem solving. In W. K. Estes (Ed.), *Handbook of learning and cognitive processes*, Vol. 5, *Human information processing*. Hillsdale, N.J.: Erlbaum, 1978.

Simon, H. A., and Feigenbaum, E. A. An information processing theory of some effects of similarity, familiarity and meaningfulness in verbal learning. *Journal of Verbal Learning and Verbal Behavior*, 1964, *3*, 385–396.

Singer, R. N. (Ed.). *Readings in motor learning.* Philadelphia: Lea & Febiger, 1972.

Singer, R. N. *Motor learning and human performance*, 3rd ed. New York: Macmillan, 1980.

Singer, R. N., and Dick, W. *Teaching physical education.* Boston: Houghton Mifflin, 1974.

Skinner, B. F. *The behavior of organisms.* New York: Appleton, 1938.

Skinner, B. F. *The technology of teaching.* New York: Appleton, 1968.

Skinner, B. F. *Contingencies of reinforcement: A theoretical analysis.* New York: Appleton, 1969.

Slamecka, N. J. Studies of retroaction of connected discourse. *American Journal of Psychology*, 1959, *72*, 409–416.

Slamecka, N. J. Retroactive inhibition of connected discourse as a function of similarity of topic. *Journal of Experimental Psychology*, 1960, *60*, 245–249.

Smode, A. Learning and performance in a tracking task under two levels of achievement information feedback. *Journal of Experimental Psychology*, 1958, *56*, 297–304.

Spence, K. W. *Behavior theory and conditioning.* New Haven, Conn.: Yale University Press, 1956.

Sperling, G. The information available in brief visual presentations. *Psychological Monographs*, 1960, *74*, No. 6. (Whole No. 498).

Spilich, G. J., Vesonder, G. T., Chiesi, H. L., and Voss, J. F. Text processing of domain-related information for individuals with high and low domain knowledge. *Journal of Verbal Learning and Verbal Behavior*, 1979, *18*, 275–290.

Staats, A. W. An outline of an integrated theory of attitudes. In M. Fishbein (Ed.), *Readings in attitude theory and measurement.* New York: Wiley, 1967.

Staats, A. W., and Staats, C. K. Attitudes established by classical conditioning. *Journal of Abnormal and Social Psychology*, 1958, *57*, 37–40.

Staats, A. W., Staats, C. K., and Crawford, H. L. First-order conditioning of meaning and the parallel conditioning of a GSR. *Journal of General Psychology*, 1962, *67*, 159–167.

Stelmach, G. E. (Ed.). *Motor control: Issues and trends.* New York: Academic Press, 1976.

Stevens, J. C., and Savin, H. B. On the form of learning curves. *Journal of the Experimental Analysis of Behavior*, 1962, *5*, 15–18.

Struening, E. L., and Guttentag, M. *Handbook of evaluation research.* Vols. 1 and 2. Beverly Hills, Calif.: SAGE Publications, 1975.

Taylor, C. W. *The second University of Utah research conference on the identification of creative scientific talent.* Salt Lake City: University of Utah Press, 1958.

Taylor, J. A. The relationship of anxiety to the conditioned eyelid response. *Journal of Experimental Psychology,* 1951, *41,* 81–92.

Tennyson, R. D., and Park, O. C. The teaching of concepts: a review of instructional design research literature. *Review of Educational Research,* 1980, *50,* 55–70.

Tennyson, R. D., Woolley, F. R., and Merrill, M. D. Exemplar and non-exemplar variables which produce correct concept classification behavior and specified classification errors. *Journal of Educational Psychology.* 1972, *63,* 144–152.

Thomson, D. M., and Tulving, E. Associative encoding and retrieval. *Journal of Experimental Psychology,* 1970, *86,* 225–262.

Thornburg, H. D. *Development in adolescence.* Monterey, Calif.: Brooks/Cole, 1975.

Thorndike, E. L. Animal intelligence: An experimental study of the associative processes in animals. *Psychological Review Monograph Supplements,* 1898, *2,* No. 4 (Whole No. 8).

Tiemann, P. W., and Markle, S. M. *Analyzing instructional content: A guide to instruction and evaluation.* Champaign, Ill.: Stipes, 1978.

Tighe, T. J., and Shepp, B. E. (Eds.). *Perception, cognition and development.* Hillsdale, N.J.: Erlbaum, 1983.

Tolman, E. C. *Purposive behavior in animals and men.* New York: Appleton, 1932.

Trabasso, T., and Bower, G. H. *Attention in learning.* New York: Wiley, 1968.

Travers, R. M. W. *Essentials of learning,* 5th ed. New York: Macmillan, 1982.

Trembath, R. J., and White, R. T. Mastery achievement of intellectual skills. *Journal of Experimental Education,* 1979, *47,* 247–252.

Triandis, H. C. Exploratory factor analyses of the behavioral component of social attitudes. *Journal of Abnormal and Social Psychology,* 1964, *68,* 420–430.

Triandis, H. C. Towards an analysis of the components of interpersonal attitudes. In C. W. Sherif and M. Sherif (Eds.), *Attitudes, ego-involvement, and change.* New York: Wiley, 1967.

Triandis, H. C. *Attitude and attitude change.* New York: Wiley, 1971.

Triandis, H. C., and Triandis, L. M. Race, social class, religion and nationality as determinants of social distance. *Journal of Abnormal and Social Psychology,* 1960, *61,* 110–118.

Tulving, E. Subjective organization and effects of repetition in multitrial free-recall learning. *Journal of Verbal Learning and Verbal Behavior,* 1966, *5,* 193–197.

Tulving, E. Episodic and semantic memory. In E. Tulving and W. Donaldson (Eds.), *Organization of memory.* New York: Academic Press, 1972.

Tulving, E., and Donaldson, W. (Eds.). *Organization of memory.* New York: Academic Press, 1972.

Tulving, E., and Osler, S. Effectiveness of retrieval cues in memory for words. *Journal of Experimental Psychology,* 1968, *77,* 593–601.

Tulving, E., and Pearlstone, Z. Availability versus accessibility of information in memory for words. *Journal of Verbal Learning and Verbal Behavior,* 1966, *5,* 381–391.

Tuma, D. T., and Reif, F. *Problem solving and education.* Hillsdale, N.J.: Erlbaum, 1980.

Tyler, R. W. *Basic principles of curriculum and instruction.* Chicago: University of Chicago Press, 1949.

Underwood, B. J. Laboratory studies of verbal learning. In E. R. Hilgard (Ed.), *Theories of learning and instruction.* Sixty-third Yearbook, Part I. Chicago: National Society for the Study of Education, 1964. (a)

Underwood, B. J. The representativeness of rote verbal learning. In A. W. Melton (Ed.), *Categories of human learning.* New York: Academic Press, 1964. (b)

Underwood, B. J., and Schulz, R. W. *Meaningfulness and verbal learning.* Philadelphia: Lippincott, 1960.

Vanderplas, J. M. Perception and learning. In M. H. Marx (Ed.), *Learning: Interactions.* New York: Macmillan, 1970.

Watson, J. B. *Psychology from the standpoint of a behaviorist.* Philadelphia: Lippincott, 1919.

Watson, J. B., and Rayner, R. Conditioned emotional reactions. *Journal of Experimental Psychology,* 1920, *3,* 1–14.

Watts, G. H. and Anderson, R. C. Retroactive inhibition in free recall as a function of first- and second-list organization. *Journal of Experimental Psychology,* 1969, *81,* 595–597.

Welborn, E. L., and English, H. Logical learning and retention: A general review of experiments with meaningful verbal materials. *Psychological Bulletin,* 1937, *31,* 1–20.

Welford, A. T. *Fundamentals of skill.* London: Methuen, 1968.

Wellman, H. M., Ritter, K., and Flavell, J. H. Deliberate memory behavior in the delayed reactions of very young children. *Developmental Psychology,* 1975, *11,* 780–787.

Wertheimer, M. *Productive thinking.* New York: Harper & Row, 1959.

Wessels, M. G. *Cognitive Psychology.* New York: Harper & Row, 1982.

Westie, F. R., and de Fleur, M. L. Autonomic responses and their relationship to race attitudes. *Journal of Abnormal and Social Psychology,* 1959, *58,* 340–347.

Wheeler, D. D. Processes in word recognition. *Cognitive Psychology,* 1970, *1,* 59–85.

Whimbey, A., and Lochhead, J. *Problem solving and comprehension: A short course in analytical reasoning,* 2nd ed. Philadelphia: Franklin Institute Press, 1980.

White, R. T. Research into learning hierarchies. *Review of Educational Research,* 1973, *43,* 361–375.

White, R. T. The validation of a learning hierarchy. *American Educational Research Journal,* 1974, *11,* 121–136.

White, R. T., and Gagné, R. M. Past and future research on learning hierarchies. *Educational Psychologist,* 1974, *11,* 19–28.

White, R. T., and Gagné, R. M. Formative evaluation applied to a learning hierarchy. *Contemporary Educational Psychology,* 1978, *3,* 87–94.

White, R. T., and Wittrock, M. C. Cognitive strategies in problem solving. Unpublished manuscript, 1982.

White, R. W. Motivation reconsidered: The concept of competence. *Psychological Review,* 1959, *66,* 297–333.

Whitely, J. D. Effects of practice distribution on learning a fine motor task. *Research Quarterly,* 1970, *48,* 576–583.

Wickelgren, W. A. *How to solve problems.* San Francisco: Freeman, 1974.

Wittrock, M. C. Replacement and nonreplacement strategies in children's problem solving. *Journal of Educational Psychology,* 1967, *58,* 69–74.

Wittrock, M. C. Learning as a generative process. *Educational Psychologist,* 1974, *11,*

87–95.

Worthen, B. R. Discovery and expository task presentation in elementary mathematics. *Journal of Educational Psychology Monograph Supplement*, 1968, *59*, No. 1, Part 2.

Worthen, B. R., and Sanders, J. R. (Eds.), *Educational evaluation: Theory and practice.* Worthington, Ohio: C. A. Jones, 1973.

Yates, F. A. *The art of memory.* London: Routledge and Kegan Paul, 1966.

Zajonc, R. B. The concepts of balance, congruity, and dissonance. *Public Opinion Quarterly*, 1960, *24*, 280–286.

Author Index

Subject Index